Geology and the Urban Environment

Geology and the Urban Environment

DAVID LEVESON

Original illustrations drafted by
Margaret Leveson

New York / Oxford
OXFORD UNIVERSITY PRESS
1980

Library of Congress Cataloging in Publication Data

Leveson, David, 1934–
  Geology and the urban environment.

  Bibliography: p.
  1. Urban geology.   2. Land use—Planning.
I. Title.
QE39.5.U7L48   1980   550'.9173'2   78-31256
ISBN 0-19-502578-4

Printed in the United States of America

In stopping to take breath, I happened
to glance up at the canyon wall. I wish
I could tell you what I saw there, just
as I saw it, on that first morning,
through a veil of lightly falling snow.
Far up above me, a thousand feet or so,
set in a great cavern in the face of the
cliff, I saw a little city of stone . . .

Tom Outland
in *The Professor's House*
by Willa Cather

Preface

Geology, since its inception, has always been intimately involved with the interrelationships that exist between humans and the earth. Indeed, it might reasonably be claimed that all areas of geologic investigation are immediately or ultimately relevant to human well-being. Frequently, however, because of the press of the great amount of material that must be covered in basic undergraduate courses in physical and historical geology, there is a tendency to relegate the examination of many of the more obviously practical aspects of earth science to a series of parenthetical asides and afterthoughts. As an antidote to this tendency, and also in response to the current flowering of awareness of the significance to humankind of the natural world, the practical or "human-oriented" aspects of the earth sciences have been gathered together and fashioned into curricula in "environmental geology." The offering of such courses is an important step in revealing to students the major roles that the earth and geology play in their lives. However, for the inhabitants of towns and cities (who now constitute the majority of people in the industrialized world), there are few chances to develop an intimate acquaintance with the "natural" world, and the importance of the earth commonly seems abstract and removed from personal experience.

In response to the tangible reality of this feeling, the Geology Department of Brooklyn College of the City University of New York decided to offer a first-level environmental geology course specifically designed for an urban audience, entitled *Geology and the Urban Environment*. The aim of the course has been to introduce the student to the pervasive influences of the earth and of geology upon the character of cities and upon the civilizations of which cities are the nuclei. Moreover, the course emphasizes how the success of cities of the future, as human, liveable environments, must involve appreciation of the opportunities the earth offers and the constraints it imposes. To achieve an understanding of the interrelationship between the earth and the urban environment, examination of basic aspects of geology, land-use planning, and the physical, social, aesthetic, and economic attributes of cities is required.

As the author developed lectures for *Geology and the Urban Environment* over a number of years, it became apparent that no appropriate text for the course existed. Texts designed for courses in environmental geology lacked sufficient reference to cities, were often over-technical, and did not attempt to explore many important areas of influence of the earth upon urban environment as it is perceived by urban inhabitants. Collections of papers in environmental geology share these shortcomings and in addition are burdened by an absence of a continuous development of ideas at a consistent level of difficulty.

This book is an attempt to provide the broad understanding of both cities and the earth that is necessary for a full appreciation of the interrelationship between geology and the urban environment. Part I (Cities and Urban Necessities) examines the growing importance of urban environment as the home of most of humanity, discusses the influence of the earth upon the origin and evolution of cities, and describes how cities succeed or fail in their attempts to obtain water, dispose of wastes, gather construction materials, and find stable ground upon which to build. Part II (Short-term Geologic Hazards) investigates problems posed by earthquakes, unstable ground, floods, volcanic eruptions, sedimentation, and erosion. Part III (Long-term Geologic Hazards) considers the possible effects upon cities of climatic change and shortages of natural resources. Part IV (Geology and the Human Potential of the City) investigates how the earth affects the aesthetic, psychological, and social aspects of urban environment, sketches the evolution of the physical form of the city and its relationship to the earth, introduces concepts of urban and regional planning, and suggests the proper relationship between the earth and cities of the future.

Case studies of individual cities are introduced throughout the body of the narrative. A comprehensive list of references facilitates further investigation. The glossary provides a ready reference for technical terms not explained in the text.

The author believes that the breadth of material presented in this book will make it useful to students of geology, geography, environmental science, urban studies, and land-use planning by revealing to them the ties that interconnect their respective disciplines and reminding them of the common debt all people owe to the earth.

DAVID LEVESON

Acknowledgments

I wish to express my gratitude to some of the many people who encouraged and aided me in the preparation of this book. First and foremost, thanks are due to my wife, Meg, for her herculean labors in drafting illustrations and for her careful, critical reading of the initial manuscript. J. Walter Graham, Professor Emeritus of the University of Toronto, and Lionel Bier of the Art Department of Brooklyn College contributed invaluable advice on archeological matters, Arthur Margon of the New School of Liberal Arts of Brooklyn College provided expertise on urban history, Bob Shatkin of the Brooklyn Public Library gave continual help in finding and suggesting references, David Seidemann, William Harris, Robert Wallace, E. Lynn Savage, and Charles Weil of the Geology Department of Brooklyn College, and Donald Coates of the Department of Geological Sciences of the State University of New York at Binghamton made helpful suggestions on geochemical, oceanographic, geologic, and organizational aspects of the text, and Arnold Wendroff, William Wendroff, George Kuchar, and Mike Kuchar contributed technical and sociological information relevant to geology and the urban environment. Special thanks go to members of the editorial staff of Oxford University Press for their splendid help in readying the book for publication: Joyce Berry for her detailed, creative editing of the manuscript, Jim Anderson for his interest and advice, and Deborah Bowen for her assistance in obtaining illustrative material. I also wish to thank Ellis Rosenberg, now of Plenum Press, for his encouragement in early days.

Contents

I

Geology and Urban Necessities

All cities acknowledge the presence of their natural environment. The original choice of site, subsequent growth, architectural character, style and quality of life, the ultimate destiny of a city all are affected by the needs of the inhabitants on one hand, and on the other by the opportunities that the earth presents and the restrictions that the earth imposes. For every city a choice is possible: harmonious accommodation may be reached in which natural opportunities are made best use of and natural restrictions respected, or strenuous efforts may be exerted to ignore or override the natural world if it interferes with certain visions or desires. In either case, the natural environment must be dealt with, successfully or unsuccessfully; the necessities (and niceties) of life have to be furnished; the hazards of the universe avoided or lessened in their impact.

Many urban necessities are well-rooted within the sphere of geologic influence. Water must be provided, wastes disposed of, provision made for enclosure and protection from the elements, avenues of communication and transport kept open. Failure to ensure these services signals failure of the city. The role of geology in securing urban necessities is considered in Part I in separate chapters dealing with the nature of cities and geology, the origin and development of cities, water supply, waste disposal, building materials, and foundations. Geologic processes that pose hazards to cities are discussed in Parts II and III. Separation of these topics is to some degree arbitrary: excavation for building foundations may cause landslides; the way in which wastes are disposed of is of vital concern to those who must ensure adequate water supply; measures taken to supply water and to control floods may complement each other; withdrawal of water from the ground may cause subsidence; extreme water shortage may be a hazard more severe than some floods. If a useful distinction be sought between topics discussed in Part I and those elaborated in Parts II and III, it may be based on the observation that, with respect to urban necessities, the role of the earth is usually (but not always) passive, whereas hazards, for the most part, develop when the earth actively and perhaps violently disturbs the urban environment, or when humans seriously violate or contradict the equilibria, rates, or directions of earth processes.

1. Cities and Geology

To most people, urban environment is the epitome of the artificial, the opposite of nature. The acres of concrete and asphalt, the piles of brick, the elaborate networks of curtained steel that pierce the sky seem the antithesis of forest and meadow, snowfield and lake—and in most senses, so they are. But to the geologist, whose curiosity focuses on the rocky sphere of the earth, substances like concrete, brick, asphalt, steel, grass, forest, sand, and water all share one thing in common: they rest on and respond to the basic materials and structures of the ground below. Cities, like marsh and desert, are part of the skin or clothing of the planet. In and of themselves, buildings, roads, cables, and tunnels are inert; they lack breath and heartbeat; no living sap runs through their veins. Yet, like the beehive or the coral reef, they are the direct and necessary by-product of biologic life. It is somewhat strange, therefore, that artifacts and the most elaborate and ambitious of our constructions—*cities*—are considered unnatural, something apart from nature. Most cities, unfortunately, may be poorly conceived, shoddily built, irrational, wasteful, even anti-life in that they discourage the full realization of human potential. Some few other cities have, through the ages, housed and fostered the best in humans, become the sources from which civilization has

flowed. But in either case, cities are no more unnatural than the feathered hemispheres that couch eggs or the daubs of mud constructed by a wasp. The common feeling that cities are something apart from nature, the common striving to make cities independent of nature constitute an attitude that is destructive both to the spirit of those that inhabit cities and to the physical and aesthetic integrity of cities. This attitude may stem in part from the belief that humans are separate and apart from other creatures: special creations destined and entitled to rule what they survey. But it has become abundantly clear that humans are not and cannot be creatures apart. Like other life forms, they must win their living from the world about them and must occupy or create an environment whose vagaries or extremes do not exceed the tolerances of their needs and senses. As human beings are natural, such demands are natural. The question that must be posed is, how can urban environment, which will soon be the environment of most people, best fulfill human goals? The answer, some of whose details form the concern and substance of this book, is that urban environment must integrate itself with and stem organically from the natural world of which, like it or not, it is a part.

Before the relationship between the earth, geology, and the city can be explored, some

3

agreement has to be reached as to what is meant by those terms. The popular image of a city is a relatively dense concentration of large numbers of people, houses, shops, factories, roads. However, just what constitutes adequate density and sufficient numbers to warrant calling a place a city varies considerably in different parts of the world. In Denmark, for instance, a place in which 250 people live in close proximity is called a city, whereas in Korea, unless at least 40,000 people are grouped together, a place is not a city. The density of population in central Singapore is 971,000 per square mile; Los Angeles has 5000 people per square mile. Even if density and numbers seem sufficient, a place may not be considered a city. The population of Rye, New York, is similar to that of Santa Fe, New Mexico, yet to the inhabitants of southern New York state, Rye is a village, whereas to the inhabitants of New Mexico, Santa Fe is a city. The reason: the importance of Rye is obscured by its proximity to New York City, whereas Santa Fe is a state capital, one of the larger settlements in the region, and a noted historic and cultural center. Staten Island, situated in New York Harbor, is part of New York City, but Edgewater, New Jersey, which is closer to Manhattan than is Staten Island, is not part of New York City. In medieval times, the term city was usually restricted to the area within an enclosing town wall. Today, few city walls remain intact; only their memory may be preserved in the names of roads or sections: Wall Street, Bishopsgate.

From this welter of contradictions, it might well be concluded, with much justification, that a city is whatever local people choose to call a city. However, for many purposes, including those of this book, a somewhat more specific, working definition is required. Here, a *city* shall be a relatively dense grouping of large numbers of people and structures, unified by and located within a definite political boundary, and whose primary concern in *not* connected with agriculture. Furthermore, ide-

ally, a city is characterized by social heterogeneity and the opportunity for rich cultural, economic, and political experience and exchange.

If a city, by definition, is restricted to the area within a particular political boundary, its influence and many of its characteristics spread considerably further, affecting what may be called a *metropolitan region*. The Standard Metropolitan Statistical Area of the U.S. Bureau of the Census consists of an integrated economic and social unit containing at least one city with 50,000 inhabitants, together with adjacent counties of metropolitan character. At least 75 percent of the labor force must be non-agricultural, and at least 50 percent of the population must live in areas with at least 150 people per square mile. Hans Blumenfeld (1967), noted urban theorist, prefers to define a metropolitan region in terms of commuting distance from a major city center: people living within two hours travel-time (about 100 miles in North America) of the city center will be profoundly affected by its presence. (Fig. 1.1) suggests that few areas in the United States lie outside the spheres of influence of metropolitan centers.

Another extremely useful term is the word *urban*, which refers to areas that have most of the physical and economic characteristics of cities but which need not lie within city boundaries. Urban is the opposite of rural, rural pertaining to the countryside. *Urbanization* refers to the conversion of rural into urban areas. The rapid growth of cities and the spread of urbanization in recent years has given rise to the phenomenon of the joining or coalescing of what were previously separate urban areas. Patrick Geddes, a pioneer in urban planning, coined the word *conurbation* to describe the "enormous urban sprawls, where the identity of towns disappears, and political boundaries wander aimlessly in solidly built-up areas. . . ." (Jones, 1966, p. 33). Groupings of conurbations, such as those that are forming along the eastern seaboard of the United States from Boston through

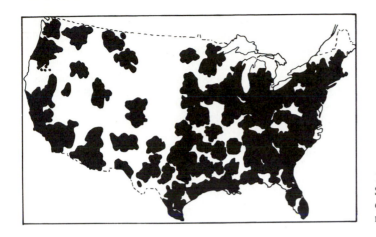

1.1 Map of the mainland United States, showing areas within commuting distance of metropolitan centers in 1960.

New York and Philadelphia to Baltimore and Washington (Fig. 1.2) may eventually constitute a "supercity" or *megalopolis*. Constantine Doxiadis (1968), a famous town planner, foresees, within the not too distant future, the merging of megalopoli to form a single, world-embracing city: *ecumenopolis* (see Fig. 16.13).

If satisfactory definition of a city is elusive, then the definition of *geology* is

agreeably simple, if not over-informative. Geology is the science that seeks to understand earth materials, structures and processes, unravel the history of how they have come to be what they are, and obtain a glimpse of what changes are likely to occur in the future. Encompassed within the sphere of geology (sometimes also called earth science) are a great range of specialties that consider such diverse topics as the

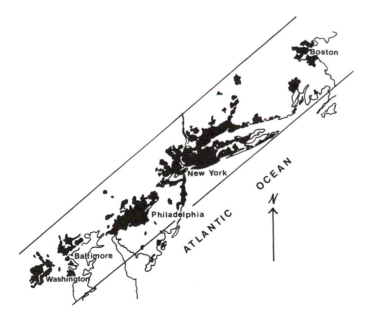

1.2 The urbanized areas along the northeastern coast of the United States may eventually coalesce to form a megalopolis.

origin and evolution of life, the atomic structure of minerals, the mechanisms of volcanic eruption, the formation of landscape, the nature of the earth's interior, and a host of other exotic and fascinating corners of human investigation of the natural world. Many of the fruits of geologic research have been of direct, practical importance to human beings: locating water and ores, evaluating foundations, estimating the probability of natural catastrophes, aiding in the successful disposal of wastes, understanding the effects of earth materials upon human health. Traditionally, however, most geologists have not been concerned with cities. Rather they have and perhaps for the most part still consider the city an intrusion upon and hindrance to an understanding of the earth. Cities, like lakes, like grass, like trees, obscure the rocks below— except where investigations and excavations for tunnels, shafts, roadways, or foundations have provided access to subterranean mysteries. However, with or without the formal participation of geologists, the interaction between the builders of cities and the earth upon which cities are built has provided a small but significant rivulet of geologic information and discovery that has helped nourish the flowering of earth

Table 1.1. Percentages of population in selected urban areas. (Sources: Hall, 1966; Jones, 1966; Population Reference Bureau, Inc., 1976.)

AUSTRALIA		JAPAN	
1933	64%	1920	18%
1947	69%	1930	24%
1954	79%	1940	38%
1961	82%	1950	38%
1974	86%	1955	56%
CANADA		1960	64%
1921	50%	1974	72%
1931	54%	UNITED STATES	
1941	54%	1800	6%
1951	63%	1850	15%
1956	67%	1900	40%
1961	70%	1920	51%
1974	76%	1930	56%
DENMARK		1940	57%
1921	43%	1950	64%
1930	59%	1960	70%
1940	64%	1974	74%
1950	67%	USSR	
1955	69%	1926	18%
1974	80%	1939	32%
		1959	48%
		1974	60%

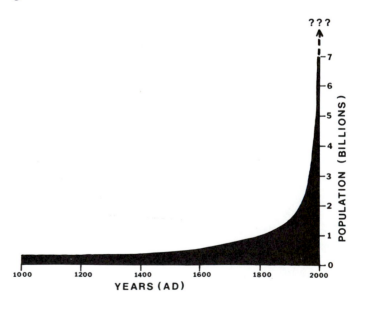

1.3 Increase in world population, A.D. 1000–2000.

science. In return, geologic information, where heeded and sufficient, has guided cities toward rational, economical growth.

Now the time has come to expand the relationship between cities and geology, to make it a formal, conscious part of the fashioning of urban environment. The human race is undergoing radical changes. The number of people populating the planet has begun to soar upward at an ever-increasing rate (Fig. 1.3). Moreover, as their numbers increase, continually larger proportions of humankind are moving to cities (Fig. 1.4), and more specifically to large cities (Figs. 1.5 and 1.6). Table 1.1 demonstrates that this trend is particularly true of industrialized countries. However, even in non-industrialized countries where the bulk of the population remains rural, the large cities that do exist are expanding rapidly. If current trends persist, it may well be that within 100 years, 95 percent of the world's population will be urban. This seemingly inevitable increase and urbanization of the world's population has numerous, diverse ramifications that present the human race with major social, economic, political, and environmental problems. Their satisfactory solution is both imperative and urgent. The crisis is sharpened by the fact that people can no longer fall back upon tried remedies and traditional approaches. The scope and scale of the problems engendered by our in-

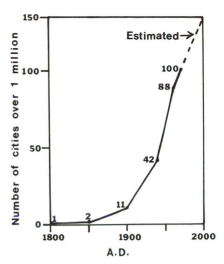

1.5 Increase in the number of cities in the world with populations over one million, from 1800 to 2000.

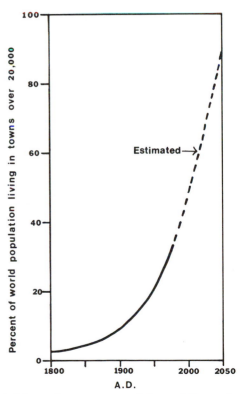

1.6 Increasing percentage of the world's population living in towns with more than 20,000 inhabitants.

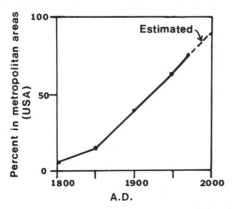

1.4 Increasing percentage of U.S. population in metropolitan areas, from 1800 to 2000.

creasing numbers and rapidly accelerating demands upon the finite resources of the planet become more serious with the passage of each day. Many of these problems are intimately related to the qualities of the earth: its structures, materials, and processes. In urban areas, ''man has so thoroughly intruded that he has overwhelmed many of nature's physical systems. . . .'' (Coates, 1976, p. 1) As will be seen, ignorance of the earth can lead to discomfort, unnecessary expense, waste, and even catastrophe. Understanding and respect of the earth can help preserve and improve the quality of human existence.

The relationship between the earth and the city involves necessities, hazards, and opportunities.

NECESSITIES

The most fundamental earth-related necessities for urban expansion are space, raw materials, energy, water supply, and waste disposal.

Figure 1.7 reveals that of the earth's total surface area, by far the largest part is covered by the waters of the oceans, and half of the remaining area is uninhabitable ice-cap or extreme desert. Only about one-seventh of the earth's surface is ''usable land'' and potentially the site of urban expansion. Of this usable land, only one-tenth of one percent is already built-up, but in less than a century, the built-up regions may cover ten to twenty-five times as much area. The increase is significant on two counts: First, each acre that is urbanized is withdrawn from land devoted to food production, forest, recreation, or wilderness. Second, there is increasing pressure to expand urban areas onto lands inherently unsuitable and sometimes dangerous for human habitation due to the likelihood of events such as earthquake, landslide, flooding, or volcanic eruption. Thus, it becomes extremely important to understand thoroughly the best uses to which each piece of land may be put in the light of its natural geologic and bio-

logic properties. This is true with respect to both the choosing of the original location of the city and its subsequent growth.

By the year 2000, the amount of building that must take place to accommodate the increase in the world's population may well equal or exceed the total, cumulative amount of building undertaken since the start of civilization some six thousand years ago. To accomplish this feat and to ensure the day-to-day functioning of cities once they are built, vast quantities of raw materials and energy will be required, most of which will involve the quarrying or mining of earth materials. Locating the necessary substances—stone, sand, gravel, clay, limestone, metallic and non-metallic ores, coal, oil, gas, uranium—will require considerable investment of geologic expertise.

Today, in the United States, the daily per capita demand for water in urban areas is more than 150 gallons. Multiplying this figure by the hundreds of millions of people who are or who will be inhabiting urban areas suggests the magnitude of the problem of guaranteeing adequate water supply. To ensure that the supply is of acceptable quality requires that water, once used, must be restored to appropriate cleanliness through treatment and by controlled disposal of harmful wastes. Both water supply and water quality depend heavily upon local and regional geological and meteorological conditions. For many cities, adequate water and means of waste disposal are already among the most serious problems faced and, until solved, severely restrict the potential for urban expansion.

HAZARDS

The term hazard suggests immediate, unpredictable danger that may occur at any moment or at least in the near future as measured with respect to the length of an individual's lifespan. Immediacy, however, in terms of geologic processes that may encompass millions of years, may imply an event whose occurrence is likely to take

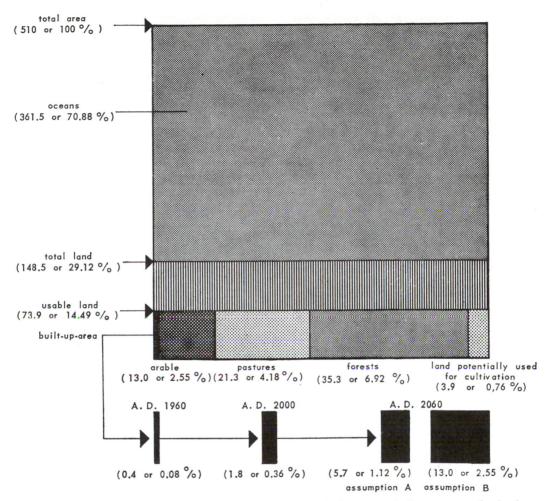

total area
(510 or 100 %)

oceans
(361.5 or 70.88 %)

total land
(148.5 or 29.12 %)

usable land
(73.9 or 14.49 %)

built-up-area

arable   pastures   forests   land potentially used
(13.0 or 2.55 %)(21.3 or 4.18 %)   (35.3 or 6.92 %)   for cultivation
                                                                                    (3.9   or   0,76 %)

A. D. 1960   A. D. 2000   A. D. 2060

(0.4 or 0.08 %)   (1.8 or 0.36 %)   (5.7 or 1.12 %)   (13.0 or 2.55 %)
                                                              assumption A   assumption B

1.7 The large square represents the earth's total surface area. The variable character of the surface is indicated by different patterns. Numbers referring to area are in millions of square kilometers. Percentages indicate percent of the total area of the surface. Four black rectangles place within only hundreds or thousands of years. Thus, later on in this book, it will become convenient to distinguish "short term" geologic hazards (immediate hazards, in the usual sense of the word) from "long term" geologic hazards (those that are "immediate" from the perspective of the span of geologic time).

beneath the square indicate extent of urbanization in 1960, 2000, and 2060. (Two assumptions on extent of urbanization are shown for 2060) Note that only 14.49 percent of the surface is usable by humans; of this area, less than half is considered habitable.

Certain earth hazards are obvious: active volcanoes, rivers that flood frequently, hillsides that slide, zones that are repeatedly ravaged by earthquakes, "tidal" waves, or coastal storms. Contrary to rational expectation, affected areas are often heavily urbanized. Other threats from the earth are more subtle—either because they are in-

frequent, or because they act slowly: settling of the land with consequent tilting or
breaking apart of artificial structures; loss of
soil or retreat of a coastline due to erosion;
burial of roads and houses by river sediment, sand dunes, or wind-transported dust;
drowning or stranding of coastal settlements
due to gradual changes in the level of the
sea or the configuration of the shoreline; the
sudden, unexpected springing to life of an
extinct volcano. Some of these hazards are
beyond our ability to control, but not
beyond our ability to avoid. Other hazards
are caused by people and are the reward of
ignorance, greed, or foolishness. Still others
may be reduced to acceptable proportions or
eliminated or remedied. The key to lessening hazard in each of these cases is knowledge of the possibility of danger and of the
earth mechanisms involved. Such understanding falls within the heart of geologic
investigation.

OPPORTUNITIES

Beyond avoiding earth hazards and securing
the necessities for urban existence, proper
awareness of the earth may help guide
urban environment toward achievement of
its maximum potential. In a city, a sense of
the earth may be gained directly through the
steepness of streets, the rivers or beaches,
the outcroppings of rocks in parks, the use
of granite or limestone in building, or the
sight of mountains on the horizon. Similarly, the presence of the earth is reflected
in the layout of roads and architectural design, or variations in the use to which land
is put. In either case, a sense of the earth

helps to strengthen the connection between
human beings and the larger universe of
which they are a part (Leveson, 1971).
Consciousness of the connection between
people and things larger and more enduring
provides a comfort and sense of perspective
that is essential to psychological and spiritual well-being. Moreover, a keen and per-
sistent sense of the earth helps ensure that
the growth and design of cities takes place
in a way that will make the most of economic and environmental advantages of
urban sites and lessen irrational land use
and encounters with geologic hazards.

If urban environments are to fully benefit
from geologic opportunities, to be less subject to geologic hazards, and to win successfully the geologic necessities of life
from the earth, then the appropriate geologic information must be developed and integrated into the planning and construction
of future cities and the expansion of existing
cities. Geologists, city planners, social scientists, economists, architects, politicians,
legal experts, and ordinary citizens must
work out systems of communication that
guarantee thoughtful exchanges of information and cross-fertilization of ideas. It is
becoming increasingly clear that urban environment is becoming *the* human environment, and that what happens to cities is
what happens to people. Thus, the plight,
betterment and future of cities must be a
major focus of concern and the recipient of
the best that human ingenuity and endeavor
have to offer. The role that geology can and
must play in this struggle is the theme of
this book.

2. Geology and the Development of Cities

ORIGIN OF CITIES

The origins of the first cities are clouded by the passage of time. Traces of ancient cities are as old as the evidence of humans as civilized beings, already present at the dawn of oral and written history (Mumford, 1961). The need to congregate and to establish a social rather than an individual life, and the physical expression of such needs in the form of durable, preservable structures may be traced back at least five thousand years into the obscurity of the Stone Age. The early manifestation of humans as social, congregating creatures must, it seems, have expressed basic needs and drives of the human animal, traceable even further back to primate ancestors.

The early mammalian creatures from which man-like, or "hominoid," primates developed were inhabitants of forests. The basic necessities of life were obtained within the arboreal sphere; the ground was a place of danger, rarely touched down upon. Existence consisted of a jumping, scrambling, climbing from branch to branch, trunk to trunk. Movement took place within a three-dimensional world, an ocean of leaves, wood, air, and scattered sunlight, all-enveloping, all-containing. It was an environment without walls and with few boundaries. The mere interposition of a few hundred feet between the hunted and the hunter provided necessary obscurity, safety, comfort.

About 30 million years ago (Oligocene time), for reasons that remain conjectural, several groups of larger, more advanced primates branched off from the earlier prosimians. Some of these larger primates remained tree-dwellers: New and Old World monkeys, gibbons, and orangutan apes. Other apes descended to the ground, initiating a new mode of existence, and then branched again to give rise to gorillas, chimpanzees and, sometime before five million years ago, the earliest human-like creatures.

These human ancestors probably lived in the great tropical savannas of Africa—scattered clumps of trees in a sea of grass—seemingly unlimited, an eternal environment of abundant game and equable climate. About two million years ago, however, events began to take place far to the north that were to disrupt that relative ease of existence. Repeatedly during the Pleistocene (the Ice Age), massive sheets of ice advanced southward from the Arctic and then gradually melted back again. Accompanying the migration of the ice were radical changes in weather patterns that periodically shifted the position of the savanna belt, at times perhaps to as far north as parts of Arabia and India (McNeill, 1963). Changing patterns of weather were mirrored by rapidly changing assemblages of plant and animal life, and humans were forced to cope with change or to face extinction. By the beginning of the last great retreat of glacial ice some thirty thousand years ago, modern man (*Homo sapiens*) was established on the European continent, an environment of harsh, seasonal climatic changes and of flora and fauna radically different from the African savanna. Spurred by necessity, humans had evolved the art of toolmaking, had tamed fire, developed language, and were already endowed with an ancient heritage of custom and ritual, myth and legend.

Paleolithic men (approximately 2 million to 10 thousand years ago) were hunters, forming nomadic tribes of perhaps 20 to 60 people, whose existence depended upon the gathering of fruits and nuts and wild plants, and the following of game. During winter months, the protective shelter of caves permitted life to continue until the release of spring. Just as forests offered protection to our earliest ancestors, caves were for Paleolithic hunters protected places from which they could venture forth. Caves offered physical security, warmth, and the psychological comfort of *envelopment,* and in doing so assumed a particular significance. The dark recesses suggested access to the womb of Mother Earth. Paintings, such as those in the caves of Lascaux in south-central France produced by the Magdalenian hunters sixteen thousand years ago, were perhaps the result of rituals designed to propitiate animal spirits or to encourage their fecundity (McNeill, 1963). Spiritual life was already complex, important, and inextricably intertwined with the mundane.

Those who encountered the sea found other sources of food available: an abundance and variety of shellfish and the possibility of catching fish. The sheltered cove bisected by a freshwater stream was ideal (Tuan, 1974). There, advantages of forest and clearing, security and adventure existed side by side. Furthermore, sand and water, like forest and cave, are substances in which humans in a sense, submerse themselves, and within which they can regain the sense of haven and security that comes from envelopment (Tuan, 1974). As will be seen, the search for the reassurance that *envelopment* provides helped, later on, shape the character of cities.

A life of hunting and of gathering wild plant food can only support a limited population. Some ten to fifteen thousand years ago, the tools and techniques necessary for the domestication of animals and the cultivation of crops were developed. Geologist H. E. Wright, Jr. (1976), professor in the Center for Ancient Studies at the University of Minnesota, suggests that climatic changes attendant upon the retreat of glaciers at the end of the Pleistocene helped provide the optimal conditions for the attainment of those skills. Thus advantaged, but also thus encumbered, humans abandoned the nomadic existence of hunter and gatherer for the more rooted life of farmer and herdsman, and with food supplies more certain, larger populations could be supported. Agriculture was perhaps first established in valleys or basins of modest size traversed by permanently flowing streams (Tuan, 1974). Fertile floodplains might be successfully planted and harvested, the river itself was a possible source of food, and settlements could be built close by on gravel terraces or valley slopes not subject to flood. In such surroundings the first villages were born. The earliest constructed dwellings in some cultures were often copies of caves: holes carved into the sides of cliff or hillside or covered pits excavated in flatter ground, and suggest the halting and difficult progress of human beings in their struggle to come to grips with fickle Nature.

As humans progressed from forest to cave to valley, their struggle for survival and betterment took place in both spheres of existence: the spiritual or religious as well as the physical or mundane. Flood, famine, drought, and disease were constant dangers.

A foothold as farmer was for eons only perilously established. The universe was a strange mixture of order and chaos. The rising and setting of the sun and the moon, and the march of the stars across the night sky displayed reassuring regularity, but the ravages of storm and insect, invasions by wild beasts and other humans, the rush and recession of flowing streams, all were impressive testimony to the fragile, illusory nature of security in a world of chaos.

The earliest comings together of people were, therefore, attempts to enlarge the sphere of order at the expense of disorder. Even before the establishing of villages, certain spots became favored as meeting places, places that people came to again and again—because they offered certain obvious material benefits, or because they possessed an indefinable mystic character, an aura that hinted at links to the invisible world where power resided, power that was capable of controlling and taming the disorderly universe, power that might somehow be persuaded or bribed to act in man's favor. Caves, springs, burial sites, special trees or stones were among such places (Mumford, 1961).

When the first villages were established, their particular location was governed as much by proximity to such sacred shrines as by material considerations such as fertile land, dependable water supply, defensible position, and, at a later stage, proximity to trade routes (Mumford, 1961).

Thus, the act of establishing a dwelling place, and the grouping of such structures to form a village was a definite first attempt to take possession of the environment, to create order out of disorder (Norberg-Schulz, 1971). It was a transformation of profane space into sacred space, an act that echoed the creation of the world. (The symbolic, religious aspect of the founding of dwelling places was not lost until much later. The priesthood played a vital role in the establishing of Greek and Roman cities. Indeed, the universe-creating aspects of the founding of cities persists, in transformed guise, even today.) The very construction of an enclosure divided the universe into an *inside* and an *outside,* into *the closed* and *the open,* with all attendant associations. Enclosed space (*envelopment*) implies security, coziness, privacy, darkness, biologic life; open space suggests freedom, adventure, light, the public realm (Tuan, 1974). (The Egyptian hieroglyph for "city" also meant "mother," something warm and embracing.) Juxtaposition of the enclosed and the open, the cozy and the grand, the intimate and the public, the shuttling between residential cubbyholes and spacious public squares were to become essential elements in the appeal of urban life.

The coming together of people and the construction of villages was also rooted in practical advantage. Grouping permitted exchange of ideas, cooperative labor, and mutual support in times of defense or aggression. Early villages resembled cattle pens: a few simple structures clustered together, perhaps about a tribal shrine, and an enclosing wall with a gate of some sort. Daytime existence was largely outside the wall: labor in the fields, the tending of animals. Life inside the village was principally one of retreat—at night or in times of danger—or for the sick, the young, and the old. Activities were centered about established custom. Procedures that had proved successful were clung to, and little deviation was tolerated. That which had allowed people to live harmoniously with each other, and to maintain existence in a harsh universe was deemed moral; all else was immoral, and a perpetrator of immoral acts was subject to punishment or expulsion.

By 6500 B.C., the ice had melted back from continental Europe and climatic zones were as we know them today. In that part of the Middle East known as Mesopotamia, a grain-centered agriculture flourished that permitted considerable expansion of human population and the proliferation of villages. By 3000 B.C., a mature civilization (the Sumerian), replete with urban centers was established (Fig. 2.1). That the rise of civili-

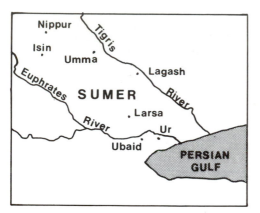

2.1 Urban centers in Sumer, ca. 3000 B.C.

zation and cities took place in the Middle East was not accident. Agriculture dependent upon rainfall is hazardous, except in those places where rainfall is seasonal, predictable, and dependable. Rainfall in the Middle East is erratic, and successful large-scale farming awaited the spread of agriculture to the irrigable valleys of the lower Tigris and Euphrates rivers, and the development of the technical skills necessary to conceive of and implement the building of dikes and canals to divert and transport water to crop-growing areas.

The evolution of the technical skills necessary for irrigation may have been stimulated by the need to identify the correct planting season in an area of erratic rainfall. Historian William McNeill suggests that astronomic observation and the development of an "agricultural calendar" were vital in order to avoid catastrophic mistakes in the timing of the planting of fields. In areas where rainfall is seasonal and predictable, mistakes in planting are less likely, and the spur to observational and intellectual growth is absent.

Improvements in irrigation techniques and in methods of plowing gradually permitted the accumulation of agricultural surpluses, which in turn permitted some to abandon the full-time occupation of producing food and to specialize in and elaborate

other skills. Earliest among such specialists or "professionals" were perhaps religious functionaries who served as intermediaries between the people and gods in an attempt to minimize natural disaster. As the valleys of the Tigris and the Euphrates became increasingly populated with farmers, fishermen, and herdsmen, conflicts of interest became more frequent and inevitable. The peaceful settlement of disputes required the emergence of a class of managers to whom authority was ceded. Increasing grain surpluses harvested from the nearly flat, stone-free soil—a soil continually renewed during frequent floods—permitted an exchange of agricultural goods in return for lumber, stone, and metals with hill peoples who lived peripheral to the valley. Surplus labor could be directed toward the building of monumental religious edifices, the extension of dikes and canals, and the development of water and land transport.

Gradually the villages became nodes in a larger social web characterized by an increasing number of religious, craft, and administrative specialists concentrated into temple communities which, for the first time in human history "technically permitted and psychologically compelled the production of an agricultural surplus and applied that surplus to support specialists, who became, as city dwellers have since remained, the creators, sustainers, and organizers of civilized life" (McNeill, 1963, p. 36).

In addition to the religious, managerial, and technical classes, kings and their military retinue were an additional burden the food-producers had to support. The origin of "kingship" as distinct from temple administration may lie in the character of pastoral life. Whereas passivity and conformity were of prime importance in agricultural settlements, prowess and the martial arts were prized by pastoral nomads who had to protect herds from predators. Also, encounters between herdsmen and cultivators often resulted in the former subjugating the latter. It may have been the descendants of

Semitic pastoral tribesmen who comprised the royal families and attendant armies (McNeill, 1963).

Thus the panoply of civilization and cities was assembled, manifest both in social relationships and the resulting physical structures: king, peasant, priest, nobleman, artisan, merchant, engineer, bureaucrat, soldier, artist, palace, temple, granary, marketplace, house, farm, dike, canal, street, fortification—all combined to form rich pageantries of thought and activity, centers of vibrant exchange of ideas, news, goods, and services. Beyond the Mesopotamian valley, civilization and cities took root in other favorable environments where irrigated agriculture was feasible. In Egypt a complex society developed along the Nile; the city of Jericho flourished in the Jordan valley; to the east great cities arose on the banks of the Indus and Hwang Ho.

Egypt, Mesopotamia, and Greece

In the foregoing analysis it was suggested that geologic stirrings of the earth—specifically the rhythms of the Ice Age—profoundly influenced the biologic and early cultural evolution of humans toward technical, intellectual, and spiritual attainment and the subsequent rise of civilization through the founding of cities. A logical and interesting next question to pursue is whether spiritual and physical differences between early civilizations and cities may have been due, at least in part, to differences in the geologic environment in which they evolved. Comparison of early Egypt, Greece, and Mesopotamia supports this possibility.

Egyptian civilization, developed within the protective confines of the Nile Valley, was long insulated against foreign intrusion by the great stretches of almost impassable desert that lay to the east, south, and west, and by the expanse of the Mediterranean to the north (Fig. 2.2). Each year the relatively predictable gentle flood of the Nile spread through the valley and then receded, leaving

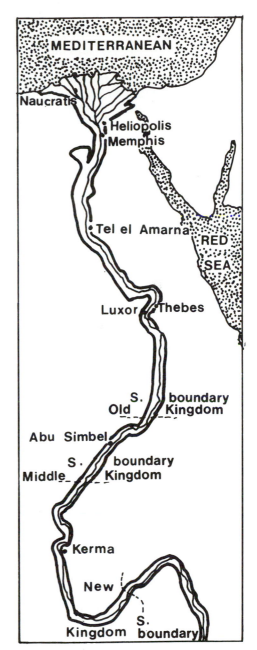

2.2 Ancient Egyptian cities along the Nile Valley. The two roughly parallel heavy lines indicate the boundaries of the Nile Valley and the adjacent desert on either side.

behind a new coating of fertile sediment. The climate was equable, generally devoid of surprise or extreme. The river itself was easily navigable; boats traveling to the north could take advantage of the current; those headed in the opposite direction could raise sails to the prevailing northerly winds. Thus, the Nile was a natural artery of transport and communication that early served to integrate the fertile lands along its shores into a single state. Indeed, control of shipping by the royal family enabled it to exert such excellent control over all the habitable regions that great cities in the form of dense aggregates of structures may not have developed until 1500 B.C.; before that, the power and proliferation of the royal household and the specialization of its parts lent the aura of *city* to the entire Nile Valley. The royal family could amass labor, construct pyramids, temples, and palaces, engineer earthworks to divert and direct the river, and administrate and adjudicate successfully even though the population was relatively dispersed. Access to excellent building stone where cliffs and slopes separated the Nile Valley from the adjacent desert permitted high development of the arts of stone sculpture and wall painting. Urbanity displaced parochialism as civilization spread along the watery ganglia of the Nile. The Egyptian mental outlook was worldly; the gods were ever-present, powerful, but essentially benign. They provided the backdrop of life and, when it occurred, their entry upon the stage was ritual rather than disruptive. In times of disaster, the Egyptians tended to place the blame upon humans rather than on their spiritual overlords.

The physical context of Mesopotamian civilization was by contrast turbulent and often harsh. The boundaries of the fertile Tigris-Euphrates Valley were often penetrated by hostile tribes that occupied less favorably endowed peripheral lands. The rivers themselves were only navigable in the downstream sense, and then only when the river level was right. Upstream travel had to

be overland, inherently more difficult and hazardous. The prodding of barbarian invasion spurred political centralization, the development of a bureaucracy and of a professional army, improved administrative technique through written communication, increase in trade, and the rise of an independent merchant class—in other words, the elements of civilization. Relative difficulty in communication and transport may have favored the concentration of the non-agricultural populace into cities. Aside from their frequent non-navigability, the Tigris and Euphrates were subject to destructive, erratic flooding and to periods of low water and drought. Furthermore, frequent shifts in the position of the river channel stranded riverside cities and rendered useless whole irrigation networks. Ur, Uruk, and Kish on the Euphrates declined before 2000 B.C. as a result of such changes in stream course (Bellan, 1971). Mirroring the physical universe, the gods were viewed as arbitrary and capricious. Even if all the demands of the gods were met, there were no guarantees that they would be favorably inclined toward the wishes and needs of humans. The rule of priest and king was correspondingly harsh and life was marred by frequent violence and terror.

The cities of Ancient Greece were forced to develop on rocky islands, mountainous terrain, or small pockets of flatter land hemmed in by mountain and sea. These environments, strikingly different from the fertile river valleys of Egypt and Mesopotamia, affected the size and form of cities and the world view of the inhabitants. The early Minoan civilization—with the exception of its center at Knossos on the island of Crete, where perhaps eighty thousand people were supported by abundant grain fields—consisted of isolated trading towns, each housing populations of less than a few thousand. By contrast, half a million people may have lived in the immediate vicinity of the city of Ur in Mesopotamia (Hammond, 1972). The classical Greek city-states, which began to emerge more than a thousand years later in the eighth century B.C., resulted from the merging of groups of villages within naturally defined agricultural areas. Isolated from each other by rugged terrain, these urban centers remained small (generally a few tens of thousands) and the inhabitants, accustomed to a life of struggle due to the necessity of winning bread from soil that was often shallow, stony, and situated on steep slopes, were typically self-reliant and independent (Mumford, 1961). As a result, Greece was long characterized by many local sovereignties, each with its own gods and laws, rather than one all-powerful, remote, central government. In practical terms, this led to the concept that the power residing in the state and in law ultimately derived from the citizens themselves and their decisions.

Choosing the Site—Spiritual Aspects

Both the spiritual and material aspects of the decision of where to build a city have been affected significantly by properties of the earth. Early man often solved the problem of where to place a settlement largely in religious terms. That is, the site had to be acceptable in terms of spiritual potential and to be pleasing to the gods. Within each culture, certain spots determined by the configuration of the topography or certain specific features of the landscape (a stone, a spring) were recognized as the right place to build. The mystical importance of site was frequently so strong that often a site was not only "holy" before the construction of a settlement but remained so through disasters that destroyed the settlement itself (Rapoport, 1969).

Athens An analysis by Vincent Scully, the well-known art historian, of the relationship between Greek sacred architecture and the landscape helps to illustrate this point: To the Greeks, the site of a temple was holy *before* the temple was built upon it. As the temple and the buildings associated with it were constructed, they had to respond to and enhance the sacred character of the place: "the natural and the man-made create one ritual whole, in which man's part is defined and directed by the sculptural masses of the land and is subordinate to their rhythms" (Scully, 1962, p. 11). According to Scully, the specific landscape elements sought for the palaces in Crete from 2000 B.C. onward were an enclosed valley in which the palace was set; a gently mounded or conical hill on axis with the palace to the north or south; and a higher, double-peaked or cleft mountain some distance beyond the hill but on the same axis. All these features are present at Knossos, Phaistos, Mallia, and Gournia; moreover, they define and focus the architectural space of each palace complex. The success of Athens, Scully suggests, may be attributed not only to economically advantageous features (fertile land, quality clay deposits, silver-bearing ore) and a defensible hilltop (the Acropolis), but also to an "ancient sanctity of place" that provided its people with "sacred symbols of the earth to focus upon." Athens lies within the basin of the Attic plain; from the site of the archaic temple of Athena Polias on the Acropolis, the Hymettos Range furnishes a profile of a double-peaked mountain; below and nearer than the bulk of the Hymettos Range, a number of conical foothills are clearly visible (Fig. 2.3). (It may be noted parenthetically that the topographic setting of Athens has an elegant, simple relationship to its geologic setting: elevation correlates directly with rock structure and material (Figs. 2.4; 2.5).

These religious or spiritual aspects of the choosing of a site may seem strange to us, but for primitive people mythologic events are more real than mundane events. In fact, for primitive peoples, ordinary events are made "real" by modeling them after mythologic events (Eliade, 1959; 1961).

The religious aspects of choosing a site and the influence of the earth upon the spiritual choice have persisted through time in diluted form, manifest in founding ceremo-

2.3 The Acropolis, Athens, with horns of Hymettos and conical hills at Kaisariani.

nies, patriotic utterances, and aesthetic declarations (see Chap. 15).

Choosing the Site—Material Aspects

The role that the earth plays in the material aspects of the decision of where to create a settlement is more commonly appreciated than its role in spiritual decisions. Cities need adequate water, ways to dispose of wastes, good building foundations, and materials suitable and plentiful enough for construction purposes. The earth may also furnish that which is necessary for the economic viability of the city: a fertile hinterland, coal, oil, and mineral deposits, energy from running water; favorable topographic configuration such as a good har-

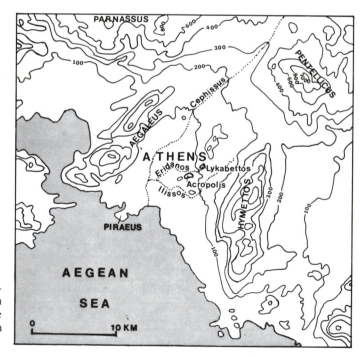

2.4 Topographic map of Athens and surrounding mountain ranges. The dotted lines are streams, contours are shown in meters.

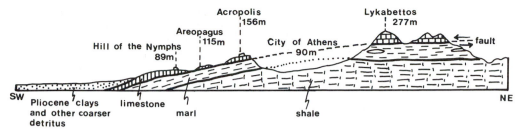

2.5 Geologic cross section of Athens through Lykabettos and the Acropolis. Note how the hills are underlain by remnants of a once-continuous, resistant limestone. The valley in which Athens sits is underlain by non-resistant shales that are exposed where the limestone has been eroded away.

bor, a mountain pass that facilitates trade, or navigable streams. Before modern forms of warfare, the defensibility of a site in terms of its topography and water supply was important. Topography sometimes also exerts considerable influence over local variations in climate that may affect the exact positioning of a settlement. Where observation indicates that a site is subject to natural hazards, such sites will be avoided if reason prevails.

A few examples will demonstrate the influence of the earth upon site selection and subsequent development in these material senses.

Athens (*continued*)   Athens lies in the middle of an irregular, undulating plain roughly 10 miles wide and 15 miles long. On three sides the plain is hemmed in by mountains whose foothills extend a considerable distance toward the central part of the enclosed area; the fourth side of the plain is bounded by the Aegean Sea. From the center of the plain several rocky hills arise abruptly; the highest (Lykabettos) to almost a thousand feet above sea level (Fig. 2.4). These hills are the last remnants of a series of sedimentary layers which once covered the entire area (Fig. 2.5). One of the hills, the Acropolis, has a relatively flat top nearly 1000 feet long and 445 feet wide, and is bounded by precipitous cliffs on all except the western side that drop more than 250 feet to the surrounding plain. Human occupation of the Acropolis was first abetted by the presence of caves and ledges on the south slope which were thickly inhabited in the Neolithic. By 3000 B.C., a hamlet existed on the ledge at the base of the northwest shoulder of the Acropolis. This "bleak site was chosen, no doubt, because of the ease with which water could be tapped as it emerged through artesian action from between the fractured geologic strata of the Acropolis" (Thompson and Wycherley, 1972, p.2). In times of siege, those who retreated to the hilly defenses of the Acropolis could retain access to this water by zigzagging their way down a deep cleft (Hill, 1953). The spring, known as Klepsydra, was later enclosed by an artificial spring house: "A deep rectangular basin of well-fitted masonry was inserted like a box into the cleft. Steps . . . led down to a paved platform which enclosed the basin . . . and users descended to this to lower their vessels over a railing into the water" (Wycherley, 1969, p. 217). Thus, the choice of the Acropolis as the nucleus from which Athens grew was due to the presence of caves, defensible topography, and availability of water in times of siege, as well as its presumed spiritual suitability.

The subsequent success of Athens, as has already been suggested, was due at least in part to several geologically controlled factors. Attica clay is one of the finest clays in the world. Its unusual plastic properties permitted the most refined shapes to be fashioned on the wheel, and its rich reddish-brown color was considered exceedingly handsome. The ancient clay pits from which it was originally taken have been worked continuously through to modern times (Noble, 1965). Marble building stone of exceptional quality was available from the Pentelicus and the Hymettos. White scars on the flanks of Pentelicus now mark the site of modern quarries located not far from the ancient diggings. Silver from the mines at Laurium (30 km southeast of Athens) was an exceedingly valuable resource that helped finance the building of Athens. Overflows from the Cephissus River just west of Athens and its tributaries deposited fertile soil which, when adequate water was available, could sustain considerable agriculture. The natural harbor at Piraeus facilitated trade and fishing.

The most serious geologic problem that Athens faced was ensuring an adequate water supply. The Athenian plain has always been fairly arid. In modern times rainfall is 16 inches per year, all of which falls between October and January, and there is no reason to assume the rainfall has been radically different in the last five thousand years. Two rivers, the Eridanos and the Ilissos, used to merge and flow through the outskirts of Athens as a "sparkling stream shaded by plane trees, so beloved of Sokrates and associated with the sanctuaries of Pan and Acheloos and the nymphs and the spring Kallirhoe . . ." (Hill, 1953, p. 215). In recent times, the growth of population and the demands of "progress" have led to their channels being filled in. However, it is likely that along much of their courses, the streams were intermittent or clouded with sediment (Weller, 1924). The major stream of the valley, the Cephissus, dries up before it reaches the sea, except in times of flood.

As the population of Athens grew, water from natural springs eventually failed to meet the demand, and hundreds of wells were dug, some more than a hundred feet deep. Rainwater was channeled through terracotta pipes and collected in cisterns. In the sixth century B.C., to supplement local supplies the tyrant Peisistratus brought water into the city from the east by means of earthenware pipes and narrow trenches dug into the earth or soft bedrock. By the fourth century B.C., aqueducts had been constructed of large blocks of soft limestone (Lang, 1968), and in Roman times, Hadrian began and Antoninus Pius completed an aqueduct and terminal reservoir on the south side of Lykabettos which have since been restored and are in use today.

Despite water shortages, problems of flooding sometimes arose. The site of the Agora (the marketplace) was ideal in that it was low enough for water to be brought in by gravity flow to supplement local wells; slightly inclined so that there was good natural drainage; and regular enough to be easily leveled for building. However, in times of heavy rainfall, water from nearby slopes rushed over the Agora, causing flooding and depositing masses of sediment. "By the end of the 6th century B.C. the need for efficient artificial drainage had become obvious, and soon thereafter it was provided by the construction of a great stone channel . . . [which] has resumed its function in modern times" (Thompson and Wycherley, 1972, p. 194).

Water   Water has been a major factor in the siting and development of cities throughout history. Four and a half thousand years ago disputes took place between the Mesopotamian cities of Lagash and Umma over water. Already at that time a canal still in use today, the Shatt-el-Hai, connected the Euphrates and Tigris rivers (Warnick, 1969). In about 1700 B.C., Hammurabi constructed a canal to bring water to Sumer and Akkad. Sennacherib (705–681 B.C.), King of Assyria, constructed dams, diverted rivers, and built canals (one 35 miles long) and aqueducts to bring fresh water to Nineveh, his capital. Ninevah sat on the banks of the Tigris, but Sennacherib found the muddy water of that river "not good enough for an emperor'' (Biswas, 1972, p. 31). About 600 B.C., in Greece, Polycrates of Samos employed Eupalinus to supervise the cutting of a tunnel through a hill which separated the town from its water source so that in times of danger, access to the water could be secure (Winter, 1971). The tunnel was eight feet across, eight feet high and 4200 feet long. Similarly, water tunnels were built in Palestine to assure supply during times of war. Palestinian cities typically were built on hilltops at the bottoms of which were the springs or streams that provided the municipal supply. Secret tunnels funneled water from the streams to reservoirs within the city walls or to the bottoms of shafts provided with stairs so that the water might be reached. At el-Jib, the Arab village eight miles from Jerusalem that occupies the site of the ancient biblical city of Gibeon (where Joshua asked the Lord to make the sun stand still), the ancient water systems unearthed by the ar-

cheologist Pritchard are an example of this type of water strategy. Gibeon was situated on a hill and surrounded by a massive city wall which, when the gates were shut, provided an almost impregnable defense. However, the wall separated the city from its water supply at the base of the hill. The wall could not be enlarged to encircle the spring without weakening the hilltop system of defense. To obtain water, two projects were undertaken. The first, constructed from about the twelfth to eleventh century B.C., was the digging of a large, 80-foot-deep shaft down to an artesian water source. The shaft, about 37 feet in diameter at the top, was dug in solid limestone and required the excavation of about 3000 tons of rock. A staircase dug into the side of the shaft gave access to the pool of water at the bottom (Fig. 2.6). The second project, about the tenth century B.C., was the digging of a cave and two tunnels into the side of the hill (Fig. 2.7). One tunnel brought water from a

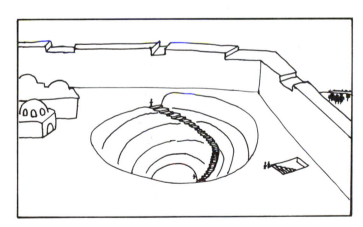

2.6 Hypothetical reconstruction of the large water-shaft at Gibeon (el-Jib), near Jerusalem.

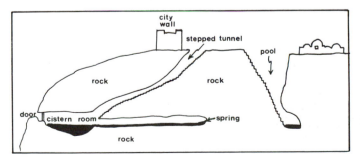

2.7 Cross section of the walled city of Gibeon showing the ancient water projects.

spring into a cistern room within the cave; the other tunnel, with stairs cut into its floor, gave access to the cistern room from within the city wall. A small, easily defended door opened into the cistern room from the side of the hill to give alternate access to the water in times of peace (Pritchard, 1962).

Jerusalem's water supply was similarly secured by means of a tunnel built by Hezekiah, King of Judah, (circa 700 B.C., which led from the Gihon spring outside the city walls to the pool of Siloam inside the walls (Fig. 2.8). The tunnel, which is still intact, runs 1776 feet through solid limestone. It was excavated simultaneously from both ends. An ancient inscription discovered in 1888 reads: "When three cubits were still left to be pierced, the voice of one was heard calling to another, for there was a cleft in the rock from the south side. And on the day on which the boring was finished, the stonecutters struck one towards the other, pick against pick. Thereupon the waters flowed from the entrance to the reservoir, 1200 cubits away. And the height of the rock above the heads of the stonecutters was 100 cubits." (Robins, 1946, p. 47).

The Gihon spring is the only defensible spring in the immediate vicinity, and was one of the major factors in the founding of the earliest settlement at Jerusalem. During later times, the spring water was augmented by the diversion of rainfall to open reservoirs and rock-hewn cisterns, permitting the expansion of the city during the period from the eighth to the first centuries B.C. (Amiran, 1975). However, in the days of the Second Temple, Jerusalem's rapid growth brought about serious problems of water supply, until a series of aqueducts were built to convey water to the city from other sources. They consisted of three groups of springs issuing from hillsides south of the city at slightly higher elevations, thus permitting gravity flow to the city. The difference in elevation was so small, however, that the aqueducts had to be constructed along meandering, lengthy

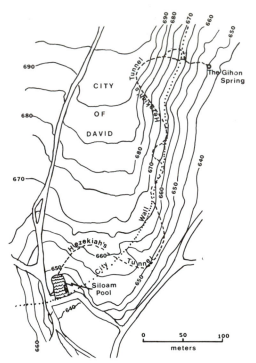

2.8 Contour map of the City of David, Jerusalem, showing the location of Hezekiah's Tunnel and the former city wall. Contour interval is 5 meters.

routes to avoid numerous topographic obstructions. One of the aqueducts, the Wadi Biyar route, ran through a tunnel whose floor rested on impermeable rock and whose walls and ceiling were cut into highly permeable, water-rich rock. Thus, the aqueduct was supplied not only from the spring at its beginning, but also through seepage from the tunnel walls and roof along much of its course (Fig. 2.9). The famous Solomon's Pools south of Bethlehem were part of the aqueduct-reservoir system. It was only recently, during the days of the British Mandate in Palestine, that the aqueducts were abandoned as a water source for Jerusalem, replaced by modern pumps and iron pipes. The Biyar Aqueduct, however, was rebuilt by the British to supply Solomon's Pools, and remains the prime source of water for them (Mazar, 1975).

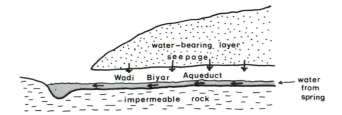

2.9 Diagrammatic cross section of the Wadi Biyar aqueduct.

The Wadi Biyar type of aqueduct was based on the Persian *qanat* system used to supply water for irrigation and municipal supply centuries earlier and later copied throughout the Roman Empire. Actually, qanats probably originated in Armenia sometime before 700 B.C. A qanat is an artificial channel which carries water long distances underground either from a spring or from water-bearing strata (Fig. 2.10).The supply tunnel, which is 2–4 feet wide and 4–7 feet high, frequently extends for more than 25 miles underground and in places reaches depths of up to 400 feet. The tunnel was constructed by digging a series of vertical well-shafts down to a water-bearing layer. The shafts were then connected by a slightly inclined tunnel that carried the water to the desired location. Qanats had several advantages over surface water-channels that compensated for the difficulty of their construction. Normally, considerable amounts of water are lost by evaporation as it travels in surface channels through dry or desert regions. If water travels underground, this loss is not only avoided, but the water remains cool and free of surface contaminants. The qanats of Iran comprised 170,000 miles of underground channels, and in 1968 still supplied 75 percent of all the water used in Iran (Wulff, 1968). Until the recent construction of the Karaj Dam, the two million inhabitants of Teheran depended upon a qanat system for water.

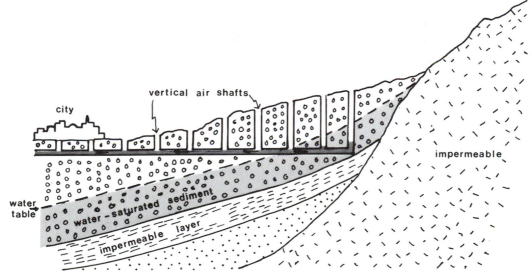

2.10 Diagrammatic cross section of a Persian qanat. Not to scale.

The aqueducts that supplied Rome are legendary. For the first four and a half centuries of its existence, Rome obtained water either from the Tiber or from wells and springs. Late in the fourth century B.C., these sources became insufficient, and Appius Claudius Crassus undertook the building of the first aqueduct in 312 B.C. Construction continued for more than 350 years. The structures were built on a very gentle gradient, just enough to convey water by the pull of gravity. In this way, water could be brought great distances, 60 miles or more. The aqueducts wound their way around and through mountains and across valleys (Fig. 2.11). Some of the aqueducts ran underground for tens of miles; one more than fifty miles, and the bridges and arches that carried them across valleys reached heights of over 100 feet. The magnificence of the Roman aqueducts may be further appreciated when it is noted that the much acclaimed Old Croton Aqueduct, which was constructed in 1837–43 to bring water to New York City was only 37 miles long. Indeed, the Romans were proud of their engineering skills. Strabo wrote that ''while the Greeks bore the reputation of being discerning choosers of sites for the foundation of cities, aiming at beauty, defensive siting, harbors and fertile soil, the Romans showed good discrimination in points neglected by the Greeks, such as the construction of roads and aqueducts, and of sewers that could wash the filth of the city into the Tiber . . . almost every house has cisterns, waterpipes, and copious fountains. . . .'' (Strabo, *Geography* v. 3–8 *in* Dudley, 1967, p. 3).

Great feats of engineering were not restricted to the Old World. The ancient Peruvians built, possibly before the Christian era, a conduit 125 miles in length to bring water from the mountains to the capital (Warnick, 1969).

The position of the first settlement of Los Angeles, El Pueblo de Nuestra Senora la Reina de Los Angeles (1781), was determined by considerations of water supply.

2.11 Sketch of a reconstruction of the Roman aqueducts near Campannelle.

Instead of being located along the coast, the Pueblo was founded well inland from the Pacific at the Glendale Narrows, where the flow of the Los Angeles River was most dependable. (Details of the role of water supply upon the growth of Los Angeles are given in Chapter 3).

Las Vegas, which means ''the fertile plains'', originated as an oasis community centered about springs in the Mojave Desert. It later flourished as a water-supply depot for the transcontinental railroad.

Water in the form of hot springs has been the determining factor in the origin and growth of some cities. For example, the city of Bath in England owes its existence to the quarter of a million gallons of water at 120° F which gushes each day from springs that have been flowing constantly since before the Roman conquest of Britain. Legend has it that Prince Bladud (who was later to be the father of King Lear), when evicted from his father's court after contracting leprosy, became a swineherd. While watching his pigs one day, he noted that the pigs, who also suffered from skin diseases, were miraculously cured after wallowing in a hot steamy swamp. Following their example, Bladud himself was cured and was able to return to his father's court. When he became king, he established a health spa at the swamp and gave it his own name, Bladud,

2.12 An aerial view of Bath, England showing two Georgian crescents and a circle.

from which the name Bath derives (Buchanan, 1976). Establishment of the Roman spa at the site occurred shortly after the Claudian invasion of Britain in A.D. 43. The Roman town was called Aquae Sulis after Sulis Minerva, the Roman goddess of healing. An extensive bathing establishment was built over the hot springs and a magnificent temple was dedicated to the goddess. The spa flourished for almost four hundred years until the Roman legions were finally recalled. With the departure of the Romans, the buildings began to decay and the hot springs covered over with by mud and reverted to swamp. Burial of the hot springs was caused by flooding and deposition of sediment from the nearby River Avon, on whose floodplain the springs are located. Throughout the later history of the springs, there was a constant rebuilding at higher levels as the Avon continued to construct its floodplain. The Roman ruins and the springs were ignored or unsuspected for 500 years until the tenth century, when Bath briefly regained importance as the center of a monastic community. In medieval times, five open unsavory baths were maintained. Finally, in the eighteenth century, Bath regained its glory as a famous health and social resort, and was completely rebuilt (out of the famous Bath stone, a limestone of exceptionally good quality) to become one of the most beautiful cities in Europe and a masterpiece of Georgian town planning. Today it remains a major tourist attraction and a gracious provincial city (Fig. 2.12).

Topography

Topographic features that have facilitated transport, invasion, and the development of trade routes have played an important part in the location of cities (Pirenne, 1925; 1956).

London, which originated in the first century A.D., developed forty miles inland from the sea along the Thames at the first place where the river could be forded and eventually bridged. At this point the river had a gravel bed which provided trading vessels with a firm landing ground on either bank. Two hills, Ludgate Hill and Cornhill, which were forty feet above the floodplain over which the Thames meandered and well above the dangers of rising floodwaters, provided safe places for settlement (Barker and Jackson, 1974).

River fords also played a part in the origin and development of Paris and Rome, where the presence of islands in the Seine and the Tiber facilitated river-crossing and later the building of bridges.

Toronto originated on the shore of Lake Ontario about five miles from the mouth of the Humber River. The Humber River was navigable by small craft to within a short distance overland from the Holland River, which flows north into Lake Simcoe (Fig. 2.13). Toronto was thus a key point on the portage route that connected the Great Lakes of the north with the east-west waterway formed by Lake Ontario and the St. Lawrence River. Road and rail connections in later years have maintained this pattern of transportation (Fig. 2.13) (Blumenfeld, 1967).

Coastal configurations that provide good harbors, especially when navigable rivers or bays are present to provide access to interior hinterlands, help account for the origin and growth of many cities. Boston on the Charles River, New York on the Hudson, Wilmington and Philadelphia on the Delaware, Norfolk and Baltimore on Chesapeake Bay, New Orleans on the Missis-

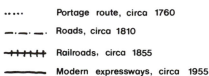

.....   Portage route, circa 1760

—·—·—·   Roads, circa 1810

+++++   Railroads, circa 1855

————   Modern expressways, circa 1955

2.13 Map showing the relationship between the site of Toronto and the position of transportation routes through time.

sippi, and San Francisco, Seattle, and Vancouver are a few North American examples.

Many other cities, such as Québec, Montréal, Buffalo, Cleveland, Detroit, St. Louis and Memphis, owe much of their success to strategic location on inland waterways. New York had a particular advantage over the rival cities of Boston and Philadelphia: those two cities suffered from an absence of good passes or routes through the Appalachian Mountains, but New York, after the completion of the Erie Canal in 1825, was linked to the Midwest via the Hudson and Mohawk rivers and the Great Lakes (Fig. 2.14).

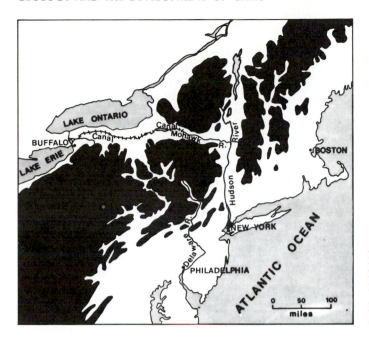

2.14 Transport route connecting New York City to the Great Lakes. Note the advantage New York has over Boston and Philadelphia. Mountainous areas are shown in black.

Energy

A number of cities were established and flourished (at least until the advent of the steam engine) due to the presence of energy in the form of waterfalls or rapidly flowing streams. Many mill towns developed along the east slopes of the Appalachians where narrow, rushing streams provided power for flour mills and sawmills, and eventually textile mills. Lowell, Lawrence, Nashua, Manchester, Chicopee, and Haverhill are examples in New England. The towns of Niagara Falls, in New York and Ontario, owe their prosperity to the harnessing of the flow of the Niagara River for the production of hydroelectric power. (Sightseers are also an important source of revenue.) Niagara Falls owes its origin to the presence of the relatively strong Lockport Dolomite above the weaker Clinton Shales and Albion Sandstone. Where the channel of the river leaves the dolomite and encounters the shale it has excavated an impressive gorge more than 150 feet deep.

Some cities developed because of valuable concentrations of raw materials. Birmingham, Alabama (founded in 1871) is a large industrial steel center due to the happy coincidence of extensive iron, coal, and limestone deposits. In Pennsylvania, Scranton and Wilkes-Barre were founded on the strength of profitable coal seams. Butte, Montana is centered upon its great copper mine. The site of Gary, Indiana was chosen by the United States Steel Company: it lay halfway between the iron ore of Minnesota and the coal of Pennsylvania, and had access to the Great Lakes via the Calumet River (Galantay, 1975). In fact, as Alan Bateman an economic geologist, says "It is no accident that great manufacturing cities sprang up in the United States around the Great Lakes, in Pennsylvania and in Alabama, and in England, the Ruhr, northern France, and Belgium. There coal and iron met, and the product of their union reached the far places of the globe." In more recent times, cities such as Houston could not have achieved their rapid growth without the "smell" of oil (1950, p. 367).

Venice

Venice is an example of a city whose origin and unique character were fostered by a set of coastal processes that were later to threaten it with extinction. In Roman times, a line of sand bars called *lidi* protected a series of lagoons at the head of the Adriatic (Fig. 2.15) against storms. (A section of these sand bars is now called the Lido, and is famous as a summer resort.) The lagoons were gradually silting up from sediment brought to the sea by the Po and Adige rivers, but a general rise in sea level that was occurring simultaneously actually increased the depths of parts of the lagoons and made them more navigable. Fishermen sailed the interconnected lagoons and others made a living gathering salt from trapped, evaporating bodies of sea water. (The expression "sailing the seven seas" actually referred to sailing through these lagoons; the connections between the lagoons are now blocked by the Po and Adige deltas (Lane, 1973). The origin of Venice in A.D. 568 was due to the Lombard invasion of Italy which started a migration of refugees from mainland cities, some of whom escaped danger by settling along the lagoons. The area that is now Venice was at that time mostly open water with a cluster of small islands, the largest of which was called "Rivoalto," the future Rialto. Venice developed as a city through the coalescence of island parishes, the dredging of intervening waterways to form canals and the creation of new land through judicious placement of the dredged material. The canals and the open lagoons facilitated traffic. Marine tides flushed away unwanted wastes. The one thing lacking was fresh water, which initially had to be brought from the mainland in boats. Wells were sunk, but as late as the 15th century, whenever extra-high, wind-driven tides salted the

wells, bargemen sold fresh water by the quart.

Venice's greatest natural hazard, oceanic flooding, became serious early in the history of the city, for the islands rise little above sea level. Flooding was exacerbated as the canals were blocked by dumped ballast and stoneyard wastes, and by the presence of rotting, sunken ships which served to trap silt. As early as A.D. 1224 there was a magistracy in charge of keeping canals and channels clear. Eventually, rivers that flowed into the lagoons had to be diverted to reduce the problem of siltation and also to prevent the growth of aquatic vegetation (canebreaks) that thrived on the brackish water and acted as sediment traps. In the fourteenth century, prohibitions were enforced against burning the pine forests (which helped prevent erosion and sedimentation and strengthened natural coastal flood defenses) and against the indiscriminate removal of sand for ballast from coastal areas.

With time, however, the problem of flooding was aggravated by other factors. Some of these were beyond human control: a general rise in sea level, natural subsidence of the area, Adriatic storm surges and seiching, tidal effects, heavy rainfall (see Chap. 11). Others were caused by man, such as subsidence of the land due to excessive withdrawal of water from the sediments on which Venice rests (see Chap. 12).

In 1783, massive sea walls (*murazzi*) were constructed. These lasted until the storm of November 1966 when the sea broke through them and submerged historic Venice under six feet of water. The Lido was completely covered; waves dashed against the Ducal Palace and San Marco. After this disaster, an attempt was made to lessen the likelihood of flooding. The murazzi were rebuilt. The pumping of groundwater to provide water for the industrialized mainland, for irrigation, and for the municipal water supply of Venice, which had caused a quadrupling of annual

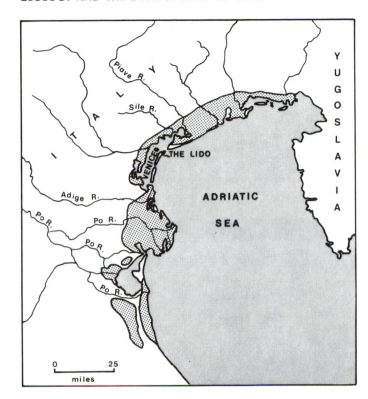

2.15 The configuration of ancient and modern coastlines in the vicinity of Venice, Italy. The dotted areas indicate land created since the founding of Venice in A.D. 568.

subsidence, from one-half inch each ten years to two inches every ten years, was halted, and aqueducts were designed to bring water from the Piave and Sile rivers. Proposals have been made to inject salt water under pressure into the sediment to halt or reverse subsidence.

The particular configuration of the sea coast and the natural processes that led to the founding of Venice and which underwrote its greatness will, however, continue to threaten it with destruction, for forces are at work that are beyond the power of human beings to halt.

THE GEOLOGIC VIEW AND THE MODERN CITY

The influence of geology upon cities goes beyond the contributions it makes to under-standing geologic opportunities and constraints. The basic assumptions that underlie the geologist's approach to the earth have themselves affected the course of history and the human environment.

The geologic approach, consistent with a Western scientific viewpoint, assumes that the universe is at some level orderly rather than capricious; that a bank of accumulated experience is of some use in estimating future or past experience. This assumption was formally stated in 1795 by James Hutton, a Scots doctor-cum-naturalist, as the *Doctrine of Uniformitarianism*. It suggests that the present is the key to the past; that is, that knowledge of present earth materials and processes will permit fruitful speculation on the past conditions of the earth.

One of the most important implications of Uniformitarianism was its effect upon the human concept of time. In the eighteenth century when Hutton formulated the idea, the prevailing opinion was that the universe had originated roughly 6000 years earlier. God had created heaven and earth, proclaimed Bishop Ussher (1650), at nine o'clock in the morning in the year 4004 B.C. His opinion was echoed by sophisticated and credulous alike. James Hutton, however, as he walked the hills and valleys of his native Scotland, came to a radically different conclusion. He had observed natural phenomena carefully and become familiar with the processes that were operating to erode rock and transport and deposit sediment. He realized that the earth was undergoing constant change, sometimes rapid and violent, as when flooding rivers rage through narrow valleys, more often imperceptibly gradual, as when granite slowly disintegrates into sand. He then posed a key question: what would be the effects of such changes in the course of sufficient time? His conclusion was that the natural world could be attributed to the cumulative results of processes such as he had observed. How much time was required? "Time without end," said Hutton. Thus, the Doctrine of Uniformitarianism from the moment of its conception violated prevailing opinion. Bishop Ussher's fifty-eight centuries of biblical time were to be exchanged for an infinity of geologic time, opening the door to intellectual and social revolution. In the years that followed dissemination of Huttons' ideas, the concept of "time without end" was tempered somewhat. Lord Kelvin (1897) considered the age of the earth to be on the order of 20–40 million years; Arthur Holmes in 1911 opted for 1700 million years; today, the age of the earth is thought to be about 4.6 billion years.

The idea of the great length of geologic time, the length of time since the earth was formed, paved the way for ultimate acceptance of Darwin's *Origin of Species by Means of Natural Selection* (1859). Darwin's thesis was that the characteristics of animal and plant species were not fixed, but changed through time in response to changes in their environment. This concept of the evolution of species was in direct contradiction to religious belief that each creature's form had been created by God and was forever unchangeable. Most unacceptable was Darwin's inclusion of humans in his scheme of evolution. The suggestion that humans, like other animals, were natural creatures and had gradually evolved from simpler forms of life, was both sacrilege and an affront to vanity. Hutton's Uniformitarianism together with Darwin's Evolution constituted an irresistibly powerful attack upon literal interpretation of the Bible and were significant factors contributing to the decline of religion.

Also implicit in Darwin's thesis was the concept that many species failed to respond adequately to changes in environment and became extinct. Fossilized remains of extinct forms of life were abundant in the rock record. One of the strongest factors causing species to evolve or to become extinct was competition. To survive and be successful, an individual or a species had to be "fit." Simplistic interpretation of "survival of the fittest," coupled with a decline in religious belief and influence, was used to excuse much of the unrestrained exploitation common in the capitalist-industrial society of the nineteenth and early twentieth centuries. The intolerable conditions that arose within rapidly expanding Victorian cities and ruthless opportunism on the part of the powerful precipitated many of the political and social revolutions that have characterized the twentieth century. Thus, the philosophic foundation of geology played an indirect but major role in creating tangible and intangible aspects of somewhat earlier urban environments that have remained important in the heritage of modern cities.

3. Water Supply

Fresh water, in sufficient quantity and of adequate purity, is a determinative factor in the foundation, expansion, and prospering of cities. Where water supply has diminished or has not expanded at a rate commensurate with urban growth, cities, and sometimes the civilizations of which they are the mainstays have stagnated or withered and died. In modern cities where water is abundant, its uninterrupted availability is taken for granted by most people. Curiosity as to where water comes from is rare. Even where great feats of engineering have been employed to provide water, only lapses in the continuity of supply or noticeable declines in quality cause comment. This lack of curiosity is in itself curious for without water, man cannot exist. Lack of reverence for the commonplace is perhaps an unhappy characteristic of our age. However, as population multiplies and society becomes increasingly industrialized, ensuring the "commonplaceness" of abundant, sufficiently pure water is becoming a matter of growing concern. It is imperative that the occurrence of water on earth be understood properly if effective planning is to be made for its withdrawal, treatment, and use. Expansion of cities or the founding of new cities without due regard for hydrologic constraints invites eventual expensive corrective measures. With respect to urban planning, hydrologist W. J. Schneider emphasizes that "in the evaluation of viable development alternatives, the planner must be aware of the physical system. This awareness includes at least rudimentary understanding of hydrology and other physical sciences. Just as the planner must be aware of the relation of hydrologic factors to his planning, so must the hydrologist be knowledgeable in the processes of urban planning. Together they must develop the development-alternative/resource-impact relationships necessary for sound decision making" (Schneider *et al*, 1973, p. H4).

Understanding the mechanics and geology of water supply may help make its use a conscious act. If water use is thoughtful, misuse may be minimized. Furthermore, users will be made richer by increased awareness of their own ties to the natural world.

In this chapter attention is focused on the quantitative aspects of water supply. Problems of water quality (except those related to saltwater intrusion) are discussed in greater depth in Chapter 4; the role water has played in the founding and subsequent development of cities has been considered briefly in Chapter 2; future problems of supply are discussed in Chapter 14.

NATURAL OCCURRENCE

The earth is generously endowed with water. Oceans cover more than 70 percent of the surface of the globe, reach depths of 36,000 feet, encompass a volume of 317 million cubic miles and embrace an area of 139,500,000 square miles. The saline character of ocean water, however, makes it useless to humans for drinking and for most home, agricultural, and industrial purposes. In comparison, the "fresh" water of the world is of minute quantity, constituting only 2.8 percent of the total water on earth. Moreover, about 60 percent of all fresh water is locked up as glacial ice in Antarctica and Greenland (plus a scattering of much smaller, local glaciers in mountainous regions) and is not of practical use to humans. Almost all the remaining fresh water sits or flows on the surface of the land as lakes or streams, or has filtered beneath the earth's surface into the myriad minute openings and crevices in soil, sediment, and uppermost rock formations. Water on the surface in streams and lakes is easily obtainable; water under the ground (*groundwater*) requires considerably more effort to extract. However, the importance of groundwater is emphasized by the fact that the groundwater that lies within one-half mile of the surface constitutes a reservoir of fresh water roughly thirty times greater in volume than fresh water present on the surface of the land. Table 3.1 summarizes the distribution of the world's water at any given moment.

Movement

Water is in almost constant motion, both laterally and vertically. Moreover, changes of phase to and from liquid, solid (ice) and gas (water vapor) are common and continual. The motion and phase changes that water undergoes are driven by the pull of gravity, the rotation of the earth, and the uneven heating of the earth's surface by the sun. The *hydrologic cycle* (Fig. 3.1) is a

Table 3.1. The world's water supply as estimated by the U.S. Geological Survey.

Location	Percentage of Total Water
Surface water:	
Freshwater lakes	0.009
Saline lakes and inland seas	0.008
Average in stream channels	0.0001
Subsurface water:	
Water in saturated zone, including soil moisture	0.005
Groundwater within a depth of half a mile	0.31
Groundwater at depths greater than half a mile; commonly salty, costly to extract, and extremely slow to recharge	0.31
Other water locations:	
Icecaps and glaciers	2.15
Atmosphere	0.001
Oceans	97.2

simplified summary of the complex migration of water. The ocean acts as a vast reservoir from which fresh water is evaporated into the atmosphere. This water vapor is then carried to cooler regions, where it is precipitated as rain, snow, hail, etc. Much of the precipitation returns the water directly to the oceans again, but a considerable fraction falls on land. What happens to water that falls on the land depends upon a variety of factors. If the air is warm and dry and a wind is blowing, and if the water is unable to penetrate the ground easily, much of it quickly evaporates and returns to the atmosphere. Water that infiltrates the ground may be subsequently drawn back to the surface by capillary action and then evaporated, or be absorbed by plant roots and then "breathed out" (*transpired*) through leaves into the atmosphere. (A single tree can transpire up to 40,000 gallons of water each year.) Water that escapes evaporation and transpiration may slowly migrate downward to become part of the *groundwater system*. Within the system, water gradually

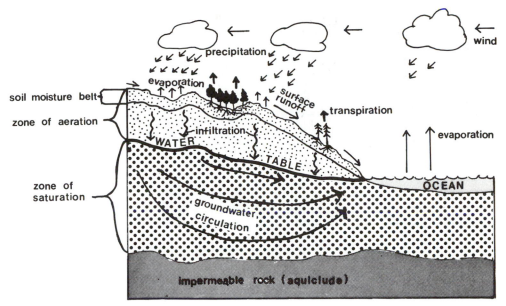

3.1 The hydrologic cycle. Water circulates from the oceans into the atmosphere, onto the land, and then back to the ocean or atmosphere by evaporation, transpiration, or movement over or under the land.

moves underground until it eventually emerges at the surface and is discharged into lakes or streams and is then carried to the oceans. A small amount of groundwater may migrate directly underground to the oceans. If the ground is unable to absorb all the precipitation that lands on its surface, either because it is already saturated with water or because it has few openings capable of admitting water, then the precipitation flows over the surface as *surface runoff* into streams and lakes, eventually returning to the oceans.

Water may complete the cycle from ocean-to-atmosphere-to-land-to-ocean rapidly or extremely slowly, depending upon the length of its journey, the nature of the materials through or over which it passes, and whether it is captured for long periods in glacial ice, buried sediment, or deep lakes.

Surface water and groundwater are the major sources of water supply and will be considered in greater detail.

Groundwater

Water that falls to the surface of the earth as rain, or water that is derived from the melting of snow or ice may seep beneath the surface of the land under appropriate conditions. The rate at which and the depth to which such infiltration takes place depends upon (a) the texture of the material through which the water must pass; (b) the degree to which the material is already saturated with water; and (c) the rate and duration of application of water to the earth's surface.

Natural land surfaces consist of soil, sediment, or bedrock. The presence of openings (*porosity*) and the degree to which the openings are interconnected by passageways of sufficient diameter for the water to pass (*permeability*) affects the ease of groundwater movement. Soil and sediment are by nature particulate; that is, composed of separate particles, between which openings exist (Fig. 3.2). The larger the particles, the larger the openings between them are likely

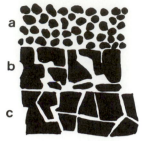

3.2 Permeability. Rocks a, b, and c are permeable (aquifers). Rocks d, e, f, and g are impermeable (aquicludes). a = poorly cemented coarse sediment; b = dissolved passageways in limestone; c = highly fractured igneous rock; d = fine-grained sediment; e = clay or shale; f = a rock with openings that are not connected; g = poorly fractured igneous rock.

to be, and the greater will be the ease with which water may pass through them. Finely particulate material may actually have a greater number and larger volume of openings than coarse material, but the passageways that connect the openings are extremely narrow. The movement of water through such passageways is very slow or non-existent due to frictional effects and a tendency for the water to stick to the surfaces of the particles. The common presence in fine-grained rocks of clay minerals that swell when wet or the presence (in rocks of any grain-size) of natural cements that bind particles together, also hinder the passage of water.

Rocks vary considerably in the number and size of openings they possess and the degree to which the openings are interconnected. Openings in rocks may be inherited from the originally particulate character of the material of which the rock is composed (silt, sand, gravel, volcanic ash), and may permit the easy passage of water if they are not filled with cements, closed by pressure, or welded shut. Other rocks contain openings formed through fracturing or jointing which may or may not be interconnected and permit the passage of water. Rock

openings may be enlarged by the dissolving action of water passing through them. Whereas almost all other types of openings are minute (a few millimeters or less), such *solution openings* may be up to tens of feet in diameter.

The rate of groundwater movement also depends upon water pressure differences between adjacent regions. The greater the difference, the faster groundwater will flow.

Substances that often contain water and permit its easy passage are known as *aquifers,* and include loose, coarse sands and gravels of alluvial or glacial origin, poorly cemented sandstones, limestones with solution openings, fractured igneous or metamorphic rocks, deeply weathered rocks, and soils relatively low in clay content. Substances that either have few openings or whose openings are not interconnected and therefore do not permit water to pass through them easily are called *aquicludes,* and include clays, shale, well-cemented sandstones, unfractured linestones, and unweathered, unfractured igneous and metamorphic rocks.

The ease of infiltration of water beneath the earth's surface not only depends upon the textural characteristics of earth materials, but also upon the extent to which these materials are already water-saturated. For each material, depending upon its texture, there is a specific rate at which water can pass through it, known as the *infiltration rate.* In fine-grained substances, the infiltration rate is somewhat diminished as water films coat the surfaces of narrow openings and passageways, substantially reducing them in diameter. If clay is present, it may swell and block the openings.

Lastly, the percentage of precipitation that manages to infiltrate is affected by the violence and duration of storms. In a gentle rainfall, when the precipitation rate is less than that of infiltration, all of the rain that escapes immediate evaporation is capable of being absorbed by the ground. If the rain is short, however, the water will not infiltrate very deeply, and will be either drawn back to the surface by capillary action and subsequently evaporated, or absorbed by the roots of plants and then transpired. Water that infiltrates only to shallow depths and is then returned to the surface to be lost by evapotranspiration is called *soil moisture* (Fig. 3.1). Only if a gentle storm lasts many hours or days will a substantial fraction of the water penetrate deeply enough to become part of the groundwater system.

If precipitation is heavy and exceeds the infiltration rate, water that is not absorbed will flow over the surface as *surface runoff*. Excessive surface runoff results in flooding and erosion and transportation of soil and sediment. In vegetated areas, there is less surface runoff and concommitant erosion: vegetation dams the surface flow of the water and provides additional time for infiltration. When rainfall is heavy for protracted periods, even the presence of abundant vegetation is ineffective in slowing surface runoff and preventing flooding.

From this brief discussion it may seen that drought can be alleviated only by prolonged rainfall. Short storms, even if they dump great quantities of water onto the ground, will not succeed in effectively recharging the groundwater system.

Water that succeeds in infiltrating the groundwater system can only migrate downward a limited distance until it encounters impermeable rock (Fig. 3.1). Such rock may be only inches beneath the surface or may not be reached until a depth of thousands of feet. Above the "floor" of impermeable rock is a volume of rock or sediment called the *zone of saturation,* all of whose openings are filled with water. Above the zone of saturation and extending to the earth's surface is the *zone of aeration,* a volume of rock or sediment whose openings are free of water or only partially filled, and through which infiltrating water passes to join the zone of saturation (Fig. 3.1). The upper surface of the zone of saturation is called the *water table*.

Position of the Water Table

Figure 3.3 illustrates the relationship between the topography of the land surface and the topography of the water table in wet and arid regions (assuming that the areas in question are underlain by uniformly permeable aquifers). Arrows indicate the direction of movement of water within the groundwater system.

Wet climates.   In areas of abundant rainfall, the water table has the same general configuration as the land surface, but is at greater depths below the surface beneath hills than beneath valleys. During and after prolonged rainfall or snowmelt, infiltrating water increases the volume of the zone of saturation, causing a general rise in the elevation of the water table. Where the water table is higher than the ground surface and the zone of saturation is exposed, water seeps from the groundwater system into lakes and streams. During times of little rain or drought, the general elevation of the water table falls due to continued seepage at places where the water table is higher than the land surface, and also from the general tendency of water within the groundwater system to seek its own level. It is important to note that streams and lakes persist during intervals between rainfalls because they rest on saturated ground and are fed by groundwater seepage as long as the water table in their vicinity is higher than their floors. If the water table subsides below the level of lake and stream beds, the latter will go dry (unless fed by a source other than groundwater).

Dry climates.   In arid regions, the water table is generally deep below the surface of the ground. Brief rainstorms add little or no water to the zone of saturation because the water is quickly evaporated. When there are more prolonged or heavy rainstorms, water may flow over the surface to accumulate in gullies and depressions, creating brief periods of streamflow and shallow ponds

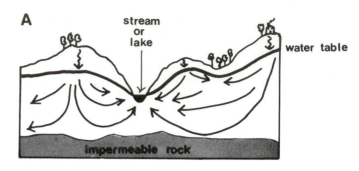

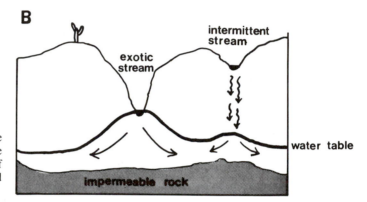

3.3 The relationship between the configuration of the land surface and the water table in areas of abundant rainfall (**A**) and in arid areas (**B**).

that persist for a few hours or days. Since these streams and ponds rest on unsaturated ground, they lose water downward. Some of the downward percolating water may reach the zone of saturation, causing local mounds in the water table and a small rise in its general elevation. So-called *exotic streams* that originate in rainy regions outside the margin of the desert but whose course carries them across deserts may lose considerable quantities of water downward. If their initial volume is not sufficiently great, exotic streams may dry up before they leave the desert region.

Effect of Wells   Wells are openings dug or drilled into the ground for the purpose of obtaining and withdrawing water. A steel pipe or *casing* is inserted into the hole to prevent its collapse or clogging. Along its

lower portion the casing is perforated to allow groundwater to enter it from the zone of saturation. The casing also prevents water seeping into the well from higher levels that may be polluted. Water enters the well and rises to a level equal to that of the local water table (Fig. 3.4). As the water table fluctuates, so will the water level in the well. For the well to be a reliable source of water, it must be deeper than the lowest elevation to which the local water table is likely to decline during dry periods. As water is withdrawn from a well, it is replaced by seepage from the zone of saturation, causing a local depression in the water table. This depression, which is usually cone-shaped, is called a *cone of depression*. Whether the cone expands and becomes deeper, remains constant, or shrinks and becomes shallower depends upon the relative

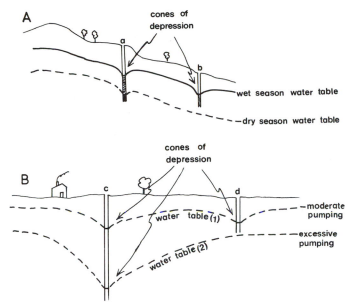

3.4 The relationship between the water level in wells and the position of the water table. (**A**) shows the effect of seasonal changes in the position of the water table on the water level. Note that whereas well (a) is deep enough to have water in all seasons, well (b) goes dry in the dry season. (**B**) shows the effect of withdrawal of water on the position of the water table (1 and 2). Note how excessive pumping of well (c) causes well (d) to go dry.

rates of withdrawal of water from the well and replenishment by seepage from the zone of saturation. Too rapid and prolonged withdrawal of water may lower the water table to the point where the well goes dry. If the cone of depression of one well expands until it intersects other wells, it will cause the water level in them to decline and may cause them to go dry. If many wells are being pumped in a region, there may be a general lowering of the water table if natural recharge by infiltration of precipitation does not equal withdrawal (unless other means of recharge are employed).

Non-Uniform Permeability The rocks and sediment underlying a region are rarely uniform in permeability, and the configuration and position of water tables are correspondingly complex. Figure 3.7A illustrates how the presence of an aquiclude (such as clay, shale, or a lava bed) may result in the formation of springs.

Figure 3.5 illustrates a series of inclined layers of varying permeability where a highly permeable aquifer is underlain by an aquiclude and overlain by a poor aquifer that is only somewhat permeable. Note in this instance that the source of the water

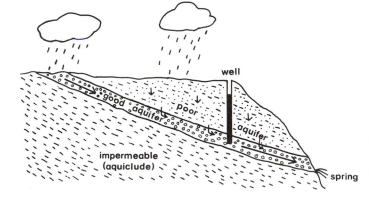

3.5 A cross section showing an inclined, highly permeable aquifer overlain by a poorly permeable aquifer and underlain by an aquiclude. Water in the good aquifer is derived from its outcrop and also by infiltration through the poor aquifer.

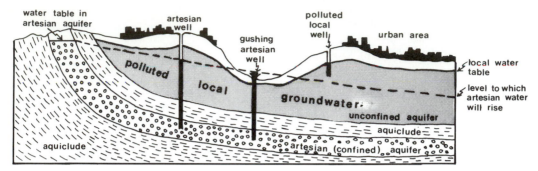

3.6 Cross section of an artesian aquifer. Note how polluted local groundwater is prevented from entering the artesian aquifer by the overlying aquiclude. Note also the level to which the artesian water rises in wells.

discharging at the lower end of the highly permeable aquifer is derived both from direct infiltration at its upper outcrop and also from infiltration from the overlying poor aquifer. The abundance of water issuing from the good aquifer therefore depends upon local rainfall as well as rainfall in more remote regions.

Where good aquifers are underlain *and* overlain by aquicludes, an artesian condition may exist.

Artesian Wells and Springs

Figure 3.6 illustrates an inclined aquifer, underlain and overlain by aquicludes, that outcrops in a rainy region. Water infiltrating the outcrop has saturated the aquifer. Since the aquifer is confined by aquicludes, water in its lower parts is under considerable pressure due to the weight of the water in its higher parts. If the aquifer is penetrated, either by a well or by natural fractures, water will flow upward, seeking its own level (the level of the water table in the upper part of the aquifer). Due to frictional effects, the level of the water table will not be reached, but water will rise under pressure toward the surface, and may actually gush into the air. Such water is called *artesian water,* the well an *artesian well,* and the geologic terminology for an inclined, confined aquifer

that outcrops in a rainy region is an *artesian condition*. A major advantage of artesian water, aside from its tendency to rise toward the surface, thus eliminating or lessening the necessity of pumping, is that it is not dependent upon local rainfall. Thus, where an artesian condition exists, water may be obtained despite inadequacies of local rainfall or pollution of local shallow groundwater.

A variety of geologic conditions may result in the presence of *springs*. Figure 3.7 illustrates three common types of springs: (A) where groundwater travels laterally along the contact of permeable and impermeable rock; (B) where hydrostatic pressure forces groundwater up a fracture zone to the surface; (C) where erosion has intersected an artesian aquifer.

Surface Water

Surface water exists naturally in the form of lakes and streams. Such bodies of water are fed by surface runoff during and after rainfall, by melting snow and ice, and by the groundwater system. Loss of water takes place by outflow, evaporation, downward percolation into unsaturated sediment or rock, and withdrawal of water by humans. Permanency and volume (or surface elevation) of lakes and streams depends upon the

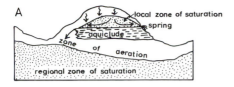

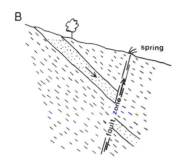

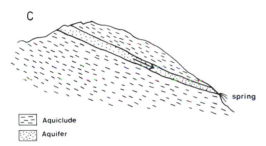

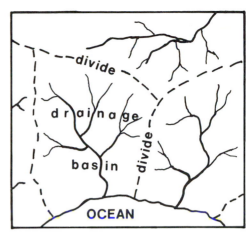

3.8 Map illustrating divides (dashed lines) outlining drainage basins.

3.7 The origin of springs. In each cross section, dot patterns represent aquifers, dashed patterns represent aquicludes. In (**A**) the spring is caused by lateral diversion of groundwater by an aquiclude; in (**B**) by migration of groundwater up a permeable fault zone; and in **C** by erosion of the land surface down to an artesian aquifer.

rate of water nourishment compared to the rate of water loss.

The land surface area that feeds a stream or system of streams upstream of a given point is known as its *drainage basin* or *watershed* (Fig. 3.8). The topographic highs that separate one drainage basin from another are called *divides*. Within a drainage basin, all precipitation that is not lost by evapotranspiration will make its way above or under the ground into the basin's streams. Changes in *discharge* of a stream

(volume of water passing a given point in a given time-interval) are of special interest to humans. Such changes affect water supply, waste disposal, erosion, sedimentation and flooding. A variety of interrelated factors control discharge: frequency, duration, and amount of rainfall; amount and rate of snowmelt; degree of evapotranspiration; degree of surface runoff; volume of water contributed by tributary streams; distribution, degree of saturation, and permeability of aquifers; and the location and unused capacity of storage basins.

DROUGHT AND OVERDRAFT

During times of drought, or when water withdrawal is excessive, surface waters diminish in volume and discharge. Also, as the groundwater system drains at a greater rate than it is recharged, the water table subsides and ponds, lakes, and swamps gradually dry up, streams become intermittent, and whole communities of living creatures are destroyed. As the water table falls below the depth to which wells have been drilled, wells will go dry unless deepened. Where waste materials are dumped into streams, reduced streamflow may inadequately dilute them, resulting in concentra-

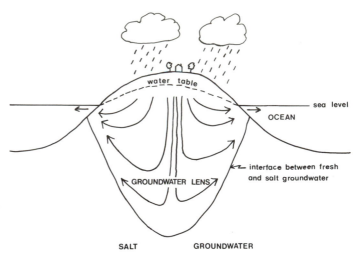

3.9 Cross section showing relationships between fresh and salt groundwater and the circulation of fresh groundwater within a "lens."

tions of pollutants that may threaten municipal water supplies. Similarly, estuarine waters whose salt content varies according to the inflow of fresh stream water may become too saline to support life forms that have limited tolerance to increased salinity. Sediments that are normally water saturated may compact as they are dewatered, causing the ground surface above them to subside, damaging or destroying buildings and other structures. (See the section on Subsidence in Chap. 12.) In coastal regions, where fresh groundwater is in contact with salt groundwater, declining water table levels may result in *saltwater intrusion.*

Saltwater Intrusion

Figure 3.9 is a cross section of an island (or peninsula) showing the relationship between fresh groundwater beneath the land and the salt groundwater that exists in permeable rocks and sediment beneath the ocean floor. The assumption is made that the region is underlain by uniformly permeable material. Since fresh water has a lower density than salt water (in the ratio of 40:41), the fresh groundwater tends to float on top of the salt groundwater, forming a discrete body that is lens-shaped in cross section. The boundaries of the fresh groundwater lens are stable as long as the water passing through the zone of aeration and infiltrating the zone of saturation matches the fresh groundwater lost through seepage into the ocean. (The circulation of groundwater is indicated by arrows.) The height of the water table above sea level is controlled by the magnitude of the vertical dimension of the freshwater lens. Because of the density relationship between fresh and salt water, the elevation of the water table above sea level is $1/41$ the vertical thickness of the fresh groundwater lens. For example, if the bottom of the lens is 400 feet beneath sea level, the water table will be 10 feet above sea level.

Figure 3.10 illustrates the effects of excessive withdrawal of water or drought. As water drains out of the lens or is withdrawn in excess of recharge, the water table is lowered from position 1 to 2 to 3, and the bottom of the lens rises from position 1 to 2 to 3, diminishing the thickness of the lens. (Recall that for every foot that the water table declines, the bottom of the lens rises by 40 feet.) As the lens diminishes in thickness lakes and streams dry up, and salt groundwater replaces fresh groundwater, advancing under the lens as a *saltwater intrusion.* When the intrusion reaches well

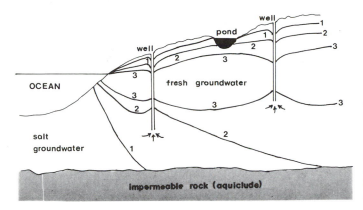

3.10 Cross section showing the effects of excessive loss of water from a fresh groundwater "lens." Numbers indicate successive positions of the interface of salt and fresh groundwater and of the water table as the fresh groundwater lens shrinks. Compare with Fig. 3.9.

intakes, they become contaminated with salt water. Saltwater intrusion has been a major problem for coastal cities whose water supply depends upon withdrawal from local groundwater. Examples will be described in the case studies of the water-supply systems of New York City and Miami later in this chapter.

Water Conservation

The harmful effects of drought and of overdraft and pollution of water supplies may be overcome by diminishing the rate of consumption, increasing efficiency of use, treating waste water, increasing recharge of aquifers, and finding alternate sources of supply.

The actual consumption of water by public systems and industry is minimal; that is, most water is returned to surface or underground sources after use (see section on Water Use). Losses due to evaporation from reservoirs (which may be considerable) may be avoided by storing water underground in natural sand or gravel layers, caverns, or excavated chambers. The greatest losses occur during irrigation, and are caused by evapotranspiration. Improved efficiency (such as water fed to plant roots through underground pipes) may be possible in some instances. More economical use of water in irrigating is particularly important since, by the year 2000, the amount of water used for

this purpose will have to double to feed the world's increasing population. Proposals have been made to cut down on amounts lost through transpiration by non-economic native vegetation. For instance, the eradication of cottonwood trees along the courses of western streams is being investigated. However, the aesthetic and ecologic damage resulting from the destruction of these remnants of the natural landscape must be considered.

Increased efficiency in water usage in urban areas may be accomplished by metering and the establishment of realistic pricing. Too much water is wasted because "it doesn't cost anything." (See the New York City case study.)

Adequate treatment of "used" water permits its reuse and prevents contamination of water sources. In metropolitan areas, since less than 10 percent of withdrawn water need be of highest purity, the separate distribution of high- and lower-purity water would permit greater recycling. Partially treated, "used" water, and that obtained from lower-quality sources (water that is somewhat saline, for instance) could be used for industrial purposes, fire-fighting, and street-cleaning, for example. Japan is a leader in wastewater recycling. In 1973, Japanese industry obtained 62 percent of their water by treating and reusing their own industrial wastes. Furthermore, adequate treatment of polluted water and appropriate disposal of pollutants will decrease the amount of water required for dilution of wastes. Where water is in short supply, decisions may have to be made regarding the relative importance of maintaining, for example, fish and wildfowl habitats compared to other possible uses for water.

In areas where water is drawn largely from groundwater sources, maximizing the *recharge* of aquifers is essential. Where excessive withdrawal of groundwater has resulted in ground subsidence or salt-water intrusion, additional impetus is given to ensuring adequate recharge. Aquifer recharge may also allow storage of excess water and provide a means of disposing of floodwaters. Two principal methods of artificial recharge are the use of *recharge wells* and *water spreading*.

Recharge wells conduct treated waste water or excess surface water downward to aquifers. Pressure may be used to force the water underground. *Barrier injection wells* are designed to prevent salt-water intrusion by increasing fresh groundwater pressure in the vicinity of encroaching salt groundwater (Fig. 3.11). Problems encountered in the use of recharge wells are (1) clogging of the well perforations and (2) clogging of the aquifer by introduced silt, air, and growths caused by micro-organisms. The use of recharge wells has, therefore, been restricted to a few areas such as Los Angeles, where local conditions are favorable and actual experience has proved the practicality of the method (Walton, 1970).

Water spreading involves the spreading of waste water or excess surface water over the surface of permeable sediment or rock to allow it to infiltrate the groundwater system. This is accomplished by the excavation of "recharge basins," ponding of water by dikes or small dams, the flooding of designated areas, or the distribution of the water to a series of closely spaced, shallow, flat-bottomed ditches or furrows. The swelling of soil particles and microbial growths tend to slow down infiltration. The adding of organic matter and chemicals to the soil and

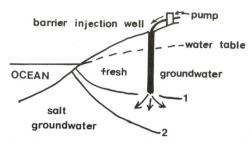

3.11 Cross section showing how the pumping of fresh water underground through a barrier injection-well causes the interface of salt and fresh groundwater to retreat from position (1) to position (2).

the alternation of wet and dry periods have been effective in countering these problems.

The development of new sources of water supply, such as desalinization of ocean waters or brines and attempts at inducing additional precipitation over specific watersheds are in their infancy. To be of significant help, water produced by desalinization must become competitive in price with other sources. The high energy requirements involved in desalinization and the necessity of pumping the desalinized water to where it is needed or to elevations from which it may be distributed by gravity have kept the process uneconomical until the present. Desalinization is, however, a source of supply for coastal cities where other sources of water are insufficient. In inland areas, desalinization poses the additional problem of disposing of the salts that have been separated from the water so that they do not re-enter water sources.

Bringing water to drought-stricken or chronically dry areas from well-watered regions is a classic solution to shortages. Water importation is discussed in the case studies of New York City and Los Angeles and in Chapter 14.

When drought strikes an area that normally has excess water, alternate sources may be hard to find on short notice. Shortages in southern England brought about by the drought of 1976 engendered considerable hardship and prompted consideration of importing water from other areas by rail, truck, and boat and the eventual development of permanent means of conveying or diverting water from one drainage basin to another in future times of need. However, convincing taxpayers of a region that is usually rainy, such as England, to spend great sums of money to avoid hypothetical future droughts is not an easy task. Israel, on the other hand, which is located in a perpetually arid region, has less to fear from drought than many countries situated in rainier areas. Its water resources are under state control and can be transferred from one part of the country to another as needed. Moreover, water use in Israel is so efficient that farming requires only one-third the amount per unit of irrigated land compared to California, its closest competitor in terms of economical use.

WATER USE

The demand for water and the uses to which it is put vary widely according to the climate of a region, the degree to which it is urbanized and industrialized, the types of agriculture practiced, and the cultural habits of the people. In this discussion, attention will be focused on urban water use in the United States. However, it should be noted that whatever water problems threaten American cities, they pale before those facing the urban shantytowns of Latin America, Asia, and Africa, where 200 million people must use unsafe, disease-laden water.

The term *withdrawal use* refers to water withdrawn from its source and used elsewhere. After such use, part of the water may be returned to the same or to another source and be available for withdrawal and use again. During use, part or all of the water may be evaporated, transpired, or incorporated into plants, animals, or manufactured products. It is thus effectively removed from the water environment for substantial periods of time, and is consid-

ered *consumed*. *In-channel use* refers to surface water used without withdrawal for navigation, disposition and dilution of waste water, freshwater discharge into estuaries to maintain proper salinity, sports-fishing, and so forth. Unless otherwise designated, the term *use* will signify withdrawal use.

In the United States during 1975, 420 billion gallons of water per day (bgd) were withdrawn for all purposes other than creating hydroelectric power—an average per capita withdrawal use of 1900 gallons per day (gpd), 1600 gpd of it fresh water. Of that amount, 58 percent was used by industry, 34 percent for irrigation, 7 percent for public supplies, and one percent for rural supplies other than irrigation. Use of the water resulted in 96 billion gallons, or 23 percent, of it being consumed. Consumption losses took place mainly through evaporation during irrigation (83 percent of the total consumed).

Roughly 40,000 organized systems of water distribution today serve about 80 percent of the population of the United States, and 172 million people are supplied by public water-supply systems, mostly within metropolitan areas. Municipal water systems supply 115 million people in 17,000 towns and cities (Leopold, 1974). Per capita withdrawal from public water supplies in 1975 was 168 gallons per day. According to Luna Leopold, conservationist and former chief hydrologist of the U.S. Geological Survey, the average use per person in an American home varies between 20 and 80 gpd. Typical uses are:

Flush a toilet	6 gallons
Tub bath	30–40 gallons
Shower bath	20–30 gallons
Wash dishes	10 gallons
Run washing machine	20–30 gallons

Watering a garden of 8000 square feet requires 30,000 to 80,000 gallons per year (the equivalent of 80–500 gpd), depending upon whether the area is humid or desert. A tap that drips one drop per second wastes 4 gallons a day; a running toilet can waste 36 gallons a day.

Industrial users drawing upon municipal water-supply systems require an average of 56 gpd per capita. Commercial use, for places of business, amounts to a per capita use of 20 gpd. Public use for fighting fires, cleaning streets, watering parks, and providing water for swimming pools, fountains, and public buildings amounts to 10 gpd per capita. Another 10 gpd per capita is lost through leaks and breaks in underground pipes.

Per capita use of water from public systems in large U.S. cities in 1975 varied from 101 to 442 gpd, depending upon the extent to which industry was self-supplied or drew upon public supplies. Nine-tenths of the water self-supplied by industry is used for cooling purposes during the production of energy. Twenty-nine percent of the self-supplied water is saline.

Quality

Depending upon the use for which water is intended, the definition of acceptable water quality varies. Water meant for drinking must be free of objectionable dissolved solids, chemical additives, biologic contaminants, and particulate matter. Water for industrial purposes (and for some home and public uses, such as toilet-flushing, lawn-sprinkling, street-cleaning, and fire-fighting) need not meet such strict standards. The use of water changes many of its characteristics, a particular use often making it unsuitable for other uses without appropriate treatment. Geologic factors in water pollution will be discussed in Chapter 4. It may be noted, however, that the pollution of water effectively diminishes water supply. Unpolluted water may be used many times before it is returned to streams, lakes, or aquifers. Water that is polluted with respect to specific uses is of diminished value, and its efficient reuse is hindered. Also, the return of polluted water to its source in unac-

ceptable quantities may degrade the general supply.

Sources

Approximately 75 percent of American cities obtain water from the groundwater system through wells. However, utilities supplied by surface-water sources, although few in number, supply twice as much water (64 percent) as utilities using groundwater sources (36 percent). Industries using their own sources obtain 5 percent from the groundwater system and 95 percent from surface sources. Irrigation water is 40 percent groundwater and 60 percent surface water. Small quantities of water, on the order of a fraction of 1 percent are obtained through reclamation of sewage. Geographically, the use of groundwater compared to surface water is highest in arid and semiarid regions of the West and Southwest.

Five of the thirty-five largest cities in the United States obtain water from the Great Lakes; ten from major rivers. Three cities, Miami, San Antonio, and Memphis, use local groundwater systems. The remaining seventeen cities obtain water from a combination of underground and surface sources, often importing supplies from reservoirs and small streams considerable distances from their incorporated boundaries. New York's supply comes from as far as 125 miles from the city. San Francisco, Los Angeles, and Oakland pipe water from the slopes of the Sierra Nevada, and the Colorado River supplies part of the needs of Los Angeles and San Diego.

Trends

Studies of water withdrawal and water consumption in the United States during the period 1950–1975 reveal that, although the population increased by only 78 percent, water withdrawn for public supplies increased by 135 percent, self-supplied water used for the production of electricity increased by 376 percent, and water consumed increased by more than 56 percent. In the same period, fresh groundwater use increased by 150 percent, fresh surface water by 63 percent, and saline surface water by 560 percent. During the period 1970–75, withdrawal for all other uses other than production of hydroelectric power increased by 14 percent, to 420 bgd (Murray and Reeves, 1977). Estimates of future water use are that it will rise from 420 bgd in 1975 to 450 in 1980; to 800 bgd in 2000;

and to more than 1300 bgd in 2020. Currently, municipal water systems supply 24 bgd. If urban population increases as predicted, more than 48 bgd will be required by municipal systems in 1985, and 74 bgd in 2020 (Schneider and Spieker, 1969).

Hydrologic effects of urbanization. Table 3.2 summarizes the effects of progressive urbanization on water quantity and quality. A specific example of this progression of events is given in the case study of New York City.

Table 3.2. Hydrologic effects during a selected sequence of changes in land and water use associated with urbanization (From Savini, J., and Kammerer, J. C., 1961)

Change in Land or Water Use	*Possible Hydrologic Effect*
Transition from pre-urban to early-urban stage:	
Removal of trees or vegetation, Construction of scattered city-type houses and limited water and sewage facilities	Decrease in transpiration and increase in storm flow. Increased sedimentation of streams
Drilling of wells	Some lowering of water table
Construction of septic tanks and sanitary drains	Some increase in soil moisture and perhaps a rise in water table. Perhaps some waterlogging of land and contamination of nearby wells or streams from overloaded sanitary drain system
Transition from early-urban to middle-urban stage:	
Bulldozing of land for mass housing; some topsoil removal; farm ponds filled in	Accelerated land erosion and stream sedimentation and aggradation. Increased flood flows. Elimination of smallest streams
Mass construction of houses; paving of streets; building of culverts	Decreased infiltration, resulting in increased flood flows and lowered ground-water levels. Occasional flooding at channel constrictions (culverts) on remaining small streams. Occasional over-topping or undermining of banks of artificial channels on small streams
Discontinued use and abandonment of some shallow wells	Rise in water table
Diversion of nearby streams for public water supply	Decrease in runoff between points of diversion and disposal
Untreated or inadequately treated sewage discharged into streams or disposal wells	Pollution of streams or wells. Death of fish and other aquatic life. Inferior quality of water available for supply and recreation at downstream populated areas
Transition from middle- to late-urban stage:	
Urbanization of area completed by addition of more houses and streets, and of public, commercial, and industrial buildings	Reduced infiltration and lowered water table. Streets and gutters act as storm drains creating higher flood peaks and lower base flow of local streams
Larger quantities of untreated waste discharged into local streams	Increased pollution of streams and concurrent increased loss of aquatic life. Additional degradation of water available to downstream users

Table 3.2. Hydrologic effects during a selected sequence of changes in land and water use associated with urbanization (From Savini, J., and Kammerer, J. C., 1961) (*Continued*)

Change in Land or Water Use	Possible Hydrologic Effect
Abandonment of remaining shallow wells because of pollution	Rise in water table
Increase in population requires establishment of new water-supply and distribution systems, construction of distant reservoirs diverting water from upstream sources within or outside basin	Increase in local streamflow if supply is from outside basin
Channels of streams restricted at least in part to artificial channels and tunnels	Increased flood damage (higher stage for a given flow). Changes in channel geometry and sediment load. Aggradation
Construction of sanitary drainage system and treatment plant for sewage	Removal of additional water from area, further reducing infiltration recharge of aquifer
Improvement of storm drainage system	
Drilling of deeper, large-capacity industrial wells	Lowered water-pressure surface of artesian aquifer; perhaps some local overdrafts and land subsidence. Overdraft of aquifer may result in salt-water encroachment in coastal areas and in pollution or contamination by inferior or brackish waters
Increased use of water for air conditioning	Overloading of sewers and other drainage facilities. Possibly some recharge to water table, owing to leakage of disposal lines
Drilling of recharge wells	Raising of water-pressure surface
Wastewater reclamation and utilization	Recharge to groundwater aquifers. More efficient use of water resources

Will There be Enough Water?

The trend of rapidly rising water use raises the question of whether the United States and its cities will be able to meet future demands for water. The mainland United States receives about 30 inches of precipitation each year, equivalent to 4235 bgd. More than two-thirds of that amount is rapidly lost to the atmosphere through evaporation and transpiration. The remaining amount finds its way into lakes and streams and contributes to the groundwater system, and is the potential available for withdrawal. Comparison of this figure, 1200 bgd, with the projected water use for the year 2020, 1300 bgd, suggests that the need will exceed the supply. The comparison, however, is invalid. Much water that is withdrawn for use is returned to water sources and is then used again, one or more times, before it is consumed or returned to the ocean. On the other hand, of the 1200 bgd theoretically available for withdrawal, only about 700 bgd is the practical maximum available if surface waters and the groundwater system are to remain intact. The major problem in the near future is not a lack of adequate precipitation over the United States, but rather that regional variations in available water do not coincide with regional variations in demand.

Whether a water deficiency or surplus exists in a given area may be determined through comparing precipitation and evapotranspiration. Where precipitation exceeds evapotranspiration, a natural water surplus exists, manifested by the presence of permanent streams. Where precipitation is less than potential evapotranspiration, a natural water deficiency exists, and only temporary

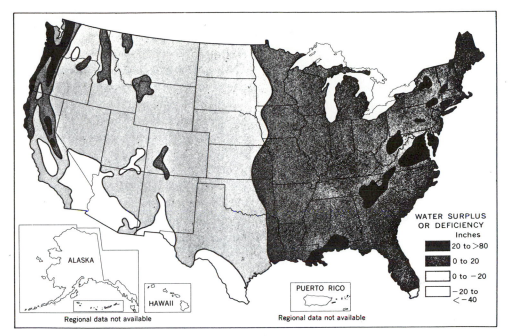

3.12 Areas of water surplus or deficiency (calculated by subtracting potential evapotranspiration from the average precipitation) within the United States.

or exotic streams are present. In general, the eastern half of the United States, together with the Pacific Northwest, the western flank of the Sierra Nevadas, and local uplands within the Rocky Mountains are areas of water surplus. The rest of the country suffers from water deficiency (Fig. 3.12).

Stream flow is the major source for water withdrawal and a convenient measure of available water without lowering lakes and reservoirs or depleting the groundwater system. The patterns of streamflow reveal that it is neither uniform from place to place nor constant in time (Fig. 3.13). Geographic variations in streamflow do not match present or prospective water-use patterns (Piper, 1965), and temporal variations range from excesses that result in floods (which not only cause damage but also waste water) to droughts that place a limit on the *assured capability* of water-supply systems.

Moderate seasonal variation can be either an advantage or disadvantage, depending upon whether high flow coincides with periods of maximum use. Regulation of seasonal variation through the use of reservoirs to store and release water can make 25–75 percent of a given area's natural streamflow usable. On a nationwide basis, perhaps 700 bgd of the 1200 bgd streamflow may eventually be usable.

Table 3.3 and Figure 3.14 show the results of a regional analysis of water supply and demand in the United States for the year 2000. In only three regions may a water surplus be expected in the year 2000. In seven regions, projected economic and social evolution will require virtually complete regulation of streamflow. In the remaining nine regions, even with complete regulation, growth will be moderately to severely handicapped. Several factors, however, might serve to modify this analysis:

Table 3.3. Summary of projected demand and supply of water as of the year 2000, by regions [In million gallons a day per square mile]. (From Piper, 1965)

Region	Demand						Supply	
	Consumed in Use (1)	Consumed on Site[1] (2)	Depletion by Reservoirs (3)	Subtotal (4)	In-channel Commitment (5)	Total (6)	Potentially Assured (7)	Total Streamflow (8)
New England	0.0256	0.0144	0.0134	0.0534	0.429	0.482	0.640	1.086
Delaware-Hudson	.0548	.0301	.0214	.1063	.641	.748	.556	.912
Chesapeake	.0296	.0148	.0118	.0562	.488	.544	.473	.769
South Atlantic-Eastern Gulf	.0430	.0758	.0067	.1255	.244	.370	.469	.783
Eastern Great Lakes	.0372	.0228	.0110	.0710	2.107	2.178	.414	.847
Western Great Lakes	.0469	.0413	.0109	.0992	.572	.671	.362	.483
Ohio	.0293	.0049	.0041	.0383	.249	.287	.326	.777
Cumberland-Tennessee	.0149	.0083	.0088	.0320	.784	.816	.612	1.003
Upper Mississippi	.0303	.0298	.0079	.0680	.262	.330	.227	.344
Lower Mississippi	.0598	.1584	.0085	.2267	1.569	1.795	.368	.811
Upper Missouri-Hudson Bay	.0412	.0375	.0078	.0865	.0491	.1356	.0399	.0583
Lower Missouri	.0277	.0055	.0059	.0391	.417	.456	.113	.433
Upper Arkansas-Red	.0326	.0082	.0074	.0482	.0268	.0750	.0501	.0880
Lower Arkansas-Red-White	.0328	.0240	.0159	.0727	.262	.335	.193	.698
Western Gulf-Rio Grande-Pecos	.0619	.0450	.0081	.1150	.0556	.1706	.0752	.172
Colorado	.0564	.0106	.0048	.0718	.0623	.1341	.0384	.0443
Great Basin	.0339	.0276	.0059	.0674	.0209	.0883	.0339	.0446
Pacific Northwest	.0600	.0056	.0113	.0768	.535	.612	.341	.610
Central and South Pacific	.2483	.0320	.0147	.2950	.295	.590	.244	.511
Mean	.0516	.0320	.0086	.0922	.271	.363	.210	.388

[1] Land-treatment measures and wetlands only.

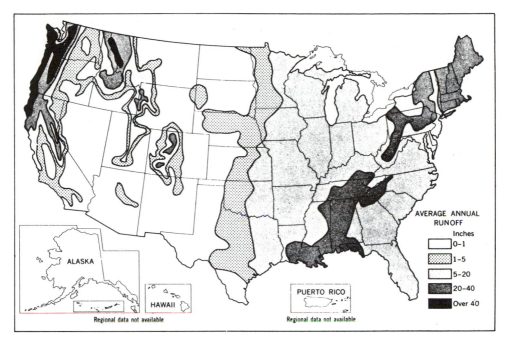

3.13 Average annual surface runoff within the United States.

3.14 The conterminous United States, showing water-supply and water-use regions, each of which is dominated by a single major source of water or encompasses several sources that are similar in magnitude and variability.

(1) streamflow from Canada is not included as available water; (2) increased use of groundwater results, in the long run, in a reduction in streamflow; (3) it is assumed that sewage would undergo considerably greater treatment than today and would therefore require minimal dilution; (4) the predictions of water requirements may not be accurate.

Geologists W. J. Schneider and A. M. Spieker consider the outlook for water supplies in U.S. urban areas from a historical point of view. Typically, the history of municipal supply has been a constant cycle of shortages and subsequent development of resources. Because of the expense involved, efforts to expand water systems seldom manage to keep ahead of increasing demand for more than short periods. This type of marginal operation results in crisis when unexpected events such as drought or groundwater contamination occur. As the demand of cities for water doubles and triples within the next half century, whether there is enough water will depend upon adequate planning and development, conservation and recycling of water, and treatment of wastes to alleviate pollution. It must also be kept in mind that self-supplied industry in urban areas often requires many times the water needed by municipal systems, and is in competition for the available supply. Also, the use and abuse of water in one urban area often affects the quantity and quality of water available to other areas. Regional planning rather than uncoordinated unilateral development must be undertaken and implemented if chaos is to be avoided. Despite the strain on existing systems and the problems posed by expanding demand, the outlook for water for the cities may be regarded as "cautiously optimistic" (Schneider and Spieker, 1969).

The following case studies of the water-supply systems of the Miami, Los Angeles, and New York metropolitan areas illustrate the complex interplay of factors involved in obtaining adequate water for large urbanized regions.

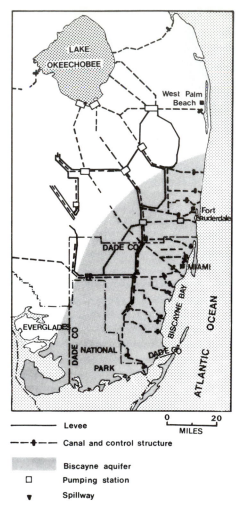

3.15 Elements of the water-management system of southeast Florida.

Miami

The city of Miami is located in the southern part of Dade County, in southeast Florida (Fig. 3.15) and constitutes part of a planning area known as Metropolitan Dade County. The countryside is almost flat: most of the area is less than 10 feet above high tide and the highest points have elevations of only 25 feet. Rainfall averages 60 inches per year, two-thirds of which falls from June to October, usually as brief and intense localized storms. Natural drainage is poor, and in much of the area the water table is at or near the surface, resulting in large areas of swamp, such as the Everglades, the Mangrove Swamps, and the Coastal Marshes. These areas are frequently flooded during the rainy season. Coastal areas are also subject to flooding from storm surges (see Fig. 11.13). Development of the land for agricultural and urban use has made it necessary to dig canals to drain saturated lands and to minimize flooding.

Geologically, the area is underlain by almost flat-lying limestones that are 15,000 feet thick (Fig. 3.16). The uppermost part of the limestone, which is highly permeable, is a coarse-grained, shelly rock containing many cavities. It forms the Biscayne aquifer, an excellent source of fresh water except where it is invaded by salt water along the coast. The aquifer, which is wedge-shaped, is about 10 feet thick in the western part of the area and about 120 feet thick at the coast. Underneath lie about 800 feet of fine-grained, poorly permeable limestone that acts as an aquiclude. Beneath this aquiclude is the Floridan aquifer, a permeable limestone containing only brackish and salt water.

The urbanized area of south Dade County has spread rapidly, increasing three-fold during the period 1940–1970. By the year 2000 it is expected to triple again. The population of Miami has increased from 249,276 in 1950 to 365,082 in 1975. Population in the entire Miami area is expected to rise from 1,438,600 in 1975 to four million in 1995. Continued urban spread without severe environmental degradation will be hindered by interrelated hydrologic problems of drainage, flood protection, waste disposal, pollution, water supply, and efforts to preserve certain areas as natural wetlands.

A regional water system managed by the Central and Southern Florida Flood Control District maintains and operates a system of levees, canals, control structures, pumping stations, and water storage areas (Fig.

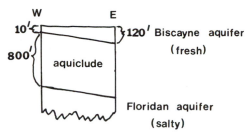

3.16 Stratigraphic column showing part of the sequence of geologic formations in the vicinity of Miami, Florida. Not to scale.

3.15). The water-supply works of metropolitan Miami are part of the system. The major elements of the system are: (1) During the rainy season, excess surface water collects in three water-conservation areas bounded by levees and in Lake Okeechobee, helping to prevent flooding of urban and agricultural areas. Water impounded in this way is also available for use during times of drought (Fig. 3.17). (2) A system of canals drains the urbanized coastal area, maintaining the water table at a low position during the rainy season to prevent flooding (Figs. 3.15; 3.17B). During the dry season, the canals conduct water eastward from the conservation areas and Lake Okeechobee to replenish the Biscayne aquifer (from which municipal supplies are drawn) and to prevent saltwater intrusion. Structures, regulating flow in the canals are closed during the dry season (Fig. 3.17A) to block the flow of water into the ocean and during the rainy season, are opened to reverse the process. (3) Regional water supply is obtained from the Biscayne aquifer. Municipal wells such as those in the Orr-Southwest well-field complex withdrew 50 mgd in 1950; 150 mgd in 1970. Total water use in the Miami area is expected to rise from 230 mgd in 1969 to 1400 mgd in 1995. Water is lost from the aquifer not only by withdrawal from wells, but also by groundwater seepage from the aquifer along the coast. It is recharged by precipitation and by the downward percolation of water from the conser-

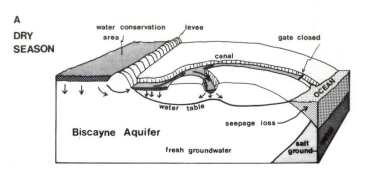

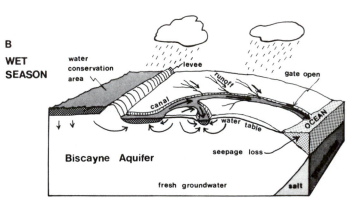

3.17 Block diagrams illustrating the functions of the water-management system of the Central and Southern Florida Flood Control District. In (**A**), the dry season, canals feed water into the Biscayne Aquifer and prevent salt-water intrusion. In (**B**), the wet season, canals carry off excess surface runoff and drain water from the Biscayne Aquifer to maintain a lowered water table.

vation areas. During the dry season, water seeping under the levees of the conservation areas supplies the canals with water, which then flows eastward and sinks into the aquifer. If necessary, during prolonged drought, water can be transferred from Lake Okeechobee through the conservation areas to coastal areas where it is needed. The lake water, however, must serve agricultural interests and Everglades National Park as well as municipalities.

One of the major problems with water supply in the Miami area is saltwater intrusion (Fig. 3.18). In 1900, local wells served 1680 people. By 1925 the population had increased to 30,200. New wells had been sunk in 1907 to meet increasing demands, but by the early 1920s the water table had been so lowered that the wells had to be abandoned because of saltwater contamination. New wells were drilled in another area, but excessive water withdrawal

together with drainage designed to prevent flooding again lowered the water table, again causing encroachment of salt water. It became evident that strict regulation was necessary. Since 1952, water management has stabilized saltwater intrusion by ensuring adequate recharge of the aquifer. However, in times of extreme drought, as in 1970–71, adequate recharge was not possible, and the water table sank below sea level over half of Dade County (Fig. 3.19). As a result, salt water temporarily advanced half a mile inland of its normal position and eight of Miami's supply wells had to be shut down. The normal position of the fresh-salt groundwater interface ranges from less than half a mile inland in northern parts of the area to eight miles inland in southern parts of the area. The exact position of the interface fluctuates seasonally as the level of the water table changes. As urban demand and amounts of water withdrawn from the

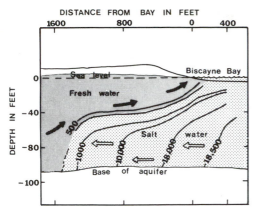

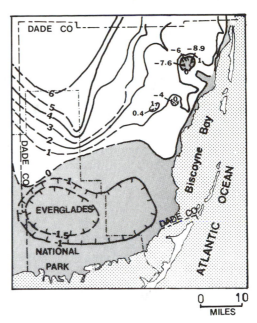

3.18 Cross section showing (schematically) the pattern of salt-water intrusion in the Biscayne Aquifer. The numbers indicate salt concentration in parts per million.

Biscayne aquifer rise, saltwater intrusion and contamination of well fields will increase.

The Orr-Southwest well-field complex furnishes water to much of Miami as well as to Coral Gables, West Miami, South Miami, Key Biscayne, and adjacent areas (Fig. 3.20). In the vicinity of the well field,

3.19 Contour map showing the elevation of the water table in Dade County, Florida, near the end of the prolonged drought of 1970–71. Numbered lines indicate elevation of the water table in feet above sea level. The shaded area indicates where the water table was below sea level.

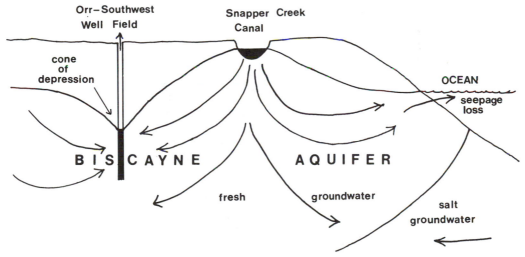

3.20 Schematic cross section illustrating how water infiltrating into the Biscayne Aquifer from the Snapper Creek Canal feeds the Orr-Southwest Well Field and also inhibits salt groundwater intrusion.

the Biscayne aquifer receives much of its water through infiltration from the Snapper Creek Canal. The cone of depression associated with the field does not induce saltwater intrusion because of adequate seepage from the controlled reach of the canal. As new well fields are required, however, they should be located far enough inland to reduce the threat of saltwater intrusion and the need to maintain high water-levels in the canals. (Maintaining high water-levels to inhibit saltwater intrusion involves the loss of fresh water by seepage to the ocean).

Increased conservation is important if future water needs are to be met. A number of water-management alternatives have been proposed: (1) backpumping storm runoff, (2) increasing number of control gates, (3) increasing canal depths, (4) storing water in the Floridan aquifer, (5) treating and recycling waste water, and (6) injecting brackish water into the Biscayne aquifer to retard saltwater intrusion.

1. Storm runoff could be backpumped through canal networks to conservation areas. The additional stored water would permit increased releases through forward pumping as well as increased seepage under the levees to canals, thus retarding saltwater intrusion and providing long-term recharge for municipal well fields. In this way, the population of Dade County could rise to 2.5 million without straining water resources (Edgerton, 1973). The backpumped water, however, would have to be free of excessive nutrients, pesticides, or toxic metals.

2. The number of control gates along inland stretches of the canals could be increased. Such structures maintain higher water levels in the canals during dry periods, thus preventing overdrainage of groundwater and its loss to the ocean (Fig. 3.19A).

3. Increasing the depth of canals (and thus canal volume) would permit greater storage of floodwaters behind coastal gates, necessitating fewer releases of fresh water into the

ocean. The depth of canals cannot be increased by lowering their floors because the channels are at or close to sea level. However, canal walls can be built higher. This will become feasible as agricultural areas are urbanized and low-lying lands are raised to meet county flood-protection regulations.

4. Excess floodwater could be injected into the deep-lying Floridan aquifer (where theoretically it should maintain a lens of recoverable fresh water) instead of being allowed to flow to the ocean (Fig. 3.21). This type of storage would eliminate evapotranspirational losses, which in the area amount to more than 40 inches of the annual 60-inch rainfall.

5. Treated waste water could be a significant source of fresh water. In 1970, sewage treatment plants in Dade County discharged 90 mgd of wastewater to the ocean and 10 mgd to inland canals, and it is estimated that by 1990, 325 mgd will be produced. Properly treated waste water could be injected into the Biscayne aquifer or transferred to conservation areas or wetlands.

6. Brackish water from the Floridan aquifer could be injected into the salt front of the Biscayne aquifer, thus retarding inland movement of the fresh-salt groundwater interface (Fig. 3.21).

Miami has been described as "an excellent example of a large metropolitan water system where careful planning has averted shortages and assured an adequate supply to meet future demands. . . ." (Schneider and Spieker 1969, p. A3) Whether an adequate water supply will continue to be maintained depends in part upon "promiscuous" urban sprawl and largely uncontrolled development encroaching further upon areas vital to recharging the Biscayne aquifer (Carter, 1976). Westward urban spread has begun to intrude upon such areas and upon areas where new well-fields are to be established in or near the East Everglades area. Happily, in 1957, Dade County voters chose to place nearly

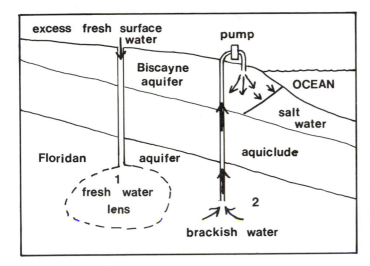

3.21 Schematic cross section illustrating two proposed methods of conserving fresh water in the Miami, Florida region. (1) Excess fresh water could be stored underground in the Floridan Aquifer. (2) Brackish water from the Floridan Aquifer could be used to prevent salt groundwater intrusion into the Biscayne Aquifer.

all governmental functions of county-wide significance under a newly created Metropolitan Dade County Commission. Among its powers, the Metro commission provides or regulates all local water and sewer systems, and, as part of a new metropolitan master plan, has rezoned areas necessary to aquifer recharge that were previously slated for development. Whether the plan will continue to be implemented and adhered to depends upon whether the people of Greater Miami decide to "try to create a well-planned semitropical garden spot or simply try to adjust to life in another sprawl-city, U.S.A., with all its trials and problems. . . ." (Carter, 1976).

Los Angeles

The history of water supply in the Los Angeles region encompasses a complex and controversial struggle between competing economic, social, legislative, and regional interests.

Water has always been a subject of controversy in California. Water is present in abundance, but it is distributed extremely unevenly, both in space and time, and the distribution (Fig. 3.22) does not match the pattern of demand. The total annual runoff in the state is 70 million acre-feet (an acre-foot is the amount of water required to cover an acre of land to a depth of one foot, and is equivalent to 43,560 cubic feet or 325,581 gallons) which far exceeds the present estimated demand of 33 million acre-feet and the projected requirements for the year 2020 of 48 million acre-feet for agricultural and urban use. The major sources of water, however, are in northern California, while the major urban and agricultural areas are in the central and southern parts of the state. More specifically, 80 percent of the population live in metropolitan areas from Sacramento to the Mexican border and 70 percent of the total streamflow occurs north of Sacramento. Furthermore, large variations in runoff from year to year are typical, and both floods and drought occur often. Annual precipitation varies from less than 2 in. per year in some desert areas to more than 100 in. on the windward slopes of high mountains.

The Los Angeles metropolitan area is located in a series of flat, gently seaward-sloping interconnected plains and valleys bounded on the southwest by the Pacific Ocean and surrounded on the three remaining sides by mountains that rise sharply to elevations of more than 10,000 feet (Fig.

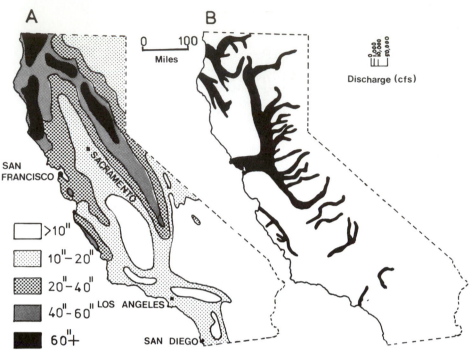

3.22 Annual rainfall (**A**) and stream runoff (**B**) in California. In **B** the width of the lines indicates average stream discharge in cubic feet per second.

3.23). Locally, hilly regions penetrate and partially separate the flat areas from each other. Collectively, the semi-elliptical area between the crests of the peripheral mountain ranges and the Pacific Ocean form a watershed known as the South Coastal Basin (Fig. 3.24). Precipitation within the watershed occurs when moisture-bearing breezes from the ocean are forced upward and cooled as they cross the mountainous areas. At sea level along the coast, annual precipitation is about 10 inches; at the base of the mountains (1100 feet), 20 inches; along the mountain summits, (3400–10,000 feet), it varies from 25 to 50 inches. Beyond the mountains to the north and east, the breezes descend to the lower elevations of the Mojave desert where annual precipitation is less than 6 inches. In more general terms, the 2410 square miles of mountains and foothills receive an average of 24 inches of precipitation each year, equivalent to 3,100,000 acre-feet of water. Of this, evapotranspirational losses account for all but 500,000 acre-feet, which flows over the surface or seeps underground. In the 2140 square miles of plain and valleys rainfall averages 16 inches a year, equivalent to 1,860,000 acre-feet. Of this amount, 1,400,000 acre-feet are lost through evapotranspiration, and 190,000 acre feet flow into the oceans. As a result, the mean annual supply of surface and groundwater available for consumption is on the order of 770,000 acre-feet. This supply can only be increased to the extent that some of the 190,000 acre-feet that flow to the ocean can be impounded and conserved. During times of flood, reservoirs and water-spreading grounds permit excess water to penetrate into the ground and augment groundwater storage. Urbanization, however, reduces in-

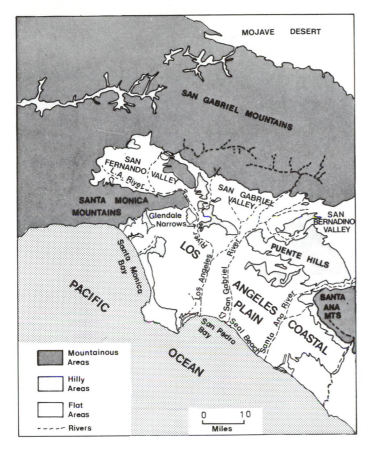

3.23 Topography and geography of the Los Angeles region.

filtration, through the creation of impervious surfaces such as paving and roofs, and the channeling of storm water into drains and sewers.

In the city of Los Angeles itself, average annual precipitation is 15 inches, but the amount for individual years has varied from 38.18 to 5.59 inches. Within the period 1893–1904, five years had an annual precipitation of less than 9 inches. From 1944 to 1951, the average annual precipitation was only 10 inches.

Geologically, the South Coastal Basin is complex, but may be thought of as a series of water-bearing, sediment-filled structural basins underlain and partially isolated from each other by non-water-bearing rock series (Fig. 3.25). Three large inland basins that

underlie the San Fernando Valley, the Upper San Gabriel Valley, and the Upper Santa Ana Valley, have been filled by sediment washed down from the mountains and deposited as alluvial fans. Except in times of flood, most streams flowing from the mountain slopes to the valley floors disappear beneath the surface within a short distance as the water percolates downward through the coarse sediment. Once underground, the water migrates away from the mountains toward the gaps in the walls of these inland basins where they are joined to the coastal basins that underlie the Los Angeles coastal plain. As the water migrates through the gaps it is forced to the surface, to flow in the channels of the Los Angeles, San Gabriel and Santa Ana rivers.

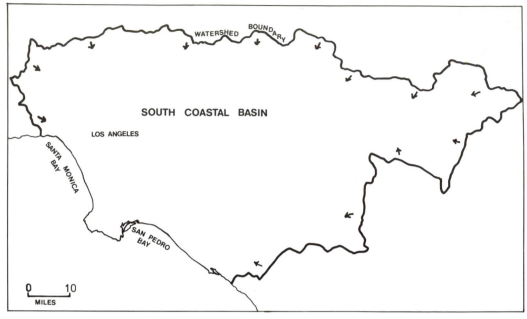

3.24 The boundary of the South Coastal Basin watershed. Arrows
indicate the general direction of surface runoff.

These and other rivers have filled the structural basins underlying the coastal plain
with alluvial sediment, and much of the
water flowing over the plain infiltrates this
sediment and continues its migration underground, causing the rivers to diminish in
volume downstream. Toward the coast,
much of the plain is capped by impervious
clay that confines the underlying aquifers
and prevents groundwater from emerging at
the surface. The confined aquifers contain
water under pressure and create an extensive artesian zone along the coastal plain.

All of these interconnected basins have
an immense storage capacity, estimated at 7
million acre-feet total, sufficient to maintain
the flow of surface rivers through long
periods of drought.

The original settlement, founded by the
Spanish in 1781 as El Pueblo de Nuestra
Senora la Reina de Los Angeles, was sited
just below the Glendale Narrows where the
flow of the Los Angeles River is most dependable. For many years, the river was
sufficient for the needs of the population.
However, when the transcontinental
railroads were completed in the 1870s and
1880s, the population began to rise rapidly:
to 11,183 in 1880, 50,395 in 1890, 102,479
in 1900, and close to a quarter-million in
1905. This burgeoning population coupled
with the severe drought of 1893–1904
brought the water supply close to its limits.
During the drought, wells were dug in the
coastal plain, and underground galleries
were constructed to improve the underground migration of water through the
gaps connecting the coastal plain basin with
the inland structural basins. The expanded
water supply, however, was sufficient for
no more than 300,000 people. The area of
artesian flow was diminishing rapidly, and
the level of the water table was sinking. To
meet the ever-increasing urban and agricultural needs of the area, it was decided early
in 1905 to import water from Owens Val-

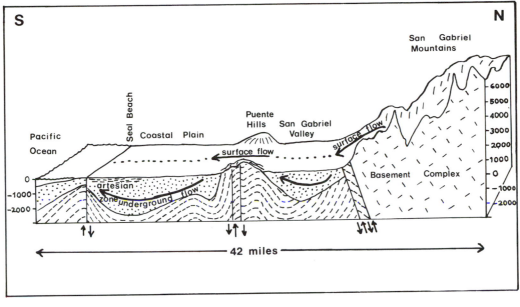

3.25 Block diagram illustrating the geology of a N-S strip across the South Coastal Basin. Long arrows indicate the pattern of surface runoff and groundwater circulation. The dotted line on land surface indicates path of stream runoff after a spell of wet weather. Numbers indicate elevation (in feet) above or below sea level. Short arrows indicate fault movement.

ley, 250 miles to the northeast (Fig. 3.26).

Owens Valley receives abundant water from streams draining the eastern flank of the Sierra Nevada (Fig. 3.27). Forty small streams, fed mainly by melting snow from the high mountains are tributary to the south-flowing Owens River. The valley itself is underlain by a structural basin filled with permeable volcanic debris and covered with coarse alluvial fans. Both the volcanic debris and the alluvial fans absorb and store great quantities of water that is released to the river and maintains its flow during the dry months from September to April.

The decision to convey water from Owens Valley to Los Angeles was not expected to gladden the hearts of farmers living in the valley. To forestall effective opposition, representatives of the Los Angeles Water Department secretly bought or obtained options to buy immense amounts of land (and associated irrigation ditches) bordering the Owens River before the plan was announced on July 29, 1905. On September 7, 1905, a bond issue of $1.5 million was passed by the voters of Los Angeles to consummate the land purchases and to begin surveys for an aqueduct and storage facilities. On June 12, 1907, $23 million for actual construction had been approved. The Los Angeles Aqueduct, completed in 1913, conducted water from the Owens River and from wells in channels built alongside hills, across deserts, and through mountain tun-

3.26 The major rivers, lakes, dams, reservoirs, and aqueducts of Arizona and California.

nels into reservoirs in San Fernando Valley. At first, the aqueduct provided more than enough water, and the city decided to enlarge itself by annexing the San Fernando Valley and other adjacent areas so that the surplus water could be used for irrigation. (The early law of the pueblo stated that water could not be sold to areas outside the city limits. Thus, the San Fernando Valley had to become part of Los Angeles in order to use the water.) It was perhaps more than coincidence that landowners in the Valley had been among the strongest advocates of construction of the Los Angeles Aqueduct.

From 1910 to 1920, the population of Los Angeles increased from 319,189 to

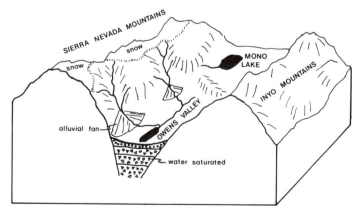

3.27 Schematic block diagram of the Owens Valley–Mono Lake region of California showing topography before construction of the Los Angeles Aqueduct.

576,637, and additional water had to be secured. Owens Valley farmers, however, opposed Los Angeles' terms for purchase of the water, and violence erupted, leading to the dynamiting of the aqueduct in 1924. Eventually California Governor Young mediated the dispute between the city and the farmers, and Los Angeles bought most of the private land in the valley to ensure a continuing supply. In 1940, an eleven-mile tunnel was constructed through the mountains at the head of Owens Valley to tap the waters of the Mono Lake area to the north (Fig. 3.27), effectively extending the length of the Los Angeles Aqueduct works to 350 miles.

The drought years of the 1920s and increasing population brought many communities adjacent to Los Angeles to the point of crisis, and the residents permitted their areas to be annexed by the city so that they could use water imported from Owens Valley. Thus, Sawtelle, Hyde Park, Eagle Rock, Venice, Watts, and Barnes City became part of Los Angeles. As the city enlarged through such annexations, so did its financial base, permitting it eventually to undertake costlier and more ambitious projects to expand its water supply system. However, towns such as Santa Monica, Pasadena, Beverly Hills, and Long Beach resisted annexation. Instead, they continued to draw upon local supplies, making use of stored floodwaters and pumping groundwater, thus severely lowering the water table. By 1933, the water table was substantially below sea level, and by the 1940s, saltwater intrusion had become a serious problem, having progressed to up to two miles inland in some places. In an attempt to combat the intrusion, a program was developed to pump fresh imported water into the groundwater system through a series of recharge wells. By 1965, twelve wells had been installed along the coast; ultimately the program calls for 75 recharge wells.

As it became clear in the 1920s that additional sources of water would have to be sought for Los Angeles and other urban areas of southern California, investigation was begun into the possibility of importing water from the Colorado River (Fig. 3.26). The Colorado River drains a vast area of the Rocky Mountains and then flows through the intensely arid regions of the Southwest. The flow is highly variable, varying from 25 to 5 million acre-feet per year, with an average annual flow (at Lee's Ferry) of 16,270,000 acre-feet. With the water is carried 100,000 acre-feet of sediment each year. The most convenient point from which water could be brought from the Colorado River to the coast of southern California lies about 200 miles from Los Angeles, along the stretch of the river forming the boundary between California and Arizona. A series of dams (including Hoover and Parker) and reservoirs, 242 miles of aqueducts, tunnels, hydroelectric works, and pumping stations to raise the water 1357 feet above the intake level would have to be constructed. The project also involved building an aqueduct to San Diego and a canal (the All-American Canal) to bring water to the rich soil of the Imperial Valley. Furthermore, to do all this, the permission and participation of the federal government and of local and state governments with legitimate interests in Colorado River water would have to be obtained. In order to coordinate the many coastal cities of southern California interested in the project, a new political institution, the Metropolitan Water District (MWD) of southern California was formed in 1928. In the same year, despite vigorous opposition from Arizona, Congress appropriated $165 million for the project, to be paid back by 1987. On September 29, 1931, the voters of the MWD approved a $220 million bond issue by a margin of five-to-one, and by 1941 the first deliveries of Colorado River water to the Los Angeles region were made.

The estimated capacity of the Colorado Aqueduct is 1,212,000 acre-feet per year. This amount, together with 770,000 acre-feet from the South Coastal Basin, 130,000 acre-feet from the San Diego watershed, and 325,000 acre-feet from the Owens-Mono area was considered by the MWD, in 1948, to be nearly enough to meet the estimated future demands of the region until 1980–2000, assuming a population of 8,000,000 and irrigation of several hundred thousand acres. Beyond 1990, the MWD envisoned receiving an additional 1,500,000 acre-feet annually from the California State Water Project (SWP), upon its completion. The SWP is an ambitious, complex program designed to supply water-deficient areas in the southern parts of the state from the water-rich areas in the northern part of the state, and to prevent flooding, provide recreational areas, and generate power. The principal components of the SWP already constructed (1974) include a series of dams on the Feather River (Fig. 3.26), the Oroville Dam and Reservoir, the California Aqueduct, electric power facilities, and works in the Sacramento Delta area to prevent direct outflow of river water into San Francisco Bay and the Pacific Ocean.

However, a number of events conspired to undermine these projected sources of additional water. Controversy arose between Arizona and California over the amount each was legitimately entitled to withdraw from the Colorado River, and in 1963 the U.S. Supreme Court issued a decree that by 1985 will lower California's allocation by 962,000 acre-feet or more per year. Of that amount, 662,000 acre-feet will be taken from the allotment of the MWD of Southern California. Seeking to compensate for the loss and preparing for estimated future needs, the MWD turned to the State Water Project for an additional entitlement of 500,000 acre-feet. The remaining 162,000 acre-feet was to be obtained through additional importations from the Owens-Mono area. But when, in 1972, Los Angeles began to increase its withdrawals from the Owens-Mono area, residents of Inyo County, in which most of Owens Valley lies, claimed that Los Angeles was violating the California Environmental Quality Act of 1970 and went to court and demanded that

an environmental impact study be made (*The New York Times*, Sept. 19, 1976, p. 21). Environmentalists contended that the valley would be turned from a place of beauty into a desert, and that the reduction in vegetation attendant upon withdrawal of additional water would aggravate dust storms. (Before construction of the Los Angeles Aqueduct, 100 years ago, the floor of Owens Valley was covered by a lake 70 feet deep. Today, the 200 square-mile lake floor is completely dry, and when the wind blows over it, as much as 50,000 tons of dust are lifted into the air.) Moreover, it has been charged that Los Angeles wastes water, and that it has been drawing heavily upon the cheap water from Owens Valley not because of shortages, but in order to keep water rates low. As of 1977, the case was still in court, and continued sporadic violence, including dynamiting of the aqueduct, indicates that the antagonisms raised by the issue of water are long-lived.

As for the State Water Project, the wisdom of continuing its expansion has been called into question: (1) Estimates of the future population and water requirements of the MWD may be exaggerated; the rate of population increase has already slowed considerably, in part because of the environmental deterioration of the urban areas of southern California. If this is so, the SWP may prove to be a financial drain on taxpayers if customers for the water are lacking. (2) Reductions in the amount and quality of water entering San Francisco Bay from the Sacramento Delta may disrupt the delicate ecologic balance of the bay, turning it into a polluted "dead" body of water, and permitting eastward saltwater encroachment. (3) Continued damming of wild rivers in northern California diminishes precious scenic and recreational resources, and floods archeologically valuable Indian sites. Also, the damming of these sediment-laden rivers that flow into the Pacific would cut off the sediment needed to maintain the delicate balance of natural processes upon which the continued existence of ocean beaches depends. (Erosion by longshore currents would, without natural beach nourishment, quickly result in the disappearance of the beaches.)

It has been suggested that instead of continuing the traditional approaches of damming and diverting water, new, alternate sources of water be found. Wastewater reclamation may permit the annual storing of hundreds of thousands or even millions of acre-feet of water in the groundwater system for future use. Already, municipal sewage is being reclaimed and used to recharge groundwater and to create recreational lakes at a cost of $19–$31 an acre-foot. This is far cheaper than the estimated future cost of SWP water at $40–$60 an acre-foot (not including inflationary increases). Desalinization of salt water is still expensive, but the cost has already been lowered from $1600 to $320 per acre-foot. If cheap sources of power can be found, technological breakthroughs may make desalinization competitive with other sources of water. An immensely significant potential source of both power and water in southern California are the geothermal resources of the Imperial Valley. Beneath it are great masses of sediment, up to 20,000 feet thick, containing billions of acre-feet of saline brine at temperatures up to 700° F and under hydrostatic pressure of over 2000 lbs per square inch. Wells sunk into this material permit the fluid to fountain upward as a mixture of steam and boiling brine at velocities close to the speed of sound. The heat in the brine could provide the energy for its own desalinization and the production of excess electricity. If technical problems are overcome, it may be feasible to develop as much as 10–15 million acre-feet of brine each year for 100–300 years, yielding 5–7 million acre-feet of distilled water and 20–30 thousand megawatts of electric power at an attractive price (Rex, in Seckler, 1971).

The California Department of Water Resources has recently acknowledged that traditional approaches must be rethought, and it may be expected that the continuing history of water supply for the urban areas of southern California will reflect changing attitudes and values as well as changing technological capabilities.

New York City

The New York City region receives ample precipitation, mostly in the form of rain, distributed fairly evenly throughout the year. Average annual precipitation is about 42 inches, with extreme variations from about 30 to 50 inches. Evapotranspirational losses are on the order of 20 inches a year. Problems of water supply have been concerned not with an abundance of water, but with an abundance of clean, uncontaminated water.

The five boroughs of New York City (Fig. 3.28) straddle two hydrologically distinct areas. Brooklyn and Queens (which comprise the western end of Long Island) and southeastern Staten Island (Richmond) are situated on the Atlantic Coastal Plain, and are underlain by up to 2000 feet of unconsolidated sand, gravel, silt, and clay. Manhattan, the Bronx, and the central spine of Staten Island are underlain by metamorphic rocks which either outcrop at the sur-

3.28 The five boroughs of New York City: Manhattan, The Bronx, Brooklyn, Queens, and Staten Island (Richmond).

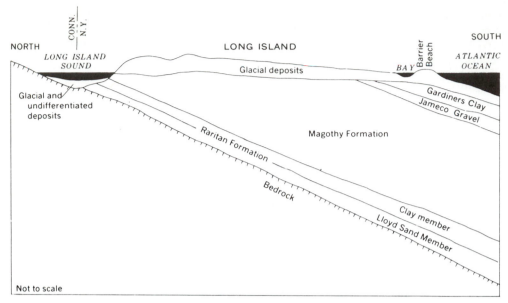

3.29 Diagrammatic cross section showing the general relationships of
the major rock units of the groundwater system.

face or are covered by thin coats or pockets
of soil or glacial debris. Northwestern
Staten Island is geologically distinct from
the rest of the city and will not be considered here.

Brooklyn, Queens, and Southeast Staten
Island. This region is underlain by a wedge
of sediment that thickens from 0 feet in the
northwest to 2000 feet in the southeast (Fig.
3.29). The sediment rests on an impermeable basement of metamorphic rock, and
consists of two major parts: (1) gently inclined layers overlain by (2) glacial debris.
The inclined layers include two relatively
impermeable aquicludes, the Gardiners Clay
and the Raritan Clay, which confine the intervening Jameco Gravel and Magothy Formation, both aquifers. These aquifers consist of thick layers of permeable sands and
gravels interspersed with local impermeable
silts and clays. Beneath the Raritan Clay is
a second, deeper aquifer, called the Lloyd
Sand Member, (sands and gravels), which
rest on the impermeable metamorphic basement. Overlying the inclined layers is a

more or less horizontal layer of permeable
sands and gravels deposited by melting glacial ice as morainal till, or by meltwater
rivers as outwash plain (glaciofluviatile) deposits. These morainal and outwash-plain
sediments will be refered to collectively as
"the glacial aquifer."

Precipitation enters and travels through
the glacial aquifer with little difficulty.
Water enters the Jameco and Magothy
aquifers by percolation through the glacial
aquifer or slowly by leakage through the
Gardiners Clay. The Lloyd aquifer receives
water by slow leakage through the Raritan
Clay. Salt water penetrates all of the
aquifers as a series of wedges (Fig. 3.30A).
The water table lies within the glacial aquifer. Due to the inclination of the layers, and
to the confining presence of (1) the Gardiners and Raritan clays, (2) the local impermeable clay and silt layers within the
Magothy, and (3) the underlying metamorphic basement, groundwater within the
Magothy and Lloyd aquifers is under artesian pressure. Water within the glacial

aquifer, however, is not artesian. The patterns of groundwater movement are shown in Figure 3.30A.

Details of the history of the development of Long Island's water supply may be conveniently divided into four phases. Before the arrival of European settlers (Phase 1), the Indian inhabitants obtained water from surface streams and lakes. Contamination was minimal and an overall equilibrium between recharge and discharge of the groundwater system was maintained. As a result, the positions of the water table and of the fresh salt groundwater interfaces was stable (Fig. 3.30A). With the arrival of European settlers (Phase 2), houses were constructed, each of which typically had a shallow well and cesspool (a cavity in the ground for household wastes). As the population increased, public wells dug deeper into the glacial aquifer replaced many private wells. Recharge/discharge equilibrium with the groundwater system was maintained, but the aquifer gradually became polluted in the vicinity of the cesspools (Fig. 3.30B). To obtain unpolluted water, deeper public wells were dug into the Jameco and Magothy aquifers (Phase 3), and waste water continued to be disposed of into cesspools connected to the glacial aquifer. Ninety percent of the water entering the glacial aquifer (whether precipitation or polluted waste water) migrates laterally and discharges into streams or the ocean. Only 10 percent percolates downward to recharge the underlying inclined aquifers, and eventually, withdrawal of water through wells from the Jameco and Magothy aquifers exceeded recharge by water percolating downward from the glacial aquifer. As a result, there began a gradual net depletion in the volume of fresh groundwater, a lowering of the water table, and a slow landward migration of salt groundwater into the Jameco and Magothy aquifers (Fig. 3.30C). With urbanization (Phase 4), significant areas of the land surface were paved over and large-scale installation of sewers began. Storm waters and waste waters now were channeled di-

rectly into the sea rather than into the groundwater system, and recharge of the Jameco and Magothy aquifers was severely hindered. Rapid salt water intrusion and a serious lowering of the water table resulted (Fig. 3.30D). Comparison of Maps A and B in Figure 3.31, which show the elevation of the water table in 1903 and in 1936 (before and after extensive urbanization) reveals the magnitude of the hydrologic changes that had taken place. The water table had fallen in places to more than 35 feet below sea level. Saltwater contamination of local wells was most serious in Brooklyn, where urbanization had proceeded most rapidly and extensively, and it became clear that another source of water would have to be found. In 1947, almost all pumping of local wells in Brooklyn was forbidden, and the borough's water mains were linked to the aqueduct system that was already supplying Manhattan and the Bronx with surface waters from upstate New York. (Withdrawal of local groundwater for purposes of air conditioning was permitted, provided the water was reinjected back into the groundwater system after use.)

Hydrologic changes in Queens began to repeat the same pattern of excess withdrawals, water-table lowering, and saltwater intrusion and contamination of wells. By 1959, most areas of Queens (except southern Queens, where 750,000 residents still receive local groundwater) were provided with water imported from upstate. Parts of Staten Island had begun to receive water from upstate in 1917.

It is interesting to note that after the cessation of withdrawal of local groundwater, recoveries of up to 35 feet in the elevation of the water table and a major retreat of saltwater intrusions have taken place (Fig. 3.30C). Ironically, in low-lying parts of Brooklyn and Queens, subways and basements constructed when the water table was low have suffered increasingly from flooding as the water table has begun to rise toward its pre-urbanization levels. Expenditures of hundreds of thousands of dollars

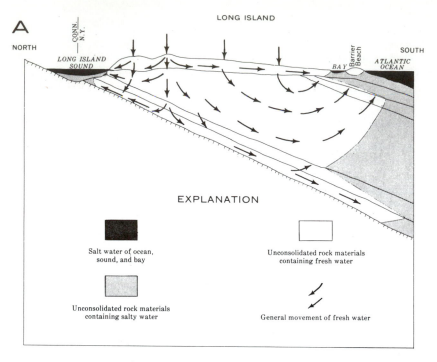

A

NORTH
CONN.
N.Y.

LONG ISLAND

SOUTH

LONG ISLAND
SOUND

Barrier Beach

BAY

ATLANTIC
OCEAN

EXPLANATION

Salt water of ocean,
sound, and bay

Unconsolidated rock materials
containing fresh water

Unconsolidated rock materials
containing salty water

General movement of fresh water

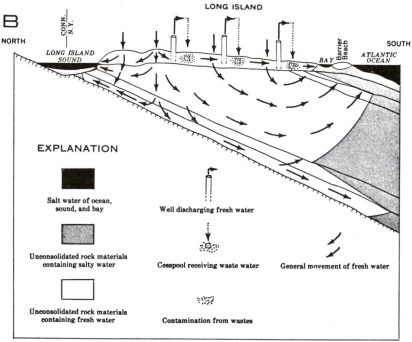

B

NORTH
CONN.
N.Y.

LONG ISLAND

SOUTH

LONG ISLAND
SOUND

Barrier Beach

BAY

ATLANTIC
OCEAN

EXPLANATION

Salt water of ocean,
sound, and bay

Well discharging fresh water

Unconsolidated rock materials
containing salty water

Cesspool receiving waste water

General movement of fresh water

Unconsolidated rock materials
containing fresh water

Contamination from wastes

3.30 Diagrammatic cross sections showing generalized groundwater conditions in Long Island, New York (**A**) before the arrival of European settlers (phase 1). (**B**) after the arrival of European settlers (phase 2). Each house was served by a shallow well and disposed

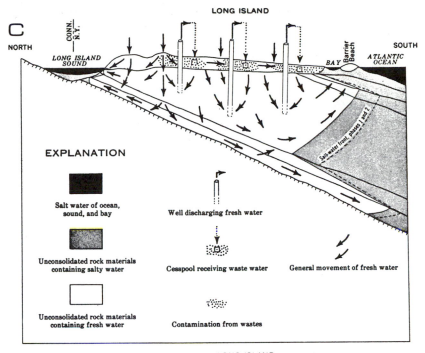

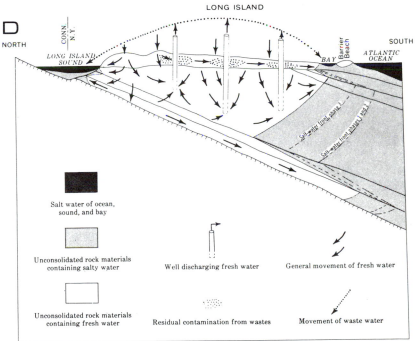

of wastes through cesspools. (**C**) as population increased (phase 3).
Water was obtained from deep public wells; wastes were disposed
of in cesspools and septic tanks. (**D**) after large areas were paved
over and sewers were installed (phase 4).

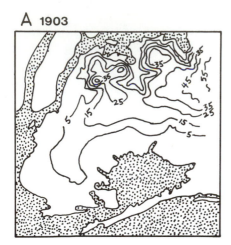

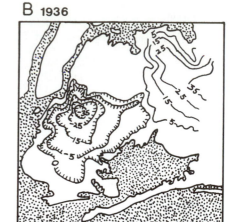

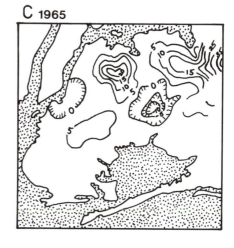

3.31 Three maps showing the elevation of the water table under western Long Island (**A**) in 1903, (**B**) in 1936, (**C**) in 1965. The numbered lines are groundwater table contours showing elevations in feet above or below (hachured lines) sea level.

have been necessary to repair damage to schools, hospitals, and private houses. In the East New York section of Brooklyn, cessation of pumping of groundwater in 1974 resulted in a water-table rise of 8–10 feet above sea level by 1976, and a further rise of 2–4 feet in the next several years is expected (Soren, 1976). Alleviation of the problem is difficult because if pumping is resumed, saltwater intrusion will recommence. Also, the quality of the groundwater is poor, and if pumping were resumed, the problem of what to do with the polluted water once it is brought to the surface would not be easily solved.

Manhattan, the Bronx, Central Staten Island. Manhattan and the Bronx are underlain by generally impermeable gneisses, schists, and marbles. Central Staten Island is underlain by serpentine. Collectively, these materials may be referred to as "the bedrock." During the last part of the Pleistocene, the bedrock was covered by southward flowing glacial ice that scraped away most loose surface materials. Upon its retreat, the melting ice left a thin cover, with locally thicker pockets, of glacial till over much of the bedrock, and subsequent weathering converted the uppermost materials into soil. The glacial till and the soil

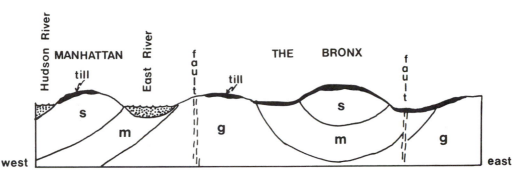

3.32 Simplified E-W geologic cross section across Manhattan and the Bronx. s = the Manhattan Formation (mainly schists and gneisses), m = Inwood Marble, g = Fordham Gneiss.

constitute a discontinuous, shallow groundwater reservoir resting on the impervious bedrock. Local narrow zones of groundwater penetrate the bedrock where it has been shattered by faults (Fig. 3.32).

Before the region was settled by Europeans, numerous streams, ponds, and lakes provided clear, pure water for the needs of the native Indian population. With the arrival of settlers, additional water was obtained from wells sunk into the surficial glacial materials. After use, the water was dumped back onto the surface, into the lakes and streams, or disposed of in shallow cesspools. In Manhattan, as the number of inhabitants grew, the surface waters became polluted by water draining from privies and graveyards and the dumping of dead animals and other refuse into ponds and lakes. By the early nineteenth century, the demand for water began to exceed the supply. Fires swept through Manhattan in 1828 and 1835, and an epidemic of cholera killed 3500 people in 1832. New York's population was now close to 300,000 and it became clear that new sources of water would have to be found. In 1842 a dam across the Croton River and a 37-mile-long aqueduct to carry water southward to the city were completed (Fig. 3.33). Within a few years, additional reservoirs were needed and added to the Croton System, but even so, by the end of the nineteenth century, waters collected

within the Croton Watershed were insufficient for the needs of the growing city. By 1917, water began to flow into the city from the Catskill Mountains through a series of aqueducts and tunnels more than 120 miles in length. During the period 1917–1950, the Catskill System was expanded through the further construction of dams, reservoirs, aqueducts, and tunnels. Yet as early as 1928, well before the system was completed, it was seen that more water would soon be needed, and plans were drawn up to tap the Delaware Watershed. The Delaware River, in its lower reaches, borders on New Jersey, Pennsylvania, and Delaware, and in 1929, New Jersey filed suit to prevent New York from depleting the flow of the river by diversion of part of its headwaters. The court ruled that New York could withdraw only 400 mgd rather than the 600 mgd it had planned upon, and that it must, furthermore, release enough water to assure a minimum flow in the Delaware River of 1750 cubic feet per second (as measured at Montague, New Jersey). Work was begun in 1955 on construction of the Delaware System, and by the 1970s, water was flowing to New York from reservoirs as far away as 128 miles. Today, New York City receives about 95 percent of its water supply from eight distant watersheds that drain an area of 1969 square miles and provide a dependable yield of 1805 mgd. The water travels

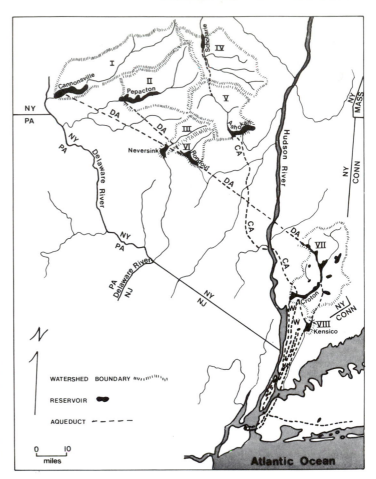

3.33 The watersheds, reservoirs, rivers, and aqueducts of the New York City Water Supply System. Watersheds I (West Branch), II (East Branch), III (Neversink) and VI (Rondout) constitute the Delaware System; IV (Schoharie) and V (Esopus) constitute the Catskill System; VII the Croton System; VIII the Bronx River System. Major aqueducts are the Delaware Aqueduct (DA), the Catskill Aqueduct (CA), and the Old and New Croton Aqueducts (W).

along more than 1000 streams, is captured in 27 reservoirs, and carried through 350 miles of aqueducts and tunnels. (An additional 5 mgd can be obtained from wells on Staten Island, and 55 mgd from surface and underground sources on Long Island. Privately owned water-supply companies in Queens can provide 50 mgd.)

The quality of the water imported from upstate is excellent. The watershed is underlain mainly by insoluble schists, gneisses, sandstones, and shales, and the precipitation is able to retain its "soft" character, free of objectionable minerals. On the other hand, it contains little of the natural flourides necessary to decay-resistant teeth. The watershed areas are main-

tained as forests to prevent soil erosion and silting of reservoirs. For towns located within the watershed areas, New York City builds and operates sewage-disposal plants. Since elevations of reservoirs within the watershed area are up to 840 feet or more above sea level, most water is able to reach consumers in the city by gravity flow, without pumping (Van Burkalow, 1959).

Imported water was first brought to Manhattan in 1842, to the west Bronx (1874) and the east Bronx (1895) upon their annexation, and to Staten Island in 1917. A factor in Brooklyn's decision to become part of New York City in 1898 may have been the threat of water shortages.

Rapid increases in population of areas adjacent to New York City coupled with the drought of 1961–66 and the increasing problem of saltwater intrusions into the groundwater reservoirs of Nassau and Suffolk counties have forced consideration of ways to increase the water supply for the entire New York metropolitan region. Construction of the so-called "Third Water Tunnel" designed to carry water from Hillview Reservoir in Yonkers under the East River to Queens has been stalled due to New York's financial crisis. In the hope that the Third Water Tunnel will be able to feed water into Nassau County's water-supply system, Long Island officials have joined New York in asking for Federal funds to complete the project.

Looking to the future, the federal government has stated that the New York metropolitan region will face a water shortage of at least 390 million gallons a day by the year 2000. If adequate water conservation measures are not implemented, the shortage could be as high as 590 mgd. To solve this problem, proposals have been made to dam and divert waters from the Hudson (upstream of its brackish estuarine reaches), Susquehanna, Housatonic, Passaic, and other rivers, and to tap the waters of Lakes Champlain and Ontario. Major objections to the proposals have been raised in terms of destruction of wilderness areas, depletion of stream flow for other areas served by these water bodies, and the effects of altered salinity in estuarine areas. Moreover, it has been claimed that addition of Hudson River water to the currently almost pristine New York City supply would drastically reduce its quality due to the presence in the Hudson of partially treated sewage and industrial effluents.

One of the most radical proposals has been to turn Long Island Sound into a freshwater lake by constructing dams at each end of the sound, flushing or pumping out the salt water, and filling the basin thus created with fresh river-water (Fig. 3.34). However, sewage nutrients carried into such a lake by rivers flowing from Connecticut would convert it into an algae-covered cesspool unless excellent waste-water treatment plants were installed. Vigorous objection has also been raised by residents of shore communities both in Connecticut and Long Island.

General criticism has been made of the nature of the demand for water in New York City (Boyle, 1971). With the exception of commercial and industrial establishments, water metering is optional, and most private users of water pay a flat rate, regardless of the amount they use. As a result, there is little attempt to conserve water or to repair minor leaks. Leakage from public

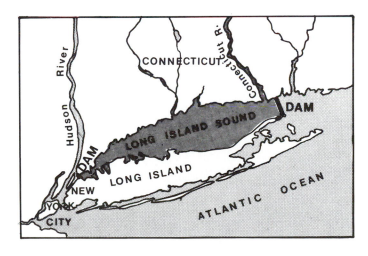

3.34 The location of proposed dams that would turn Long Island Sound into a freshwater lake.

water mains is notorious. The Mayor's Select Committee on Water Main Breaks reported in 1976 that in 1969 and 1970, the city abandoned programs for leak detection and valve maintenance on the ancient (much of it nineteenth century) 6300-mile underground water-distribution system as funds were cut out of the budget in a shifting of municipal priorities. This is especially serious because the normal life expectancy for a water main is approximately 80 years, and many of the mains approach or exceed that age. The Committee urged an orderly replacement of all nineteenth-century mains by the year 2000. It is highly unlikely that this target date can be met.

If universal metering was required and a realistic pricing policy adopted, it has been estimated the city would save 200 mgd. Repair of leaky mains would save as much as 400 mgd. Such savings amount to about one third of the city's daily needs. Other methods of water conservation together with treatment and reuse of waste water would further augment the city's supplies and delay the necessity of obtaining additional water through expensive and perhaps ecologically disruptive engineering projects. In addition, the Regional Plan Association has suggested that the Federal government's projected population increases for Long Island may be too high, and that future water needs may be less than expected.

4. Waste Disposal

One of the major products of modern, affluent society is waste material. Vast quantities of solids, liquids, and gases are released or discarded as useless or unwanted. In urban areas, where large numbers of people and great industrial and manufacturing complexes are concentrated, the question of how to dispose of such materials economically, without poisoning and disfiguring the environment, has become a major problem. In 1970, urban areas of the United States were producing about 1400 million pounds of solid wastes each day, enough refuse to cover 400 acres of land to a depth of ten feet (Schneider, 1970). The cost to local governments for the collection and disposal of these wastes, about $3 billion each year, was exceeded only by expenditures for schools and roads. It has been estimated that on the average, every man, woman, and child in the United States is producing nearly a ton of refuse each year (Ehrlich and Ehrlich, 1972).

Intermeshed with the problems of waste disposal are the problems of treatment or disposal of polluted water and its effect upon water supply. As population and per capita use of water increases, there is a growing need for multiple reuse of water. Reuse of water makes it imperative that its quality be maintained or restored so that the supply will remain adequate. The degree of purity required obviously varies: water used for street cleaning, flushing toilets, industrial cooling, or putting out fires need not meet standards for drinking. However, most municipal water-supply systems do not segregate water intended for different uses, and therefore the highest standards of purity must be attained.

It is significant that problems of waste disposal and pollution multiply exponentially as population increases. Where population is small and scattered, wastes may be discarded relatively simply by releasing them into large bodies of water where they are diluted and neutralized, or through the construction of septic tanks and cesspools. In cities, however, land for dumping is scarce and expensive, the quantity of wastes becomes too great for adequate dilution in surface waters, and there is no room for proper spacing of septic tanks and cesspools. For example, in the Lake Tahoe region on the California-Nevada border, where the population expanded from 10,000 in 1960 to 50,000 in 1977, urbanization is actually being brought to a halt because of overloading of the new sewage treatment plant. Enlargement of the plant is not foreseen in the near future. When industrial and commercial wastes are considered in addition to municipal wastes, the problem is further aggravated. Sophisticated and sometimes costly methods of disposal have to be employed.

Efficient waste disposal and avoidance of pollution involves an array of economic, technologic, political, and legal considerations. Emphasis in the following discussion will be placed on the geologic factors involved and the maintenance of water purity. Since water sources and sites of waste disposal commonly lie outside of city limits, discussion must range beyond the boundaries of urbanized regions. For convenience, problems of water quality, and the disposal of solid wastes, liquid wastes, radioactive wastes, and thermal pollution will be treated separately, although in reality they overlap.

WATER QUALITY

The Federal Water Pollution Control Act of 1948 amended by the Water Quality Act of 1965 requires that all states and the federal government establish water-quality standards for interstate streams and coastal waters so that the public health or welfare shall be protected and the quality of water enhanced (Feth, 1973). In 1962, the U.S. Public Health Service published a set of Drinking Water Standards that have been widely accepted by local health agencies either in toto or as a model for their own regulations. Because for the most part, raw surface waters are used for public water supply without treatment other than disinfection, it is of the utmost importance that such sources be of adequate quality. To this end, a subcommittee of the Federal Water Pollution Control Administration (1968) developed raw-water criteria for public water supplies. Such criteria include statements as to physical characteristics (color, odor, temperature, turbidity), microbiological constituents (coliform organisms and fecal coliforms), inorganic chemical constituents or characteristics (twenty metals, non-metals and radicals, plus alkalinity and hardness), organic chemicals (including oil, grease, pesticides, and herbicides) and radioactivity. The Subcommittee notes, however,

that it is "difficult and sometimes impossible to develop uniform numerical criteria suitable for national application. . . ." because of natural regional variations in water quality aside from man-made pollution and the inevitable effects on water quality of human occupance and activity.

The National Community Water Supply Study (McDermott, 1970) investigated the quality and dependability of water supply in the United States, surveying 969 public systems that provide water for a total of 18 million people. Twenty-two cities with populations over 100,000 were included in the survey. Acceptable water quality was that which met the Public Health Service's Drinking Water Standards. It was found that 41 percent of the 969 systems, delivering water to 2.5 million people, provided water of inferior quality. Potentially dangerous water was being delivered to 360,000 people. The quality was deficient in that it was bacterially contaminated, contained excessive chemical constituents (organic or inorganic), or was of insufficient clarity. Poor treatment and distribution facilities, inadequately trained operators, insufficient inspection of facilities, insufficient sampling and analysis of water, and impure water sources were listed as the causes. The report noted that 12,000 different toxic chemical compounds are in industrial use today (with more than 500 new chemicals being developed each year), and that wastes from these chemicals enter the groundwater and surface waters at continually increasing rates. Furthermore, very little is known about the environmental and health impacts of the chemicals. The report also states that the current Drinking Water Standards are inadequate and must be up-dated. For example, asbestos minerals associated with health problems have been detected in substantial quantities in some municipal water supplies in and near Duluth, Minnesota (Mazzella and Morrison, 1974). The Standards do little more than mention viruses, neglect numerous inorganic chemicals known to be toxic, and identify only one index that is supposed to cover the entire family of organic chemical compounds. It was concluded that "we can no longer afford to 'wait and see what happens.' We must begin to *investigate before we introduce* new compounds into the environment. . . ." (McDermott, 1970, p. 11). In 1974, the Safe Drinking Water Act was passed, placing all of the 40,000 public water supplies in the United States under federal supervision. However, passage of the law does not alter the fact that remarkably little is known about the toxicity of many substances that may enter the systems. An attempt to catalog hazardous substances is being undertaken as mandated by the Toxic Substances Control Act of 1976. However, beyond listing substances, ways must be found to identify, detect, and isolate dangerous materials and to determine in what quantities their presence is acceptable. Thus, the control of drinking-water quality remains primitive.

Sources of water contamination include the application of herbicides, pesticides, and fertilizers to agricultural lands, release of industrial waste products, waters draining from mines and through mine dumps, storm waters polluted in their passage through urbanized areas, inadequately treated sewage, contaminants leached from solid waste disposal sites, and saltwater encroachment. Also, gaseous pollutants dissolved in rain and snow together with the settling of poisonous, wind-transported dusts add significantly to the deterioration of water quality.

Self-Cleansing of Water

Natural self-cleansing of water takes place in several ways. In lakes and rivers, sunlight bleaches out some pollutants. Other pollutants settle to the bottom or are consumed by bacteria. Consumption of organic wastes by aerobic bacteria (bacteria that require oxygen) depends upon the presence in the water of dissolved oxygen (DO). Oxygen enters water where the water is in contact with air and also through the life pro-

cesses of aquatic plants. If a great deal of organic debris enters a water body, the demand for dissolved oxygen needed to accomplish the decay of the debris (biochemical oxygen demand, or BOD) may exceed the supply of DO. If this happens, organic debris accumulates and settles to the bottom rather than being consumed. The debris may then be attacked by anaerobic bacteria (bacteria that thrive in the absence of DO), resulting in foul-smelling putrefaction. The absence of adequate DO also may cause the death of sensitive species of fish and plants.

The problem of DO deficiency is exacerbated when nutrients such as phosphorous and nitrogen compounds from fertilizers, detergents, and so forth, enter water. The nutrients encourage the growth of algae and other weeds. When such plant material dies, it is decayed by aerobic bacteria, which leads to a serious loss of DO. Frequently, there is not enough DO to allow complete aerobic decay and anaerobic bacteria begin to attack the plant remains. The noxious compounds that these bacteria produce cause the quality of the water to deteriorate rapidly. The process of over-fertilization-excessive plant growth-DO deficiency-anaerobic decay is called *eutrophication*.

Self-cleansing of groundwater may take place mechanically, biologically, and chemically in the course of its passage through soil, rock, and sediment—assuming the water does not move rapidly through large open fissures, such as are commonly found in limestone or dolomite. Harmful bacteria are effectively removed by entrapment and adsorption onto the surface of grains; for example, percolation through 200 feet of coarse gravel has been sufficient to remove coliform bacteria, and bacteria in sewage have been removed by infiltration through 3–7 feet of coarse soil. Similarly, viruses have been removed in less than 200 feet of flow through gravel, and viral contamination of groundwater is no more of a hazard than is bacterial contamination (McGauhey, 1968; Alberding *et al*, 1976). The bacterial decomposition of organic solids is

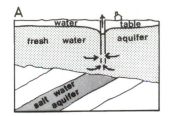 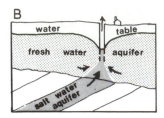

4.1 Cross sections to illustrate contamination of a fresh water aquifer by salt water from a saltwater aquifer due to over-pumping. (**A**) before overpumping; (**B**) after overpumping.

usually acceptable because it results in an increase in the ions normally present in the groundwater. Alteration or removal of such solids and of nutrients is accomplished by contact with the microbial population of the soil and also through adsorption by clays, ion exchange, precipitation, and filtration (Born and Stephenson, 1969).

Dangerous changes in groundwater that cannot be self-cleansed are produced by buildups of salt and by addition of certain industrial wastes and agricultural chemicals.

In considering the geologic aspects of maintaining or enhancing water quality, it is important to note that lakes and streams and underground water systems are intimately interconnected. Polluted surface water can cause a deterioration in the quality of groundwater; polluted groundwater can seep into and contaminate surface waters. Falling water-tables can diminish the volume of lakes and streams and hence their ability to adequately dilute and disperse waste materials. Likewise, diminished volume of surface water bodies can affect the recharge and patterns of circulation of groundwater.

Problems of saltwater intrusion in coastal areas due to withdrawal of fresh water in excess of recharge were discussed in Chapter 3. Saltwater contamination may also occur through upward migration of salt water from brine-bearing aquifers and is likely to take place if the freshwater aquifers are overpumped and the hydrostatic pressure in them is significantly reduced (LeGrand, 1968) (Fig. 4-1). Wells drilled into or through deep salty aquifers will facilitate the upward migration of salt water and leakage into freshwater aquifers if well

casings are absent, corroded, or improperly installed (Deutsch, 1965) (Fig. 4-2).

Other major aspects of achieving and maintaining adequate water quality are intimately related to the proper disposal of waste materials, and are considered in the following sections of this chapter.

SOLID WASTES

The disposal of solid wastes has become a major urban crisis. By 1985, unless it develops acceptable alternatives, New York City will have no place to put the 30,000 tons of garbage that it generates each day. Since 1965, Philadelphia has been dumping its garbage in southern New Jersey. However, New Jersey has gone to court to have out-of-state garbage banned. Connecticut will run out of landfill space for half of its refuse production by 1980. Such examples may be repeated for cities across the country.

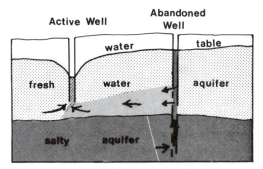

4.2 Cross section illustrating migration of salt water from a salty aquifer into a freshwater well via openings in an abandoned well.

Ordinary urban solid wastes include garbage (food wastes), rubbish (combustible paper, wood, and cloth wastes, non-combustible metal, dirt, glass, ceramic, and mineral wastes) ashes, street sweepings, dead animals, abandoned vehicles, and construction material wastes. In addition, there are solid wastes from industrial and processing plants, solids and sludge from sewage treatment plants, and pathological, or radioactive, or other hazardous wastes from institutions or industries. In the United States, the per capita production of solid waste is 6–8 pounds per day. For a city of a quarter of a million people, this means that about 900 tons of solid wastes must be dealt with every day. Costs of disposal ranged from $10 to $30 per ton in 1970. To suggest the magnitude of the problem, each year in the United States, solid wastes include 55 billion cans, 26 billion bottles and jars, and 65 billion metal and plastic bottle caps.

Ideally, the cost of solid-waste disposal could be partially offset by extraction of valuable substances such as metals, the production of gas for generating electric power, use of sewage sludge for improving soils, and the high-temperature, high-pressure conversion of other wastes to building materials. Such practices, however, for the most part still remain on a local, experimental basis.

Disposal methods of most solid wastes include incineration, open dumping, feeding garbage to swine, composting, creating sanitary landfill (Fig. 4.3), and ocean dumping.

Open Dumps and Sanitary Landfill

A recent survey of 1118 U.S. cities revealed that one-third of them piled up solid wastes in open dumps. In 1960, more than 1400 cities used solid wastes to create sanitary landfill (American Public Works Assc., 1966).

In sanitary landfill, layers of compacted wastes are alternated with and covered by layers of soil. This prevents exposure of the

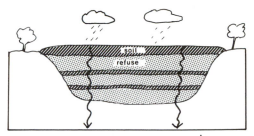

4.3 Cross section of a sanitary landfill showing alternate layers of soil and refuse. Arrows indicate downward migration of precipitation through the sanitary landfill. As the water percolates through the refuse, it may become contaminated (a leachate).

wastes to insects and wildlife, stops material from being blown and scattered, controls odors, and lessens fire hazard.

Sanitary landfill (Fig. 4.3) commonly takes place either in excavations on flat sites, or in ravines, canyons, quarries, or gravel pits. It may also take place in wet areas such as swamps, marshes, tidal areas, or ponds or quarries containing standing water. The depth of fill usually ranges from about 7 to 40 feet. Each time refuse is deposited, it is compacted and covered with a minimum of 6 in. of compacted soil. The thickness ratio of refuse to soil cover is from 4:1 to 8:1. The final layer of soil cover is at least two feet thick.

Suitable material for cover is clean sandy loam relatively free of organic matter, large stones, or excessive clay. Too high a clay content creates quagmires in wet weather, causing equipment to bog down, and in dry weather develops cracks through which odorous gases may escape and into which insects and rodents may enter. Large stones may impede equipment and vehicles. If the grain size of the cover is too uniform (examples are pure sand or silt or crushed rock), it will not compact well. Cover may be obtained from material excavated to form the disposal site or, if that material is unsuitable, may have to be imported from elsewhere. New York City found it could develop suitable cover by mixing dredged sand with digested sewage sludge.

In the construction of open dumps or sanitary landfill, surface drainage is essential to conduct water away from the sites to prevent erosion of the dump or fill and to avoid water pollution. Precipitation or surface runoff that does come in contact with the refuse will percolate downward, dissolving or *leaching* out organic and inorganic constituents. When such contaminated water (the *leachate*) reaches the water table, it will then become part of the groundwater system, polluting it. Eventually associated streams, lakes, or springs may also become polluted (Fig. 4.4).

The degree to which the groundwater system becomes polluted depends upon a number of factors. The faster that water passes through the refuse, the less chance it has to adsorb contaminants. If the water table is higher than the base of the dump and the water actually sits in the refuse for a considerable length of time, contamination will reach a maximum. The dumping of refuse into ponds or water-filled quarries may require that the water be heavily chlorinated.

In arid regions, the percolation of water downward through dumps is minimal. Instead, it is adsorbed by the refuse and eventually evaporated back into the atmosphere. Little or no contamination of the groundwater system takes place, but there is the danger, however, that a cloudburst will de-

stroy the fill cover and flush contaminants to the water table (Flawn *et al,* 1970).

If the leachate does percolate through refuse, the ease with which it passes through the zone of aeration before it reaches the zone of saturation will have an effect upon its quality. If the zone of aeration is sandy or silty, particulate contaminants can be filtered out, but chemical contaminants will pass through the material. If the zone of aeration is clayey, some purification of chemical contaminants may take place by ion exchange with the clays. Also, clays or shales may retard the movement of the leachate sufficiently so that it will be "perched" (restricted to local shallow zones of saturation; see Fig. 3.7A) and thus not able to enter deeper aquifers in significant quantities. The typical rates of groundwater flow through clayey sediments where the hydraulic gradient is low are on the order of one-tenth to one-half a foot per year. Thus, in fifty years the leachate will still be restricted to within 5–25 ft of the fill (Flawn *et al,* 1970). Thirty feet of impermeable material is considered an ideal minimum distance between the base of landfill and the shallowest aquifer.

To summarize, groundwater contamination will be minimal under one or more of the following conditions: (1) in dry climates, where little precipitation comes in contact with the refuse and evaporation rates are high, (2) if the refuse is so impermeable that little precipitation is able to penetrate it,

4.4 Schematic cross section showing leachate from sanitary landfills migrating underground to a stream channel. Note that a greater amount of leachate is produced by the landfill that is partially beneath the water table (right side of diagram).

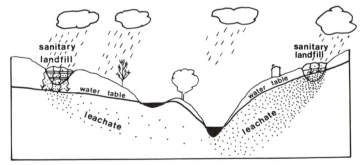

(3) if the base of the refuse sits well above the water table, and (4) if passage of the leachate to the general zone of saturation is hindered by a clayey zone of aeration. Conversely, groundwater pollution will be greater in wet climates, especially if the water table is high and the refuse actually sits in water, or if the zone of aeration is highly permeable.

It is clear that disposal sites must be placed with adequate knowledge of geologic materials and structures and the pattern of groundwater circulation. Local and state governments in many areas have developed codes or recommendations regulating solid-waste disposal. In Los Angeles, for instance, the types of solid wastes allowed at a particular disposal site depends upon the suitability of the site in terms of its geology, hydrology, and topography. In Ontario, under the Waste Management Act of 1970, open-pit dumps and open incinerators are illegal and are being phased out and replaced by sanitary landfill.

Subsequent use of completed sanitary landfill must be compatible with the likelihood of eventual settlement and the persistence of dangerous leachates. Within two years, settlement up to 25 percent of the thickness of the fill may take place. In New York, "it was found that about 90 percent of the total settlement occurs in the first 2 to 5 years. The remaining 10 percent may be over such a long period that it has little bearing on the grade planned for the site" (American Public Works Assc. 1970, p. 133). Fill placed on wet ground or in water will settle more and take a longer time to become stable. Until settlement has stopped, occasional regrading may be necessary, especially if there is a tendency for depressions to develop in which precipitation may accumulate and then percolate into the fill.

Since movement of groundwater may be quite slow, noxious leachates may not become obvious for a number of years, perhaps long after the fill site has been abandoned. Thus, periodic inspection and monitoring of fills and derived leachates is important even when the site is no longer used. Lining the fill pit before it is used and covering the completed fill with impermeable material, such as clay, provides additional safety. Also, subsurface barriers may be constructed to direct leachates to points where they may be collected and treated. In earthquake areas, the possibility of seismic disturbance of landfill must be considered as well.

Ocean Dumping

Due to increasing costs and the difficulties of disposing solid wastes on land, a small but growing number of communities are beginning to dump such wastes into the oceans (Council on Environmental Quality, 1973). For example, in 1968, about 48 million tons of waste were disposed of at 250 sites in the Atlantic and Pacific oceans and the Gulf of Mexico. In addition, one hundred artificial "dump" reefs composed of junked autos, cinder blocks, and other debris were created by private concerns. These figures do not include materials disposed of more than twelve miles offshore or along the coasts of Alaska or Hawaii.

The major type of waste dumped into the oceans is *dredge spoils,* material dredged from the floors of waterways to keep them clear for navigation. (Without dredging, many vital waterways would soon become impassable.) Unfortunately, many estuaries and coastal regions have become polluted by municipal and industrial wastes, and it is estimated that one-third of the dredge spoils are significantly contaminated. The second largest category of wastes dumped into the ocean are industrial wastes, which may be highly toxic. The problem is exacerbated by the location of and increase in industrial production in the United States. Forty percent of manufacturing is concentrated in estuarine regions. Industrial production is increasing at about 4.5 percent annually and the production of industrial wastes increases commensurately. Another source is sludge produced in the treatment of sewage. In 1968, 200,000 tons out of a total of 30 million tons of sludge—which may be both toxic and pathogenic—was disposed of in the sea. The rate of increase of such disposal is suggested by the amount carried out to sea from New York City in 1968 (99,000 tons) as compared to the estimated amount for the year 1980 (220,000 tons)—an increase of 120 percent in 20 years. Additional material being dumped into the oceans include municipal wastes, construction and demolition debris, and explosives.

The detrimental effects of ocean dumping are becoming increasingly evident. Most wastes sink to the bottom; others are dissolved, float, or remain suspended in the water for long periods of time. Poisonous materials enter marine flora and fauna, sickening or killing them. Economic losses from the pollution of shellfish or other edible marine creatures are mounting. When organic wastes are added to ocean water, the bacteria that decompose them use up DO; if the amounts of wastes are excessive, the DO will be depleted and decomposition by aerobic bacteria will stop. Nutrients released into the water, such as compounds of nitrogen, potassium, phosphorus, sulfur, and iron, encourage excessive growth of algae. When the algae die, their decomposition places great demands upon the DO content of the water, and the water's ability to "cleanse" itself is destroyed. As a result, dead and partially decomposed algae may wash up along the shores, reducing the aesthetic value of beaches. Pathogenic bacteria added to the water may make coastal regions unsuitable for swimming, and changes in the turbidity, temperature, and chemical characteristics of the water may destroy or shift marine habitats.

As yet, little is understood of the mechanisms of dispersal and concentration of solid wastes dumped into the ocean and of their effect on marine and estuarine ecosystems. W. S. Broecker, a noted geochemist

states that an unbalanced emphasis has been placed on the construction of facilities and the development of technological expertise to counter pollution without sufficient basic research on natural geochemical and biochemical processes. Engineering geologist S. J. Williams suggests that "before major and costly policy changes are initiated, exhaustive environmental monitoring must be conducted to determine present geologic, chemical, and biologic conditions at the disposal sites and environmental conditions prior to dumping activities." Until such understanding is arrived at and while evidence of the detrimental effect of indiscriminate ocean dumping accumulates, the procedure must be eliminated or else curtailed and strictly regulated. To this end, the 1972 Marine Protection, Research and Sanctuaries Act banned the ocean dumping of chemical and biological warfare agents and of radioactive materials, directing the Environmental Protection Agency and the U.S. Army Corps of Engineers to prohibit dumping of substances whose effects on marine ecosystems is not understood, of materials that float rather than sink, and of oily substances. Disposal of other wastes that are less dangerous but still harmful are regulated.

A number of alternatives to ocean dumping have been suggested. Incineration of solid wastes may reduce their volume up to 90 percent and thus reduce the land area required for sanitary landfill. The shortage of land for sanitary landfill near large coastal cities may make it economically feasible to transport solid wastes by rail to moderately distant areas that have been strip-mined. Sanitary landfill to restore such areas may perform an environmentally beneficial function. The Department of the Interior estimates that there are two million acres of abandoned, unreclaimed strip-mined areas available as potential solid-waste disposal sites.

Incineration of refuse may be able to produce gas for electric power generation. On October 5, 1975, the Empire State Electric

Energy Research Corporation, a non-profit organization comprised of New York State's eight major electric power suppliers, announced its intention to construct and operate a laboratory-scale model of equipment needed to convert solid wastes and sewage sludge into gas. The gas would be used for the generation of electric power. Fossil fuel resources would be conserved, and at the same time a partial solution would be found to the serious municipal waste-disposal problem.

The use of sewage sludge as a crop fertilizer has been undertaken in places such as Janesville and South Milwaukee, Wisconsin. Milwaukee itself has pioneered in selling dried sludge, under the trade name Milorganite, as a soil conditioner and fertilizer. The sludge is monitored continuously to guard against the possible buildup of toxic substances. To prevent possible contamination of surface water or groundwater, the sludge should not be applied to land that slopes steeply, has a high water table, is very sandy, or is less than two feet above bedrock.

Additional reduction of solid wastes may be accomplished through the separation and recycling of paper, glass, aluminum, and ferrous metals (see also Chapter 14). New York State plans to build 21 recycling plants by 1985 that could recycle almost half of the state's garbage (compared to the less than one percent recycled now). Six plants are under construction. New York City's Environmental Protection Agency task force hopes that such plants could produce steam to heat buildings and provide gas to supply energy needs for Kennedy Airport. In Brooklyn, New York, the Ashmont Metal Company plans to construct a plant that may be the world's first facility to produce high-quality commercial steel from metal scrap removed from incinerated municipal refuse. The plant will reduce the need for barge transport of ash by a third and landfill needs by 25,000 tons a year. However, community objections to the presence of the proposed heavy industry initially delayed the start of the project, and as of December 1978 it had not yet begun. The total value of recoverable materials in New York state's annual garbage is approximately $31 million worth of aluminum, $60 million of iron and steel, $13 million of paper, $32 million of glass, $19 million of non-ferrous metals, and $12 million of fuel production.

Dredge spoils could be reduced in amount by reducing the necessity for dredging. If inland coastal erosion is lessened, sediment accumulation that hinders navigation will become less of a problem. Also, as inland waters are cleaned up to obey more stringent federal and state standards, dredge spoils will be less polluted and environmentally damaging.

Last, regional rather than local attack on waste-disposal problems will permit less costly, more efficient solutions through elimination of competition between and duplication of facilities.

LIQUID WASTES

Polluted liquids added to groundwater and to surface waters range from dilute pollutants, such as water released from storm and sanitary sewers to concentrated industrial contaminants injected underground through disposal wells. Geographically *non-specific* (non-point) sources of contaminants (Fig. 4.5A), as opposed to *specific* (point) sources (Fig. 4.5B) are the major cause of water pollution, and include materials dissolved or picked up during water runoff, both in agricultural and urban areas. Major specific sources of pollution are sewage and industrial effluents.

The Federal Water Pollution Control Act Amendments, which became law on October 18, 1972, have as their aim the restoration and maintenance of the chemical, physical, and biological integrity of the nation's waters, so that by July 1983, wherever possible, water quality will be suitable for recreational contact and for protection and propagation of fish and wildlife. To achieve

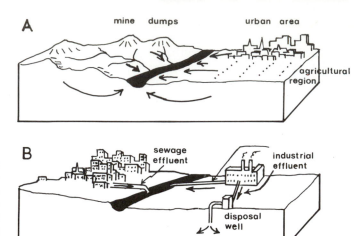

4.5 Block diagrams to illustrate (**A**) non-point sources of contaminants (runoff from mine dumps and urban and agricultural regions) and (**B**) point sources of contaminants (sewage and industrial effluent pipes).

these objectives, the Act establishes a national goal of eliminating discharges of pollutants by 1985. Implementation is to be effected by an expanded system of federal grants to plan and construct publicly owned waste-treatment plants, a permit program to restrict pollutant discharges from point sources, and major research and demonstration programs to work toward eliminating pollution from non-point sources.

To control pollution from industrial sources, a two-level program has been set up. First, by July 1, 1975, industrial effluents must be subjected to the "best practicable technology currently available." This may be defined as the average of the best existing performance by well-operated plants within each industrial category or subcategory. By July 1, 1983, achieving the average best technology will no longer suffice. Instead, industrial effluents must be subjected to "best available technology economically achieveable." In addition, new plants must be designed with the express purpose of bringing pollutant discharges to a minimum.

Industrial water pollution in terms of *suspended solids* is almost equal to that contributed by community sewage. The disposal of *oxygen-consuming wastes* by more than 300,000 water-using industrial plants is

three to four times that of non-industrial sources (Mackenthun, 1972). When "best available" technology is applied to industrial effluents, a fourteen- to thirty-fold reduction in discharge of oxygen absorbing wastes and suspended solids, compared to 1973, for example, will have to be achieved.

In 1973, municipal wastes accounted for more than 20 percent of the organic pollutant load in streams. The annual discharge of more than one trillion gallons of industrial wastes through publically owned facilities increased the municipal sewage problem even more. In order to cope with expected increases in the volume handled by publically owned facilities, the Federal Water Pollution Control Act Amendments set up a program to upgrade existing plants and construct new facilities: By July 1, 1977, all waste-treatment plants constructed before June 30, 1974 must provide at least secondary treatment (see section on sewage effluents), and by July 1, 1983, all publically owned plants must achieve "best practicable waste treatment technology." For new plants, the Act establishes a construction grant program to improve the planning, design, and operation of public facilities. Also, industry will be required to treat their wastes before sending them to public facilities so that they will not be incompatible with the treatment process.

The cost of these programs is on the order of $100 billion in capital expenditures by industry, and $60 billion by government for the improvement of public sewage facilities. As noted, however, water quality will be only moderately improved because there still will be pollution from urban and rural non-specific sources. For example, within urban areas, 40–80 percent of the annual biochemical and chemical oxygen demand is from non-specific sources.

Sewage Effluents

Two types of sewer systems are in common use: *sanitary sewers,* which dispose of household or domestic wastes, and *storm sewers,* which provide a system of runoff for excess rainwater, snowmelt, or for water used in street cleaning and firefighting. In many urban areas, sanitary sewers and storm sewers form a single system. An advantage of combining the two types, aside from savings in installation costs, is that the intermittent rush of water from storm sewers helps to carry sanitary wastes to and through the treatment plants (Thomas and Schneider, 1970). These plants are designed to process up to several times the normal dry-weather volume of sewage. During storms, however, the flow may increase as much as 50 or even 100 times, far exceeding the capacity of the plants. When this happens, a considerable fraction of the effluent must be allowed to bypass the plants, and significant quantities of sewage, together with storm waters that have become polluted from their contact with streets, pavements, and roofs, are discharged in a raw untreated state. This *combined sewer overflow* (CSO) is a common, serious contaminant of surface and underground water. Sewer systems installed in recent years provide separate sewers for sanitary and storm wastes. However, after a long dry spell, street wash-off can be just as polluted as sanitary sewage from oil, gaso-line, dog and bird droppings, and litter of all kinds. For example, the wash-off from a typical moderate-sized city contains 100,000 to 250,000 pounds of lead and 6000 to 30,000 pounds of mercury each year.

In many cities, even the dry-weather sewage volume cannot be handled by existing treatment plants. In some cities, treatment is primitive or non-existent. In the United States in 1970, one-tenth of all domestic sewage was discharged raw, and one-quarter received only primary treatment. Since 1956, in an attempt to remedy the situation, the federal government has participated in the financing and construction of municipal sewage plants. Section 208 of the Water Pollution Control Act of 1972 rejects the idea that industries, muncipalities, or individuals have an inherent right to dispose of wastes in the nation's waterways, and provides funds for the development of management plans so that pure water standards may be met.

Ordinarily, sewage treatment consists of two phases: *primary* and *secondary*. These are illustrated diagrammatically in Figure 4.6. Primary treatment is mechanical, designed to separate, treat, or remove solid objects from the raw sewage. The raw sewage, or *influent,* is passed through *bar screens,* a series of upright bars, spaced about one to three inches apart, which trap large objects, such as rags and sticks. These are removed by automatic raking devices, and either torn to pieces in *macerators* and remixed with the sewage, or taken elsewhere for destruction. Grit and sand—often present in sewage in large amounts, especially during and after rains—must be removed to protect pumps and other equipment from abrasion and to prevent a build-up of deposits in subsequent treatment tanks. Such removal is accomplished by reducing the velocity of the influent as it passes through a *grit chamber,* thus allowing the sediment to settle out and to be removed by a series of scrapers. The influent then passes into a *primary settling* tank, in

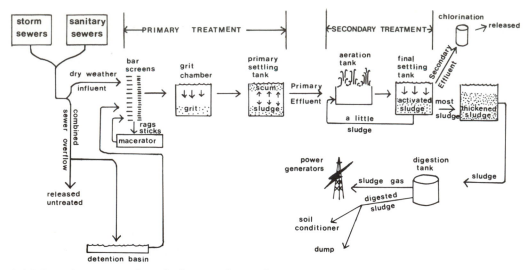

4.6 Schematic representation of primary and secondary sewage treatment.

which the lighter, organic impurities settle, forming a *sludge* which is then removed from the bottom of the tank by pumps. Skimming mechanisms remove scum and grease that float to the surface. The remaining liquid, called the *primary effluent,* has, at this point, been relieved of perhaps one-third of its gross pollutants. For roughly 30 percent of Americans served by sewers, the primary effluent is then chlorinated to kill disease-causing bacteria and to reduce odor, and then is released into the environment (Bylinsky, 1970).

Where secondary treatment is provided, the primary effluent is conveyed to *aeration tanks* or to *trickling filters.* In these tanks, the suspended and dissolved solids are acted on by aerobic bacteria, causing the pollutants to "clump" together, forming particles large enough to settle out within 3–6 hours. To ensure vigorous bacterial action, there must be an adequate supply of oxygen; this is accomplished by spraying the sewage onto gravel beds or by bubbling compressed air through it. If a trickling filter is used, the sewage seeps through a bed of stones or synthetic material where aerobic bacteria consume organic matter.

Next, the sewage is passed into a *final settling tank,* where it sits for 2–3 hours, allowing the suspended solids to settle to the bottom to form *activated sludge*—rich in aerobic bacteria. Some of the activated sludge is returned to the aeration tanks to ensure a continuing bacterial population. The clarified liquid or final effluent that issues from the settling tank may be released or chlorinated (to kill disease germs) and then released. The sludge may be disposed of or allowed to settle for 12–24 hours in a *thickener* tank, where water from within the sludge rises to the top and is removed. The volume of the sludge is reduced considerably, thus minimizing the cost for conveying it to solid-waste disposal sites. Water from the thickener is returned to the raw sewage flow as it enters the plant. Secondary treatment rids the sewage of up to 90 percent of the degradable organic waste.

In some plants, sludge is passed into closed *digestion tanks* where it is attacked by anaerobic bacteria to produce "sludge gas." This gas is rich in methane and may be burned to produce power, often sufficient to meet the power requirements of the entire treatment process. Digested sludge is relatively harmless, and with appropriate monitoring may be used as a soil conditioner. It may be feasible to disinfect the sludge by bombardment with electron beams. This treatment, which is an experimental phase, also inactivates some toxic chemicals.

One measure of the success of sewage treatment is the biochemical oxygen demand (BOD) of the final effluent. A BOD removal of 90 percent is sought so that the dissolved oxygen content of the receiving waters will not be excessively depleted.

At Bay Park on Long Island, New York, the final effluent from the sewage treatment plant is injected into a deep sand aquifer (the Magothy formation) through a recharge well. Injection of the treated water helps to maintain the volume of the fresh groundwater lens and to prevent salt groundwater intrusion. Experimental injection of unchlorinated effluent revealed that harmful coliform bacteria were effectively removed after only 20 feet of passage through the fine-to-medium sand of the aquifer. (Vecchioli *et al*, 1972).

Removal of disease-causing bacteria, either by chlorination or natural filtration is not enough to give final effluent a clean bill of health. Subtler, non-degradable contaminants such as salts, dyes, acids, pesticides, herbicides, and other pollutants remain in the water and may harmfully affect the quality of the surface water or groundwater bodies into which they are released. Realization that secondary treatment alone is not adequate to preserve environmental quality has been widespread for some time now in densely urbanized sections of Europe. Similar realization has been reached in several locations in the United States, and provision for *tertiary* or *advanced* treatment is now being implemented in some localities (Grava, 1969). Tertiary treatment, which aims at 98–99 BOD and suspended solid removal, employs special techniques to remove phosphates, ammonia, and organic industrial

chemicals resistant to bacterial action. One of the most extensive of such operations has been developed by the Metropolitan Sanitary District of Chicago.

Since removal of all contaminants from the final effluent is exceedingly rare, its injection into the groundwater system must be carefully monitored so that water sources are not ultimately polluted by its entry. To this end, reactions between the injected final effluent and the rocky substances with which it comes in contact must be understood.

In the Chicago area, proposals have been made for the disposal of combined sewer overflow produced during storms into a network of underground tunnels. Tunnels would be excavated in the Galena and Platteville formations, about 600 feet below the surface, and in the Niagara Dolomite, less than 300 feet below the surface. Water and wastes stored in the tunnels could later be pumped to the surface, treated, and discharged into streams. The tunnels would have to be adequately sealed to prevent contamination of groundwater reserves. In New York City, surface detention basins are planned to hold combined sewer overflow until it can be treated.

Pollution of surface streams by sewage effluents is most serious during dry periods, when stream volume is low. The Miami Conservancy District in Ohio, which includes the city of Dayton, plans to augment stream flow during dry periods by releasing water from surface reservoirs or by pumping groundwater. The possibility of artificially injecting air into the waters of the Great Miami River to help prevent dissolved oxygen deficiency is also being studied.

Reuse of treated waste water is especially important in areas where water shortages exist. At Pomona, California, a pilot plant reclaims about 8 million gallons per day. It is the first step in a $20 million program in the Los Angeles basin designed to reclaim 100 mgd. In Santee, California, treated effluent is conducted to and passes through a chain of five progressively cleaner lakes used for boating and fishing.

At East Lansing, Michigan, partly treated sewage effluent containing abundant nutrients passes through a series of aquatic farms where algae, water weeds, and planktonic crustaceans are grown for high-protein animal feed or fertilizers. In this way, 95 percent of the phosphates and 99 percent of the nitrates are removed. After the nutrients have been consumed, the water passes into and forms an artificial lake that has been stocked with fish and is clean enough for boating and swimming. The operation is being run as an experiment by Michigan State University's Water Quality Management Project. Some caution, however, is necessary in the use of sewage effluents. In Israel, partially treated effluents were used for spray irrigation in some agricultural settlements, resulting in 200–400 percent increases in certain human diseases (Katznelson et al, 1976). Clearly, waste water used for irrigation purposes near residential areas must be adequately disinfected.

Septic Tank Effluents

As urbanized areas expand through the construction of new subdivisions, installation of sanitary sewers frequently fails to keep pace. Individual houses are forced to dispose of domestic wastes through septic-tank systems. It has been estimated that about 50 million Americans rely upon septic tanks, and that many of these do not function properly because they are not large enough or were improperly installed and are poorly maintained, or were constructed in geologically unsuitable areas (Grava, 1969). Such failures lead to contamination of water supplies.

A septic tank is a rectangular or cylindrical watertight container (usually concrete) into which sewage is introduced and from which a liquid effluent is allowed to seep underground into the soil (Fig. 4.7). The sewage entering the tank consists of solids and liquids. Within the tank, the solids settle to the bottom and are partially converted, by anaerobic bacterial decomposition, into liquids and gases. The gases escape through a chimney or stack; the remaining solids form a sludge on the bottom of the tank or float to the top as a scum and must be periodically removed by pumping; the liquid passes through an outlet and seeps into the soil. This liquid effluent contains undesirable concentrations of organic matter, pathogenic bacteria, viruses, and phosphate and nitrate nutrients. Passage through soil or sediment (an *adsorption field*) may reduce concentrations of these substances to an acceptable level: Bacteria are trapped and die, organic material is broken down by microbial populations native to the soil, suspended solids are removed by natural filtration. Depending upon the type of soil, some nutrients may be bound and removed, but generally nutrient removal is not achieved to a satisfactory degree.

In order for a septic tank and adsorption field seepage system to work effectively, several criteria must be met. First, the tank must be large enough to retain sewage long enough to allow most of the solids either to sink or float and to undergo adequate anaerobic decomposition. In a well-designed septic tank, 60–70 percent of the suspended solid particles separate out, and the BOD of the organic matter is reduced by 30–40 percent. Second, the permeability of the adsorption field must allow for proper passage and cleansing of the effluent. Too slow a passage, through material such as clay, results in clogging and saturation of the soil and prevention of aerobic bacterial activity. Or the effluent may pond over the seepage area or back up into household drains. Clogging may be physical, caused by the entrapping of suspended solids in pore spaces; chemical, caused by reactions between the effluent and the soil that destroy the structure of the soil, or biological, caused by the deposition of products of microbial growth. If passage of the effluent is

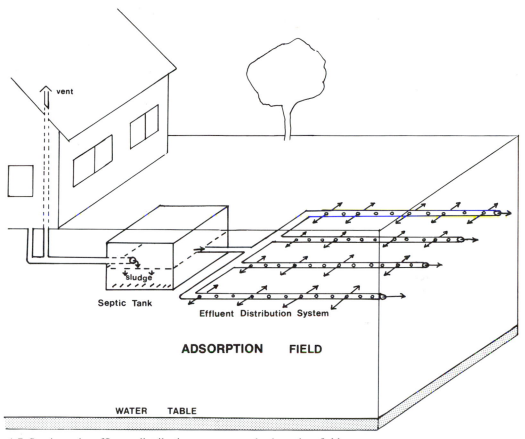

4.7 Septic tank, effluent distribution system, and adsorption field.
Note deep position of water table.

too rapid (through coarse gravel or fissured material) it may enter and contaminate streams, wells, or aquifers.

To ensure proper rate of introduction of effluent into the soil commensurate with the soil's ability to transmit it, special distribution systems are employed (Fig. 4.7). One common system is an assemblage of drainage pipes placed below ground level that conduct the effluent from the septic tank to the seepage area (*adsorption field*). The pipes are either perforated along their lengths or separated at their joints to allow the effluent to seep into the soil of the absorption field at numerous separated points

rather than at one single point. The drainage pipes are laid in excavated trenches that are then filled and packed with uniformly sized gravel or similar material. Passage of the effluent through the gravel will further aid in its distribution and gradual introduction into the adsorption field.

Other major factors in the successful operation of septic tanks and adsorption fields are the depth to and configuration of the water table and the spacing of the disposal systems and their placement relative to wells, streams, floodplains, and topography.

Septic systems are efficient only in areas

of relatively low population density. Lot size and the placement of the system within each lot must be such that the capacity of the soil to transmit and cleanse effluents is not exceeded. There should be at least 5 feet of permeable soil above (1) the maximum elevation of the water table. (2) bedrock, or (3) clay or any other impervious strata, to ensure that the effluent remains in the oxygen-rich environment of the zone of aeration. At least 12 feet of cover should overlie the gravel filled trenches, and at least 6 feet of undisturbed earth must be left between adjacent drainage pipes. The effluent distribution system should be at least 100 feet from any uncased well, 50 feet from a cased well, 50 feet from a lake or stream, 25 feet from any building, and 10 feet from property boundaries. These figures may be adjusted for different soil types.

It is important to note that the adsorption field should not consist of coarse sands or gravels free of organic substances, as they would be lacking in the aerobic bacteria necessary to decompose organic materials in the effluent.

Construction of effluent distribution systems in topographically steep regions may be difficult because the depth of the water table or of impervious strata may be highly variable. Septic-tank systems should not be used on floodplains because of the possibility of flooding or extreme fluctuation of the water table, and the ease with which contaminants may enter the stream.

Despite all of these precautions, overloading of septic tanks with dissolved inorganic materials may lead to their failure. On Long Island, effluents from more than half a million homes have contaminated much of the shallow, glaciofluviatile aquifer with unacceptably high concentrations of synthetic detergents, chlorides, nitrates, sulfates, and phosphates (Thomas and Schneider, 1970). Sigurd states that "septic tanks are to be regarded only as a second-best solution permissible under certain well-defined conditions: (a) no existing community (sewer) system within a reasonable distance and no prospects for one within the foreseeable future; or (b) the presence of unique land forms, such as extremely rough topography, which would make a collection (sewer) network prohibitively expensive . . . The owner of a house with a septic tank should be made aware that maintenance costs for such a system may be very high if something goes wrong . . . [and that] the resale value of this house is bound to be lower than that of a comparable property on a municipal line. . . ." (1969, p. 52) He also notes that "the cost of providing public sewers for each house may only be one half to one-quarter of the construction cost of bathrooms . . . ."

However, residents of the Southwest Sewer District in Suffolk County, Long Island, take a less benign view of the cost of public sewers. A proposal to install sewers for the 57-square-mile area was approved by the voters in 1969 after public officials warned of increasing pollution of groundwater and possible future water shortages. Cost estimates for the project were originally $291 million, but have now risen to $1.2 billion. Despite assurances to the people by John V. N. Klein, the Suffolk County Executive, that the cost over-run will be paid for by federal, state, and county governments, real estate values have plummeted as people have become fearful of major rises in property taxes (*The New York Times,* Feb. 26, 1978, p. R1). Furthermore, it is feared by some experts that the sewer system may prevent adequate groundwater recharge and that groundwater quality may continue to deteriorate due to non-point sources of pollution such as fertilizers and animal wastes. Lee Koppelman, executive director of the Nassau-Suffolk Regional Planning Board has stated that a lesson to be learned from the controversy is that before an area is allowed to become urbanized, there should be proper assessment of environmental impact to ensure that proposed land-use changes are environmentally sound.

Injection Wells

Under the Water Pollution Control Act of 1972, industry is being forced to meet quality standards for all waste water discharged into public waters. In the past, the most common way of disposing of liquid industrial wastes has been to store them in open pits in the vicinity of industrial centers. The materials in these ponds (carbonates, hydrates, silicates, sulfates, oils, tars, acids, and brines, all of which often contain toxic substances) are subject to leaching that transports them into underground and surface water systems. In an attempt to find an environmentally and legally acceptable method to dispose of these wastes, industry is becoming increasingly interested in the potential for injecting them deep underground (Federal pollution controls do not apply to underground water). Several hundred industrial waste-water injection wells have already been constructed in 28 states, and about 30 new waste wells are being added each year. The injection of radioactive wastes, wastes from saline-water conversion plants, and effluents from sewage treatment plants is also being considered.

Injection through deep wells is designed to emplace the wastes into natural pore spaces or fracture systems, or into artificially created fracture systems at depths of hundreds or thousands of feet. At such depths, it is hoped that the wastes will be isolated below zones of active groundwater circulation and will not be sources of contamination. However, lack of adequate knowledge about the circulation of deep groundwater, together with changes in rock permeability due to thermal, chemical, and mechanical alterations induced by the injection of the wastes, makes contamination a distinct hazard. Other hazards are possible contamination of mineral resources (including fossil fuels) and the triggering of earthquakes.

Of particular importance is knowledge of the way in which wastes may be altered with time, including changes in temperature (radioactive substances may produce heat at rates faster than it can be dissipated); chemical changes produced by reactions of the injected material with other injected wastes, with fluids native to the injection zone, and with mineral and organic constituents; mechanical changes, such as conversion of the liquid into a gel or a precipitate (Piper, 1969). These changes may increase or decrease the toxicity of the wastes and also affect the surrounding environment. Changes in the viscosity of the wastes and the enlarging or clogging of openings and passageways will also affect their mobility and the likelihood of contamination of water supplies.

Knowledge of the normal mode of circulation of groundwater before injection is essential. A useful concept is that of *residence time,* the length of time fluids take to migrate through a given volume of rock, soil, or sediment. The zone of aeration and the upper part of the zone of saturation are characterized by rapid circulation, with residence times of a few hours to a few years (Fig. 4.8). This zone is suitable only for the disposal of very dilute, relatively inoffensive wastes, such as septic tank effluents. Below it, at depths varying from hundreds to thousands of feet, is a zone of "delayed circulation" (Piper, 1969) in which the residence time is measured in decades or even centuries. Water from this zone constitutes the major underground supply, and injection of wastes is not advisable except when carefully controlled and monitored. In the zone of "lethargic flow," residence time ranges from hundreds to thousands of years; the groundwater in the zone is commonly saline. Depths at which such conditions exist are generally greater than 5000 feet. It is there that injection and storage of moderately concentrated and intractable wastes may best take place. Zones in which the groundwater is *stagnant* seem to be ideal for the disposal of the most noxious, permanently dangerous wastes. However, little is known about such zones. Furthermore, the

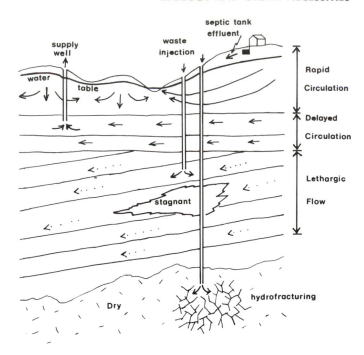

4.8 Cross section illustrating rates of circulation of groundwater and appropriate methods of disposal of wastes.

act of injection might induce circulation of fluids within formerly stagnant zones.

Another alternative is to inject wastes into dry impermeable zones, such as salt beds or salt domes. The material of such zones, which may exist close to the surface or at great depths, requires fracturing, solution, or excavation so that they will accept the fluids. One way of creating fractures is to inject fluids under sufficient pressure so that the rock "hydrofractures" (Fig. 4.8). The danger exists, however, that the fractures may extend to the boundary of the dry zone, connecting it hydraulically with zones in which fluids circulate. Such procedures, therefore, must be undertaken with caution.

Waste injection in earthquake areas may trigger seismic activity. A series of earthquakes near Denver, Colorado, were linked to the disposal of fluid wastes through a 12,000-foot-deep well at the Rocky Mountain Arsenal (See Chapter 7).

If wells are faultily designed or maintained, contaminants from a shallow aquifer may migrate through the wells into the deeper aquifers. In the Baltimore Harbor area in Maryland, for instance, water from a shallow aquifer contaminated by sulfuric acid and copper sulfate corroded the well casings and leaked into a deeper aquifer (Thomas and Schneider, 1970).

Monitoring Groundwater Pollution

In order to ensure continuing supplies of high quality groundwater, it is important to delineate within aquifers the interfaces between contaminated and pure groundwater, and to follow their movement through time. In this way, contamination of pure water may be avoided, and the best locations for new wells and waste-disposal sites may be planned. Contaminants may be natural, such as saline water adjacent to coasts or within saline aquifers, or artificial. It is also important to keep track of the extent to which contaminants may be altered or dispersed during their travels. In order to do

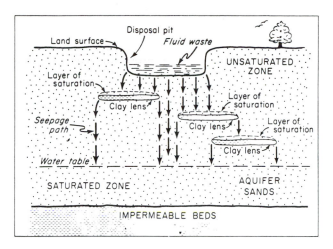

4.9 Cross section of disposal pit, showing seepage paths through an unsaturated zone containing lenses of clay.

so, general knowledge of groundwater movement in a given region is essential. *Monitoring wells* placed in strategic locations near potentially contaminated water are also useful (LeGrand, 1968).

Movement of liquids within the zone of aeration is downward toward the zone of saturation, except where deflected laterally by the presence of impermeable layers (Fig. 4.9). Within the zone of saturation, movement is more complex, as described in Chapter 3 on Water Supply. Stated simply, in well-watered regions, underground movement is generally toward lakes and streams or the ocean. In arid regions, movement is downward from surface bodies of water toward the water table. Within artesian aquifers, movement is generally downward, parallel to the slope of the aquifer.

Complications arise when water is withdrawn from or injected underground through wells. In the vicinity of withdrawal wells, the water table is drawn down into a *cone of depression* and groundwater is sucked toward the well. Where liquids are being pumped underground, a *mound* forms in the water table, and water flows away from the well (Fig. 4.10). Leachates from solid-waste disposal sites or from contaminated surface water may enter water-supply wells (Fig. 4.11), and overpumping may induce upward migration of water from a contaminated aquifer (Fig. 4.10).

The strategic placement of monitoring wells involves locating *pollution plumes*—the paths of travel of polluted water plotted on a map (Fig. 4.12). The edge or front of

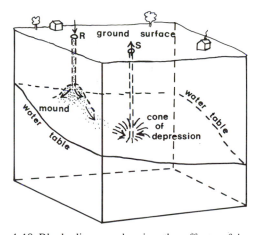

4.10 Block diagram showing the effects of injection and withdrawal of fluids upon the configuration of the water table. Injection of fluid produces a mound; withdrawal of fluid produces a cone of depression. Note the migration of injected fluids from the bottom of the injection well (R) toward the intake end of the water-supply well (S).

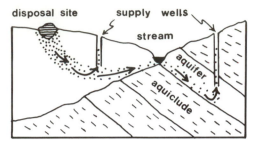

4.11 Leachate from a disposal site migrates underground toward a water-supply well and a stream. Note that contaminated water from the stream may migrate down an aquifer, polluting another well.

the plume is not a sharp line, but rather a zone across which contamination increases—from undetectable to concentrated and highly objectionable. Monitoring wells should be placed to intercept the plume before it reaches the water supply. The progress of contamination can thus be checked, and, if remedial measures are taken, its diminution can be monitored. Where vertical movement of contaminants is likely, as in saltwater intrusion, the wells must be placed

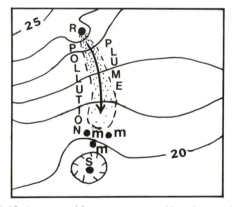

4.12 A water-table contour map. Note how polluted water from an injection well (R) migrates down the slope of the water table toward a water-supply well (S), forming a "pollution plume." Monitor wells (m) are placed between the injection well and the supply well to check the progress of the plume and to provide warning of possible contamination of the supply well.

at appropriate depths. Usually, more than one well must be emplaced to determine adequately the location and advance of contaminants.

Radioactive Wastes

Disposal of radioactive wastes becomes increasingly important as the trend continues toward nuclear power and as the volume of radioactive wastes rapidly mounts. Currently (1978) in the United States, about 3500 metric tons of radioactive wastes from commercial nuclear operations sit in temporary storage awaiting permanent disposition. By 1985, the figure would rise to 25,000 tons, and by the year 2000, to more than 125,000 tons. To these figures must be added the accumulations of military wastes. Unless the problems of safe disposal of such wastes are solved, the whole future of nuclear power may be in serious jeopardy.

Radioactive wastes demand special attention because they emit heat and give off dangerous radiation for long periods of time. For high-level (most concentrated long-lived) wastes, temperatures of 600°–900° F may be achieved. Deadly radiation may persist from 500 to 500,000 years. Clearly, radioactive wastes must be disposed of carefully so that they do not come in contact with living organisms, water supplies or economically valuable minerals.

Disposal of low-level radioactive wastes (those that are dilute and present only short-term hazards) has been commonly achieved by first removing the most dangerous constituents and then releasing the treated effluent into large bodies of surface water or into the groundwater system (de Laguna, 1968). Such effluents, however, are increasing in quantity and are being concentrated in estuaries (Cronin, 1967). Fine-grained sediments in the Hudson River estuary near New York Harbor contain radioactive materials whose source, in part, is a nuclear reactor located more than 35 miles upstream (Simpson *et al*, 1976). The concentration of such wastes in the Lower Hudson, while not immediately hazardous, is as much as a hundred times that in most parts of the river. This is of concern because estuaries are rich in aquatic organisms which may ingest and further concentrate the radioactive substances. Such organisms may belong to food chains which include humans. W. S. Broecker, a well-known geochemist, notes that in general the fate of radioactive substances in groundwater and surface-water circulation is not well understood. Moreover, what constitutes an acceptable level of radioactive contamination of water in terms of human health is in itself a controversial issue (Feth, 1973).

A workable alternative to disposal of low-level radioactive wastes into surface water or shallow groundwater may be to inject into deep-lying, permeable formations (de Laguna, 1968).

Wastes of intermediate hazard have in the past been released into the ground at shallow levels. Due to fears that eventual contamination of groundwater might take place, this practice was discontinued, and the wastes are now being injected through deep wells into shale. Geologic requirements are a layer of shale at least 300 feet thick, lying less than 3000 feet underground and overlain by a rock cover sufficiently impermeable so that the shale is isolated from the earth's suface. Liquid wastes are injected forcefully into the shale, fracturing it and providing avenues of entry.

A variety of proposals have been made for the disposal of high-level radioactive wastes. These proposals include rocketing the wastes into space; storing them on the earth's surface in massive mausoleums; dumping them into the oceans; embedding them in glacial ice in the polar regions; placing them deep underground in stable geologic environments. Each has advantages and disadvantages in terms of safety, cost, and technical feasibility. Sending radioactive wastes into outer space would remove them forever from the human environment. The procedure is costly, however,

and the danger exists of rocket failure and the consequent return to earth in an unpredictable and uncontrollable fashion of the radioactive substances. Building massive containment structures, perhaps similar to Egyptian pyramids, is being actively considered. Material stored in this way would be retrievable at some future date for use or for re-disposal. In the event of social upheaval or war, however, there is the possibility that the structures might be damaged or breached and the radioactive substances released. From 1946 to 1970, the U.S. Atomic Energy Commission disposed of low-level nuclear wastes by dumping them into the ocean in containers. An examination of two dumping sites by the Environmental Protection Agency revealed that at both locations oceanic sediments had been contaminated by leakage. Ocean dumping of high-level wastes is considered unacceptable because leakage of such substances might wreak havoc upon aquatic organisms. The risk involved in burying containers of high-level radioactive waste in glacial ice is that the heat from the containers might trigger ice movement. Also, there is no guarantee that climatic changes might not cause the glacial ice to recede beyond the point of safety with respect to isolation of the wastes.

Underground storage of high-level radioactive wastes has received the most active consideration. Impermeable rock formations in geologically stable environments and completely isolated from groundwater circulation, are required. The formations must be large and geographically widespread, so that transporting wastes over long distances can be avoided. An extensive study was made of the possibility of storing high-level wastes in 300-foot-thick salt formations that lie 1000 feet beneath Lyons, Kansas. Storage in salt has several advantages: its melting point is high enough (1400° F) to withstand heat and radioactive wastes, and it is impermeable to groundwater and flows plastically (especially at elevated temperatures) so that any fractures that develop are self-sealing. It also provides a good shield against radiation. The site at Lyons, however, suffers from two disadvantages: the area is not as geologically stable as first thought, and the presence of several thousand abandoned well and mine shafts in the vicinity raises the possibility that water might make its way eventually into the salt formations. The salt and potash formations in southern New Mexico are now being considered. Also, the possibility of emplacing wastes into hard impermeable rock such as granite or basalt is being investigated. Such rocks have the advantage of being insoluble, but are brittle and fractures that develop are not self-healing.

Recently five U.S. Geological Survey scientists stated that in general interactions between host rocks, heat-generating wastes emplaced in them, and any water that the host rocks may contain are not well understood, which contributes considerable uncertainty to evaluating the risk of geologic disposal of high-level wastes (Bredehoeft *et al*, 1978). Furthermore, with respect to disposal in salt, a panel of eminent earth scientists has noted that salt beds probably contain significant amounts of water in inclusions and between grain boundaries. Upon being heated to comparatively low temperatures (150° C), the fluid inclusions are likely to burst and release the water, perhaps allowing it to enter groundwater circulation (Carter, 1978).

Other methods of disposal that may be successful include (1) pumping the wastes into deep cavities where they gradually heat up and convert themselves and some of the surrounding rock into a glassy ball, and (2) the conversion of high-level liquid wastes into glass (*vitrification*) before burial (Kubo and Rose, 1973; de Marsily *et al* 1977; Holden, 1978). The French have already started a plant to vitrify liquid wastes.

Whatever methods of disposal are ultimately taken, they are not likely to be inexpensive. The cost of disposing of U.S. civilian and military wastes until the year 2000 is estimated at $23 billion.

Thermal Pollution

A subtle but significant type of "waste" is heat emitted during the thermal generation of electricity and as a by-product of other industrial processes. The release of such heat into the atmosphere or into bodies of water results in local rises in temperature that are called *thermal pollution*.

The magnitude of the problem is suggested by the amount and rate of increase of water needed for cooling in generating electricity. Typically, water taken from a lake or stream or the groundwater reservoir is passed through the cooling system and then returned at elevated temperatures to its source. In 1970, the average withdrawal of water in the United States for all purposes was 370 billion gallons per day (bgd). Of this amount, 167 bgd was used by thermo-electric plants to condense spent steam from generators. By 1980, it is estimated that 200 bgd of fresh water and 50 bgd of saline water will be used for this purpose. Electrical generating capacity in industrialized countries increases at about 7 percent a year (a doubling time of ten years), and the amount of water required increases commensurately. Furthermore, the amount of heat generated by nuclear plants is greater than that generated by coal- or oil-burning facilities of similar capacity, and the likelihood is that the proportion of nuclear-powered plants will increase in the near future. The Hudson and Connecticut rivers, Lake Michigan, and the Columbia River Basin are places that have already faced problems of thermal pollution from nuclear power plants. Consolidated Edison of New York abandoned plans for a nuclear plant on the Hudson River at Verplanck some 20 miles north of New York City when public concern became focused on the possibility that the plant would harm the Hudson River fishery (Carter, 1974).

The temperature of water used for cooling purposes in the generation of electricity is commonly raised by 6–9.4° C. The production of electricity by geothermal plants, which are powered by natural hot water and steam resources, results in very high heat discharges; for example, the Wairakei plant in New Zealand discharges approximately 6.5 times as much heat per unit of power produced as would a modern coal plant (Axtmann, 1975).

The industrial use of water for cooling is quantitatively far less than that used in the generation of electricity. However, temperature changes produced by water released by factories may be extreme. In the vicinity of steel mills in Ohio, stream temperatures of 47° C in the summer and 29° C in the winter have been recorded (Feth, 1973).

Thermal pollution of surface water or underground water has a number of serious consequences. A few bacteria and algae can survive in water above 60° C; in general, more complex, higher organisms do not thrive in water above 35° C. Fish are rare above 30° C, and diatoms, an important link in aquatic food chains, decrease in numbers as the water temperature rises above 20° C. Many desirable fish, such as Atlantic salmon, lake trout, northern pike, and wall-eyes require water below 10° C for reproduction (Cole, 1969). Thus, small changes in water temperature may radically affect aquatic organisms. As water temperatures increase, the amount of dissolved oxygen, which is vital to many aquatic life forms, decreases. Indeed, as water temperatures rise, the oxygen requirements of most life forms increases. Further, the ability of water to rid itself of organic pollutants through the action of aerobic bacteria depends upon sufficient dissolved oxygen. Increases in water temperature also foster the growth of blue-green algae. These algae are not important as a source of food for aquatic organisms and may impede the growth of other, more desirable types of aquatic life. The salinity of water may be altered by temperature changes: the solubility of many salts increases; moreover, water evaporates at a greater rate at higher temperatures, thus increasing the concentration of salts in the remaining liquid. Changes in salinity affect aquatic life and also the usefulness of the water to humans.

Ways of lessening or preventing local thermal pollution are being investigated. Passing heated water through air-cooling towers or letting it stand in ponds can reduce its temperature before it is returned to its source. Other possibilities include using the hot water to heat houses and swimming pools (see Chapter 14), or to create warm lakes for algae or fish farming. Where feasible, surface and underground water sources might be drawn upon alternately during different seasons. In winter, cold surface waters might be used for cooling and then injected underground. During the warm months, the "used water" that was stored underground during the winter might be cooler than surface waters heated by the summer sun, and could be withdrawn for use.

Chicago—Waste Disposal and Water Supply

Because water supply within the Greater Chicago area is drawn from local sources, adequate waste-disposal methods and treatment facilities are vital. To accomplish these aims, a series of major engineering projects have been undertaken over the last century, with ultimate success.

Chicago was incorporated in 1837. It could claim 4100 residents and covered an area of about 100 square miles. Water was drawn from wells and from adjacent Lake Michigan. In the first decades of its history, Chicago suffered from frequent epidemics that took a high toll of life. In the 1830s disease was considered by most to be divine punishment; by the 1850s, it was felt that disease stemmed from noxious vapors given off by filth, such as excrement, dead animals, and garbage, and that it was essential to draw upon water sources that were uncontaminated by such materials. The existence of disease-causing bacteria was not yet recognized, and water that was visually acceptable and without odor was considered safe. After a severe cholera epidemic in 1852, which was attributed to wells contaminated by sewage seeping from outhouses, muncipal leaders sought to terminate the use of well water and to make Lake Michigan the city's sole source of water. To this end, in 1854, an expanded water works was constructed whose intake from the lake was situated 600 feet from the shoreline so as to avoid obviously polluted water along the shore (O'Connell, 1976). To reduce the health hazard from sewage that was accumulating in outhouses close to private dwellings, a board of sewerage was authorized to construct a sewer system that would dispose of not only domestic wastes, but also industrial wastes and surface drainage. Prior to this, much of the sewage was dumped into the Chicago River, which then carried it to Lake Michigan (Fig. 4.13A).

The chief engineer, Ellis S. Chesbrough, believed that the best method of disposing of the sewage would be a canal to transport it from the Chicago River southwest to the Des Plaines River, which would then carry it to the Illinois River, a tributary of the Mississippi. To construct such a canal would have meant cutting through the divide that separates the Chicago River from the Des Plaines and Illinois rivers (at the town of Summit, west of Chicago), thereby reversing the flow of the Chicago River (Fig. 4.13B). Chesbrough believed that such a canal would be prohibitively expensive, and he decided that the best alternative was simply to drain wastes into the Chicago River. By the time they reached Lake Michigan, it was hoped, they would be diluted and would not unduly contaminate the water supply. Adequate dilution, however, did not take place, and water in the vicinity of supply intakes in the lake was smelly and distasteful. To improve the water quality, construction of an intake tunnel that was to extend two miles from shore was begun in 1864. The water obtained through this tunnel was indeed of better taste and appearance, and a second tunnel was completed in 1874. During the same period, in an effort to re-duce the amount of sewage entering Lake Michigan from the Chicago River, pumps were installed in the South Branch of the river to reverse its flow and to conduct the sewage to the Illinois and Michigan Canal and thence to the Des Plaines River. That canal, however, which was constructed in 1848 as a shallow waterway for barge traffic, was ineffective in removing the wastes. Deepening of the canal was undertaken, but still it remained an inadequate conduit. Engineering projects to divert pollutants from the North Branch of the Chicago River were also ineffective. During the summer of 1879, such quantities of sewage flowed into Lake Michigan from the Chicago River that the city's water-supply system was contaminated for thirty consecutive days. In 1885, a huge storm dumped six inches of rain onto the city within two days, flushing sewage into the lake far beyond the intake pipes. As a result of this pollution, approximately 12 percent of Chicago's three-quarters of a million people died from water-borne diseases such as cholera, typhoid, and dysentery.

After these catastrophes, Chicago's water supply was examined in the light of the discovery of the bacterial origin of many diseases. It was revealed that the water was impure and a menace to public health, and support grew for a canal along the lines originally envisioned by Chesbrough, to reverse the flow of the Chicago River and convey the sewage to the Des Plaines and Illinois rivers. In 1887, the Drainage and Water Supply Commission submitted to the city council plans for a canal, and recommended the establishment of an autonomous Sanitary District (ultimately the Metropolitan Sanitary District of Greater Chicago) to finance, construct, and maintain the canal (O'Connell, 1976). The Sanitary District would encompass not only Chicago, but also neighboring communities, and required state approval. Downstate lawmakers, however, were afraid that great quantities of sewage from the Chicago area would pollute the Des Plaines and Illinois rivers and contaminate downstate water supplies. To

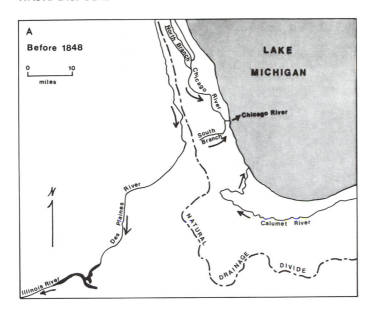

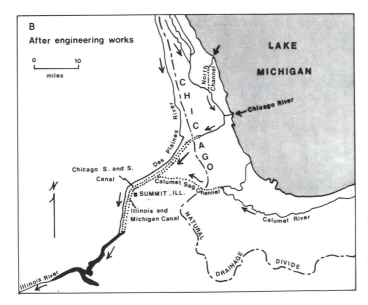

4.13 (**A**) Drainage directions in the Chicago region before 1848, before canal construction. Arrows denote direction of flow. (**B**) Drainage directions after major engineering works.

overcome these objections it was decided to make the project more attractive by designing the canal to carry large ships, thus forming an effective link between the Great Lakes and the Mississippi River and bringing enormous projected economic benefits

to downstate Illinois, Iowa, and Missouri. In 1889, the State of Illinois passed a bill giving the Sanitary District the power to construct the Sanitary and Ship Canal. To ensure adequate dilution of sewage, the canal was required to have a minimum flow of 300,000 cubic ft per minute and a potential capacity of 600,000 cubic ft per minute (compared to the 60,000 cubic ft per minute capacity of the old Illinois and Michigan Canal). Due to administrative and political difficulties, construction was delayed until 1892, and in 1900, Missouri sued to prevent the canal from opening because it was felt that the sewage would pollute Saint Louis's water-supply intakes (about 300 miles downstream of Chicago). Nevertheless, work was completed in 1900 (Fig. 4.13B), and the Supreme Court ruled in 1906 that Missouri had failed to prove that Chicago's sewage was adversely affecting the quality of drinking water in Saint Louis. In 1907, a second Canal, the North Shore Canal, was connected to the North Branch of the Chicago River to carry wastes from northern suburban communities away from Lake Michigan. In 1911, construction of the Calumet Sag Channel was begun. It extended from the Calumet River westward to a juncture on the Sanitary and Ship Canal, diverting additional polluted waters away from Lake Michigan.

To improve the quality of water supply before the completion of the canals, a new water intake located four miles from the shoreline of Lake Michigan was opened in 1894. However, a bacterial analysis revealed that the lake water was of uncertain quality, and it was concluded that even after sewage was diverted from the lake, bacterial counts would remain unacceptably high. Thus, in 1916, chlorination of the city's entire water supply was started. The typhoid death-rate, which was 67 per 100,000 before the completion of the Sanitary and Ship Canal, and 14 per 100,000 after the cessation of sewage disposal into Lake Michigan, dropped to 1 per 100,000 after chlorination (the lowest typhoid death-rate in the nation). Further purification through filtration was achieved in 1947, when the South District Filter Plant opened. In 1964, the Central Water Filtration Plant, the largest plant of its type in the world, began to provide filtered water for the rest of Chicago and for many northern and western suburbs.

The reversal of flow of the Chicago River and the diminution of flow from the Calumet River into Lake Michigan prompted a suit by neighboring states on the Great Lakes to prevent Chicago from draining Lake Michigan. As a result, diversion had to be reduced from 10,000 to 3000 cubic ft per second, and dilution of sewage in the canals and downstream rivers became inadequate. This problem was aggravated as population in the area continued to grow and the amounts of sewage increased. In the 1920s and 1930s, treatment plants were constructed to provide primary and secondary treatment before the effluent was released. In recent years, in an attempt to meet more stringent standards applied to surface water bodies, the Sanitary District built an experimental plant at Hanover Park, Illinois, that utilizes tertiary treatment. This pilot operation provided information now being utilized in the upgrading of older plants and in the construction of new plants. By 1977, all sewage will receive tertiary treatment.

In order to cope with *combined sewer overflow* after heavy storms and to help alleviate problems of flooding, a construction program of subterranean tunnels has begun. Excess storm waters will be diverted to these tunnels and stored until they can be released in controlled amounts to sewage treatment plants. The importance of avoiding CSO is suggested by an estimate that 45 percent of all annual waterway pollution in the Chicago area comes from overflows of combined sanitary and storm sewers. Aside from pollution, these overflows caused $30 million damage to land and structures during August and September 1972. The Metropolitan Sanitary District proposes a system of 125 miles of deep rock-tunnels together with two underground and one surface reservoirs at a cost of $1.3 billion (Fig. 4.14). Pumping stations will transfer the stored waste water to treatment plants during off-peak hours. Three pilot tunnels, totaling 43 miles in length, were mined by machine at depths of 223–245 feet below grade in dolomite (a tough magnesian lime-

4.14 The Chicago Deep Tunnel Plan for waste-water disposal. Black circles are storage reservoirs; open squares are treatment works; heavy solid lines are completed tunnels; dashed lines are proposed tunnels.

stone) and shale. The tunnels are about 16–18 feet in diameter. Grouting (injecting liquid cement into openings in the surrounding rock) reduced groundwater infiltration from a maximum of 2000 gallons per minute to 100 gallons per minute. The underground reservoirs will be excavated at a depth of 330 feet, measure 500–1200 feet wide and 2.5 miles long, and have a capacity of about 83,000 acre-feet.

To deal with the disposal of solid materials that remain after sewage treatment, the Sanitary District has adopted several solutions. A program has begun to utilize the solids as fertilizer while they are still suspended in water—thus eliminating the problems of separating and drying the solids. Solids that are separated and air-dried are sold as a soil builder-fertilizer called "Nu-Earth." The product is high in organic matter and humus. Bacterial tests indicate that "Nu-Earth" contains lower fecal coliform concentrations than are present in most soils. In another program, the municipal sewage sludge is being used to reclaim strip mined land for normal agricultural purposes (Halderson *et al*, 1975).

5. Building Materials

Just as people themselves are ultimately wrought from soil, water and air, so the cities they inhabit are fashioned from the materials of the earth. Metals, the nerves and bones of modern urban structure, are usually won from the earth in an impure, chemically complex form. To separate the metals from unwanted elements then requires the application of considerable technical genius. In the case of wood, life itself—manifest in the growth of forests—is the agent that gathers together raw materials and molds them into a useful substance. Stone, gravel, sand, clay, on the other hand, require fewer and simpler transformations to assume properties and forms useful in constructing the interiors and exteriors of cityscape. It is to these rocky, earthy materials that our attention shall be turned. Conventional "earth" building materials include building stone, crushed stone, sand, gravel, aggregates for concrete and mortar, clays for brick and tile, and lime and plaster.

Building materials contribute not only the sinew and flesh of cities, but are also a significant element in whatever the physical world donates to the character or "soul" of a city. The aesthetic role will be explored in Chapter 15. Building materials typically are required in great quantity or bulk and must be obtained at low unit cost. A major element of cost is transportation from quarry or pit to construction site. Thus, a city is favorably blessed if building materials may be obtained close to or within city limits. However, the possibility of extraction of these materials within urban areas requires a knowledge of their presence, both physical and legal access to them, and suitable plans for the use of excavation sites after they are exploited.

Building Stone

Building stone may be obtained from rock found lying loose at the earth's surface or, more commonly, it may be extracted from quarries. If sufficiently large and unweathered loose stones can be found, the cost and technical difficulties of quarrying can be avoided. The builders of the prehistoric stone circles at Avebury and Stonehenge in England made use of huge sandstone boulders (Fig. 5.1). A number of major buildings erected in Boston during the eighteenth century were constructed out of scattered pieces of Quincy Granite. Glacially deposited limestone blocks were used to build the campus of the University of Saskatchewan in Saskatoon (Legget, 1973). Smaller loose stones, such as flint nodules weathered out of chalk and found in fields or along the coast, have been widely used

A

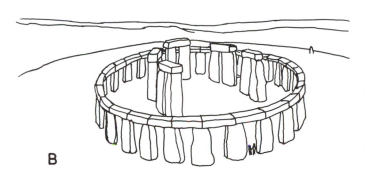

B

5.1 (**A**) Sandstone boulders, Fyfield Down, England. Boulders from this locality were transported to Stonehenge and Avebury to construct stone circles. (**B**) The prehistoric stone circle at Stonehenge, England.

as building stone in southern England (Fig. 5.2A). Another traditional source has been the dismantling of abandoned buildings.

Successful stone quarrying depends upon the availability of suitable stone, its ease of extraction, and the distance the stone has to be transported. Quarries may be dug into the side of a hill, or a pit may have to be excavated into the ground. Weaknesses in rock, such as joints and bedding planes, may facilitate removal, but if they are too closely spaced may undesirably restrict the size of the blocks. Once obtained, each piece of stone is cut or shaped to the correct dimension and form for its intended use. Such shaped, or *dressed,* stones are known as *dimension stones* (Fig. 5.2B). The use of dimension stones has diminished in recent years as new building materials have been developed and architectural techniques have changed. In older buildings, *walls* were the structural elements that bore the brunt of the weight. If they were inexpensively available, dimension stones, because of their strength, durability, fire resistance, and attractive appearance were used in considerable quantities to construct walls, especially for large or high buildings. Otherwise, walls were made of wood, adobe, bricks, and in Roman and modern times, concrete. Today the major weight-bearing element of large structures is a skeleton of steel or concrete, on which walls are "hung" to provide the protective shell of the building. In such "curtainwall" construction, dimension stone, because of its weight and cost, is rarely used other than as a relatively thin outer layer or decorative *facing* (Fig. 5.2C).

A wide variety of igneous, metamorphic, and sedimentary rocks are used as building stone. Important factors in determining usefulness include strength, resistance to weathering, appearance, and ease of dressing, or shaping.

In general, fine-grained rocks are stronger than those of coarse grain. Porous rocks,

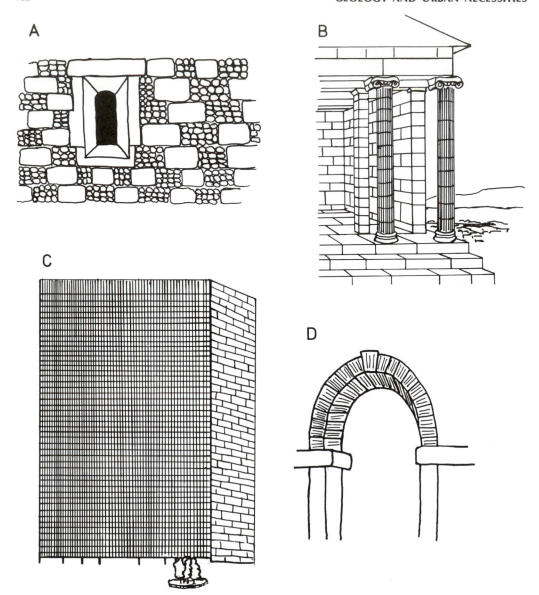

5.2 (**A**) Flint nodules (small ovoids) used in the construction of a church wall in southern England. (**B**) The use of dimension stone. (**C**) Stone facing on a modern skyscraper. (**D**) The use of layered stones in an arch. Note radial orientation of layering.

especially sandstones, are stronger dry than when wet (by a factor as high as two); provision should be made, therefore, that such rocks have good drainage. The strength of layered rocks varies considerably depending upon the way they are set relative to the maximum stress applied to them. For greatest strength, the layering should always be perpendicular to the maximum stress direction. In walls, layered stones should be set with their layering horizontal. In an arch, they should be set so that the layering is oriented radially (Fig. 5.2D).

The weathering of building stones may alter their appearance, remove their substance, and diminish their strength. However, some rocks have the ability to develop a protective skin resistant to atmospheric attack. As wet quarried rocks dry out, water carrying dissolved salts moves toward the surface, where it evaporates. The salts, which are left behind, fill and seal the pores of the rock. If such a rock is cleaned, this protective skin may be destroyed and the rock left vulnerable to weathering. Thus, building stone should be cleaned only after careful examination of the particular stone (Legget, 1973).

The durability of stone may be judged conveniently by visiting the quarry site and examining samples of fresh and weathered rock. Better yet, since conditions under which the rock is to be used may differ considerably from those at the quarry site, it is helpful to examine old buildings made of the same rock and located in areas similar to those in which the new buildings will be placed.

Crushed Stone

As the use of dimension stone has decreased, a corresponding increase in the demand for crushed stone has taken place. Annual production in the United States amounts to hundreds of millions of tons, of which about two-thirds is used in construction and the remainder in the cement and lime industries. The most common source is limestone; small amounts are produced from basalt (trap-rock), granite, quartzite, and sandstone. Compared to dimension stone, the cost of crushed stone is low, and is determined largely by how far it must be transported. General characteristics sought for in crushed stone are strength (resistance to impact or failure by compression),

hardness (resistance to abrasion), correct proportions of different fragment sizes, and absence of a tendency to absorb water. It may be obtained by crushing quarried bedrock, or by crushing boulders, cobbles (rounded rocks 2.5–10 inches in diameter), or large-size gravel.

Pieces of crushed stone have an advantage over natural gravel in that they are angular rather than rounded, allowing individual fragments to interlock and hold together. Size and sorting also may be easily controlled. An absence of fine materials is important where good drainage is required.

Crushed stone is commonly used in railroads and road beds (*ballast*), as fill where good drainage is required, and as a coarse aggregate for the making of concrete. Broken stone placed on a slope to protect it from water erosion is known as *riprap* (natural boulders may also be used). Railroad ballast, the material that supports the railroad ties and transfers the train loads to the subgrade, must be elastic, so that it will return to its original position after the train passes, and resistant to wear. Crushed quartzite, silica-cemented quartz sandstone, and cinders are excellent ballast.

The excavation and crushing of stone may on occasion produce a significant health hazard. Residents of prosperous suburban Montgomery County, Maryland, near Washington, D.C., have recently become alarmed by reports of air contaminated with cancer-causing asbestos fibers expelled during the operation of a local quarry. The stone, serpentine, is used as pavement for roads, parking lots, and driveways (Rohl *et al*, 1977).

Sand and Gravel

Sand and gravel are naturally occurring loose sediment whose particle diameters range in size from about one-twentieth of a millimeter to two millimeters in sand and from about 2 to 64 millimeters in gravel. Sand and gravel accumulate under a variety

Table 5.1. Location and characteristics of major sand and gravel deposits.

Geological Environment	Location	Particle Characteristics	Miscellaneous
Stream terraces	Sides of streams; floodplains	Sand, gravel; well-graded; well-rounded	If ancient, may be weathered and contain impurities
Channels of intermittent streams	Semiarid regions	Sand, gravel; often well-sorted; sub- to well-rounded	Abrasion in transport eliminates weak materials; renewal of supply after each flood
Permanent streams	Stream channels	As above	Dredging required
Floodplains	Within a stream valley	Generally fine-grained; locally coarse	Washing out of fines may be required
Alluvial fans	Valleys at the base of mountains	Boulders to sand; coarse at head of fan; fine at edges; angular to sub-rounded	Suitable if excessive clay absent
Marine	Ocean floor; near coasts	Sand, often fine-grained, well-sorted; gravel	Dredging may be required
Outwash from continental glaciers	Plains of great areal extent	Boulders to clay; coarser near glacial boundary, finer away from boundary	
Outwash from mountain (alpine) glaciers	Narrow valleys	As above	
Glacial moraines	Any area once covered by glacial ice	Mixtures of sand, gravel, boulders	
Talus	Base of steep slopes	Angular, unsorted	Crushing of large fragments may be necessary
Sand dunes	Shorelines, deserts	Fine to medium sand, poorly graded	

Note: *Grading:* well-graded mixtures have a good distribution of grain-sizes; poorly graded mixtures are uniform in grain size or lack certain sizes of grains.

of natural conditions. Table 5-1 lists common geological environments in which these sediments may be found and some of the characteristics of each type of deposit.

The most common uses of sand and gravel are in making mortar, asphalt mixes, and concrete, creating permeable foundations where good drainage is important, providing a substrate under floors to prevent upward migration of moisture, and as a filtering medium. Characteristics sought for vary according to the specific use. For instance, sands used for filtration should be of uniform particle size and have a high silica content. Sands for concrete should be free of organic materials and soluble salts and contain only small amounts of clay and silt. Excessive quantities of particles smaller than two millimeters reduce permeability and should be avoided where good drainage is required. Fine materials may be eliminated by washing them out. Where the distribution of sizes of fragments in sand or gravel deposits is not suitable for a given purpose, *grading* may be improved by blending in materials of appropriate sizes. Such materials may be sand or gravel obtained elsewhere or crushed rock. Blending will be of increasing importance as sand and gravel deposits become less available.

Even though, in many regions, sand and gravel have in the past seemed available in endless abundance, the enormous quantities required by modern society have made continuing supply a serious problem. In the United States, for example, the current annual demand is now in excess of one billion tons. Per capita consumption has risen from 2.5 tons in 1950 to more than 5 tons in 1970 (Legget, 1973). In Orange County, California, part of the metropolitan Los Angeles region, per capita consumption of sand and gravel in 1972 was 7.2 tons (Evans, 1973). These figures may seem more believable when it is realized that construction of an ordinary house may require as much as 50–100 tons of sand and gravel, and that 95 percent of asphalt and 75 percent of concrete consists of *aggregate* (particles of stone).

Because of high transport costs, sand and gravel deposits near urban areas are of prime importance, and a continual search is in progress for workable deposits at minimal distances from cities. Transport of 20 miles may add 50 percent to the cost. In Los Angeles County in 1973, moving sand and gravel for a distance of about five miles cost $0.72 per ton; for a distance of 30 miles, the cost was $1.90 per ton. Total cost of the sand and gravel, including transportation, was $2.00–$3.50 per ton.

As a city expands, it is important that sand and gravel deposits are used *before* they are built over or assigned to uses incompatible with extraction. By 1958, San Diego County, California, lost a valuable sand deposit used in aluminum and brass casting due to encroaching housing developments. The same type of sand underlies much of the city of San Diego, but it is unlikely that further deposits will be worked within the city boundaries. Beach pebbles used for water filter systems have been lost as shorelines in the area have been made available for beaches or parks. Los Angeles recognized the loss of mineral deposits due to urbanization and has attempted to integrate extraction of sand and gravel into the whole scheme of urban expansion. Detailed test borings were made in the San

Fernando Valley to outline the location of usable deposits, and suitable areas were set aside and zoned as pit sites. After the deposits have been exhausted, the pits will be used for solid-waste disposal and then graded and restored for urban use (Goldman, 1959).

Aggregates, Cement, and Plaster

Aggregates are the stony particles which, when bound together by an appropriate matrix, form construction materials such as concrete, mortar, and asphaltic mixtures. Coarse aggregates are crushed stone or natural gravel or pebbles that will not pass through a screen with quarter-inch openings. Fine aggregates are materials that will pass through a quarter-inch screen. Where natural aggregates are not inexpensively available, artificial aggregates, such as blast-furnace slag or fly ash (collected from factory chimneys) may be used. Concrete to be used for special purposes may require aggregates other than those mentioned above.

Concrete is made from three components: aggregate, cement, and water. The aggregate, which may comprise 70–80 percent of the concrete, provides body and strength; cement binds the particles together; and water causes the cement to set or harden. Luckily, the geologic occurrence of natural aggregates is widespread (see Table 5.1). However, special care must be exercised that such materials are physically and chemically suitable for the purpose for which they are intended. Transportation is a major factor in the cost of aggregates, and local supplies must be found and protected wherever possible. Sufficient supplies for the vast amounts of concrete used in urban construction has become a major problem.

The modern use of concrete dates from about 1850. However, much ancient Roman construction utilized a kind of concrete made from *pozzuolana,* a volcanic ash found near Naples. When mixed with lime, this ash formed a cement that would set under water. Broken stone and tile fragments cemented by pozzuolana constituted a concrete that was used in many Roman buildings, water cisterns, and other edifices.

Natural cements, certain clay-rich limestones which, when baked and ground, will set when water is added, are not common, but are highly valued in some areas. The Carthaginians used cement well before the Christian era. Pozzuolana, already mentioned in connection with ancient Rome, is still used in modern Italy and other countries, although other natural or artificial materials are sometimes substituted for volcanic ash. The discovery of a *natural hydraulic cement* (cement other than pozzuolana that will harden under water) occurred in England in 1756 when John Smeaton burned clayey limestone and discovered its setting properties.

Artificial or *Portland cement* was invented by Aspdin in England in 1824 and has almost entirely displaced natural cements. It is generally used to make concrete or mortar or for patching, and is made from a mixture of limestone plus clay or shale and a small quantity of iron oxide. The mixture is baked until it partially fuses, and then is ground to a fine powder. Upon addition of water, the cement powder hardens. By altering the ingredients, variations in strength, speed, evenness of setting, and resistance to different types of water and soils may be obtained. Limestones used in making cement must be free of magnesia and sulfur or loose particles of silica. Clays must be free of gravel or other solid particles. Cements used with aggregates containing silicate minerals or silica must be low in alkalis, otherwise reactions will cause expansion, cracking, and loss of strength.

Mortar, used to bond together bricks or other masonry, is made by mixing cement, sand, and lime. Lime is manufactured by heating limestone until the carbon dioxide is driven off, leaving behind calcium oxide (lime) and whatever impurities were present in the limestone. The usual impurities are siliceous and clay materials, which, if present in sufficient amounts, cause the lime to set slowly and to have little strength unless mixed with sand. Lime sets after it has been *slaked* (mixed with water to form calcium hydroxide) and exposed to the atmosphere.

The mineral gypsum (hydrous calcium sulfate) is important in the building industry. It is used to make plasterboards, building plasters, and to retard the setting rate of Portland cement. Workable deposits are moderately common, occurring either as relatively pure layers in sedimentary rock sequences, as gypsum sands, or as *gypsite,* an impure, earthy form. *Plaster* is obtained by heating gypsum until most of the combined water is driven off. The remaining amorphous substance is commonly called *plaster of paris,* which, when water is added, sets in 6–8 minutes. A retarder that will delay setting for an hour or two is usually desirable. The impurities in gypsite usually serve this purpose. One of the most notable deposits of gypsum was located beneath the city of Paris, hence the name "plaster of paris."

Clay Bricks and Tile

In very early times it was realized that certain muds could be molded into shapes useful for building purposes and then hardened through exposure to the heat of the sun. Such *adobe bricks* are still extensively used in arid regions of the world. Suitable *adobe clays* are widespread in occurrence, and a minimum of technological skill is required to shape and harden them. A major drawback is that adobe is easily washed away by prolonged or heavy rainfall. "Burned clay" or "kiln-baked bricks," however, are impervious to the effects of wetting. The clays used in this process, known as *brick clays,* are easy to mold when wet (have the right *plasticity*) and will shrink minimally and uniformly when dried and heated. Also, good brick clays have a sufficient range between the temperature at which they "vitrify'' (become hard without losing their shape) and the temperature at which they begin to ''melt'' (become soft and lose their shape). If the temperature range is too small, less control over brick quality will be possible during firing. Brick clays should be uniform, clean, non-calcareous and free from gravel.

Clay may also be shaped or extruded into hollow building tile, roof and flooring tile, flue linings, drain and sewer pipes, and other structural products. Compared to bricks, tiles are made of finer-grade clays and more rigidly controlled during firing.

Clay may be formed or accumulate in a wide variety of geological environments. It results from the chemical decomposition of biotite, feldspar, pyroxene, and amphibole, all common mineral constituents of many rocks. Once it forms, the clay may stay where it is (residual deposits) or be transported and deposited, commonly on ocean floors, lake beds, floodplains, areas of glacial outwash, and deltas. Wind-transported deposits (loess clays) are widespread throughout the Great Plains of the United States.

6. Foundations

The weight of buildings, bridges, roads and other structures is transmitted to the earth through specially designed structures called *foundations*. The ground on which they rest is also known as a foundation. In order to distinguish between the two meanings of the word, the latter will be called the *foundation bed*, and the former the *structural foundation*. Our primary concern here will be the foundation beds and how they affect the choice and design of structural foundations.

Foundation beds are (1) exposed bedrock (or bedrock easily exposed by minimal excavation), (2) bedrock covered by a layer of loose sediment or soil thin enough so that structural foundations may penetrate it (in an extreme case, structural foundations have been carried through as much as 250 feet of loose material to underlying bedrock), or (3) a layer of sediment or soil so thick that foundations cannot reach the underlying bedrock (Fig. 6.1).

Bedrock Foundations

Where bedrock is available, the building rests directly on or is embedded directly into solid rock. Of primary interest is the ability of such foundations to safely support weight without failing or deforming (*bearing capacity*). The principal factor in determining bearing capacity is the *compressive*

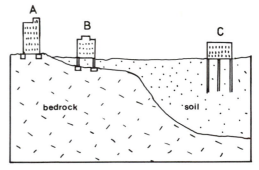

6.1 Foundation beds: **(A)** bedrock; **(B)** bedrock covered by a thin soil layer; **(C)** thick soil layer.

strength of the rock, or the degree to which it can resist compressive stress. In crystalline rocks (most igneous and metamorphic rocks and some sedimentary rocks) whose texture is one of interlocking grains, the better the interlocking the higher will be the compressive strength (Fig. 6.2A). The compressive strength of most sedimentary rocks, in which the grains are held together by a "cement," will depend upon the composition of the cement and how well it is distributed between and attached to the grains (Fig. 6.2B). Silica, for example, is a strong cement; clay is a weak one. If the bedrock is layered or jointed, its compressive strength will vary considerably (as much as 50 percent), depending upon

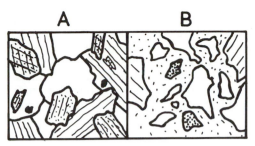

6.2 **(A)** Interlocking grains. **(B)** Cemented grains (dot pattern is cement).

whether stress is applied perpendicular or parallel to the planes of weakness. Compressive strength will be greatest when stress is acting at right angles to any layering or jointing (Fig. 6.3). Strength is also affected by the extent to which a rock is "held together" by surrounding rocks. The weight of overlying rock not only presses down on deeper rocks, but is also transmitted to them laterally through the surrounding rock medium. Such lateral support gives them a higher compressive strength than rocks at shallower depth.

Additional significant factors affecting compressive strength are degree of weathering, the presence of water within the rock, and grain size. Weathering or alteration of rocks can radically decrease their compressive strength. Similarly, rocks saturated with water have considerably less strength than when dry. Porous and permeable rocks become wet more easily and are therefore likely to be weaker than those of low

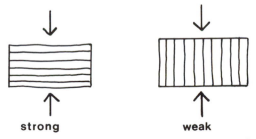

strong   **weak**

6.3 The relationship between orientation of layering and compressive strength.

porosity. Fine-grained rocks are generally stronger than coarse-grained rocks.

Rocks with high compressive strength are basalts, fine-grained granites, quartzites, and compact, well-cemented sandstones and limestones. Those of lower strength include course-grained granites, shales, porous sandstones and limestones, chalk, tuff, and siltstone.

In estimating the reliability of a given bedrock for a proposed building, a considerable safety factor is allowed. For instance, if laboratory tests show that the rock will withstand stress up to 720 tons per square foot, the building code may assign it a bearing capacity of only 25–40 tons per square foot.

The presence of faults or folds may also affect the safety or suitability of bedrock. Active faults can result in displacement of the bedrock and damage to structures. Folds affect the passage, distribution, and pressure of groundwater; synclines in particular tend to accumulate groundwater, and may cause problems in construction and maintenance.

Soil Foundations

To a geologist, "soil" is a mixture of weathered rock, decaying organic matter, and soluble salts capable of supporting plant life. For engineering purposes, soil is all material that may be excavated easily without blasting, and thus includes the geologist's "soil," together with other loose sediment and soft or poorly consolidated rock. In the discussion of foundations, soil will be used in the engineering sense.

Soil originates in diverse ways and has diverse properties. A knowledge of its mode of formation permits a more accurate estimate of how it is likely to vary both laterally and vertically (its *continuity*), and how it will behave under changing conditions.

Soil that overlies parent materials from which it was derived is called *residual soil*. *Transported soils* have been removed from

their site of formation and deposited elsewhere. In general, the thickness of transported deposits is greater than that of residual deposits, except in moist tropical
regions.

Glacial Soils Large areas in high latitudes
(and smaller areas at high elevations) were
until relatively recent times covered by
flowing glacial ice. Loose material over-rid-
den by the ice was compacted into *hardpan,*
or *basal drift,* a substance often as strong as
rock. Hardpan is desirable as a foundation
bed but is difficult to excavate. Rocky materials incorporated into the moving ice and
eventually released where the ice melted
were deposited as unsorted, unstratified
till—a mélange of boulders, sand, gravel,
silt, and clay. If a boulder is encountered in
exploratory drilling in till, it may be mistaken for bedrock; to avoid such mistakes,
the drill should penetrate any rock encountered for perhaps as much as ten feet or
more. Where glacial meltwaters were
dammed and formed lakes, quantities of
fine silt and clay accumulated in well-
sorted, well-stratified layers, and streams carrying away the meltwaters deposited gravel,
sand, and finer materials in stream channels
and floodplains. Glacial deposits are likely
to be heterogenous in grain size, porosity,
and permeability; display frequent lateral
and vertical variation in drainage properties;
and compact or settle in varying degree

under the weight of buildings or other structures. Where such deposits have buried a
pre-existing land surface of high relief,
depth to bedrock may vary greatly, and
careful exploration must be carried out before construction can be started (Fig. 6.4).
In Manhattan, for example, canyons up to
300 feet deep filled with glacial deposits
have been found.

Alluvial Soils Loose material transported
and deposited by running water may be
called *alluvial soil,* or *alluvium.* Such materials accumulate in stream channels and on
floodplains, deltas, and alluvial fans. Compared to glacial soils, alluvial soils (other
than channel deposits) are more likely to be
well-stratified and have a somewhat greater
lateral constancy. Thus, fewer drill-hole
samples to judge the nature of subsurface
deposits are called for.

Colluvium Debris that moves downhill
due to the pull of gravity or that is washed
down by water flowing over the surface
(*sheet wash*) accumulates to form deposits
known as *colluvium.* Such deposits are
usually restricted in areal extent and commonly are unsorted and unstratified.

Aeolian (Wind-Transported) Soils Deposits of wind-transported dust (*loess*) are
likely to have a porous but cohesive texture.

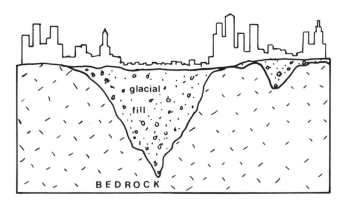

6.4 Variable depth of bedrock in
area covered by glacial debris.

Wetting causes loess to compact, a property called *hydroconsolidation,* and results in the settling of any structure built upon it. Hydroconsolidation may also occur in some alluvial soils. If properly compacted, loess may acquire considerable strength and resistance to erosion (Krynine and Judd, 1957). Wind-blown sand often accumulates into *dunes.* Dunes may reach as much as 300 feet in height, and, unless they are stabilized, will migrate in the direction of the wind. Migrating dunes may pass over and temporarily bury objects of considerable size. Structures built on dunes may find their foundations exposed when the surrounding sand is blown away. Dune stabilization is commonly accomplished by planting grasses, heather, or conifers, or by binding the sand with crude oil.

Soils Rich in Organic Materials   Large areas of the earth's land surface are underlain by saturated or almost saturated soils rich in decaying vegetation. Such areas include swamps, marshes, bogs, and muskeg. The soil (called *peat*) may be rich in recognizable plant material or, if decay is advanced, in black slimy substances. Peat has a very low bearing strength and can only support light structures. Muds and silts deposited in coastal areas may contain high percentages of micro-organisms. These organic muds and silts (which are usually water-saturated) have low bearing strength.

SOIL CHARACTERISTICS

A variety of soil characteristics are important in determining their engineering properties. The study of these properties and the problems associated with them fall in the domain of *soil mechanics.* Important soil characteristics include the size, shape, arrangement, and composition of grains, as well as cohesiveness, porosity, permeability, moisture content, and the position of the water table. These characteristics will determine such properties as bearing and shear strength, plasticity, potential for

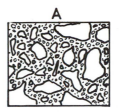 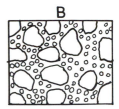

6.5 (**A**) Well-graded soil. (**B**) Poorly-graded soil.

swelling, shrinking, liquefaction, and consolidation.

Grain-size may be determined by passing the soil through a series of sieves or by measuring the settling velocity of grains in a liquid medium. Descriptive terms such as clay, silt, sand, and gravel, are then applied to grains that lie within certain size-ranges. The exact numbers that define each size-range vary according to the particular classification used: in many classifications, *gravel* is coarser than 2 mm; *sand* is between 0.04–2.0 mm; *silt* is between 0.002–0.04 mm; *clay** is finer than 0.002 mm. Soils are almost always mixtures of several of these grain-size categories. A soil in which a range of grain sizes are present is called *well-graded.* Small grains may fill the spaces between larger grains, thus decreasing the soil's porosity and permeability and increasing its density (Fig. 6.5). Soil in which most of the grains are the same size, or in which certain sizes are missing is called *poorly graded,* and will have correspondingly higher porosity and permeability and lower density. In some instances, coarse sediment may be improved by adding sand or gravel (Hunt, 1972).

The *grain-shape* of coarse grains is commonly described as rounded or angular, and affects both the strength and porosity of

---

* It should be noted that the word *clay* has several uses: (1) it refers to a certain size-range of materials (those finer than 0.002 mm); (2) it refers to the family of *clay minerals.* Not all clay-size materials are made of clay minerals; however, clay minerals are always of clay-size; (3) it is used to describe clay-size materials which when wet display a plasticity due to the abundant presence of clay minerals.

soil. Fine-grained sediment very often contains high percentages of clay minerals, which are typically tiny flat or scale-like fragments.

Under some conditions, sand grains may accumulate in an open, loosely packed structure which can later collapse into a more tightly packed *grain-arrangement.* The result is a reduction in overall volume (by reducing the porosity), which causes subsidence of the ground surface. Moisture causes sand grains to stick to one another, increasing the stability of the grain arrangements; upon drying out, this tendency to stick together (*cohesiveness*) is reduced, and the sand becomes less stable.

Moisture content in fine-grained soil is especially significant. As clay dries out, films of water separating the grains from one another are eliminated. The grains come into closer contact, which increases the effectiveness of attractive electrostatic forces, pulling the grains into even closer contact. The electrostatic attraction plus the actual loss of water cause the clay to shrink. If clay is submerged in water, it may swell or expand as the grains are separated by water films and the electrostatic attraction between the grains decreases. Or materials such as the clay mineral *montmorillonite* may be present. When grains of montmorillonite are wetted, the grains themselves absorb water and expand. Such expansion can lift and damage heavy structures. Volume changes in fine soil brought about by changes of moisture content may be described as the soil's *shrink-swell potential.* If a wet clay is subject to load pressure, the water may be squeezed out of the clay, causing it to decrease in volume or to *consolidate.*

Whether a soil responds to deformation elastically, plastically, or by rupturing is of considerable interest to soil engineers. A material is said to behave *elastically* if the change in volume or shape resulting from stress is temporary; that is, the material reverts to its original state when stress is no longer applied. *Plastic flow* occurs when a material permanently changes shape or volume, without rupturing, as deforming stress is applied. When soil experiences a deforming stress, the changes in volume and shape are only partly reversible; the extent to which they are non-reversible is a measure of the soil's plasticity.

The *consistency* of soil; that is, whether it behaves as a liquid, a plastic solid, or a brittle solid (one that ruptures rather than flowing plastically), is affected by moisture content. *Atterberg limits* refer to such changes in consistency with moisture content (Fig. 6.6). If moisture is added to a dry fine-grained soil, it will eventually change from a crumbly substance to one that behaves plastically. The moisture content of the soil when this change occurs is referred to as its *plastic limit.* If more water is added to the soil, it will eventually behave like a liquid; the moisture content of the soil when this change takes place is called its *liquid limit.* The range of moisture content over which soil behaves plastically (which is greatly dependent upon its clay mineral content) is called the *plasticity index,* and is obtained by subtracting the plastic limit from the liquid limit. Knowledge of Atterberg limits and derived indices permits an engineer to predict changes in the strength of a soil as it gets wet.

Electrostatic forces, which play a significant role in holding clay particles together, may be disturbed if the clay is kneaded or *remolded,* resulting in a loss of cohesion and a decrease in compressive strength.

Some clays, called *quick clays,* accumulate in lakes fed by glacial meltwaters, and develop an open, honeycomb-like structure which allows the clay to hold a high percentage of water while still behaving as a solid. If quick clays are disturbed (remolded) by the motion of landslides, earthquake vibrations, or vibratory motions such as pile-driving, their strength diminishes sharply, and they flow as liquid mud. Such behavior is an example of extreme *sensitivity,* in which the ratio of the strength of the quick clay before and after remolding is as

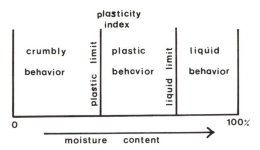

6.6 Atterberg Limits.

much as 100:1. Glacial clays deposited in sea water show a similar propensity to flow when disturbed.

A *quicksand condition* develops when fine-grained sand is saturated with water under pressure. It may develop at the base of a hill or where artesian water reaches the surface (Fig. 6.7). Water pressure in the pore spaces between the grains forces them apart, imparting a fluidity to the sand/water mixture that completely eliminates its strength and may actually cause it to flow. Vibrations (such as those produced by earthquakes) acting on water-saturated fine-grained sand or silt may cause a similar, temporary *liquefaction*. The vibrations increase the pore pressure of the water, force the grains apart, and cause the sediment to lose its strength. However, strength will be regained after the vibrations cease and the pore pressure returns to normal.

STRUCTURAL FOUNDATIONS

Two major types of building foundations are in common use: spread foundations (spread footings), and piles. The type chosen depends upon the weight of the building, the use to which the building is put, and the nature of the foundation bed.

Spread footings spread the weight of a building over a larger area, decreasing the pressure or *unit load* (expressed in units such as tons per square foot) on the ground. The footings are placed under those parts of a building (columns, walls) that transmit its weight to the foundation bed. The maximum unit load allowed at the base of the footing should be no more than one-half or one-third of the strength of the underlying material. If weight is transmitted vertically downward by columns, *individual footings* are used (Fig. 6.8A); if it is transmitted by a foundation wall, a *continuous footing* can be used (Fig. 6.8B). If the foundation bed is a soil with very low bearing capacity, it may be necessary to spread the weight of the building over a *mat* or *raft* foundation which underlies the entire structure (Fig. 6.8C). When such foundations are used, careful evaluation of the position of the groundwater table must be made, for if it is higher than the mat, the water will exert an upward hydrostatic pressure.

If the surface and near-surface soil has too low a bearing strength, concrete piers or

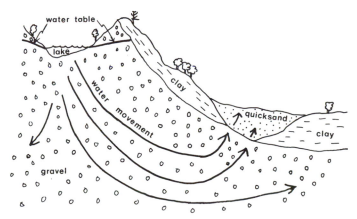

6.7 Quicksand condition: fine-grained, saturated sand through which water migrates upward.

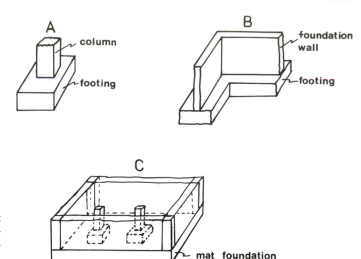

6.8 Types of spread footings: (**A**) individual footing; (**B**) continuous footing; (**C**) mat foundation.

piles may be used. Concrete piers, formed by filling drilled or excavated holes with concrete, transmit the weight of the building to a reliable deep soil or rock material. Friction between the pier and the soil that surrounds it also takes up part of the weight of the structure. The Woolworth Building in New York City rests on piers that extend 115 feet beneath street level to the underlying Manhattan Formation (schists and gneisses) (Krynine and Judd, 1957). Piles, which may be made of timber, concrete or steel are hammered into the ground. The weight of the building is supported by the friction between the pile and the surrounding soil (a *friction pile;* Fig. 6.9), or by the firm rock or soil upon which the pile rests at depth (a *point-* or *end-bearing* pile; Fig. 6.9). If wooden piles are employed, they must be driven under the water table, or intermittent exposure to air will cause rotting. Piles driven into sensitive clay may cause the clay to fail, and in general, piles should not be used where clay is present unless they can be driven through the clay to reach underlying firm material. If the use of such point-bearing piles is not possible, spread footings should be employed.

Determining the ground conditions is vital to the successful design of major struc-

tures. The rule-of-thumb is that the ground should be tested to a depth that is at least twice the width of the proposed building. The number of test holes required depends upon the lateral and vertical variation of the soil or bedrock. Depth to bedrock may vary radically in glaciated areas. A knowledge of groundwater conditions, the position of the water table, the permeability of ground materials, and the position of buried streams, lakes, swamps, and former shorelines may be of considerable importance. Such infor-

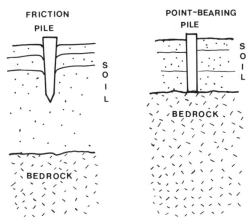

6.9 Friction pile and point-bearing pile.

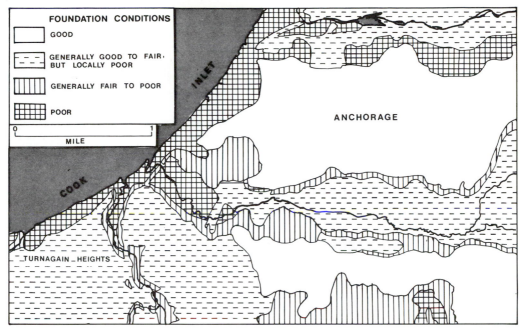

6.10 Anchorage and vicinity, Alaska, showing foundation conditions. (After Schmoll and Dobrovolny, 1974)

mation may be gained from geologic maps, borehole and water-well records, and foundation records of nearby buildings. Historic maps may reveal the extent of artificial ground. In Manhattan, maps dating back to 1783 were examined to gain information about the site of the World Trade Center. Ideally, all such data should be collected and made available by government or private organizations. In some areas, such information has been synthesized, and maps showing depth to bedrock and foundation and excavation conditions have been prepared (Fig. 6.10).

FOUNDATION PROBLEMS

Foundation problems are related to excavation, ground stability, groundwater, and chemical properties of the ground.

Excavations into bedrock usually present few problems except where planes or zones of weakness are too steeply inclined and may precipitate landslides. Excavation of soil presents a much greater danger of loose material sliding into the hole. Vibration from construction equipment and rain-soaked ground amplify such problems. Increased stability may be achieved by lessening slope angles, cutting benches into the slope and ensuring good drainage.

Damage to structures placed on expansive soils (usually clay, sometimes shale) runs to $2.25 billion annually (Snethen, 1976). Robert F. Legget, a renowned engineering geologist, says that every basement in Winnipeg, Canada, has been cracked by expanding clay. If the presence of expansive soils is not recognized during design and construction, damage may be severe. Perhaps the best method of dealing with expansive soil is to replace it with compacted non-expansive materials.

Frost-heaving (caused by the expansion of groundwater as it turns to ice) also exerts an upward pressure on structures. Frost-heaving may be minimized by ensuring adequate drainage or by insulating the ground so that it does not freeze.

Settlement, the vertically downward movement of a structure built on compressible soil, is a common foundation problem. Settlement occurs to some extent whenever a structure is built on soil. It is *excessive* settlement that is of concern, especially when the amount of downward movement is not uniform (*differential settlement*) due to differing soil conditions or uneven transferal of weight to the soil. Excessive settlement is most likely in the presence of poorly compacted sediment or clay that is capable of plastic flow. Perhaps the most famous example is the Leaning Tower of Pisa in Italy, which has tilted 16 feet since its completion in 1350, and continues to tilt an additional 0.04 inches yearly. A layer of clay 28 feet beneath the tower's foundation slab is responsible.

Buildings erected on loess are particularly likely to settle. As mentioned earlier, loess loses its open texture on contact with water, and is reduced considerably in volume. Such *hydroconsolidation* may be lessened by keeping the loess as dry as possible, either by providing drainage or by covering the ground near the building with an impervious pavement. Ground underlain by organic materials such as peat is also highly compressible.

Settlement may be avoided in some cases by using *floating foundations.* The procedure involves the excavation of sufficient material so that the weight of the structure and its foundation is no greater than the weight of the excavated material (Fig. 6.11). Thus no additional load is placed on the substrate (the building and its foundation "float"), and no settlement should take place. Many buildings in Boston, Tokyo, London, and other cities underlain by weak soils rest on such foundations. Another alternative is to "precompress" the soil, perhaps by allowing a load of sediment to rest on the ground for a considerable time before construction is started.

Structures placed on artificial ground such

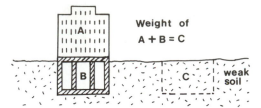

6.11 Floating foundation. The weight of building **A** plus foundation **B** is equal to the weight of excavated soil **C**.

as sanitary landfill, filled-in quarries, land reclaimed from lakes, swamps, or the ocean, or on fill used to even out rugged topography, may often settle. Such material and any underlying soil should be thoroughly compacted and well drained. Sanitary landfill may settle by as much as 25 percent of its thickness within two years. The extent of urbanization over artifical ground in the boroughs of Manhattan and Brooklyn in New York may be seen in Figures 11.25; 11.26. Throughout the world, the ground level in cities rises with time as buildings are destroyed or dismantled and then built over. In Prague, the present street level is as much as twenty feet higher than the original ground surface; parts of Boston rest on seven feet of rubble. Archaeological excavation of "mounds" dramatically reveals such vertical layering of cities built on cities.

Downward movement of structures may also take place when liquids or solids are removed from beneath the earth's surface, causing *ground subsidence* (see Chap. 12).

Foundations on sloping ground may be damaged by downslope movement of earth materials. If the soil cover is thin, structures may be anchored to solid bedrock. The stability of the foundation will be lessened, however, if planar features such as joints, foliation, or bedding are inclined and parallel to the surface. Foundations on loose soil may be subject to *creep,* the slow downhill movement of loose material that results from freezing and thawing, root wedging, and other processes.

Drainage may be a major factor in ground

6.12 Raising the Briggs House, northeast corner of Randolph and Wells Streets, 1857.

stability and in foundation design and construction. Where the water table is high, or an aquifer is situated at shallow depths, groundwater may flow into an excavation, causing its sides to become unstable and subject to landslide. Water can also interfere with foundations. Groundwater may exert an upward hydrostatic shove or "floating" action that may tilt or crack floor slabs or walls. Basement structures could be affected, and should be thoroughly waterproofed.

Chicago

Chicago faced a particularly severe drainage problem in the mid-nineteenth century. Much of the city was built on land only slightly higher than adjacent Lake Michigan, and the water table was only slightly beneath the land surface. For long periods each year the streets were "a vast sea of black mud," and the city was "destined to be a prairie Venice, a maze of drainage canals. . . ." (Jackson, 1972, p. 72). However, instead of building drainage canals, the city pulled itself up by the bootstraps. Over a period of twenty years, the street level was raised by as much as twelve feet, existing buildings were placed on jacks and elevated (Fig. 6.12), and new subsurface drainage facilities were installed. "The raising of Chicago soon became one of the great wonders of the nation. . . ." (Mayer and Wade, 1969, p. 96).

Building skyscrapers on Chicago's wet spongy soil called for special construction techniques (Condit, 1964). The soil consists almost entirely of sand and clay interspersed with pockets of water and is highly compressible. In the late 1800s, architect John Wellborn Root developed the "floating raft" foundation—a 20 inch-thick slab of concrete reinforced with layers of steel rails on which the weight of the building might rest. To avoid differential settlement, all parts of a building were constructed simultaneously. This type of construction was used for the 10-story Montauk Block (1882) and the 16-story Monadnock Building (1891). The basement of the 10-story Auditorium Building (architects Denkmar Adler and Louis Sullivan) was sunk seven feet below the mean water level of Lake Michigan. Not only did the floor have to be waterproofed, but it was specially constructed to resist the intense upward hydrostatic pressure. The soil beneath the building was compressed before construction. To avoid settlement of the 13-story Stock Exchange Building (1894), Adler and Sullivan placed reinforced concrete footings on timber piles driven 55 feet down to glacial hardpan. The concrete piers supporting the west side of the building were poured in watertight drums to resist high-pressure groundwater seepage; this was the first use of *caisson* foundations for buildings. (A caisson is a watertight chamber sunk into the ground or into a body of water into which concrete can be poured.) In the 100-story John Hancock Center (1970), the footings rest on 239 caissons, 57 of which reach down to bedrock at depths of up to 191 feet beneath grade level. The remaining 182 caissons rest on hardpan found at depths up to 88 feet (Condit, 1974).

Lowering the water table and drying out the ground may cause a number of problems. Wooden piles exposed to moist air may rot and have to be replaced by other materials—an expensive proposition. Buildings put up on a mixture of sand and finer material may subside as the finer material is washed away by the receding groundwater. If clay is present, drying out may cause shrinkage and deep cracks. Nevertheless, the water table is often purposely lowered to prevent flooding of subways or other underground structures.

Trees may cause unwanted lowering of the water table and subsequent ground settlement. Where foundation problems are likely, trees should not be planted closer to buildings than a distance equal to the height of the trees (Legget, 1973).

Mexico City

Mexico City has suffered spectacular drainage and settlement problems. The oldest continuously inhabited city in North America, it is situated in an enclosed valley (7350 feet in elevation) surrounded by high mountains (Fig. 6.13). Underlying the valley floor is sediment washed down from the surrounding mountains and loose volcanic ash deposited by wind and water—water-saturated montmorillonitic clay, sand, pumice, and organic debris. This mixture, as might be suspected, is highly compressible. Furthermore, the valley has interior drainage; that is, there is no natural drainage outlet to the sea, and streams flowing within the valley used to empty into a central lake (the former Lake Texcoco), a shallow body of water dotted with small islands. In the twelfth century, the islands were settled by Aztecs. In 1521, Spanish invaders destroyed the city, and drained much of the lake by digging a series of canals. Aztec building stones were used to construct a new, Spanish city. Despite the drainage canals, the city was subject to frequent and severe flooding during the summer rainy season because there was still no drainage connection from the valley to the world outside. Finally, in 1900, the Canal de Desaugue was completed. It carries valley waters 30 miles through the mountains to join the Pánuco River, which empties into the Gulf of Mexico. An additional, unique drainage device serving Mexico City is the Carocol, (meaning snail), a long, inward-coiling, spiral canal. Water draining into the canal flows toward its center and is eliminated through evaporation.

As a result of water drainage and a consequent lowering of the water table, Mexico City has undergone severe and uneven subsidence. Between 1898 and 1950, the ground surface sank up to 17 feet in some places. In addition to foundation problems caused by the ground sinking unevenly, differential settlement has arisen due to the high, variable compressibility of the soil. The Palace of Fine Arts, a massive structure built between 1905 and 1934, has settled ten feet, and its entrance is now several feet below street level. The sinking, which continues today, is attributed to the high water content of the underlying soil. Modern sky-

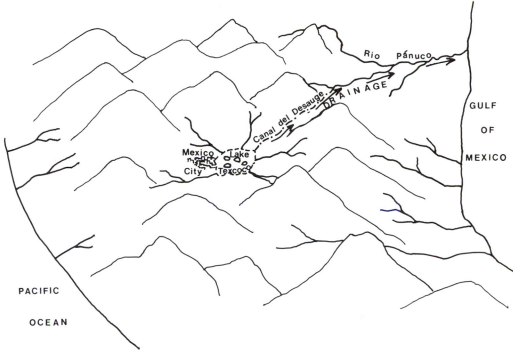

6.13 Diagrammatic sketch of the physical setting of Mexico City.

scrapers in Mexico City have been built successfully on piles that extend to firmer layers, such as sand, found 100 feet below the ground surface. Special techniques have been employed to counteract the flooding that occurs when excavations are dug to install foundation slabs and basements. Floating foundations have also been successfully used to reduce settlement and to lessen the effect of earthquake vibrations. Strict control over pumping of groundwater is now enforced to minimize further subsidence.

The *chemical properties* of the ground may affect the useful lifespan of building materials. Corrosion or decomposition of metallic pipes, cables, pilings, and caissons may be quite rapid, depending upon soil moisture and acidity, oxidation-reduction potential, and the presence of dissolved minerals and certain bacterial organisms. A given soil may be tested for corrosiveness by measuring its electrical resistivity: the lower the resistivity, the more likely it will be corrosive (Flawn, 1970). Sulfates in groundwater may react chemically with cements, weakening concrete. Where this danger exists, sulfate-resistant cements must be used (Legget, 1967).

Bridge Foundations

Bridges may be supported at their ends by *abutments,* or in their central portions, by *piers* (Fig. 6.14A,B). These supports rest on spread footings or piles which, like building foundations, may be attached to solid rock or rest on loose soil. However, bridge foundations differ from those of buildings in several ways. Besides transmitting the *vertical* load to the ground, some bridges may exert a substantial *horizontal* component of thrust or push (Fig. 6.14C). In suspension bridges (Fig. 6.14D), the superstructure is anchored to rock or

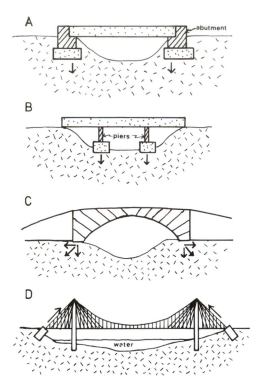

6.14 Bridge foundations. (**A**) abutments; (**B**) piers; (**C**) horizontal thrust from arch; (**D**) suspension bridge (note pull).

concrete, upon which it exerts a considerable pull. Exploration of foundation beds is particularly important because of the concentrated loads placed on bridge supports and the fact that the load may deviate from the vertical. Obtaining adequate information is vital because underneath or adjacent to surface valleys there is the distinct geologic likelihood of buried, older valleys, where the depth to bedrock may vary considerably. In glaciated regions, boulders, which may be mistaken for bedrock or cause construction difficulties, may also be present.

Piers built to stand in flowing water must be able to resist the pressure of the water and the possible impact of floating debris and ice. Their presence also partially blocks the channel, causing the velocity of the water to increase and the water level to rise

as it flows through the constricted passageways between the piers or between the piers and the abutments or shores. This increase in velocity causes the stream to erode or scour (deepen) its channel, possibly exposing and weakening bridge foundations. In some instances, emplacement of a bridge has actually caused a stream to shift its channel.

Where steam floods reach great volume, bridges may actually be submerged for short periods and must be designed to withstand such inundations. Bridge abutments, which are often built on valley slopes, must be able to resist any tendency for downhill movement of loose earth materials.

Special techniques must be employed where bridge supports are to stand in water. Water may be excluded from the construction site by emplacing a *cofferdam,* a vertical enclosure commonly constructed of piles placed in watertight contact with one another, and from which water is removed by pumping (Fig. 6.15). If boulders are encountered during the sinking of the piles, great additional expense may be involved in construction. Keeping the interior of the cofferdam water-free depends partly upon how easily water may seep into it from the sediment or rock underlying the stream, which in turn depends upon the composition and structures of those materials. Gravel and sand are highly permeable and can allow seepage; clay has low permeability and often helps seal a cofferdam.

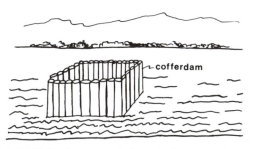

6.15 Cofferdam to exclude water from construction site.

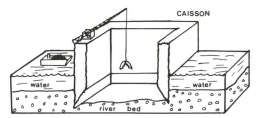

6.16 Sinking of a caisson.

Another construction technique is the use of *caissons*. A caisson is a watertight vertical box with wedge-shaped bottom edges that is open at one or both ends (Fig. 6.16). By weighting the box or removing material from beneath its edges the caisson is sunk into the soft river bed. Water may be removed by pumping or by using compressed air to push the water out. If the latter method is employed, workers and materials enter and leave the chamber through airlocks. Once a caisson is in position, it is filled with concrete. The sinking of a caisson may be complicated by the nature of the foundation bed: lateral variations in strength may cause uneven sinking or tilting. During the construction of the Brooklyn Bridge, sinking of caissons into the floor of the East River was hindered by the presence of numerous glacial boulders—most of them diabase fragments torn by ice from the Hudson River Palisades. (Diabase is a dark, tough igneous rock similar to basalt.) To avoid crushing the cutting edges of the caissons all boulders had to be located and removed before each increment of downward movement—"an unbelievably tough and disagreeable task. . . ." McCullough, 1972, p. 200).

Pavement Foundations

Express highways, local streets, sidewalks, parking lots, and airport runways occupy a considerable fraction of the area of a city. To function properly and to have a life-span commensurate with their cost, such paved surfaces must be placed on appropriate foundations. The problems most frequently encountered include settlement, expansive soils, and frost heaving. These and other problems are best solved by ensuring adequate drainage, compressing the soil before loading it with the pavement, and, occasionally, removing objectionable bed material and substituting non-expansive permeable sediment or crushed rock.

TUNNELS AND SUBWAYS

Beneath cities, underground railways that provide daily transport for millions, together with tunnels that carry roads through mountains or link the opposite shores of streams or lakes, are essential elements of the urban fabric. In addition to such people-carrying tunnels, there are tunnels beneath cities enclosing aqueducts, sewage mains, and electric, gas, and phone lines. Without these underground passages, the surfaces of cities would be so awash with pipes, cables, tracks, wires, and additional traffic that today's crowded, cluttered streets and skies would seem unencumbered and pristine in comparison.

Tunnels are constructed basically in two ways. Where the ground is sufficiently strong and the route deep enough, they can be *driven* or bored, using mining techniques. Where the ground is soft and the route shallow, an open trench may be excavated, the tunnel constructed in it, and the trench refilled—a method of construction referred to as *cut-and-cover*.

If tunnels are driven through the ground, supports and a lining (which may amount to a quarter of the total cost) may be necessary to prevent movement or collapses of surrounding rock or soil into the tunnel. The need for a lining, and the mode of excavation depend upon factors that include depth beneath the surface, the strength and cohesiveness of the ground material, the presence of stress within the material that might cause it to expand into the tunnel opening, and the orientation of folds, bedding, foliation, joints, or faults with respect to the tunnel. The amount of rock removed (by design or through necessity) beyond that required by the dimensions of the tunnel adds greatly to the cost. Advance knowledge of conditions and materials likely to be encountered during excavation is important in planning the exact route. Precise information is difficult to obtain, but exploratory drilling, geophysical testing, and careful examination of existing geologic reports can be extremely helpful.

Pressure tunnels, designed to transport water under pressure, must be lined to prevent leakage and possible violent escape of water to the surface as a *blowout*. The importance of such tunnels is suggested by New York City's supply system, which employs them along with aqueducts to bring water to the city from as far away as 128 miles. Individual pressure tunnels are up to 85 miles in length. To cross under the Hudson, a tunnel was emplaced in solid granite 1000 feet beneath the surface to avoid the treacherous river and glacial sediments within the river gorge. New York is still engaged in tunnel-building to ensure adequate water supply for the future. The Third Water Tunnel is to be only 13.7 miles long, running from Hillview Reservoir in Yonkers through the Bronx, Manhattan, and Queens, but will cost well over a billion dollars by the time it is finished.

The presence of groundwater plays a major role in the ease, expense, and safety of tunneling and the choice of techniques used in excavating. Where possible, tunnels are located above the water table. But this is often not possible, especially if the tunnel has to run under a stream or a lake. An influx of groundwater is likely if the rock is highly permeable (such as when zones of fissures are encountered) or if an aquifer is intersected. If the tunnel is being driven through soft ground, groundwater problems are likely to be even more serious. Water problems may be dealt with through pumping (to remove water or lower the water table); grouting (sealing rock fissures or pores by pumping cement into them); or by

compressing air within the tunnel so that the pressure within is higher than the pressure of the water trying to enter the tunnel. Lowering the water table, however, may cause surface structures to settle, and may also affect the elevation of suface lakes and the reliability of streams and springs. The use of compressed air is avoided whenever possible because accidental, rapid decompression is dangerous to the lives and health of workers in the tunnel.

When tunneling takes place after urbanization, as is unfortunately often the case, the digging of the tunnel becomes a not inconsiderable element of the urban environment. Excavation of the eleven-mile Manhattan-Queens subway line in New York has subjected residents of elegant East 63rd Street to a continuing nightmare. They have had to face daily dynamite blasts, the roar of drills and pumps, flooded basements, broken windows, cracked walls, massive traffic disruptions, property values that have plummeted (at least temporarily), and a disheartening loss of business for many local merchants. Graceful trees and front stoops have been removed and replaced by the paraphernalia of modern construction: giant cranes, trailers, portable toilets, wire fences, and wheelbarrows. For much of the estimated ten years that it will take to complete the line and the associated stations, the feeling of repose which lent much to the attractiveness of the neighborhood will be lost in a quagmire of noise, dirt, and disruption.

The duration and extent of the disruption, the cost of the project, and the engineering techniques employed have been materially affected by the nature of the Manhattan schist through which this section of the line is to run. Abundant fractures in the schist call for the emplacement of steel columns and arches every five feet to support the walls and roof of the tunnel. Also, because the tunnel is below the water table, there is a continual influx of groundwater which must be stemmed by concrete patching and removed by pumping.

The first subway built in New York caused considerably less disruption. It was built in 1867–70 by Alfred Ely Beach, editor of the *Scientific American*. Beach decided upon secrecy to avoid having to obtain franchise rights by bribing "Boss Tweed," the head of the Tammany Hall Democratic machine. To accomplish the covert construction of the subway, Beach rented the basement of a clothing store at the corner of Murray Street and Broadway, and, with the aid of a special hydraulic tunneling shield that he invented for the purpose, had workmen dig a 9-foot diameter tunnel through the sandy soil beneath Broadway 312 feet to Warren Street. The only external sign of activity was workmen bringing sacks of dirt out of the basement. When the subway was completed, it included an opulent waiting room, frescoes, a fish-tank, a fountain, and a single richly upholstered 22 seat subway car. The car was alternately blown through the tunnel and then sucked back again by a giant fan. When Beach announced the existence of his subway, Boss Tweed was furious. The public and the press, however, were ecstatic, and thousands paid the 25-cent fare to try out the ride. Beach envisioned the Murray Street-Warren Street Line as the first step in a system that would extend north to Central Park, and sought permission and support from the New York State Legislature. The Legislature approved the project and appropriated $5 million for its construction. However, Governor John T. Hoffman, a political ally of Boss Tweed, vetoed the bill. With the collapse of Tammany Hall and the defeat of Governor Hoffman, the Beach Transit Bill was finally passed in 1873. But delay took its toll. Lack of money ($5 million was no longer sufficient due to inflation) and fears that the tunnels would undermine the foundations of large buildings, caused the abandonment of Beach's subway. The pneumatic tube was soon forgotten. In 1912, a construction crew working on the BMT subway chopped through the wall of the Beach tunnel and rediscovered the earlier line intact. Beach's subway now forms part of the BMT City Hall Station.

The first official New York subway, for which excavation began in 1900, ran from City Hall Park near the Brooklyn Bridge to West 145th Street via Times Square and Grand Central Station. Most of the tunnel was constructed using the cut-and-cover technique with drilling and blasting to get through the hard bedrock. Within two years, approval was given for extensions into the Bronx and Brooklyn. The lines in Brooklyn were "laid out in fields from which hardly a house could be seen, but the houses followed the rails (and even the plans for rails). . . ." (Day, 1964, p. 108). Today, the New York City subway system runs for 237 miles, 132 of which are in tunnels, includes 458 stations, and carries well over a billion passengers each year.

The Bay Area Rapid Transit District subway line (BART) which serves the earthquake prone San Francisco metropolitan area, has a 3.6 mile stretch which runs along the floor of the bay between San Francisco and Oakland (Fig. 6.17). The underwater Transbay Tube, in which the subway runs, reaches depths up to 135 feet below the surface. The tube does not cross any faults known to be active, but to cushion it against earthquake shocks, the tube sections (which were prefabricated) were laid in a trench dug into soft soil, gravel, and mud, and covered with a five-foot layer of sand and gravel. To allow for possible movement during an earthquake, the tube's connections to its terminal buildings are flexible (like giant universal joints) and permit movement of several inches up or down, in or out, and sideways. Parts of BART run on elevated tracks 20–30 feet in the air. The track roadbed rests on girders pinned to support columns using a special design to ensure that they won't be shaken off during an earthquake. Building subway stations in downtown San Francisco, where the soil is saturated with water (31 percent by weight), also presented special problems. Excavation was hindered by great in-

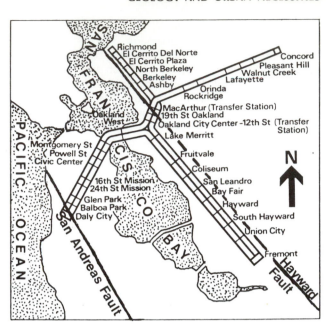

6.17 Map of the San Francisco Bay Area Rapid Transit (BART) system and major regional faults.

fluxes of water. Lowering the water table by pumping was not possible because it might have caused nearby buildings to settle and fail. To overcome the problem, a narrow trench was dug around the proposed excavation site and filled with a special wet clay "soup" (*slurry*) which held back the water. Concrete pumped into the trench forced the slurry out, and when it hardened, formed a wall inside which excavation could take place. To counteract the upward thrust of the groundwater, the foundations of the stations include concrete bases seven feet thick.

Construction of the Rotterdam subway in Holland was also hindered by the presence of a high water-table, necessitating a unique mode of construction. A trench was dug and lined with sheet-steel planking, and groundwater was allowed to seep into and fill the trench. The tunnel sections, which were made out of prefabricated concrete, were temporarily sealed shut at each end, floated into position, and then allowed to fill with water and to sink into the trench. After being joined to adjacent sections, they were then pumped dry and covered over.

The width and length of the subway cars and how much they tilt and sway may be affected by the nature of the material surrounding the tunnel. Urbanist Hans Blumenfeld has compared the Montréal and Toronto (Yonge Street) subways. The Montréal line runs a considerable part of its route in tunnels dug through solid rock. In Toronto, which rests on glacial till and lake clays that overlie the deeper Dundas Shale, cut-and-cover construction was used. An open trench was dug down to the shale, and a concrete box was laid in the trench, which was then refilled (Fig. 6.18). The tracks run through the buried concrete box. The Montréal tunnels are narrow (to minimize excavation through solid rock) and only allow passage of cars 8 feet 3 inches wide; the Toronto cars are a more spacious 10 feet 2 inches wide. The use of narrow cars in Montréal permitted the excavation of a single tunnel only, 23 feet wide and 16 feet 3 inches high at the center, which contains two sets of tracks. The Toronto tunnels are much wider, and some of the tracks run in separate tunnels. In Montréal, to further reduce tunneling costs, steeper gradients and

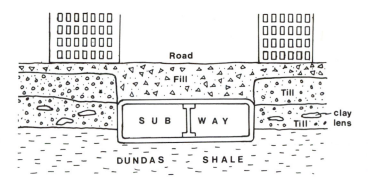

6.18 Cross section of the Yonge Street line of the Toronto Subway system.

tighter curves were employed. As a result, subway cars there are relatively short (to allow a shorter turning radius) and have rubber wheels that permit them to climb steep grades—which in places are as much as 6 percent.

The London "Underground" railway is one of the world's largest subway systems. In 1975, 278 stations were served by 251 miles of track. Ninety-seven of these miles are in tunnels: 74 miles of "tube" constructed by boring through the earth from underground working sites and 23 miles in cut-and-cover trenches. Construction of the Underground was facilitated by the presence of the London Clay, through which much of the tunnel system runs. The clay is almost the ideal substance to excavate, having the consistency of a "medium cheese" (Legget, 1973). The system may be said to have begun in the mid-nineteenth century when a London solicitor, Charles Pearson, saw the potential of underground travel as a way of avoiding street congestion. His vision was realized in 1863 when the Metropolitan Railway Company opened a four-mile stretch of sub-surface steam railway that ran from Paddington Station to Farringdon Street. In 1870, the Tower Subway was constructed by boring a tunnel under the River Thames. Electric underground railways came into existence in 1890. During the bombing of London in World War II, the Underground became temporary home for great numbers of people seeking shelter. With the start of massive air raids in Sep-

tember 1940, 177,000 people sought refuge there; subsequently an average of 60,000 people slept in the tubes each night. During this unhappy time, for many people, tunnels became the urban environment.

Today, subways in fifty cities around the world serve a combined urban population of 150 million. In the last twenty years, the number of cities with rapid transit systems has doubled, and in less than ten years from now, another thirteen cities will be added to the list. Accompanying this growth has been the development of a new urban-planning philosophy. New York regional planner Boris Pushkarev states that patterns of land development and forms of transportation "are intimately linked: compact urban forms encourage public transit; disperse forms of settlement require the automobile.If it is in the public interest to encourage public transportation . . . it is not enough to build new subway systems: *one must also build the kinds of cities that go with them.*" (1977, p. 21). Such a city will make full use of the third dimension: depth. Underground space can be utilized for structures not requiring natural light, such as parking garages, movie theaters, and warehouses (Macaulay, 1977). Stations in Tokyo are already integrated with large shopping arcades. In this manner, the use of underground railways meshes with other aspects of urban existence, liberating them from the stigma of crime, danger, and claustrophobic isolation. Also, since they are shielded by the natural insulation of the earth, underground facilities require minimal expenditures of energy for heating and cooling. Furthermore, they free surface areas for other uses.

In Kansas City, Missouri, for instance, the presence of extensive underground quarries within flat-lying, thick-bedded limestone has permitted subsurface development on a scale that has made the city "the capital of underground space" (Stauffer, Sr., 1973; Parizek, 1978). Numerous warehouses, factories, and offices already occupy more than 15 million square feet at depths of 30–200 feet beneath the surface. The excellent insulation of the quarry galleries make them particularly ideal for frozen-food storage; Kansas City has about one-tenth of such storage space in the nation, most of it underground. Similarly, ease of controlling humidity makes the space ideal for paper storage and printing, and for the setting of lacquers and glues.

An added advantage to the use of such quarries is that the income derived from "secondary" use makes underground quarrying more economically competitive with surface quarrying and unsightly surface workings and abandoned surface quarry sites may be avoided. If secondary use is planned in advance, the quarry galleries may be shaped and excavated in a manner commensurate with their future use.

A key geologic factor that has made extensive underground development possible in Kansas City is the presence of impermeable shale above the limestone. The shale prevents groundwater from reaching the limestone, thus keeping the quarry galleries dry and virtually eliminating potential weakening and collapse of the limestone due to solution.

Some subsurface conditions may not permit extensive underground development, and alternative designs must be sought. For example, the proposed Dade County Rapid Transit System for the Miami, Florida, area will have to be elevated or built at street level because of the high level of the water table within the underlying limestones. Thus, as cities seek to expand underground, knowledge of subsurface geologic conditions will become increasingly vital.

Looking further into the future, if Doxiadis's (1968) vision of a globe-encircling city, *ecumenopolis,* becomes reality, the role of underground transit in particular may leap in importance. Already, a Rand Corporation engineer, Dr. Robert M. Salter, has affirmed the feasibility of a coast-to-coast super-subway system in which trains would cross the continent in less than an hour, including a stop at Dallas. The train would be electromagnetically supported in a vacuum to reduce friction. A super-subway system linking cities such as New York, Dallas, and Los Angeles would cost on the order of $250–$500 billion, but would be economically viable with a $6 fare if four million riders rode each way daily. Thus, theoretically, one could live in California and commute daily to New York. For such fantasies to be translated into reality, detailed investigation of subsurface geologic conditions across entire continents would be necessary.

Short-term Geologic Hazards

By most of humankind, the earth is considered benign, the source of life, the universal mother. She may at times be stingy or grudging in her gifts, but is generally revered as a source of reassurance, stability, and continuity. However, in some parts of the globe and on certain unhappy occasions, the innate, blind power of the earth is revealed: volcanoes erupt, rivers flood, earthquakes shake and tear the ground, the waters of the ocean invade the land. Amidst the resulting disruption and chaos, humans view the altered face of their familiar world and in some form or another ask the question: how have the gods been offended? To a geologist, the ''gods'' are the natural equilibria and processes of the planet, and they have not been offended, merely active. Geologic processes are hazardous—cause inconvenience, expense or physical danger to humans—only if they or their works or possessions are in the wrong place at the wrong time. Human occupance of ''hazardous'' terrain stems in large part from the fact that such terrain is *not usually* hazardous. That is, the processes that are hazardous tend to be intermittent, and vary considerably in their rate and magnitude. If, for example, volcanoes erupted continuously or the volume of flow of a stream was constant throughout the year, there would be little hazard attendant upon these processes. Elements of surprise and unpredictability would be absent, regions of danger would be obvious and unchanging, and with a minimum of good sense could be avoided. Nature, however, does not operate in such a simple way. Volcanic eruptions are intermittent, erratic, and variable in violence; the volume of flow of a stream does rise and fall, reaching on occasion unwanted and unsuspected maxima and minima.

Thus, it is this irregularity and relative infrequence of the extremes of rate and magnitude that geologic processes can achieve that are the chief source of hazard. Humans have short

memories. Whether for reasons of incurable optimism or as a means of retaining psychological stability, individuals and groups who have not had first-hand experience of disaster commonly operate as if they were immune to catastrophe. For reasons that encompass necessity,
lack of choice, ignorance, perversity, greed, and conscious acceptance of risk, people in increasing numbers place houses on floodplains or in the beds of intermittent streams, construct
hospitals and schools in active earthquake belts, inhabit the slopes of volcanoes, excavate and
steepen unstable mountain slopes, and so on. Such dangerous and expensive practices would
certainly be less common if people had personal acquaintance with the dangers involved.
Since it is unlikely (fortunately) that most people will have other than vicarious experience of
the more dramatic natural geologic catastrophes, the average person will remain skeptical, un-
interested, or ignorant of the possibility of his or her own involvement. On the other hand, the
more common and less dramatic—but ultimately often more costly—geologic hazards which
affect great numbers of people either have not crossed the threshold of their consciousness, are
not understood for what they are, or are considered inevitable and unavoidable. It therefore is
clearly the responsibility of both public and private institutions, which have collective experience, to be aware of the dangers and to initiate appropriate responses.

The first step is awareness of the possibility of danger, which can be appreciated only
through understanding geologic processes. Out of such understanding, a far-sighted point of
view may be developed, enabling the recognition of geologic hazards. Codes and regulations
relating to land-use can be enforced. New and improved modes of construction and design can
be developed where necessary. Inadequate structures can be strengthened or relocated or dismantled. Where possible, methods of hazard prediction and control can be implemented. The
issuance of warnings can be made routine. Insurance and aid programs can be instituted.

Urban regions are particularly vulnerable to geologic hazards because of the density of
structures and population. Furthermore, many geologic hazards are triggered by human interference with the natural environment. As urban areas expand at an accelerating pace, the
threat posed by geologic hazards increases accordingly. It is estimated that during the period
1970–2000, property damage and the dollar equivalent of life-loss directly attributable to geologic processes and to loss of mineral resources from urbanization will amount to more than
$55 billion in California (Urban Geology Master Plan for Calif., 1973). This amount is greater
by 10 percent than losses expected from fire during the same period. Especially significant is
the estimate that $38 billion of these projected losses could be avoided if all feasible loss-
reduction measures were rigorously applied. The cost of such measures in California is estimated at $6 billion. It is evident, therefore, that the recognition of geologic hazards and the
development of appropriate responses are desirable not only for humanitarian reasons but for
economic reasons as well.

The geologic hazards considered in Part II are those caused by earthquakes and tsunamis,
landslides, volcanism, stream and coastal flooding, erosion and sedimentation, and subsidence

and collapse. For sake of convenience, each hazard is discussed separately, but it cannot be overemphasized that often there is a spatial and temporal relationship between hazards of different types. Earthquakes commonly are accompanied by landslides and tsunamis; subsidence can generate earthquakes and landslides; erosion and sedimentation are opposite sides of the same coin. In broader perspective, volcanism, earthquakes, and any instances of sea-level change, together with accompanying landslides, tsunamis, and much erosion and sedimentation may all be attributed to movements of lithospheric plates.

Long-term geologic hazards, which result from cumulative processes over hundreds or thousands of years are investigated in Part III.

7. Earthquakes and Tsunamis

In the last thousand years, more than three million people have lost their lives due to the seismic instability of the earth. A single earthquake in Shenshi, China in 1556 killed 830,000 people. In the eighteenth century, the city of Lisbon, Portugal was destroyed as the ground trembled; tens of thousands perished. In 1906, San Francisco was largely demolished by an earthquake and fire that killed 700 people. In Tokyo, 140,000 were killed in 1923 as the city was shaken and then consumed by fire. Nineteen thousand died in Guatemala in 1976; houses crashed to the ground and landslides roared down mountain slopes. During the 25-year period from 1926 to 1950, earthquakes killed 350,000 people and caused losses of ten billion dollars.

Death and damage due to seismic activity will increase as population multiplies and urbanization spreads. If an earthquake similar to the one that hit San Francisco in 1906 were to reoccur there today, more than 10,000 deaths and 40,000 injuries could be expected (Fig. 7.1). Furthermore, the likely catastrophic failure of three dams in the San Francisco Bay Area would expose 50,000–130,000 downstream residents to flooding. Bridges across the Bay and the underwater subway tube probably would be severely damaged, as would freeways and other avenues of transport and com-munication. Fully half the hospital facilities would most likely be knocked out of service. As the number of people living in the Bay Area rises from 4.6 million in 1970 to perhaps 7.6 million in the year 2000, the potential for catastrophe looms ever larger. (In 1906, the population of the Bay Area was only about 800,000.)

Great earthquakes (considered in terms of energy release rather than damage pro-duced) occur approximately every two years; twenty *major* and 200 *moderate* earthquakes occur each year. Although less lethal because they occur more often, mod-erate earthquakes cause greater cumulative damage than larger earthquakes. In Califor-nia it is estimated that between 1970 and 2000, losses due to earthquake shaking will total $21 billion (*Urban Geology Master Plan for Calif.*, 1973). Other heavily popu-lated areas throughout the world face simi-lar hazard.

CAUSES AND CHARACTERISTICS OF EARTHQUAKES

When sufficient stress is applied to rocks they may bend (*fold*), develop simple frac-tures (*joints*), or form fractures along which displacement parallel to the fractures takes place (faults) (see Fig. 7.13). Most earth-quakes occur when portions of the earth's

7.1 San Francisco City Hall after the earthquake of 1906.

lithosphere (upper brittle shell) that have been subjected to increasing stress from the plastically deforming asthenosphere give way and rupture along faults. (Those few earthquakes associated with volcanic eruptions or other local earth disturbances will not be considered here.) Not all fault displacements reach the surface of the earth; however, when rocks break or fault, even at depth, energy in the form of vibrations radiates outward in all directions and may encircle the globe. The actual place where the faulting occurs is the *focus* of the earthquake; most foci of destructive earthquakes are less than 25 miles beneath the earth's surface. The point on the earth's surface directly over the focus of an earthquake is called the *epicenter*.

Earthquakes last only a matter of seconds or minutes. For example, the main earthquake that leveled much of Managua, Nicaragua in 1972, and killed thousands of people lasted only ten seconds. During only a few moments thousands of square miles of the earth's surface may shift laterally or vertically as much as ten or twenty feet or even more. The ground often displays a rolling, wave-like motion that can trigger incipient landslides; vibrations may compact soil or sediment, causing irregular subsidence and the opening up of fractures and fissures. If fine, water-saturated sediment is disturbed it may liquify and flow. An earthquake beneath the ocean can cause abrupt movements of the ocean floor that generate "tidal waves" (*tsunamis*) (Fig. 7.2). Improperly

7.2 Boats thrown ashore by the tsunami generated by the Alaska
earthquake of 1964.

designed and built or injudiciously situated
structures are likely to break apart or collapse.

After a major earthquake, numerous *aftershocks* of gradually diminishing magnitude and frequency may take place over
periods of days or months. Such aftershocks
are quite capable of causing fresh damage
and commonly hinder recovery efforts.

When the distribution of earthquakes is
examined by plotting the locations of epicenters on a world map, it may be seen that
the major earthquake, or *seismic,* zones
(Fig. 7.3) are located along the boundaries
of lithospheric plates (Fig. 7.4). It is movement of the lithospheric plates with respect
to one another that causes the buildup of

stresses that finally result in the failure of
rocks through faulting. Such movements
have been in progress for tens or hundreds
of millions of years and are, in terms of our
short life-span, permanent.

Earthquakes that occur away from plate
boundaries may be due to isostatic readjust-
ments of the earth's crust (in response to the
redistribution of sediment over the earth's
surface, to the erosion of mountain ranges,
or to the melting or accumulation of ice) or
to internal stresses built up in lithospheric
plates during their lateral movement. Whatever the ultimate cause of the stresses, they
are of a magnitude and duration that places
them beyond the power of human interference. The stress-producing mechanisms

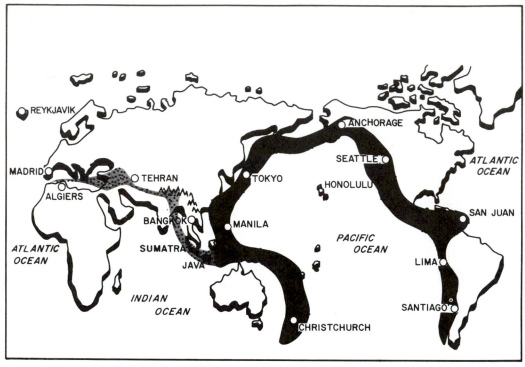

7.3 World map showing major zones of earthquake activity. Ninety-seven percent of all earthquakes take place within these zones.

cannot be stopped, but eventually it may be possible to control, to some extent, the frequency and magnitude of the earthquakes they cause. Until that time, we must learn how to live with earthquakes and to lessen seismically induced damage.

Hazards

Large-scale earthquake hazard is primarily an *urban phenomenon,* since vibratory ground motion, ground failure (slippage of the ground or loss of its ability to support heavy structures), and ground displacement due to faulting cause the most damage where humans and their structures are concentrated. Injury and death may result from partial or total collapse of urban structures, or from the impact of falling objects. On the

other hand, a person in a flat, open field during an earthquake is likely only to be knocked off his or her feet.

Very often, damage due to ground shaking, ground failure, and auxiliary hazards such as collapse of dams, fire, disease, tsunamis, or landslides is greater than damage due to displacement of the ground along faults.

Factors determining the degree of hazard include the magnitude of the earthquake, proximity to the epicenter, the type of rock material upon which structures are erected, landslide susceptibility, extent and type of earth displacement, design of structures and the competence with which they are built, land-use policies, and the extent and intensity of urbanization. Each of these factors is discussed below.

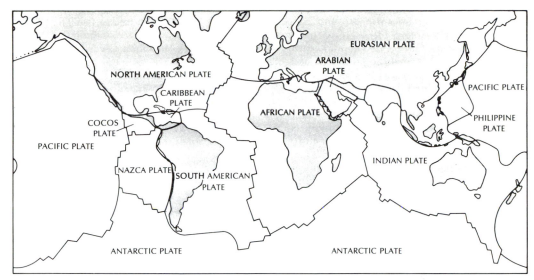

7.4 World map showing the boundaries of lithospheric plates. Within the earth's mantle is a plastic zone (the *asthenosphere*) which undergoes continual, slow movements. These movements exert an irresistably powerful drag upon the overlying rigid *lithosphere*. As a result, the lithosphere has broken into a dozen or so large fragments (*plates*) that gradually move a few inches a year, slowly colliding, splitting apart, or riding past one another, carrying with them the whole or parts of continents and ocean basins. At the margins or junctions of the plates are found the sites of most earthquakes, volcanic eruptions, and accompanying landslides.

Magnitude and Intensity

The *magnitude* of an earthquake refers to the amount of energy released during a seismic event as calculated from amplitudes of ground motions indicated on seismographs. An open-ended scale of relative magnitudes has been devised by seismologist Charles Richter, on which any earthquake may be assigned a number called the "Richter magnitude" (M). Earthquakes that are felt only near their epicenters are M = 2. Those causing local damage range from about M = 4.5 to 5.0. The Caracas quake of 1967 (M = 6.5) and the San Fernando earthquake of 1971 (M = 6.6) are considered moderate. Major earthquakes are M = 7.0 to 7.75. Great earthquakes, such as those in San Francisco in 1906 (M = 8.3) and in Anchorage, Alaska, in 1964 (M = 8.4), range from M = 7.9 to 8.5. The greatest earthquakes known, such as the Japanese earthquake of 1933 and the earthquake under the eastern margin of the Indian Ocean near the East Indies (1977) were M = 8.9. The Richter magnitude scale is arranged so that each number represents a release of energy about 30–35 times as great as the preceding number.

Table 7.1. Frequency of occurrence of earthquakes of different magnitudes. (After B. Gutenberg and C. F. Richter, 1954)

Magnitude	Frequency (per year)
3.0–3.9	49,000
4.0–4.9	6,200
5.0–5.9	800
6.0–6.9	120
7.0–7.9	18
8.0–8.9	1

Table 7.2. Modified Mercalli scale of earthquake intensities. (After J. T. Alfors *et al*, 1973)

THE MERCALLI INTENSITY SCALE
(As modified by Charles F. Richter in 1956 and rearranged)

If most of these effects are observed   *then the intensity is:*

Earthquake shaking not felt. But people may observe marginal effects of large distance earthquakes without identifying these effects as earthquake-caused. Among them: trees, structures, liquids, bodies of water sway slowly, or doors swing slowly. — **I**

Effect on people: Shaking felt by those at rest, especially if they are indoors, and by those on upper floors. — **II**

Effect on people: Felt by many people indoors. Some can estimate duration of shaking. But many may not recognize shaking of building as caused by an earthquake; the shaking is like that caused by the passing of light trucks. — **III**

Effect on people: During the day felt indoors by most, outdoors by a few. Some awakened at night.
Other effects: Hanging objects swing.
Structural effects: Windows or doors rattle. Wooden walls and frames creak. — **IV**

Effect on people: Felt by everyone indoors. Many estimate duration of shaking. But they still may not recognize it as caused by an earthquake. The shaking is like that caused by the passing of heavy trucks, though sometimes like a jolt, as if a heavy ball had struck the walls.
Other effects: Hanging objects swing. Standing autos rock. Crockery clashes, dishes rattle or glasses clink.
Structural effects: Doors close, open, or swing. Windows rattle. — **V**

Effect on people: Felt by everyone indoors and by most people outdoors. Many now estimate not only the duration of shaking but also its direction and have no doubt as to its cause. Sleepers wakened.
Other effects: Hanging objects swing. Shutters or pictures move. Pendulum clocks stop, start or change rate. Standing autos rock. Crockery clashes, dishes rattle or glasses clink. Liquids disturbed, some spilled. Small unstable objects displaced or upset.
Structural effects: Weak plaster and Masonry D* crack. Windows break. Doors close, open, or swing. — **VI**

Effect on people: Felt by everyone. Many are frightened and run outdoors. People walk unsteadily.
Other effects: Small church or school bells ring. Pictures thrown off walls, knicknacks and books off shelves. Dishes or glasses broken. Furniture moved or overturned. Trees, bushes shake visibly, or rustle.
Structural effects: Masonry D* damaged; some cracks in Masonry C*. Weak chimneys break at roof line. Plaster, loose bricks, stones, tiles, cornices, unbraced parapets, and architectural ornaments fall. Concrete irrigation ditches damaged. — **VII**

Effect on people: Difficult to stand. Shaking noticed by auto drivers.
Other effects: Waves on ponds; water turbid with mud. Small slides and caving in along sand or gravel banks. Large bells ring. Furniture broken. Hanging objects quiver.
Structural effects: Masonry D* heavily damaged; Masonry C* damaged, partially collapses in some cases; some damage to Masonry B*; none to Masonry A*. Stucco and some masonry walls fall. Chimneys, factory stacks, monuments, towers, elevated tanks twist or fall. Frame houses moved on foundations if not bolted down; loose panel walls thrown out. Decayed piling broken off. — **VIII**

Effect on people: General fright. People thrown to ground.
Other effects: Changes in flow or temperature of springs and wells. Cracks in wet ground and on steep slopes. Steering of autos affected. Branches broken from trees.
Structural effects: Masonry D* destroyed; Masonry C* heavily damaged, sometimes with complete collapse; Masonry B* seriously damaged. General damage to foundations. Frame structures, if not bolted, shifted off foundations. Frames racked. Reservoirs seriously damaged. Underground pipes broken. — **IX**

If most of these effects are observed	then the intensity is:
Effect on people: General panic. *Other effects:* Conspicuous cracks in ground. In areas of soft ground, sand is ejected through holes and piles up into a small crater, and, in muddy areas, water fountains are formed. *Structural effects:* Most masonry and frame structures destroyed along with their foundations. Some well-built wooden structures and bridges destroyed. Serious damage to dams, dikes, and embankments. Railroads bent slightly.	X
Effect on people: General panic. *Other effects:* Large landslides. Water thrown on banks of canals, rivers, lakes, etc. Sand and mud shifted horizontally on beaches and flat land. *Structural effects:* General destruction of buildings. Underground pipelines completely out of service. Railroads bent greatly.	XI

If most of these effects are observed	then the intensity is:
Effect on people: General panic. *Other effects:* Same as for Intensity X. *Structural effects:* Damage nearly total, the ultimate catastrophe. *Other effects:* Large rock masses displaced. Lines of sight and level distorted. Objects thrown into air.	XII

*Masonry A: Good workmanship and mortar, reinforced, designed to resist lateral forces.
Masonry B: Good workmanship and mortar, reinforced.
Masonry C: Good workmanship and mortar, unreinforced.
Masonry D: Poor workmanship and mortar and weak materials, like adobe.

Table 7.1 suggests the frequency of earthquakes of different magnitudes. California, for example, in the 200 years for which records have been kept, has had three great earthquakes, more than 12 major earthquakes, and more than 60 moderate ones (Oakeshott, 1976).

The *intensity* of an earthquake refers to the degree of ground motion experienced by those present or inferred by inspection of damage at a given locality. Thus a single earthquake will have one magnitude, but many intensities, depending upon where the effects are observed. A scale of earthquake intensities in common use is the Modified Mercalli Scale (MM) shown in Table 7.2. In general, intensity diminishes as the distance from the epicenter increases; however, the nature of the material at or near the earth's surface can outweigh the distance effect. Structures placed on loose soil or sediment will often suffer greater damage from vibration than will those built on bedrock. Structures on artificial fill are especially susceptible to vibrational damage. Figure 7.5 is an isoseismal map showing zones of earthquake intensity associated with the St. Lawrence earthquake of 1925. (An *isoseism* is a line of equal earthquake intensity).

Surface Faulting

Hazard due to surface displacement by faulting depends upon the likelihood of movement, the type and magnitude of slippage, and the design and number of structures and their proximity to a fault or fault zone. Much of the earth's surface is characterized by a dense network of faults along which some movement has taken place during geologic time. Likelihood of future movement along a fault may be judged from the amount of time that has passed since it last moved: the Atomic Energy Commission, for example, considers a fault potentially dangerous if it has been active once within the last 35,000 years or more than once within the last half million years. Knowledge of such activity may be obtained from historic records or careful on-site geologic investigation.

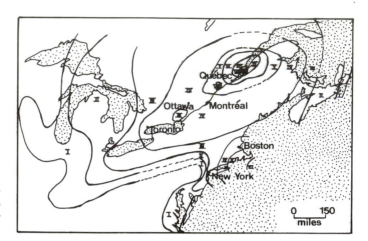

7.5 The effects of the St. Lawrence earthquake of 1925. Roman numerals indicate earthquake intensity.

7.6 Aerial photo of land use along the Hayward fault trace, San Francisco Bay Area, California. The fault runs along the left edge of the hills.

138

Displacements along a fault may range from a fraction of an inch up to tens of feet. Movement along the San Andreas Fault during the San Francisco Earthquake of 1906 was 20 feet in a horizontal sense. Vertical movements, such as took place during the 1971 San Fernando Earthquake or that may take place near Salt Lake City, may be as much as 40–50 feet during a single earthquake, and are potentially more damaging than San Andreas-type horizontal displacements.

It is thought that in the event of another earthquake of M = 8.3 in the San Francisco region, damage caused by surface faulting would occur mainly within 300 yards of the San Andreas Fault (Algermissen, Rinehart, and Stepp, 1973). Perhaps the best method of lessening such hazard along active faults is the development of land-use regulations. Land along dangerous faults may be best used as recreational areas, cemeteries, or parking lots, rather than for residential or institutional purposes (Figs. 7.6 and 7.7). Another alternative is to require buildings to be set back appropriate distances (50–100 feet) from active faults.

Ground Shaking

In many instances, ground shaking causes the most widespread damage of all earthquake-associated hazards. Such damage is greatly affected by building design and construction. Earthquake magnitude, distance from the epicenter, and the response of surficial geologic materials to bedrock motion control ground shaking. Bedrock vibration occurring at frequencies close to the natural (*resonant*) frequencies of the soil or of manmade structures will amplify deformation and stress. The effect is analogous to pushing a child on a swing. If the swing is pushed rhythmically, in time with its natural period, it is easy to maintain or to increase the swinging motion. If it is pushed erratically or out-of-step, the swinging movement will diminish. Similarly, if the ground that a building rests on shakes "in time" with the natural vibration of the building, it can eventually shake the building apart. This is most likely to occur if the building rests on loose surficial material: vibrations from the bedrock may be amplified as they move through the loose material and again amplified on reaching the building.

Duration of shaking is also a key factor in producing damage since failure of a structure or its foundation bed commonly depends upon the cumulative number of vibrational cycles as well as the amplitude of the deformation. In a general way, the fundamental frequency of building vibration is related to its height (or number of stories). The natural frequency of vibration in soil or sediment is related to its firmness, thickness, and degree of saturation (Fig. 7.8). Taller buildings have lower fundamental

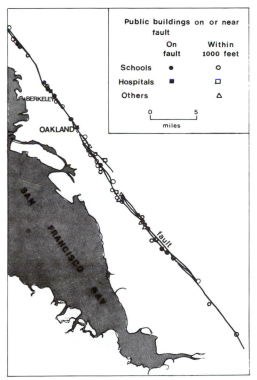

Public buildings on or near fault

	On fault	Within 1000 feet
Schools	●	○
Hospitals	■	□
Others		△

0 _____ 5
miles

7.7 Schools, hospitals, and other public buildings on or near the Hayward fault.

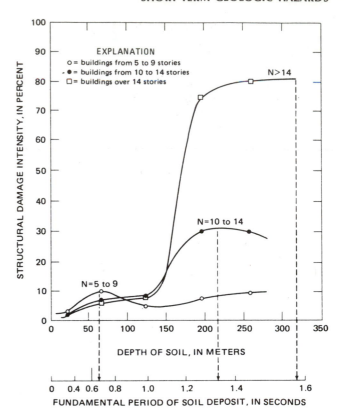

7.8 Graph showing the relationship between structural damage to buildings of different heights, soil depth, and the computed fundamental period of vibration of soil deposits. N = number of stories. Note that when the period is short, buildings from 5–9 stories are damaged most; for longer periods, damage to higher structures increases.

frequencies (longer periods), and are especially subject to damage when they stand on deep, loose material, such as alluvium or artificial fill (Nichols and Buchanan-Banks, 1974). During the 1906 San Francisco earthquake, much damage occurred in areas of thick, soft sediment in the downtown area (Fig. 7.9). A similar relationship was noted for the Caracas earthquake of 1967.

Caracas, Venezuela, 1967

On July 29, 1967, a moderate earthquake (M = 6.5) shook the northern coast of Venezuela for 50–60 seconds. During that time, about 277 people were killed and many millions of dollars of damage occurred in and around the city of Caracas. The Caracas earthquake is of special interest to inhabitants of the western United States because

the geology of northern Venezuela is in many ways similar to areas along the San Andreas Fault, and also because most loss of life and damage was connected with the collapse of high-rise apartment houses built according to specifications similar to the Uniform Building Code for earthquake-prone areas of North America (Steinbrugge and Cluff, 1968).

Maximum damage was inflicted on structures built on alluvial material, either in the valley of Caracas or along the coast. Most loss of life occurred when four high-rise buildings totally collapsed in one small area of Caracas and another collapsed partially in the coastal town of Caraballeda. There was relatively little damage to structures built on bedrock. Most of the high-rise buildings, of which about 1000 of ten to thirty stories were erected from 1958 to 1968, were con-

7.9 Aerial photo of San Francisco showing relationship of greatest
damage in the 1906 earthquake (patterned) to areas of former bay
and marshlands (former land's edge shown by solid line).

structed of reinforced concrete frames designed to be earthquake-resistant. The local
building code had been based on those used
in California, which have been recommended for large areas of Washington,
Oregon, Montana, Utah, and elsewhere.

According to Karl Steinbrugge, a renowned
structural engineer, and Lloyd Cluff, an engineering geologist, ''The quality of reinforced concrete construction was good in
the newer buildings, and engineering design
was also generally good. Damage to the

reinforced concrete frames at their joints showed an absence of confining steel; while this is considered to be poor practice by some authorities, it nevertheless is a commonly followed practice in much of the United States. . . ." (1968, p. 10).

Ground Failure

Ground failure in the form of landslides and uneven land settlement are commonly associated with earthquakes, and are illustrated in the following studies of Anchorage, Alaska, and California's San Fernando Valley. The likelihood of earthquake vibrations triggering landslides depends upon various factors, including the nature of the surface materials, steepness of slope, and surface and subsurface drainage. Further discussion of landslides is found in Chapter 8.

Anchorage, Alaska, 1964

On March 27, 1964, Good Friday, at 5:36 PM local time, an earthquake of Richter magnitude 8.4 struck south-central Alaska. It created a damage zone covering an area of 50,000 square miles and a shock that was felt throughout an area of half a million square miles (Fig. 7.10). The focus was 10 miles or so beneath the floor of Prince William Sound, just 80 miles east and slightly south of the city of Anchorage. Compared to the San Francisco earthquake of 1906, which lasted 65 seconds, the Anchorage earthquake was interminably long: the ground shook for three to four minutes. The amount of energy released was twice that of the San Francisco quake. The earth's crust was raised more than 50 feet in some places and lowered as much as 7 feet in others; horizontal displacements of tens of feet were measured. Numerous snowslides, rockfalls, and subareal and submarine landslides were triggered. A seismic sea wave (*tsunami*) generated by the earthquake swept from the Gulf of Alaska all the way to the Antarctic, causing extensive damage in

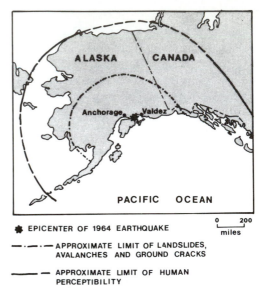

EPICENTER OF 1964 EARTHQUAKE

— · —APPROXIMATE LIMIT OF LANDSLIDES, AVALANCHES AND GROUND CRACKS

——— APPROXIMATE LIMIT OF HUMAN PERCEPTIBILITY

7.10 The epicenter of the 1964 Alaska earthquake and the area affected by the quake.

British Columbia and taking 16 lives in Oregon and California. Water levels in wells fluctuated in places as far away as South Africa. In Alaska itself, 115 people were killed. This number might have been 50 times higher if the earthquake had not taken place on a holiday when most schools and offices were deserted. Most property damage was caused by landslides. In Anchorage, hundreds of houses were destroyed and many commercial buildings collapsed. Oil-storage tanks ruptured and burned in the nearby towns of Valdez, Seward, and Whittier, and Kodiak was inundated by the ocean. The economy of much of the state was crippled from extensive damage to port and harbor facilities, the collapse of highway bridges, and the disruption of many miles of railroad lines and roads (Krauskopf, 1971).

Within Anchorage itself, sections of the city were destroyed as clays and sands of the underlying Bootlegger Cove formation lost their strength, causing overlying sediments and the structures they supported to slide laterally (Fig. 7.11). The formation

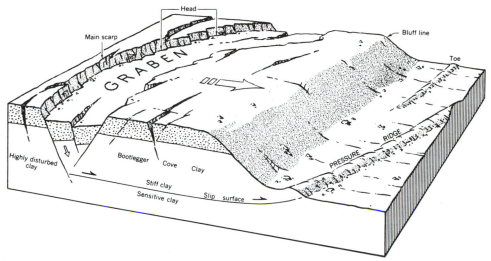

7.11 Block diagram showing how the Bootlegger Cove clay slid during the 1964 Alaska earthquake.

failed due to the presence of *sensitive clays* and to the *liquefaction* of sand lenses within the clay. Sensitive clay is clay whose strength is drastically reduced when subjected to the kneading or squeezing engendered by earthquake vibrations. Liquefaction is caused by the increase in *pore pressure* (water pressure between grains) of silt or sand that can be caused by earthquake vibrations. If pore pressure exceeds external pressure, contact between grains will be lost and sediment will liquefy, temporarily losing its capacity to support structures until the water can drain away (See also Chapters 6 and 8).

Ground failure and subsequent land slippage did not start until 1.5 minutes after strong ground shaking began. If the earthquake had been of shorter duration, there would have been few or no landslides, and investigators would have been misled as to the stability of slopes underlain by sensitive clays during earthquakes (Seed, 1973). Figure 7.12 illustrates the chaotic jumble of houses in the Turnagain Heights section of Anchorage after the Bootlegger Cove formation failed. (It is important to note that a similar clay underlies much of the heavily

populated, seismically active Salt Lake City region.)

At Valdez, which is situated at the seaward edge of a large delta composed of saturated silty sand and gravel, the earthquake triggered a massive submarine slide that destroyed the harbor facility and near-shore installations by removing their foundational support. A tsunami generated by the slide did additional damage to the downtown area. Valdez now serves as the terminus of the Alaska Pipeline.

Further discussion of the Anchorage earthquake and of the geology of Anchorage may be found in other parts of this chapter and in Chap. 8 and Fig. 6.10.

San Fernando Valley, 1971

On February 9, 1971, the San Fernando region, located in the northern part of the Los Angeles metropolitan area, was struck by an earthquake registering 6.6 on the Richter scale. Sixty-five people were killed, thousands injured, and property loss was on the order of half a billion dollars. Yet in terms of its magnitude, the earthquake was moderate. In southern California, 37 shocks

7.12 Aerial photo of the landslide area at Turnagain Heights, Anchorage, Alaska, after the 1964 earthquake.

of this magnitude or greater and two shocks greater than $M = 8.0$ may be expected in any 100-year period (Hill, 1971). In terms of lives lost, the San Fernando earthquake was the third worst in the state's history, exceeded only by the San Francisco quake of 1906 and the Long Beach quake of 1933. Most loss of lives was due to collapse of part of Sylmar Veterans Hospital, where two unreinforced masonry buildings failed. The buildings were more than 40 years old, built before the general adoption of modern codes requiring earthquake-resistant design. At Olive View Hospital, a number of new reinforced-concrete buildings were severely damaged, killing three people, and a two-story building "pancaked," its second floor

dropping onto the first. An Interstate Highway interchange collapsed, as did a number of associated bridges, killing two men in a pickup truck.

Numerous landslides accompanied the earthquake. Perhaps the potentially most lethal one occurred on the upstream face of the Lower Van Norman Dam, an old, hydraulic earthfill structure. An 1800-foot-long section of the dam slid into the reservoir, leaving the effective height of the dam only five feet above the level of the water. If the dam had failed (and it is considered that if the shaking had lasted two seconds longer, the dam *would* have failed) a destructive flood would have swept through the residential area below the dam in which

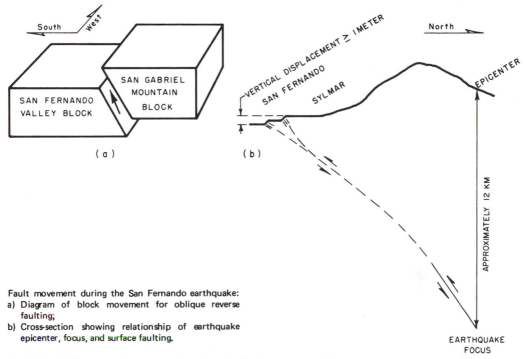

Fault movement during the San Fernando earthquake:
a) Diagram of block movement for oblique reverse faulting;
b) Cross-section showing relationship of earthquake epicenter, focus, and surface faulting.

7.13 Block diagram and cross section showing fault movement during the San Fernando earthquake.

80,000 people lived. As it was, the residents of the downstream area were evacuated for four days until the water in the reservoir could be lowered to a safe level. (It is worth noting that hundreds of old earth dams exist in seismic areas of the United States, which might fail if shaken strongly (Housner, 1973).

The Juvenile Hall landslide, which involved an area almost a mile long, was interesting in that it resulted from liquefaction of a shallow sand layer and moved laterally down a failure surface with a slope of only 2.5 percent (Nicols and Buchanan-Banks, 1974). It is reported that more than a thousand landslides, ranging in length from 50 to 1000 feet, were triggered in the hilly and mountainous terrain above the San Fernando Valley (Morton, 1971).

The cause of the earthquake was slippage along the reverse fault that separates the San Fernando Valley from the San Gabriel Mountains. Figure 7.13 is a diagrammatic block diagram (a) and cross-section (b) of the fault. Figure 7.14 is a generalized geologic map and cross section of the San Fernando area.

Building Design

Buildings normally are designed to withstand substantial vertical stress. Few buildings collapse due to their own weight. Construction designed to withstand substantial horizontal stress, however, is less common. Lateral or horizontal stress outside earthquake zones is usually due only to forces exerted by winds. During earthquakes, structures are often subjected to considerable lateral stress. The international Uniform Building Code requires that buildings be able to (1) resist minor earthquakes with-

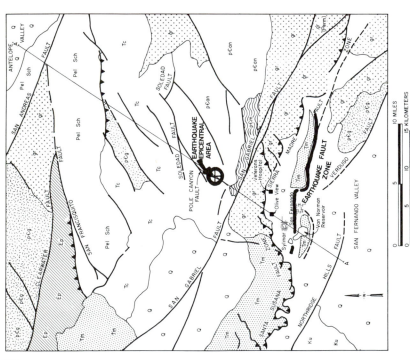

7.14 (*left*) Generalized geologic map of the San Fernando area, showing principal geologic units, the epicentral zone, and the fault zones along which movement took place. (*right*) Cross section along line A-A'.

out damage; (2) resist moderate earthquakes without structural damage, but with some non-structural damage allowed; (3) resist major earthquakes without collapse but with some structural damage as well as non-structural damage allowed. *Structural damage* may be defined as that affecting the main support system of a structure, such as supporting columns and beams or bearing walls. Non-structural, or architectural, damage affects elements such as stairways, windows, partitions, elevators, or lighting fixtures. Thus, the seismic provisions of building codes are not intended to prevent all damage (Page *et al*, 1975). Furthermore, opinions as to what is proper building design vary considerably. Post-earthquake studies in the Anchorage region indicate that "present knowledge of the dynamic behavior of soils is not sufficient to give confidence in future earthquake-resistant design and analysis. Additional research is needed on the properties of soils in relation to earthquake hazards" (Scott, 1973, p. 49). Spurred by evaluation of earthquake damage in Anchorage that indicated serious deficiencies in the building code and in structural design, Los Angeles passed an ordinance "requiring all new buildings over 10 stories or more in height to be outfitted with three strong-motion accelerographs . . . to record accurate information about earthquake ground motion and building motions for the improvement and verification of earthquake-resistant design" (Housner and Jennings, 1973, p. 245). Building codes are inadequate in other ways as well. After the 1933 earthquake in Long Beach, California, guidelines for school construction were established; however, schools constructed before 1933 were not affected. Only in 1967 did the state finally decide that pre-1933 schools should be inspected. Lack of retroactivity and enforcement of existing codes is a general problem. In San Francisco, 58 percent of the 153,400 buildings were constructuted before there was a nominal earthquake requirement (1933), and 76 percent before there was a local design code (1948). Furthermore, good engineering generally is in short supply; many engineers do not know or care that codes are minimal and inadequate (Fried, 1973). In California, for instance, many practicing engineers have been trained out-of-state, and have no practical knowledge of earthquake engineering. Even when engineering is sophisticated, workmanship is very sloppy and inadequately inspected, and suppliers of materials sometimes provide mislabelled goods. Development of adequate codes is hindered by lack of money to acquire the necessary knowledge, and by pressure from real estate interests against enactment and enforcement of strict codes (Fried, 1973). Also, local governments often permit development of marginally safe lands because they want a broader tax base. Such development is often federally funded in part. A blatant example of poor zoning is the presence of thirty-three schools and three hospitals within 1000 feet of the San Andreas Fault along the 30-mile stretch between Freemont and Albany in the San Francisco Bay Area.

As noted, damage to buildings falls into two categories: (1) damage to the structural elements that provide strength to the building; (2) damage to non-structural elements. In the 1964 Anchorage earthquake, the cost of damage to architectural elements was much greater than that to structural elements. Generally, small residential buildings of cross-braced wood-frame construction fare better than larger or masonry buildings. Adobe buildings are particularly vulnerable to collapse, as was demonstrated in the 1976 Guatemala earthquake. In the Anchorage region, "Most, but by no means all, structural failures were associated with inadequate connections of structural members." (Berg, 1973, p. 247) *Hammering* damage occurred where buildings of different heights knocked against each other; if such buildings were connected so that they would oscillate as a unit, such damage could be minimized. Unnecessary dead loads such as heavy roofs should also be avoided, and the use of lightweight materials for non-structural elements encouraged (Hauf, 1973). *Falling missiles* such as dislodged concrete panels, exterior sun-shading devices and veneers should be eliminated.

Adequate design and construction of oil storage tanks, with special attention paid to the strength of piping connections and valves is important to avoid the possibility of spills and fire.

Proper design of water systems to insure supplies for fire-fighting is of extreme importance. The earthquakes that struck San Francisco in 1906 and Tokyo in 1923 broke the water mains and subsequent fires destroyed both cities. Furthermore, disruption of water-supply systems together with broken sewer lines can lead to the outbreak of contagious disease—a serious additional hazard in cities in technologically less-advanced countries where reconstruction is likely to be slow and medical facilities inadequate.

Nuclear Power Plants

During the 1971 San Fernando earthquake, none of the 26 nuclear facilities located between 26 and 550 miles of the epicenter suffered significant damage, and there was no release of radioactive materials. However, as knowledge of seismically hazardous zones is refined and enlarged, siting of nuclear plants must be constantly re-evaluated. Federal law requires that such facilities be designed to withstand seismic and geologic hazards. Utility companies wishing to construct nuclear-fueled plants must evaluate problems associated with earthquake-generated vibratory motion, surface ground displacements caused by faulting, seismically induced flooding, and other earthquake associated phenomena. In the West, where seismic disturbance is more frequent and active faults are relatively easily located, earthquake hazard is better understood than in other parts of the country.

However, infrequency of seismic events does not mean that when earthquakes do occur, they will be of low magnitude. In the last few years, seismicity in the eastern United States has been studied more carefully so that problems associated with the emplacement of nuclear power plants may be better understood.

The Earthquake Hazard Reduction Program of the U.S. Geological Survey utilizes not only the internal research capacity of the agency, but also that of universities, the states, and the private sector. Already, plans and sites for nuclear plants have had to be abandoned. Construction of a nuclear reactor at Bodega Bay, California, for example, had to be halted due to the discovery of fault hazard. In northern New Jersey, recent movement along the Ramapo fault rattled dishes and was of concern because of the proximity of the nuclear power complex at Indian Point, New York. On March 13, 1979, the Nuclear Regulatory Commission shut down five reactors in New York, Maine, Pennsylvania, and Virginia because of questions concerning their ability to withstand earthquakes.

As of 1979, there were 72 nuclear plants in service in the United States and another 126 under construction or on order. Estimates of the number of plants in use by the year 2000 have been lowered from 1000 to 400 (Winograd, USGS 1979, personal communication). Whether this figure will prove accurate depends in part upon success in solving safety problems—not only those from earthquake hazard, but also those involving functional design deficiencies such as those that caused the March 1979 failure of the Three Mile Island plant on the Susquehanna River in Pennsylvania—and in convincing the public that risk associated with nuclear power production is acceptably small. It is to be hoped that sophisticated evaluation of seismic hazard develops more rapidly than emplacement of reactors that may fail during earthquakes of greater magnitude than that for which the plants are designed.

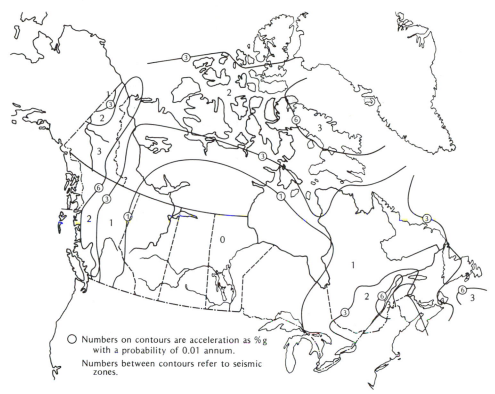

O Numbers on contours are acceleration as %g with a probability of 0.01 annum.

Numbers between contours refer to seismic zones.

7.15 Seismic zoning map of Canada, defining zones of seismic hazard in terms of probability of earthquake-induced ground acceleration attaining indicated values. For example, in Zone 2, there is a one percent chance in any given year that the ground will reach an acceleration equal to 3–6 percent of the acceleration of gravity; in Zone 3, there is a one percent chance that the acceleration will be in excess of 6 percent of the acceleration of gravity. Both earthquake intensity and earthquake frequency are shown. Zones 0, 1, 2, 3, and 4 are areas in which zero, minor, moderate, and major damage may be expected respectively at the one percent probability level.

Seismic Risk Maps

Seismic risk maps play an important role in the evaluation of earthquake hazards. Two types of seismic risk maps are commonly used: (1) those showing zones of similar probability (frequency) of earthquakes of given intensities (Fig. 7.15), and (2) those showing possible maximum earthquake intensity without indicating probability of occurrence (Figs. 7.16 and 7.17).

A comparison of seismic risk maps of the United States and Canada along their common border reveals that Canadians have the more optimistic view concerning the likelihood of earthquake damage. The difference in American and Canadian attitudes has been attributed to an absence of major earthquakes in recent years in Canada (since 1944 in Cornwall, Ontario), whereas in the United States there have been two major earthquakes in the last 15 years (1964 and 1971), both of which have caused considerable losses (Visvader and Burton, 1974).

Examination of Figures 7.15 and 7.16 indicates that a number of major urban centers lie within Zone 3, the zone of highest

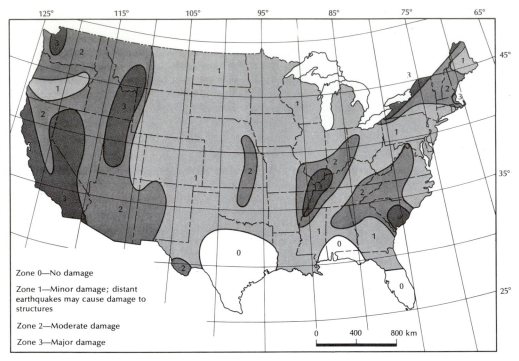

7.16 Map showing seismic risk within the conterminous United States,
The map shows expectable earthquake intensity within a given area;
it does *not* indicate probable frequency of earthquakes.

seismic risk. The population of Zone 3 in
Canada was more than 2 million in 1973.
Zone 3 areas in the United States are inhabited by more than 31 million people. It is
estimated that 70 million people in 39 states
live in regions of major and moderate risk
in the United States (Thiel, 1976). Urban
areas in the United States and Canada likely
to suffer significant seismic damage include
San Diego, Los Angeles, San Francisco,
Reno, Seattle, Vancouver, Salt Lake City,
Memphis, Charleston, Boston, Buffalo, and
Québec City, together with many smaller
urban centers. Alaska is not included in
these figures, but in that state, regions of
greatest population lie in Zone 3. The island
of Hawaii is seismically active: in 1975, an
earthquake of magnitude 7.2 cracked walls
and windows in Hilo, and was followed by
a volcanic eruption in Hawaii Volcano National Park.

The frequency of earthquakes of moderate or greater intensity is suggested by
Table 7.3, which shows the results of a
count of earthquakes in the United States
classified according to their maximum intensity.

The likelihood of future earthquakes in
specific areas of North America is suggested
by a brief review of past seismic events.

Table 7.3. U.S. Earthquakes, 1964–1970
(After von Hake, 1973)

Intensity (MM)	Number of Earthquakes
V	270
VI	81
VII	19
VIII	1
IX	1

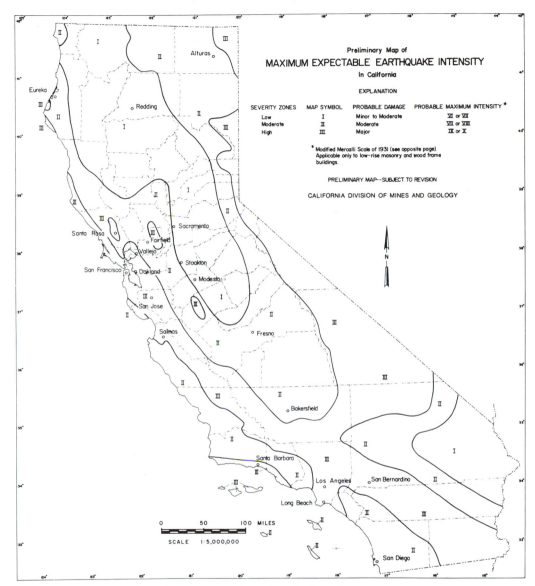

Preliminary Map of
MAXIMUM EXPECTABLE EARTHQUAKE INTENSITY
In California

EXPLANATION

SEVERITY ZONES	MAP SYMBOL	PROBABLE DAMAGE	PROBABLE MAXIMUM INTENSITY [*]
Low	I	Minor to Moderate	VI or VII
Moderate	II	Moderate	VII or VIII
High	III	Major	IX or X

[*] Modified Mercalli Scale of 1931 (see opposite page).
Applicable only to low-rise masonry and wood frame
buildings.

PRELIMINARY MAP--SUBJECT TO REVISION

CALIFORNIA DIVISION OF MINES AND GEOLOGY

7.17 Preliminary map of maximum expectable earthquake intensity
in California.

Four major earthquakes have occurred in California during the twentieth century: San Francisco, 1906; Long Beach, 1933, Kern County, 1952; San Fernando, 1971. These earthquakes took 894 lives and caused, directly or indirectly, over two and a half billion dollars damage. In the Seattle–Vancouver region, thirteen earthquakes of magnitude greater than or equal to 5 took place in the period 1899–1964. Five had a magnitude of 7 or greater. Damage was low to moderate since during most of the period the area was sparsely populated. Recent intensive urbanization makes significant damage likely in future earthquakes. The Anchorage earthquake of 1964 caused 131 deaths and almost $600 million damage (including tsunami damage). A major proportion of Utah's population lives along the fault zone at the western front of the Wasatch Mountains. Earthquakes having a magnitude greater than 6 occurred in this region in 1884, 1909, and 1934. The strongest earthquake in the eastern United States took place at New Madrid, Missouri in 1811–1812, rated at MM = XII. Earthquakes of MM = VIII took place at Memphis, Tennessee, in 1843 and Charleston, Missouri, in 1895. All of those shocks occurred within a zone of high seismicity that lies between Cairo, Illinois and Memphis in the lower Mississippi Valley. In terms of actual damage, an earthquake near Charleston, South Carolina, in 1886 (MM = X) was the most catastrophic in eastern North America. About 90 percent of the brick buildings in the city were damaged, more than 80 people died, and the seismic vibration was felt over an area of two million square miles. An earthquake centered beneath the sea floor east of Boston in 1755 caused a tsunami which disturbed shipping as far away as the West Indies. A major earthquake belt underlies the Saint Lawrence Valley between Lake Ontario and the mouth of the Saguenay River Northeast of Québec City. During the last four hundred years, there have been six shocks of MM = IX in that area. An earthquake near Québec City in 1925 of magnitude 7.0 was felt in Boston and New York City. Massena, New York was damaged by an earthquake MM = VIII in 1944.

Earthquakes along the western margin of North America may be attributed to the buildup of stress caused by the northward movement of the Pacific lithospheric plate relative to the adjacent North American plate. Earthquakes in the Mississippi and Saint Lawrence Valleys have been attributed respectively to crustal subsidence

and elevation. Seismic activity along the Wasatch front in Utah may be due to crustal stretching. Causes of the New England and South Carolina earthquakes are not well understood.

Prediction

The possibility of predicting earthquakes has been sought as a way of minimizing death, injury, and property loss. If earthquakes can be forecast, measures can be taken to plan and coordinate responses to the potential disaster: harzardous buildings can be evacuated; the water level behind large dams can be lowered; supplies and materials for post-earthquake relief and reconstruction can be assembled; and critical facilities such as nuclear reactors and oil or gas pipelines can be shut down (Carlson, 1976).

Initial investigation suggests that before an earthquake, rocks undergo a period of fracturing that results in several observable changes. An increase in volume of the rock can be detected at the surface by sensitive "tiltmeters." Water gradually migrates into the fracture system, resulting in changes in the level of water in wells. In some cases, the fracturing releases the gas *radon* and its presence in water in deep wells increases. The increased water content in the rock causes changes in the velocity with which seismic vibrations pass through it and in its electrical conductivity. Just before an earthquake, many of these anomalies disappear or are reduced. A rough correlation seems to exist between the length of time over which the anomalies persist and the magnitude of the subsequent earthquake (Hammond, 1973).

One of the most intensive attempts at earthquake prediction took place before an earthquake (M = 7.3) in Liaoning Province in northeast China in February 1975. The area was identified as early as 1970 as a region of possible risk. Roughly ten thousand people, including several hundred scientists, were engaged in the prediction attempt, using a wide variety of instruments that included some of the best equipment in use anywhere in the world today (Hamilton, 1976). Observations were made of migrations of seismic activity, ground surface tilting, changes in water level in wells, changes in electrical conductivity in rocks, and abnormal animal behavior. As the anomalies became more evident, more equipment was moved into the area. On December 20, 1974, an alarm was issued that proved false. On February 4, 1975, people were warned that an earthquake of major proportions could be expected within two days. Shops were closed and buildings were evacuated. At 7:36 P.M. that evening the earthquake occurred. According to the Chinese, ten earthquakes have been predicted successfully thus far and warnings issued. They readily acknowledge, however, that not all predictions have been correct. On July 28, 1976, an unexpected pair of earthquakes (M = 8.2 and 7.9) totally razed the industrial city of Tangshan (population 1 million).

Limited success in earthquake prediction has been achieved by Japanese scientists. Using surveying techniques to detect vertical and horizontal movements of the earth's surface, a major earthquake near Niigata was predicted in 1964. Tiltmeters gave warning of smaller earthquakes that struck Matsushiro in central Japan in 1965–67. Anomalous rock behavior permit-ted the accurate prediction of an earthquake near Hollister, California at Thanksgiving 1974. Soviet scientists have been working at developing methods of earthquake prediction for more than 25 years. It was the Soviet work that indicated that some earthquakes are preceded by variations in the velocity with which seismic waves pass through rocks.

Reliability of earthquake prediction will have to await the accumulation of sufficient data and experience. The earth is a complex system, and earthquakes in geologically different regions may be preceded by anomalies of different character and intensity. Ideally, magnitude, and the time and place of an earthquake should be known in order to develop appropriate responses. Geologist V. E. McKelvey stresses the difference between earthquake *prediction* and *warning*. A prediction is a forecast. A warning is a recommendation for response. Table 7.4 outlines responses appropriate to the different lengths of time available before predicted earthquakes.

Unfortunately, earthquake prediction may be counterproductive (Turner, 1976). In an area where an earthquake has been predicted, land values may drop, construction and repair may slow down or cease, unemployment may increase, and earthquake insurance may become difficult or impossible to obtain. Also, false or inaccurate prediction of earthquakes might result in a skep-

Table 7.4. Engineering responses to an earthquake prediction (From Thiel, 1976)

Lead Time	Buildings	Contents	Lifelines	Special Structures
3 Days	Evacuate previously identified hazards	Remove selected contents	Deploy emergency materials	Shut down reactors, petroleum-products pipelines
30 Days	Inspect and identify potential hazards	Selectively harden (brace and strengthen) contents	Shift hospital patients; alter use of facilities	Draw down reservoirs, remove toxic materials
300 Days	Selectively reinforce		Develop response capability	Replace hazardous storage
3000 Days	Revise building codes and land-use regulations: enforce condemnation and reinforcement			Remove hazardous dams from service

tical attitude on the part of the public that would undermine necessary precautions.

An interesting example of response to earthquake prediction in the United States was generated by seismologist James H. Whitcomb's statement (April 15, 1976) that there was a good possibility that an earthquake of Richter magnitude 5.5 to 6.5 would strike the Los Angeles region in the near future, possibly within a year. Whitcomb's prediction was based on anomalous seismic wave measurements (Shapley, 1976). Earlier, beginning in 1960 and continuing to the present, an ominous and geologically sudden, one-foot uplift was noted along part of the San Andreas Fault located about sixty miles north of Los Angeles (Castle et al, 1976). Whether the seismic anomalies and the bulge along the fault are related to each other is not known. At any rate, Whitcomb's prediction was taken seriously by Los Angeles politicians: there was talk in the City Council of suing him (and anyone else who made earthquake predictions) for any resulting loss in real estate values (Shapley, 1976).

The natural phenomena that suggested the possibility of an imminent earthquake in the Los Angeles region were also taken seriously by the federal government: $2.1 million in reprogrammed geological research funds was given to the U.S. Geological Survey to monitor the San Andreas Fault. Unfortunately, this money represented approximately 40 percent of the total 1976 government budget for earthquake prediction, and meant that programs in other areas would be correspondingly deprived. Seismograph networks now exist in the Puget Sound region of Washington, southern Alaska, western Nevada, Salt Lake City, and southern Missouri. Also, funding has begun for a network in the Northeast. That these efforts are already underfunded is indicated by the estimate that to create an adequate network in the southern Alaska region alone would cost about $10 million. Nevertheless, in an unsuccessful attempt to defeat the passage in the House of Repre-

sentatives of a measure to create a three-year, $210 million coordinated program to predict and reduce earthquakes, Representative Robert Bauman of Maryland claimed that the cost of the program was excessive: "If this Congress can't detect inflationary spending like that, I don't think they can detect earthquakes . . ." (*The New York Times,* Sept. 11, 1977, p. 24)

PREVENTIVE MEASURES AND RECONSTRUCTION

Skepticism (or cynicism) extends beyond attempts at prediction. California voters, in the heart of "earthquake country," have several times defeated bond issues designed to rebuild schools known to be unsafe in the event of a major earthquake. In other parts of the United States, especially in the East, the threat of earthquakes is considered fantasy. However, more than twice the average 12.5-year interval between damaging eastern earthquakes has elapsed since the last one (at Massena, New York in 1944) and another seismic event may be expected soon. Attitudes may change subsequent to a disaster. A recent study of human adjustment to earthquake hazard concludes that essentially only people who have experienced a severe earthquake consider earthquakes a real hazard (Jackson and Mukerjee, 1974). Abstract consideration of earthquake hazard does not provide sufficient motivation to change life patterns in order to eliminate, reduce, or accommodate the possibility of loss. For planning, not prediction, purposes, Karl Steinbrugge states that "the frequency of major or great earthquakes strongly affecting at least large sections of the San Francisco Bay Area, may reasonably be assumed to be from 60 to 100 years. . . ." (1968, p. 10) A survey in San Francisco frequently encountered responses such as "earthquakes don't bother me"; "Let it rock"; "We have no earthquake problem." (Jackson and Mukerjee 1974) Clearly, leadership in educating people as to the seriousness of earthquake hazard, together with the development of procedures to lessen damage and to speed effective post-earthquake recovery is lacking. California geologist Raymond Pestrong notes with respect to San Francisco that "although considered by many a relatively enlightened community with respect to its political and social mores, it appears to have advanced little in its awareness of the hazards of planning a community without regard for geological conditions. It is strangely paradoxical that some of its most scenic land, topographically, is often the most unstable structurally. The hummocky fault block terrain . . . comprises some of the most sought-after land in the Bay Area, and commands correspondingly higher prices, despite the increased natural hazards. . . ."

The reconstruction of San Francisco after the earthquake and fire of 1906 should remain an object lesson. The opportunity to rebuild a socially and esthetically improved city was abandoned in favor of rapid reconstruction that recreated grave fire and earthquake hazards and did little to ameliorate unimaginative city planning or to prevent future urban decay. (See discussion of San Francisco in Chap. 16.)

An analysis of the role of urban planning in the reconstruction of Anchorage after the 1964 earthquake describes how

Reconstruction of utilities, roads, and other public works . . . was rapid and effective. One of the most evident failures of the reconstruction program, however, was the loss of the opportunity to create the better environment suggested in some of the early feasibility studies . . . and the failure in some cases to rebuild in accordance with sound safety measures. . . . Modifications of . . . plans were immediately proposed by the various city councils in response to pressure exerted for economic reasons by certain individuals and groups. Private interest often prevailed over the public interest and over sound planning considerations. The long-range economic effect . . . was ignored in favor of the immediate expediency of reconstruction using old and outmoded methods. . . . Individual property owners clamored to reinvest and rebuild in the

same locations for the same purposes; this policy was generally followed in Anchorage . . . and was supported with federal funds. (Selkregg *et al*, 1970, pp. 236–38)

Both pre-earthquake and post-earthquake planning should be undertaken for seismically hazardous regions and should include (1) evaluation of potential disaster areas, (2) initiation of programs to minimize disaster, (3) adoption and enforcement of building codes, (4) coordination of state and federal agencies, programs and activities, (5) public education with respect to damage prevention, (6) preparation and enforcement of disaster prevention programs: zoning, subdivision regulations, fire and building codes, etc. (7) separation of immediate relief and long-term recovery programs. (Selkregg, *et al*, 1970).

Consideration of the San Francisco Community Safety Plan will illustrate the application of some of these principles.

San Francisco

Prompted by the San Fernando earthquake of 1971, California passed legislation requiring cities and counties to include within their general plans provisions for identifying and appraising seismic hazards, and measures for protecting the public from fires and geologic hazards. In response, San Francisco developed a Community Safety Plan designed to become part of the cities Comprehensive Plan. The Comprehensive Plan is a long term, general plan for the improvement and future development of the city. The Community Safety Plan was submitted to the City Planning Commission in July 1974, in the form of a proposal for citizen review, and was adopted in somewhat modified form on September 12, 1974 as Resolution No. 7241.

The Plan accepts as inevitable the proposition that San Francisco will again be subjected to severe earthquakes, and proposes programs and policies to (1) understand and identify the geologic risks; (2) determine the degree to which existing buildings and other

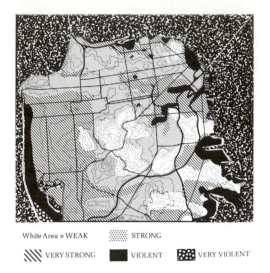

White Area = WEAK   ░░░ STRONG

░░░ VERY STRONG   ███ VIOLENT   ░░░ VERY VIOLENT

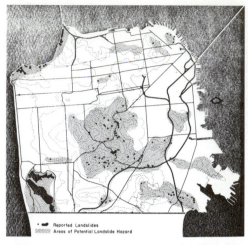

(B) Areas subject to landslide

7.18 Three maps of San Francisco, showing the effects of a future earthquake, M = 8.3.

(C) Areas subject to liquefaction

structures are likely to be damaged and the dangers posed to human life; (3) develop ways to correct existing structural deficiencies *before* a major earthquake strikes, and to ensure that new buildings are constructed to withstand seismic hazard; (4) prepare emergency plans to handle crises arising during and immediately after an earthquake; and (5) prepare plans *now* for the rational reconstruction of the city *after* an earthquake.

A series of maps were developed showing how different parts of the city would be affected geologically in the event of the repetition of the 1906 earthquake (M = 8.3). Figure 7.18A shows estimated intensity of ground shaking. The areas most seriously affected are those underlain by artificial fill placed over soft Bay muds. Figure 7.18B shows areas of potential landslides. The areas of highest risk are hill slopes underlain by weak rocks. High sea cliffs and

7.19 San Francisco, showing areas that may be inundated by a tsunami that is 20 feet high at the Golden Gate (Top), and areas that may be flooded due to failure of reservoirs (Bottom).

water-saturated dune sands are also vulnerable. Figure 7.18C indicates regions subject to liquefaction and subsidence. In 1906, a large percentage of the damage was caused by this type of failure. Particularly vulnerable are the eastern parts of the city, where buildings rest on land reclaimed by filling in shallow water and marsh areas. Figure 7.19 shows areas that would be inundated by a

tsunami of a magnitude such that it would be 20 feet high as it passed the Golden Gate Bridge, as well as sections of the city that would be flooded if hilltop or hillside reservoirs burst.

To gain further information about what happens to the ground and buildings during earthquakes, *strong-motion* accelerographs have been installed in various parts of San Francisco, as part of a wider scale program undertaken by the U.S. Geological Survey and the California Division of Mines and Geology.

In order to estimate more accurately the damage that would occur to buildings in the event of an $M = 8.3$ earthquake, potential damage estimates were made on a block-by-block basis throughout the city. The potential for severe damage is greatest in the "downtown" core of the city. It was not until 1948 that buildings being constructed were required to withstand the horizontal forces likely to occur during an earthquake. Since 1969, not only are new buildings required to meet seismic building code standards, but also buildings undergoing remodeling that affects more than 30 percent of the structure. Luckily, much of San Francisco is characterized by wood-frame residential structures that are generally resilient and relatively safe. Such buildings are, however, susceptible to fire.

In 1906, more damage was caused by fire after the earthquake than by the earthquake itself. Fire-fighting is San Francisco relies on two separate water-supply systems: the domestic system and the Auxiliary Water Supply System (AWSS). Much of the domestic system is of brittle construction without flexible joints and does not meet Fire Department standards. In 1906, this system broke in 23,000 places throughout the city and became essentially a sieve with no pressure. Although replacing the system with newer, more flexible pipes and joints is considered prohibitively costly, the Community Safety Plan urges that whenever and wherever possible it should gradually be replaced to meet standards of the Fire Department.

The AWSS which is constructed to high standards, has its own reservoir and 150 cisterns at key intersections plus two pumping stations in the Bay. At present it protects only the downtown area, a relatively small part of the city, but extension has been planned.

Abatement of existing building hazards should involve strengthening deficient structures so that they meet necessary standards. Unfortunately many of the architectural details, such as parapets and cornices on older buildings, that give San Francisco character and charm are likely to fail in the event of an earthquake. Tax relief or low-cost loans are proposed for owners who strengthen such details rather than remove them. Critical community facilities, such as schools and hospitals, that are structurally unsound or located on hazardous ground, should be relocated in geologically safer areas. Unfortunately, very little unbuilt land remains in San Francisco, so major land-use changes are not possible.

During an actual emergency, many of the most vital responses would be coordinated by the Emergency Operations Center. The Center is housed in the basement of the Youth Guidance Center, a location described as "inadequate—too small, ill-equipped and virtually unprotected." Also, many of the proposed sites of local centers are potentially hazardous. What is needed is a multi-purpose building that would house all the emergency centers: fire, police, ambulance dispatchers, together with the Emergency Operations Center. Local emergency response sites should be carefully evaluated before designation. Unfortunately, recent demands from the public for cutbacks in state spending means that these improvements are unlikely to materialize unless more federal money becomes available or a major catastrophe forces the issue.

How to reconstruct San Francisco after a hypothetical earthquake is of major concern. Immediately after a disaster there is usually a general spirit of "let's rebuild it right." However, as money becomes available, expediency becomes a prime factor, and the Bureau of Building Inspection and the Department of City Planning, as well as other city offices might be subjected to great pressure to lower standards and regulations in order to speed reconstruction (see the discussion of Anchorage above). It is emphasized that rational reconstruction will only take place if estimates of potential damage are made before they occur and plans for reconstruction are drawn up before they are needed. Funds should only be granted on the condition that they be used in accordance with the established Master Plan. If done properly, post-earthquake reconstruction can realize long-needed improvements and eliminate past mistakes.

Earthquake Control

The possibility of controlling and minimizing the magnitude of earthquakes has received serious attention. Major earthquakes occur when great lithospheric stresses accumulate and are released locally in a matter of seconds or minutes. During the twentieth century, motion between the American and Pacific plates has averaged about an inch and a quarter a year. In some places along the plate margin, movement has taken place repeatedly, at short time intervals, allowing relatively little stress to build up and resulting in only minor earthquakes. In other places, the two plates are "locked" together and move only infrequently. Infrequent movement allows stress to accumulate, and the resulting displacements and ensuing earthquakes are of much greater magnitude. In the San Francisco earthquake of 1906, horizontal displacement along the San Andreas Fault was about 15–20 feet. Since then, little movement has taken place in the Bay region, but every year that passes without significant movement allows more and more stress to accumulate, and the likelihood of a major earthquake increases.

If some mechanism could be employed to "unlock" locked portions of faults in earthquake zones, earthquakes of low magnitudes might be periodically triggered, to prevent infrequent, more destructive earthquakes. From April 1962 to November 1965, Denver suffered more than 700 earthquakes up to Richter magnitude 4.3. Previously, Denver's location was considered one of low seismicity. In November 1962, geologist David H. Evans suggested the increased seismicity might be connected with injection of contaminated waste water into the ground at the Rocky Mountain Arsenal, northeast of Denver (Evans, 1966). Waste fluids from the manufacture of products for chemical warfare and industrial use had been injected into a 12,045-foot-deep disposal well in March of that year; the earthquakes started the following month. Investigation revealed excellent correlation between pumping of fluids and the frequency of earthquakes (Hoover and Dietrich, 1969). The wastes, which were being injected under high pressure into a highly fractured gneiss, caused an increase in fluid pressure, forcing the fractures apart slightly. This permitted the rock to slide along the fractures, causing the earthquakes. Considering the implications of this phenomenon, Evans speculated that ". . . the principle of increasing fluid pressure to release elastic wave energy could be applied to earthquake modification. That is, it might be possible to relieve the stresses along some fault zones in urban areas by increasing the fluid pressure along the zone, using a series of injection wells. The accumulated stress might thus be released at will in a series of non-damaging earthquakes instead of eventually resulting in one large event that might cause a major disaster.'' (1966, p. 18)

A link between fluid injection and fault activation was postulated as a possible cause of the failure of the Baldwin Hills Reservoir, southwest of downtown Los Angeles, in 1963. Injection of water into the Inglewood Oilfield in California is correlated with surface displacement and subsidence (see Chapter 12).

In Rangeley, Colorado experiments have been conducted in activating faults through the injection of fluids (Raleigh *et al,* 1976). The starting and stopping of earthquakes met with some success, and it was concluded that earthquakes could be controlled wherever the fluid pressure in a fault zone could be controlled.

However, attempts to trigger preventive earthquakes in areas of high population density involves a high degree of risk. A deliberately triggered earthquake might be of unanticipated magnitude and cause great damage. This possibility is especially true in regions like San Francisco, where earthquake-producing stresses have been accumulating for long periods. Also, the cost of drilling wells into fault zones to inject fluids is considerable. Control of earthquakes as a practical expedient remains, as yet, beyond human capability.

TSUNAMIS

Tsunamis, popularly called tidal waves, are exceptionally high waves that on occasion wash up over coastal areas causing great damage and loss of life. Tsunamis may be generated by submarine volcanic explosions, underwater landslides, or submarine seismic disturbances (earthquakes). The latter type of tsunamis are also refered to as *seismic sea waves.*

One of the most destructive tsunamis resulted from the catastrophic eruption of Krakatau in 1883, in which the volcanic island was literally blown up. The disturbance to the surrounding ocean waters set up waves that rolled over the adjacent islands of Java and Sumatra, reaching heights of over a hundred feet and killing tens of thousands of inhabitants.

In the 1964 Alaska earthquake, 90 percent of the loss of life was caused by local tsunamis. The town of Valdez lies at the head of a narrow arm of the ocean. The earthquake triggered a submarine landslide that violently displaced the waters of the narrow inlet, generating waves that caused additional damage to the already partially destroyed town. The major tsunami from the earthquake, caused by displacement of the ocean floor, traveled out across the Pacific Ocean, causing extensive damage in British Columbia and taking 16 lives in Oregon and California. Hardest hit was Crescent City, California, where the arrival of the wave coincided with high tide, causing eleven deaths and $11,000,000 damage.

Most tsunamis are caused by submarine earthquakes that disturb a portion of the ocean floor. As the sea floor is suddenly raised or lowered, waves are formed that radiate out in all directions and are capable of traveling thousands of miles at speeds up to 600 miles per hour. Not all submarine earthquakes are accompanied by tsunamis; earthquakes that generate them have magnitudes greater than $M = 6$, relatively shallow foci, and are always followed by aftershocks. As seismic sea waves travel over the open ocean, they have heights of only one or two feet and cannot be noticed by passing ships. When they approach shallow water, however, their velocity is sharply decreased, and the confined energy of the waves forces them upward to great heights. The distance between successive wave crests can be as much as 100–600 miles, and the time interval between their arrival at a given place fifteen minutes to an hour or more. The first visible evidence of a tsunami along a shoreline is often a withdrawal of water that leaves the floor of the sea bare. This curious phenomenon often attracts people who are then overwhelmed by the arrival of the first giant wave. The first wave is followed by other waves of even greater magnitude (usually the third to eighth waves are the biggest) that may arrive over a period of many hours.

Most tsunamis originate in the oceanic trenches that ring the Pacific. The passage of the major wave generated by the 1964 Alaska earthquake is shown in Figure 7.20. Areas affected significantly by tsunamis include Japan, Hawaii and other islands of the Pacific, the Aleutian Islands, and the west-

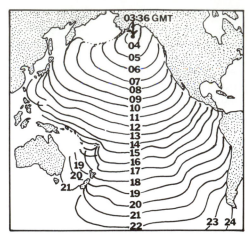

7.20 Map showing the advance of the major tsunami generated by the Alaska earthquake of 1964. Numbers refer to Greenwich Mean Time.

ern coasts of the Americas. In the last thirteen centuries, about 150 damaging tsunamis have hit Japan. The earthquakes causing them occurred off the Pacific coast of Japan or as far away as the Kamchatka Peninsula and the Chilean coast of South America. The greatest historical Japanese tsunami occurred in 1896, caused by an offshore earthquake of magnitude $M = 7$. Wave heights reached 80 feet, killing 27,000 people and destroying more than 10,000 houses and 7000 ships. An earthquake off the Chilean coast in March 1960 generated a tsunami that struck the Japanese coast 22–24 hours later with no warning. Waves up to 20 feet high left 139 dead, 872 injured and seriously affected 160,000 others.

In 1946, an earthquake off the coast of the Aleutians precipitated a tsunami that reached heights of over 100 feet, destroying the Scotch Cap Lighthouse on Unimak Island, Alaska. When the same wave reached Hilo, Hawaii, it still had sufficient energy to cause runups to 27 feet above sea level, and killed 159 people who had no warning. In 1948, the U.S. Coast and Geodetic Survey set up the Pacific Tsunami Warning System

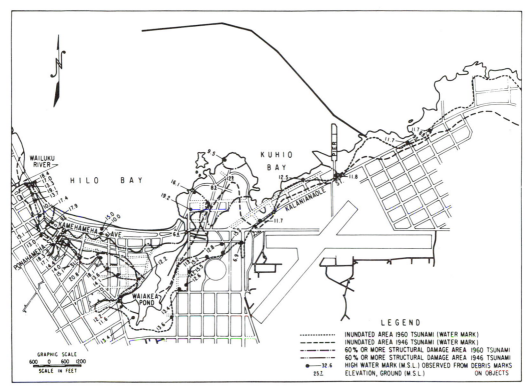

7.21 Map of areas affected by the 1946 and 1960 tsunamis in Hilo,
Hawaii.

with headquarters in Honolulu. Thanks to
the system, no lives were lost in the tsunami
of 1957. But in May, 1960, 61 lives were
lost when warnings were ignored. Major
tsunamis affecting Hawaii are listed in
Table 7.5, and Figure 7.21 shows areas affected by the 1946 and 1960 tsunamis in
Hilo.

Damage from tsunami inundation has occurred in coastal regions other than those
around the Pacific. After the Lisbon earthquake of 1755, great waves swept in on Lisbon and moved up the Tagus River, causing
very heavy loss of life. A tsunami originating south of Newfoundland and east of
Nova Scotia, accompanying the Grand

Table 7.5. Tsunamis reaching Hawaii; Runup and damage at Hilo. (After Wiegel, 1964)

Date	Tsunami Origin	Max. Runup	Earthquake Magnitude	Damage
Feb. 3, 1923	Kamchatka	20'	8.3	considerable
Apr. 1, 1946	Aleutian Is.	27'	7.4	$26,000,000
Nov. 4, 1952	Kamchatka	12'	8.3	300,000
March 9, 1957	Aleutian Is.	14'	8.0	400,000
May 23, 1960	Chile	35'	8.5	22,000,000

Banks earthquake of 1929, swept over coastal fishing villages at heights up to 15 feet and took 29 lives. As submarine geologist Francis Shepard notes, "It is disturbing to consider what would happen if a tsunami should come into a shore like Long Island, where some of the beaches have hundreds of thousands of bathers during a warm summer day. We have no record of dangerous waves coming in at these places. However, in the case of the Grand Banks earthquake . . . there had been no previous record of tsunamis in the area. . . . Let us hope that no new submarine faults suddenly come into being and send waves into this area. The effect would be almost as bad as that of a hydrogen bomb." (1964, p. 44).

The damage that tsunamis cause stems from several factors: the weight of the water may crush materials; certain goods will be spoiled by salt water; moving water produces a scouring action which can cause foundations to fail; objects caught up by the water can attain high velocities and can cause considerable damage if they hit something; the dynamic pressure of the moving wall of water itself can cause great destruction.

The actual paths of tsunami wave-fronts, once they enter shallow water, are affected by the shape and configuration of the ocean bottom and the coastline. The wave fronts are subject to considerable bending and may "bounce" or "echo" off of steep cliff faces. Tsunamis that are funneled up triangular inlets or harbors may increase considerable in height and become correspondingly more dangerous. On the other hand, natural barriers, such as offshore coral reefs, are very effective in diminishing the power of these waves.

Another phenomenon closely allied to and in some cases caused by tsunamis is "seiching." Water in an enclosed basin has a particular natural frequency of "slosh," or oscillation; such movement is known as a *seiche*. If tsunami waves enter an almost enclosed basin, and if intervals between arrivals of the waves are such that they are

able to reinforce the natural period of the seiche, dangerous internal waves may be created within the basin that can destroy harbor facilities or near-shore structures. Seiches also may be created in inland lakes by earthquake vibrations or by materials falling into a lake during landslides. Where the water is constricted, wave runup from seiches can be as much as 20–30 feet.

Short of constructing massive obstacles to the advance of tsunamis, the most effective ways of reducing death and property loss is through evaluating the likelihood of such waves, appropriate land-use zoning, and the development of adequate warning systems.

The extent of tsunami hazard at a given place may be estimated from the history of local inundations and from studies of the geographic relationship between likely points of origin and the location of the coast in question. Graphs may be constructed that suggest the number of times in a given time period that a particular value of tsunami maximum runup will be equaled or exceeded (Fig. 7.22).

From such estimates a provisional tsunami hazard map has been constructed for

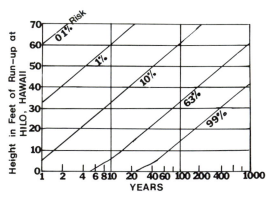

7.22 Graph showing the likelihood in any given time-span of particular values of tsunami maximum runup being equaled or exceeded. For example, in a 10-year period, there is a 10 percent chance that tsunami runup will equal or exceed 33 feet, and a one percent chance that it will equal or exceed 60 feet.

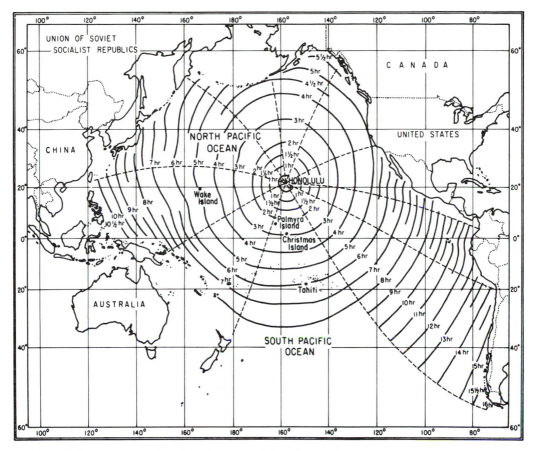

7.23 Travel times of tsunamis originating around the edge of the Pacific Ocean to Honolulu, Hawaii.

California and is available as a guide in making land-use decisions.

Where tsunami inundation has actually occurred in the past, limited or no development should be permitted. Where the history of such inundation is scanty or absent, but the theoretical likelihood is high, estimates of maximum tsunami runup probability can be used to exclude vulnerable areas from intensive development.

In the *Urban Geology Master Plan For California* it is suggested that:

"The National Oceanic and Atmospheric Administration should be requested to prepare information on the expected tsunami runup along the California coast for 20-, 50-, and 100-year recurrence intervals. Local governments should establish use zones along the coastline so that (1) no permanently inhabited structure other than those absolutely required be permitted within the 20-year recurrence runup zone, (2) low intensity uses only be permitted within the 50-year recurrence runup zone, (3) schools, hospitals, other critical facilities, and public buildings be located above the 100-year recurrence runup zone." (1973, p. 11)

The Pacific Tsunami Warning System (PTWS) in Honolulu was designed to warn the people of Hawaii of tsunamis generated by distant earthquakes. However, because of the possibility of waves generated by earthquakes associated with Hawaiian vulcanism, the system was later modified to provide warnings for local tsunamis. The Japanese also have a warning system for locally generated tsunamis; the public is informed within 20 minutes after a local earthquake. The Pacific Tsunami Warning System has recently expanded to become a pan-Pacific system in which thirteen countries participate.

Warning systems use earthquake detection and location devices and tide gauges that can distinguish the passage of tsunami waves from the ordinary fluctuations of sea water. When an earthquake occurs in an area where tsunamis are commonly generated, their arrival times can be estimated for points at varying distances from the epicenter. For a given locality, such as Honolulu, travel times of tsunamis originating at different locations around the circumference of the Pacific can be plotted (Fig. 7.23). Predictions are correct to within a minute-and-a-half per elapsed hour of travel time. Warning times vary according to the distance of the source, but may be about 20 hours and can permit evacuation of threatened areas. Even in places along the Japanese coast that are close to offshore tsunami sources, 10–30 minutes may elapse before the waves arrive, thus permitting escape to higher ground.

Unfortunately, people unaccustomed to tsunamis do not always respond to warnings or understand the nature of the danger. The Chilean earthquake of 1960 occurred at 18:56 Greenwich Mean Time. By 21:59 the epicenter had been located under the Pacific Ocean, the likelihood of tsunami established, and preliminary warnings issued in Hawaii. The first wave arrived at Hilo at 9:58 the next morning, within one minute of the predicted time. However, 61 people were killed and 282 injured. Failure to heed warnings may be attributed largely to skepticism induced by previous issuance of false alarms. Since only a small percentage of submarine earthquakes cause tsunamis, occasional false alarms are unavoidable.

Similarly, the tsunami generated by the 1964 Alaska earthquake caused unnecessary deaths in Crescent City, California. Due to previous false alarms, there was little official response to the warnings. Also, some people were unaware that more than one wave would arrive. The waves arrived at 12 midnight, 12:40 A.M., 1:20 A.M.; the *greatest* wave arrived at 1:45 A.M.

Since then, more effective use has been made of radio and television to alert the public to tsunami hazards, and special sirens have been emplaced that sound more urgent alarms.

For structures that must be built in zones susceptible to tsunamis, standard reinforced concrete construction is more likely to survive than light frame buildings or even most heavy timber buildings. Groves of trees may provide protection against the impact of objects caught up and hurled by the waves. Construction of seawalls and sheltered harbors can also reduce damage to coastal structures and ships.

8. Landslides

Bedrock, loose soil, or sediment will slide downhill when the downslope pull of gravity acting on the material exceeds its strength or shearing resistance. Relatively rapid movements of such materials are known collectively as *landslides*. Slower downslope movements are discussed in Chapter 6. Experience with landslides reveals that there are a number of distinct types that differ from one another with respect to the materials involved and the type of movement. Also, in many instances, the tendency to slide may exist for eons without any movement taking place. Movement finally occurs when a triggering mechanism upsets the delicate balance of forces.

Some Catastrophic Landslides

The coal-mining town of Frank, Alberta, was situated on the floor of an east-west valley in the southern Canadian Rockies. On the 29th of April, 1903, a mass of limestone bedrock, having a volume of perhaps 40 million cubic yards, crashed down 2000 feet from adjacent Turtle Mountain, killing 70 people and essentially destroying the town. During its brief period of movement, the avalanche attained speeds of up to 60 miles an hour, and its momentum was so great that parts of the rock mass crossed the two-mile width of the valley and reached as

high as 400 feet up the opposite slope. Such astonishing velocities and traveling power were made possible, it has been theorized, by compressed air acting as a cushion that kept the rock fragments somewhat separated from each other and from the ground—thus permitting the whole mixture of rock and air to move as a viscous fluid. Subsequent examination of Turtle Mountain revealed its inherent instability (Fig. 8.1). A joint set within the limestone roughly parallels the steeply inclined surface of the mountain. Groundwater seeping into the joints dissolved the adjacent limestone, thus enlarging the fractures. In cold weather, water in the fractures froze, expanded, and wedged the rock apart, thus weakening the connection between the outermost mass of limestone and the underlying material. At the foot of the mountain, coal-mining may have reduced essential support for the overlying limestones, causing stresses which finally triggered the avalanche. Unfortunately, the conditions existing at Turtle Mountain before the slide are duplicated at another locality in the vicinity, and another cataclysmic landslide could occur at any time (Bolt, *et al,* 1975).

In 1806, a layer of conglomerate forming the side of Mount Rossberg, Switzerland, became detached from and slid downhill along a clay-rich bed of coally limestone

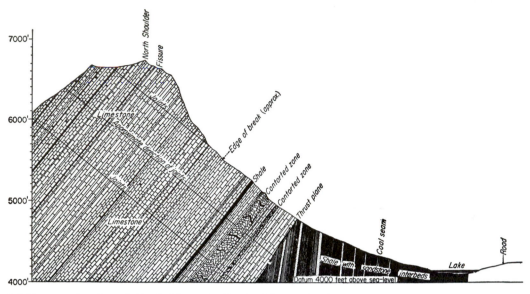

8.1 Cross section through Turtle Mountain, Frank, Alberta, showing
the relation of the 1903 landslide to the local geological structure.

(Fig. 8.2). The detached mass was more
than a mile long, 1000 feet across, and
200–300 feet thick. When it reached the
valley floor it destroyed the village of Gol-
dau and took 457 lives. The dip of the layer
on which the rock slide started was only
20°, and initial movement was slow. Within
a few minutes, however, tremendous velocities were attained, making escape impossible for the inhabitants of the valley floor.

On May 31, 1970, a water-soaked mass
of ice, mud, and rock debris started moving
down the side of Mt. Huascarán in the Peru-
vian Andes. The debris avalanche swept
along at speeds of more than 100 miles an
hour, overrunning the town of Yungay and

part of the town of Ranrahirca. Twenty
thousand people perished.

If accumulations of clay and sand become
saturated by heavy rains or melting snow,
they can turn into a viscous fluid capable of
flowing down slopes that depart only minimally from the horizontal. Such mudflows
can attain velocities exceeding five miles an
hour and can travel great distances, sweeping everything before them. In 1893, such a
mass of flowing mud rolled down a valley
in Norway, picking up houses and burying
alive 111 people.

The town of Nicolet, Québec, is situated
on high, flat ground separated by a cliff
from a narrow strip of lower ground next to

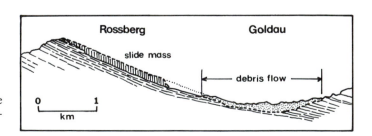

8.2 Cross section showing the
situation after a landslide at Gol-
dau, Switzerland in 1806.

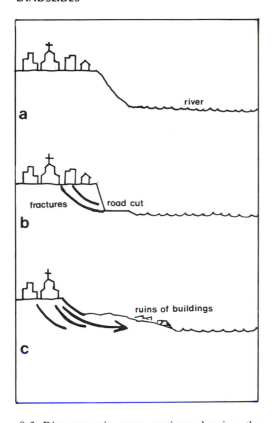

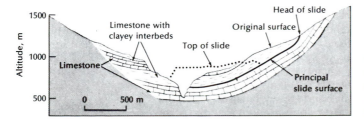

the Nicolet River (Fig. 8.3). In order to widen the narrow strip of ground along the river for a highway, the cliff-face was steepened. The cliff and the higher ground in back of it, on which the town is situated, are composed of unconsolidated silts and clays. On November 12, 1955, after heavy rains, blocks of sediment along the edge of the cliff, hundreds of feet long, began to *slump* outward and downward along curved fracture surfaces. The movement and vibration of the slumping blocks caused the wet clayey sediment to lose strength, and the whole mass broke up and flowed toward the river, carrying with it a school, houses, and pavement. Three lives were lost.

A particularly destructive landslide occurred in the Vaiont Valley, Italy, in 1963. A dam was constructed in 1960 across a narrow canyon set within a larger, broad valley (Fig. 8.4). The sides of the upper broad valley are underlain by layered sedimentary rocks that dip toward the valley floor and are traversed by fractures paralleling the slope of the land surface. The sedimentary sequence includes clays and other layers which are of especially low strength when wet. As water backed up behind the dam and filled the narrow canyon, it forced its way into the pre-existing fractures and pried them further open, wetting the vulnerable layers. After heavy rains during the autumn of 1963, the south slope of the valley began to slide. Within a matter of minutes, more than 312 million cubic yards of rock plunged into the reservoir, sending a wall of water and rock 850 feet up the slope opposite the slide area. Then, a huge wave, 330 feet higher than the crest of the dam,

8.3 Diagrammatic cross sections showing the landslide (slump) at Nicolet, Québec, in 1955. **(a)** Nicolet separated by a cliff from the river. **(b)** Excavation of road cut. Development of fractures in unconsolidated silts and clays. **(c)** Slump of part of the high area into the river after heavy rains. Note the development of new fractures, which are the forerunner of further slumping.

8.4 Cross section of the valley in which the Vaiont Reservoir is located, showing the geologic setting and the pre- and post-landslide topography.

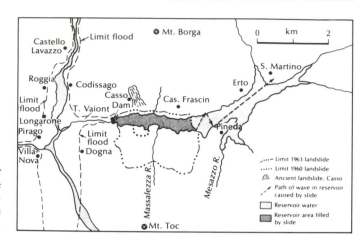

8.5 Map of Vaiont Reservoir
area, Italy, showing limits of the
landslide, the area of the reservoir filled by the slide, and the
extent of downstream flooding.

swept down and along the heavily populated
river valley below. In moments, the town of
Longarone (Fig. 8.5) and its 2500 inhabitants was destroyed. Ironically, the dam remained intact.

During the period 1962–71, 23 people
were killed in the greater Los Angeles area
as a result of being buried or struck by
debris flows. The flows, mixtures of water-
soaked soil and ravine fill (loose rock and
soil that clogs steep-sided valleys), coursed
down steep ravines after heavy rainfalls
(Campbell, 1975).

From the foregoing descriptions, it may
be seen that particularly disastrous landslides occur where towns or cities are situated on the lower slopes of mountains or
steep hills, especially if they are at the
mouths of narrow mountain valleys.

Minor Landslides

Most landslides are less dramatic and catastrophic than the ones described above. Cu-
mulatively, in economic terms, minor landslides, many of which are caused by humans, cause far greater disruption and damage. Artificially cut slopes and improper
placing of hillside fill are the chief culprits
(Morton and Streitz, 1967). *Cuts* and *fills*
are common in highway construction and in

the preparation of slopes for emplacement
of buildings.

Hilly areas of cities such as Los Angeles,
Seattle, Hong Kong, and Rio de Janeiro
have been particularly troubled. Typical urbanization of hillsides in the United States
involves creating a series of "steps" on
which buildings are constructed (Fig. 8.6).
The steep cut of each step removes support
from the uphill landmass, and placement of
buildings and swimming pools on the flat
part of the step may add weight to the un-
supported part of the slope. Heavy rains saturate and add further weight to the ground;
the water also lubricates fractures and bedding planes, facilitating slippage. In March
1978, heavy rains in the Los Angeles region
triggered landslides that caused millions of
dollars of damage.

The Palos Verdes section of the Los
Angeles metropolitan area in particular has
suffered numerous landslides (Fig. 8.8). A
court ruling found the County of Los
Angeles to be party to the reactivation of an
ancient landslide at Portugese Bend in this
area, and awarded $5,360,000 to the injured
party (an association of homeowners). Possible causes included increased groundwater
levels due to surface watering and seepage
of sewage effluent, increased rainfall, and
loading of the landslide head by highway
fill.

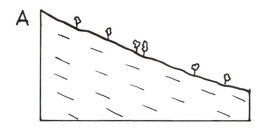

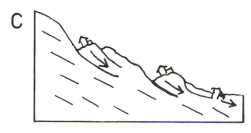

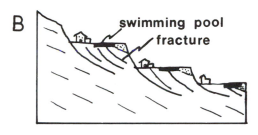

8.6 Diagrammatic cross sections showing the origin of landslides on poorly engineered hillside developments: **(a)** Natural slope of land before development. **(b)** Cut and fill alters natural slope; construction of houses and swimming pool. Note formation of fractures. **(c)** Movement along fractures, triggered by leakage from swimming pool and heavy rains.

Besides damaging buildings, landslides frequently cover and disrupt highways and railroads, break utility lines, and weaken or sweep away bridges.

LANDSLIDE CLASSIFICATION

Table 8.1 is a simplified version of a widely used landslide classification system. Figure

Table 8.1. Classification of landslides (After Varnes, 1958)

FALLS		Rockfall (bedrock)
		Soilfall (loose material)
SLIDES	Rotational movement	Slump (bedrock or cohesive units of loose material)
	Translational movement	Block glide (bedrock or cohesive units of loose material)
		Rock slide (bedrock)
		Debris slide (loose material)
		Failure by lateral spreading (bedrock or cohesive units of loose material)
FLOWS	Dry	Rockfall avalanche
		Rock slide avalanche
	Moderately wet	Debris avalanche (rock fragments, sand, clay)
		Earthflow (fine silt, clay)
	Very wet	Debris flow (rock fragments, sand, clay)
		Mudflow (fine silt, clay)

8.7 illustrates this system. Three general classes of movement are distinguished: *falls, slides,* and *flows.* It must be emphasized that different types of landslides often occur in combination with each other. The nomenclature of the parts of a landslide are illustrated in Figure 8.9.

Falls

In falls, material moves through the air, bounces, and rolls. Separate fragments move more or less independently of one another. If the material is bedrock, the fall is a *rockfall.* If the material includes rock fragments and sediment, it is a *soilfall.*

Slides

In slides, material moves down a slope along one or more discrete surfaces (such as bedding planes, joints, or faults) and follows relatively simple paths. Movement may be along either curved or planar sur-

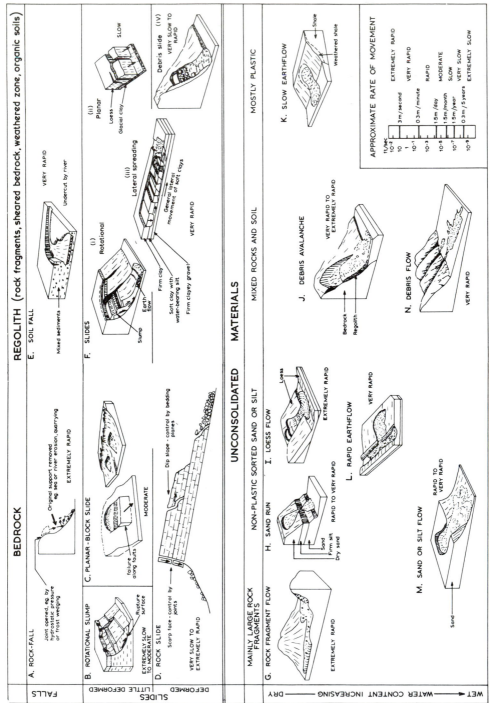

8.7 Classification of landslides.

Contents of the figure (labels read from the classification diagram):

BEDROCK (top section)
- **FALLS**
  - A. ROCK-FALL — Joint opened, eg by hydrostatic pressure or frost wedging — EXTREMELY RAPID
- **SLIDES / LITTLE DEFORMED**
  - B. ROTATIONAL SLUMP — Rupture surface, Scarp face - control by joints — EXTREMELY SLOW TO MODERATE
  - C. PLANAR - BLOCK SLIDE — failure along faults — MODERATE
- **SLIDES / DEFORMED**
  - D. ROCK SLIDE — Dip slope - control by bedding planes — VERY SLOW TO EXTREMELY RAPID

REGOLITH (rock fragments, sheared bedrock, weathered zone, organic soils)
- E. SOIL FALL — Original support removed eg sea or river erosion, quarrying — EXTREMELY RAPID — Mixed sediments, Undercut by river — VERY RAPID
- F. SLIDES
  - (i) Rotational — Slump, Earth flow, Firm clay, Soft clay with water-bearing silt, Firm clayey gravel — VERY RAPID
  - (ii) Planar — Loess, Glacial clay — SLOW
  - (iii) Lateral spreading — General lateral movement of soft clays — VERY RAPID
  - (iv) Debris slide — VERY SLOW TO RAPID

UNCONSOLIDATED MATERIALS
- MAINLY LARGE ROCK FRAGMENTS
  - G. ROCK FRAGMENT FLOW — EXTREMELY RAPID
- NON-PLASTIC SORTED SAND OR SILT
  - H. SAND RUN — Sand, Firm silt, Dry sand — RAPID TO VERY RAPID
  - I. LOESS FLOW — Loess — EXTREMELY RAPID
- MIXED ROCKS AND SOIL
  - J. DEBRIS AVALANCHE — Bedrock, Regolith — VERY RAPID TO EXTREMELY RAPID
  - K. SLOW EARTHFLOW — Weathered shale, Shale — MOSTLY PLASTIC
  - L. RAPID EARTHFLOW — VERY RAPID
  - M. SAND OR SILT FLOW — Sand — RAPID TO VERY RAPID
  - N. DEBRIS FLOW — VERY RAPID

WATER CONTENT INCREASING — DRY → WET

APPROXIMATE RATE OF MOVEMENT

ft/sec		
10⁻²	3 m/second	EXTREMELY RAPID
10		VERY RAPID
1	0.3 m/minute	RAPID
10⁻¹		MODERATE
10⁻³	1.5 m/day	SLOW
10⁻⁵	1.5 m/month	VERY SLOW
10⁻⁷	1.5 m/year	EXTREMELY SLOW
10⁻⁹	0.3 m/5 years	

170

8.8 Houses damaged by a landslide in Palos Verdes, California.

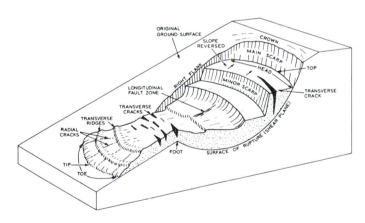

8.9 The principal features of a rotational slide.

faces. In *slump,* movement is rotational, along a curved surface that is concave upward. Several types of *translational movement* (movement in a straight line) along planar surfaces are distinguished: (1) in *block glide,* the mass remains relatively unbroken and moves as a unit, (2) *rock slides* occur when pieces of bedrock become detached and move independently of one another, (3) *debris slides* involve movement of materials that were loose before the slide began, (4) in *failure by lateral spreading,* blocks of relatively firm material are carried along on a deforming mass of underlying plastic material such as wet clay or sand.

Flows

In a flow, the mass travels in a complex constantly deforming way, similar to the motion of a viscous fluid. Such motion is made possible by the presence of water, or by air, which cushions the rapidly moving particles and separates them from the ground. Flows are capable of reaching well beyond the foot of the slope where they originate. They are classified according to size of fragment involved and degree of water saturation. Dry rockfalls and rock slides may become *rock avalanches* or *rock slide avalanches* if they build up sufficient velocity to develop fluid properties. Debris slides composed of mixtures of rock fragments, sand, and clay become *debris avalanches* if moderately wet, and *debris flows* if very wet. Flows consisting of fine silt or clay are *earthflows* if moderately wet, and *mudflows* if very wet.

Rates of Movement

Landslides may move hundreds of feet in a second or as little as one foot in several years. Typically, falls and avalanches may reach the greatest velocities; slumps and block glides may achieve velocities of several feet a day, but are often very slow; rock slides range from very fast to very slow; flows are fast or slow, depending upon the nature of the material, degree of saturation, and steepness of slope.

CAUSES OF LANDSLIDES

The cause of a landslide must be examined from two points of view: the *long-term susceptibility* of an area, in which no movement may have taken place for many thousands of years; and the *triggering*

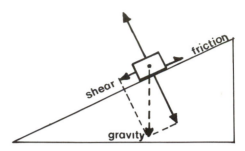

8.10 Diagram showing forces acting on a stationary object resting on an inclined plane.

mechanism, which finally sets the material into motion. Downhill movement due to gravity is possible on any surface which is not horizontal, and will occur when shearing stresses exceed retarding frictional forces (Fig. 8.10). Factors involved include steepness of slope, weight of material above a zone of weakness, existence of planes or zones of weakness, and cohesiveness of material.

Long-term Susceptibility

Where the land is steep, there will be a greater tendency for movement than where the land surface is closer to horizontal. Rock fall can only occur where slopes are extremely steep. However, flows, glides, and failure by lateral spreading may occur on very gently inclined slopes. Likelihood of failure is greatly enhanced by the presence of *planes* of weakness that are more or less parallel to the inclination of the land surface. Such planes include bedding and foliation planes, joints, and faults. *Zones* of weakness parallel to the land surface, such as plastic clay or shale or salt layers, also contribute to the tendency to slide. Porous and permeable materials can absorb water that increases their weight. Loose material composed of rounded grains, soft, platey flakes, or weathered rock is more susceptible to movement than material composed of angular, fresh fragments. Materials whose mechanical properties alter upon contact with water, such as clays that swell or become less cohesive when wet, can trigger movement.

Triggering Mechanisms

Actual movement of inherently unstable areas may be precipitated by natural or artificial events. Slope steepening may be caused by the erosion of streams, waves, or currents. When a landslide occurs, steep scarps are often created which make previously stable areas vulnerable to movement. Roadcuts, quarries, or canals can also increase slope angles. When reservoirs or lakes are drained, vital support may be removed from slopes. Weight added to unstable slopes by absorbed water or blankets of snow may cause movement. Similarly, watering of lawns, seepage of sewage effluent (especially from cesspools) and leaking street drains may initiate landslides. Artificial fill, waste piles, and ore stockpiles, placed on the head of a potential slide may trigger movement, as could construction activities in such areas. Heavy rains or melting snow may infiltrate the ground and lubricate surfaces along which slippage may take place.

Earthquake vibrations have triggered some of the most destructive landslides, sending rockfalls, slides, and avalanches roaring down steep slopes. The San Francisco earthquake of 1906, for example, triggered landslides over an area of approximately 13,000 square miles. Thousands of rockfalls followed the 1971 earthquake in the San Fernando Valley. That same earthquake triggered a slide on the upstream face of the old earthfill dam on Lower Van Norman Lake that necessitated the evacuation of 80,000 people in the downstream area.

Earthquakes can also trigger landslides on gently inclined slopes. Certain types of seismic vibrations can reduce the strength of so-called *sensitive* or *quick clays* by as much as 20–30 times. If water-saturated sands or artificial fill are subjected to vibration, increases in the pore pressure of the water can

effectively reduce the contact between sand grains so that the whole mass temporarily becomes liquid. Such liquefaction has heavily damaged structures built upon sands or fill. A description of landslides triggered by the Alaskan earthquake of 1964 is given in the case study of Anchorage (Chapter 7).

Clays

The term *clay* refers to a natural plastic substance composed of particles of diameter less than approximately one two-hundredth of a millimeter. Common constituents of clays are the *clay minerals,* a group of principally hydrous aluminosilicates.

Areas underlain by certain types of clays may be particularly vulnerable to landslides. Clays formed of glacial *rock flour* (derived from the grinding of rock fragments being transported by glacial ice) are composed of minutely ground-up particles of many minerals. If such material is deposited in salt or brackish water, the dissolved sodium chloride in the water acts as an electrolytic "glue" that holds the particles together and lends the formation strength and stability. If the clay is subsequently elevated above sea level and the salt water is flushed out by fresh groundwater, or if the sodium ions are replaced by calcium ions, the clay loses its "glue" and becomes extremely unstable. At this point the particles are arranged in a sort of open "honeycomb" that permits it to hold large quantities of water while remaining in the solid state. If this delicate structure is disturbed by earthquake vibrations, explosions, or other means, the structure may collapse and the clay turn to liquid mud. Due to such an occurrence during the Alaska earthquake of 1964, parts of the Bootlegger Cove Formation that underlies Anchorage failed by lateral spreading. That is, layers of sensitive clay within the formation lost their strength and caused the overlying material to slide laterally down extremely gentle inclines, creating substantial

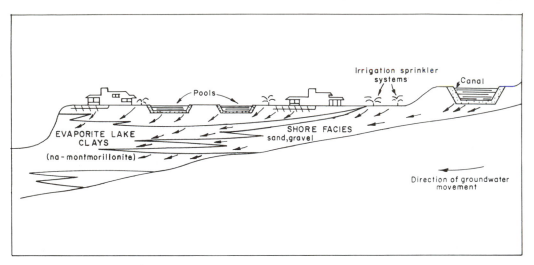

8.11 Cross section of a hypothetical California landscape analogous to Anchorage, illustrating how leakage from canals and swimming pools and water from sprinkler systems may enter the groundwater system. This water can leach sodium ions from clay layers, thus reducing the coherence of the clay and setting the stage for a major landslide.

damage. (See the case study of Anchorage, Chapter 7, for further details.)

After the Alaska earthquake, concern grew about the possibility of similar types of landslides in California during future earthquakes. Sensitive clays formed by the weathering of volcanic ash and that remain stable only in the presence of sodium chloride underlie parts of the Los Angeles Basin and other parts of California (Aune, 1966). While not so extreme in their behavior as the quick clays formed from glacial flours, much of their stability is lost if the salt is flushed out and they are wet with fresh water. For example, water transported from northern to southern California in concrete canals and aqueducts may pick up calcium from the concrete. If the structures leak, the calcium could displace sodium in the surrounding clays, increasing their sensitivity. Also fresh water pumped into the ground to facilitate recovery of oil can flush salt water from clays. In urban areas, the problem is

further exacerbrated by leakage from swimming pools and the use of lawn sprinklers (Fig. 8.11).

Reducing Landslide Hazard

Avoidance or reduction of damage from landslides may be achieved in several ways. It is important to recognize where landslides have occurred in the past because further movement may be triggered by construction or by the action of natural processes. Recent landslides may be recognized by open, unvegetated scars on a hillside, and by masses of rubble or other slipped material at the base of the hill. More ancient landslides which have been covered by vegetation may be recognized by certain types of "hummocky" hillsides or by the presence of steep cliff faces from which the material has moved away.

Whether or not past landslides have been identified, certain geologic conditions suggest the potential for future land slippage: among these are strong or cohesive material underlain by fractured or soft or non-cohesive material; steep slopes or slopes subject to erosion at their bases; accumulations on slopes of loose debris subject to sudden saturation; the presence of swelling clays, sensitive clays, or saturated sands. Construction in earthquake-prone belts should be undertaken only after careful analysis of landslide potential.

Landslide potential may be reduced by lessening of slopes, construction of retaining walls or nets where steep slopes are unavoidable, strengthening of the toes of potential landslides, and ensuring adequate surface and underground drainage. In some cases, unstable material may be removed from the head of a potential landslide before the toe is weakened or removed. Unwitting excavation of the toe of a potential landslide often precipitates movement of the upslope mass. Sometimes material may be stabilized by consolidating it artificially.

As urban areas expand into areas susceptible to landslide, revision of building codes and development of enforceable land-use policies are being sought. Following heavy rains that caused millions of dollars of damage in hillside areas of Los Angeles in January 1952, the city enacted amendments to the building code, which (1) control the steepness of slopes in cuts and fills, (2) ensure that drainage from individual lots is conducted away from cut and fill slopes and towards the streets and, (3) require the construction of erosion protection devices or the planting of erosion-preventing vegetation wherever changes in the natural grade are planned. Furthermore, on-site inspection is required before issuance of building permits in hillside areas. Existing hazardous cuts within city limits, numbering perhaps 10,000 in 1958, were not affected by the revised code, however (Smith, 1958).

Landslide hazard or susceptibility maps are an important aid in controlling landslide damage (Fig. 8.12). They are prepared from

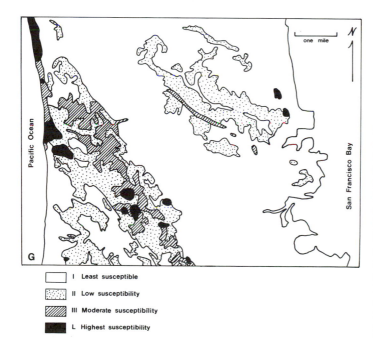

I Least susceptible
II Low susceptibility
III Moderate susceptibility
L Highest susceptibility

8.12 Relative degrees of landslide susceptibility (After Brabb *et al,* 1972). Four degrees of risk are shown: (I) Least susceptible. Large landslides possible but unlikely except during earthquakes. (II) Low susceptibility. Several small landslides have occurred; a few large landslides may occur. (III) Moderate susceptibility. Many small landslides have occurred; some large landslides likely. (L) Highest susceptibility. Consists of landslides and possible landslide deposits.

basic data maps showing slope, distribution of past landslide deposits, and from data on climate, drainage patterns, and earthquake potential.

Unfortunately, even after hazardous areas have been studied extensively, development often continues. Graphic descriptions of landslide sites on the northern Wasatch Front in Utah did not deter plans for urbanization (Pashley, Jr. and Wiggins, 1971). Cooperation between geologists, soil engineers, and urban planners to create safe land-use policies is clearly needed. The benefits of such cooperation are emphasized by landslide expert F. Beach Leighton, who estimates that a 95–99 percent reduction of landslide damage may be achieved through pre-development investigation and planning, and proper design and construction.

9. Volcanic Eruptions

Within the last five centuries, 200,000 people have been killed by the eruption of 500 of the earth's active volcanoes. This figure includes those who died of starvation subsequent to the destruction of crops and animals. In times past, human proximity to volcanoes was in large part due to the fertility of volcanic soils and, to some extent, to ignorance of the possibility of eruption. Today, through persistence of such ignorance or lack of alternative, the rapid spread of urbanization places increasing numbers of people within range of volcanic hazards. Urban development in volcanically hazardous regions is most likely where the interval between eruptions is measured in hundreds or thousands of years and where an eruption has not taken place within recent memory. Unfortunately, however, a long interval between eruptions is no guarantee that the period of quiescence will not terminate in an eruption of the most catastrophic nature. Vulcanologist Gordon Macdonald states that ''Probably volcanoes that have experienced a long period of rest should be regarded with the greatest suspicion if they show signs of returning activity, because the first eruption after such a period of dormancy is commonly of great violence, although a long rest is not a necessity for a violent eruption.'' (Bolt *et al*, 1975, p. 109)

Before the famous eruption of Vesuvius that destroyed the city of Pompeii and other towns around the Bay of Naples in A.D. 79, there had been no record of an eruption of the volcano in all of the long history of the Romans or of the Etruscans before them. Even where records of eruption do exist, people may choose to remain in familiar surroundings, where they feel at home, rather than migrate and face the unknown. The eruption of Mont Pelée on the island of Martinique in 1902 killed 30,000 people and destroyed the city of St. Pierre. The inhabitants must have known of the volcanic nature of the mountain since it had produced a rain of ash and cinders in 1851, only half a century earlier. As the behavior of volcanoes and the mechanisms of eruption are better understood, it is hoped that improved estimates may be made of the likelihood and severity of eruption of specific volcanoes so that more realistic planning for the development and use of threatened areas will become possible.

HAZARDS

Volcanic hazards are restricted to well-delineated zones where active or recently active volcanoes are located. Figure 9.1 shows the distribution of the approximately 600–800 volcanoes that are or may be active. (A volcano can be considered active

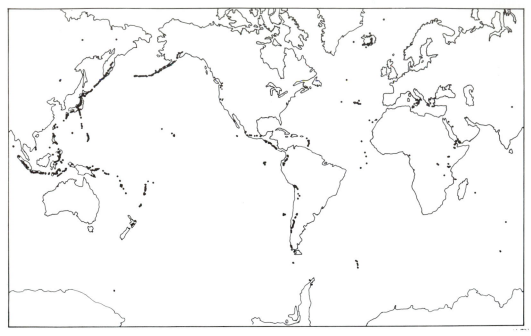

9.1 Map of the world showing the distribution of volcanoes (black dots).

and potentially dangerous if it has erupted within the last 10,000 years.) With few exceptions, known modern volcanoes occur (1) about the edge of the Pacific Ocean (including a detour into the West Indies); (2) in a discontinuous belt that runs from the Mediterranean to the East Indies; (3) along the African rift valleys; (4) along mid-oceanic ridges, particularly the Mid-Atlantic ridge; and (5) as islands in the Pacific. Outside these areas, volcanic hazard may be considered minimal or non-existent.

The hazards associated with volcanic activity are diverse. They include dangers from materials ejected during an eruption; earthquakes caused by ascent of magma; tsunamis generated by violent underwater or near-water eruptions; and floods and landslides that accompany volcanic activity or that involve volcanic materials.

During an eruption, great quantities of hot gases, molten lava, and incandescent solids (*pyroclastics*) are expelled. Most eruptions last for a few days or weeks, although some lasting as long as nine years have been observed. The violence of an eruption varies considerably. Volcanoes that produce principally gases and lava are characterized by relatively quiet, non-explosive eruptions; those producing mainly mixtures of gases and pyroclastics are violently to catastrophically explosive. Volcanoes in the circum-Pacific zone, including those in the Cascade Range, the Andes, Japan, Indonesia, and the Philippines, tend to erupt explosively. In mid-ocean areas like the Hawaiian Islands, eruptions are usually more gentle.

Lava flows commonly have temperatures on the order of 1000° and may pour down volcanic slopes at speeds up to 35 miles an hour. The movement of other, more viscous flows and those flowing over relatively flat surfaces may be almost imperceptible. The paths of lava flows, like those of other liq-

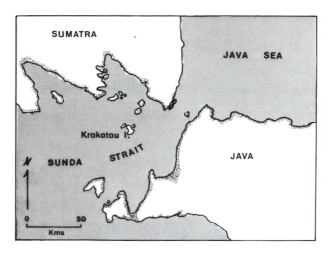

9.2 Areas inundated (dotted pattern) by the tsunami generated by the eruption of Krakatau, 1883.

uids, are generally restricted to pre-existing valleys, although the effects of flooding and damming of lava may make the course of the flows more erratic. Under favorable conditions, lava flows have been known to extend more than 100 miles from their source. Loss of life from flows is not common because their rate of advance is generally slow and their paths are more or less predictable. Advancing lava has, however, covered agricultural regions and destroyed towns and villages in Hawaii, Sicily, Mexico, and Iceland.

Eruption of pyroclastics can be much more dangerous. *Ash flows* (mixtures of gas and fine pyroclastic material) can travel 200 miles in 2–3 hours and remain hot enough for the solid particles to weld themselves together once they come to rest. In 1883, the island of Krakatau in Indonesia was destroyed by a series of violent eruptions that literally blasted a cubic mile of rock fragments as high as 17 miles into the air and left a hole in the ocean floor 900 feet deep. As the ocean waters rushed into the hole and then out again, a series of tsunamis were generated that swept over the coasts of neighboring Java and Sumatra, killing more than 30,000 people (Fig. 9.2). A similar eruption of the volcanic island of Thera

(Santorini) north of Crete in the Mediterranean (Fig. 9.3), ca. 1500 B.C., may have been one of the causes that precipitated the downfall of the Minoan Empire (Luce, 1969). The disappearance of Plato's Atlantis (whether real or mythical) may be connected with the eruption of Thera.

Destruction of the Roman cities of Pompeii, Herculaneum, and Stabiae in A.D. 79 was caused by the eruption of nearby Mount Vesuvius (Fig. 9.4). Before the eruption, warning of pending volcanic activity came in the form of a violent earthquake in A.D. 63 that caused great damage to built-up areas at the base of the volcano. The link between earthquakes and vulcanism, however, was not realized by the inhabitants and reconstruction was undertaken. Earthquakes continued intermittently over the next 16 years. Then, in A.D. 79, Vesuvius suddenly sent out huge clouds of gas, ash, and pumice. Within a matter of days, the hitherto prosperous cities of Pompeii and Stabiae were buried to a depth of more than ten feet. Human death was caused by exposure to noxious gases, by suffocation, and by the collapse of roofs weighed down with pyroclastic debris. The nearby city of Herculaneum was destroyed when it was overwhelmed by a flow of mud (composed

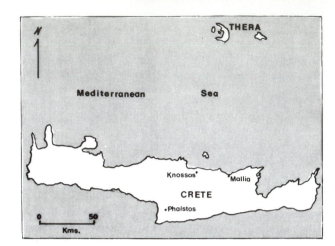

9.3 The islands of Crete and Thera (Santorini) in the Mediterranean Sea.

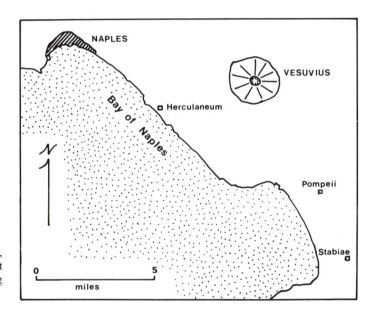

9.4 The Bay of Naples, Italy, showing the location of ancient Roman cities destroyed during the eruption of A.D. 79.

of a mixture of volcanic ash and rainwater) that swept over it from the slopes of the volcano.

A particularly deadly type of eruption destroyed the city of St. Pierre on the island of Martinique in the West Indies (Fig. 9.5). On the morning of May 8, 1902, a great cloud of hot gases and ash, a *glowing avalanche,* swept down from adjacent Mont Pelée; within two minutes the city was con-

sumed and virtually all of its 30,000 inhabitants killed. It has been estimated that temperatures within the avalanche were between 700° and 1000° C, and that its velocity was about 100 miles an hour. Warning was given in the guise of lesser eruptions that had been occurring for several weeks before the major eruption, throwing out quantities of cinder, ash, and unpleasant smelling gases. "Many people left the city,

9.5 Photograph of the ruins of St. Pierre, Martinique, with the spine
of Mont Pelée in the background, after the eruption of 1902.

and undoubtedly many more would have
done so had they not been urged by the
government to stay. An important election
was pending, and in order to vote the people must be in their home districts . . . A
government-appointed commission reported
no immediate risk to St. Pierre, and the
governor himself came to the city to reas-
sure the people. He never left!'' (Macdonald, 1972, p. 143).

Glowing avalanches generally flow along
valleys, but may have sufficient momentum
to climb several hundred yards vertically if
they encounter obstacles or are forced
around sharp bends.

Mudflows are another significant volcanic
hazard. According to Macdonald, ''During
the last few centuries mudflows have destroyed more property than any other type
of volcanic activity and have killed thousands of people'' (1972, p. 170). Three
days before the destruction of St. Pierre, a
flow of mud swept down the river valleys
on the sides of Mont Pelée. A sugarmill

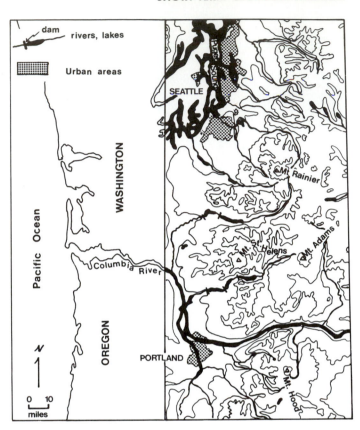

9.6 Topographic map of the Cascade Mountain Range in Washington and Oregon. Contours are at 0 (the shore of Puget Sound), 600, 1500, 3000, 6000 and 10,000 feet.

located at the mouth of one of the valleys was buried and about 30 workmen were killed. The ruin of the Roman city of Herculaneum by mudflows from Vesuvius has already been mentioned. A *volcanic mudflow* consists of a mixture of water (either hot or cold) and pyroclastic material or soil. The water may be derived from a variety of sources that include rainfall, rapid melting of snow and ice on the slopes of the volcano due to volcanic heat, and sudden draining of the lakes that are sometimes present within craters of dormant volcanoes. The pyroclastics may be derived from material that has been lying on the slopes of the volcano for a considerable time, or that has been freshly ejected. Whatever the source of the mixture, as mud it may flow at rates up to 60 miles an hour and travel more than 100

miles. During its passage, the mud is capable of picking up and transporting huge objects weighing many tons, and of sweeping away most loose objects in its path. Mudflows that move down river valleys pose a special hazard if they enter damned reservoirs (Fig. 9.6). The mud can displace the water, causing it to overflow, or may cause dam-failure and catastrophic flooding of downstream areas. Geologists D. R. Crandell and H. H. Mullineaux stress the potential danger to towns and cities situated downstream of reservoirs on rivers draining the slopes of volcanoes in the Cascade Range. The pattern of mudflow deposits formed within the last 5000 years shows that repetition of such flows could threaten dams, reservoirs, and the homes and lives of perhaps close to 100,000 people. Failure

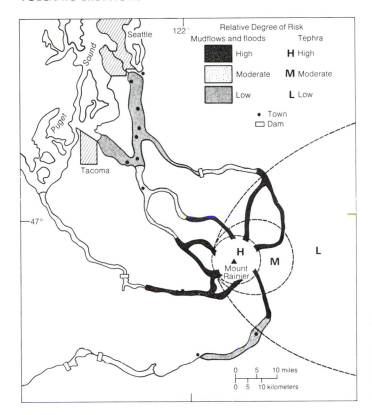

9.7 Sketch map of the area near Mount Rainier, Washington, showing relative degrees of potential hazard from mudflows, floods, and fallout of volcanic debris (tephra) in the event of an eruption.

of three large hydroelectric reservoirs along the Lewis River that flows just south of Mount St. Helens could cause serious damage to numerous small communities in the Columbia River Valley, and could perhaps also threaten the city of Portland, Oregon (Fig. 9.6). Failure of dams along the Puyallup and White rivers, which flow generally northwest from Mount Rainier, could be disastrous to towns in the lower reaches of the rivers and for the expanding suburbs of Tacoma and Seattle, Washington. Figure 9.7 shows relative degrees of potential hazard from mudflows and floods that could accompany an eruption of Mount Rainier. Similarly, eruptions of Mounts Baker, Lassen or Shasta could affect nearby communities and to the numerous summer visitors to these areas.

The Sherman Crater area of Mount Baker, Washington, emitted a column of steam on March 10, 1975, that was clearly visible from populated areas in the Puget Lowland to the west. Geologist Don Easterbrook considers that Mount Baker is now showing the most intensive heating up in more than 120 years, although as yet there is no positive evidence of lava moving into the volcano. If activity intensifies, there is serious danger that melting snow and ice may cause mudflows or avalanches in Baker Lake, threatening Baker Dam. If the dam were to fail, the towns of Concrete, Sedro Woolley, Burlington, and Mt. Vernon would be endangered.

Acid gases emitted during volcanic eruptions may cause considerable damage to crops and metal objects. When Katmai in the Aleutian Range erupted in 1912, an acid rain fell hundreds of miles away at Seward and Cordova, Alaska, that burned some people's skin. When the gases reached Vancouver a month later, acid rains damaged clothing hung on outdoor lines to dry. Similarly, fine pyroclastic material that is caught by the wind is capable of being transported great distances. An eruption in the Valley of Ten Thousand Smokes, Alaska, caused a ten-inch accumulation of ash and pumice at Kodiak, 100 miles distant. The January 23, 1976, eruption of Mount St. Augustine in Alaska sent up clouds of ash that passed over Arizona only two days later (Meinel *et al*, 1976). Dust from the eruption of Krakatau was caught by the wind and transported entirely around the globe, resulting in spectacular sunsets for several years after.

MINIMIZING THE HAZARD

Estimating of volcanic hazard involves evaluation of the likelihood of future eruption; the degree of eruptive violence; types and quantities of materials that may be expelled; the probable paths of lava flows, mudflows, and glowing avalanches; the ultimate disposition of pyroclastics; and the relationship of the above to artificial structures. Volcanoes that have erupted within human memory or whose shapes remain largely intact and unravaged by erosion can be considered potentially active. Long-term hazard exists, therefore, within any of the zones containing active or recently active volcanoes. The existence of long-term hazard, however, does not and should not deter human development of an area: thousands or tens of thousands of years may elapse between eruptions. More significant is short-term hazard, which means that an eruption can reasonably be expected within years, decades, or at most a century or two. Future eruptions may be predicted by examining records of past volcanic activity and through observation and instrumentation designed to chart physical changes that may be the precursors of eruption. Such changes include anomalous patterns of magnetic intensity and orientation, altered electrical conduc-

tivity, patterns of minor eruptions and gas emission, the occurrence of local earthquakes that may signal the ascent of magma, and the slight swelling of volcanic cones that in some cases precedes eruption. Detection of temperature changes through infrared photography may be of importance in the future.

Beyond possible prediction of eruption, estimates of damage caused by eruption may be made by careful mapping of past lava flows and pyroclastic and mudflow deposits. Similarly, the degree of violence that a particular volcano is capable of may be postulated through examining its past behavior. However, extreme departures from "usual" behavior are possible. Also, in estimating potential hazard at a specific place, the configuration of the land surface, the location of natural drainage courses, lakes and reservoirs, and the prevailing wind direction must be taken into account.

The greatest lava flow in historic times was in 1783 in Iceland and covered 560 square kilometers. However, individual flows in prehistoric times covered much greater areas. One flow in the Columbia Plateau of eastern Washington and Oregon covered an area of about 52,000 square km. As Macdonald says "Future flows of this sort could wipe out huge areas of agricultural land and whole cities. . . . (Bolt *et al*, 1975, p. 87)

Where explosive eruptions of the type that destroyed Krakatau and Thera have occurred, the possibility for repetition of such violence exists. During the eruption 7000 years ago that pulverized the ancient Mount Mazama and created the giant volcanic summit depression now occupied by Crater Lake, Oregon, 13–17 cubic miles of magma were ejected as pumice, ash showers, and glowing avalanches. The prevailing southwesterly wind spread the erupted volcanic ash in a generally north and east direction for a distance of 100 km, and an asymmetric area of 13,000 square km was buried to a depth of seven inches (Fig. 9.8). Eruptions of comparable magnitude in the Cas-

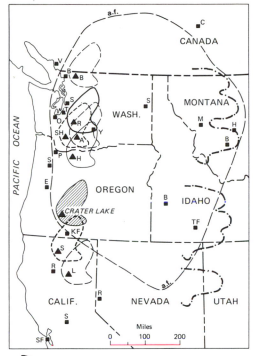

a.f. ⟩ Maximum limits of ash fall,
7000 years ago

⬭ Region covered by 6" or more of pumice,
7000 years ago

■ Major cities and towns

▲ Major Cascade Range volcanoes

⟩ Limit of future pumice fall hazard

9.8 Map of Cascade Range, showing areas covered by volcanic debris in past and future eruptions. Areas similar in shape to the one covered by six inches or more of pumice 7000 years ago from that same eruption (patterned area) are superimposed on other major volcanoes to suggest possible regions of high pumice accumulation in the event of future eruptions.

cade Range today would affect numerous population centers if the wind direction was toward the west. However, prevailing winds are generally toward the east. "A possible exception to this might be local cold air winds that blow from the mountain down valleys at night. A secondary danger stems

from accumulations of unstable ash deposits on steep slopes that are subject to debris slides and mudflows. . . ." (Easterbrook, 1975, p. 182)

Thus, the potential for catastrophic eruption of volcanoes in the Cascades presents Portland, Tacoma, Seattle and Vancouver with the possibility, albeit remote, of serious damage. Similarly, another explosive eruption of Thera could create tsunamis that could do extensive damage to low-lying coastal cities in the Mediterranean.

Volcanic eruptions cannot be prevented. Measures to avoid or lessen damage are possible in some cases. Diversion of lava flows through construction of walls or dams may be of use, but there has been little implementation of the idea. Bombing to break lava tubes or to breach lava dams or levees to allow flow into designated, less-developed areas has been tried with partial success in Hawaii. Slowing the advance of lava by spraying its surface with water to cool and harden it was the method employed in Iceland in 1973 to save the port of Vestmannaeyjar, from being engulfed by material erupted from the volcano Eldfellin (Williams, 1976). Approximately 6 million cubic meters of sea water was sprayed onto the advancing lava flows, converting 4.2 million cubic meters of the lava into solid rock. It was estimated that the economic benefit in terms of saved structures far exceeded the cost of $1.5 million.

Where developed areas are threatened by the possible failure of dams due to rapid displacement of water in reservoirs by mudflows (or other types of landslides of volcanic materials), provision should be made for draining reservoirs when eruption seems imminent.

In areas where erupted pyroclastics might accumulate, clogging the filters of water-supply systems, enough water for several days should be stored indoors. Roofs should periodically be cleared of pyroclastic debris to prevent their collapse, and drains should be kept clear to avoid flooding.

In Japan, where more than 300,000 people live in the shadow of 200 Quaternary volcanic cones (of which approximately 80 may be considered active) a comprehensive observation program and an effective warning system has been put into effect. The potential for disastrous eruptions in the Cascade Range has prompted the call for further investigation and development of ways to improve prediction and provide warning of eruption in this region. In response, the U.S. Geological Survey is studying volcanoes in the Cascades and in Hawaii in order to determine risks and to develop maps of areas likely to be affected by volcanic hazards. One such study estimates, for example, that in the east rift zone of the Hawaiian volcano Kilauea, 16 percent of which has been covered by lava since 1750, there is in any 25-year period a 4 percent chance of any given house in the area being destroyed by lava (Macdonald, 1975).

In conjunction with the methods described above, volcanic hazard may be best minimized by land-use regulations designed to avoid dense development of areas most prone to damage in the event of eruption.

10. Stream Floods and Sedimentation

The phenomenon of flooding is of concern when places important to humans are affected. Several types of floods may be defined: those caused by rises in stream level; by inadequate drainage during or after prolonged precipitation; and by coastal storms, high tides, and waves. Problems of inadequate drainage are discussed in Chapter 6; coastal and lakefront flooding are discussed in Chapter 11. Emphasis in this chapter will be on stream floods.

Flooding is one of the most costly and serious hazards to be faced in use of land resources (Fig. 10.1). Damage is of three principal varieties: that caused by (1) water immersion; (2) the impact of moving water and water-carried debris; and (3) the erosional and depositional activities of streams as their volume and velocity rise and fall. Despite increasing flood-control measures, the problems continue to increase as urban areas subject to flooding expand. About 50,000,000 acres of land in the United States are below flood levels, and the population densities in these areas are over twice the national average (Hoyt and Langbein 1955). Thus, more than 14,000,000 Americans face direct flood hazards. Examples are numerous and geographically widespread. New Orleans is entirely situated on river alluvium, protected from flooding only by levees and dikes; every large flood on the lower Mississippi threatens the city. During almost every winter and spring, cities in the Ohio River Valley, including Pittsburgh, Wheeling, Cincinnati, Louisville, Paducah, and Evansville, are inundated where protection is inadequate. In January 1937, about 1,500,000 people in the Ohio Valley were driven from their homes by a flood that caused more than $400 million damage and killed 65 people. During this flood, 10 percent of Cincinnati was under water. In Rapid City, South Dakota, a flood in June 1972 took 231 lives and caused $150,000,000 damage. Failure of a dam on the South Fork of the Little Conemaugh River 15 miles above Johnstown, Pennsylvania, took 2100 lives in May 1889. When the Fraser River in British Columbia flooded in the spring of 1948, the city of Vancouver was cut off from the rest of Canada, except by air communication, for 30 days.

The most hazardous place compared to any other area in the United States of comparable size and population density is metropolitan Los Angeles County. Between 1811 and 1954, for example, there were 21 major floods in that area.

In 1968, the U.S. Water Resources Council, on the basis of existing status of flood-control works and projected flood-plain use and development, estimated that

10.1 Hartford, Conn., flooded by overflow from the Connecticut
River, March 1936.

the total annual flood damage potential in
the United States would rise from $1.7 bil-
lion in 1966 to $5 billion in 2020. In Cali-
fornia alone, losses between 1970 and the
year 2000 are expected to be $6.5 billion if
the present level of flood-control measures
are maintained. Beyond property damage,
approximately 80 people in the United
States lose their lives each year in floods
caused by streams. In other parts of the
world, the death rate from such flooding is
considerably higher. In India, annual loss of
life is about 700, and 16 million people are
directly affected by flooding. Individual
floods in China have taken the lives of
hundreds of thousands of people.

FLOODING

In order to understand the origin of floods it
is necessary to understand the ways in
which water moves over and under the surface of the earth. It is suggested, therefore,
that the reader review the discussions of
surface and underground water in Chapter
3.

The volume of water flowing in a stream
constantly varies. As a result, the level or
elevation of the stream surface and the area
which the water covers also vary. Dry
stream beds in arid regions on occasion are
filled with roaring torrents of water. These
may be considered floods even if the water

is present only within the channel if the channel has been used for building sites. Albuquerque, New Mexico, for example, is rapidly expanding onto the beds of dry washes that drain the mountains behind the city. Permanent streams in wetter regions may for short periods achieve volumes more than 100 times greater than either minimal or average volume. When stream volume increases sufficiently, the water may exceed the "bankfull" stage: the water overflows the banks and floods surrounding low-lying regions. As the volume of a stream increases, its velocity also increases, allowing more sediment to be transported and larger particles to be moved. Flooding streams characteristically transport great quantities of mud, sand, gravel, and even boulders. Movement of such material may cause erosion, substantially altering the stream channels and their banks. As floods subside, much of the material is deposited, either within or outside the channel. Sediment deposition as well as erosion may affect the character of channels and adjacent regions.

Variation in stream volume is caused by fluctuations in the amount of water it receives (see Chapter 3). A stream is fed from a number of sources. Rainwater or melting snow and ice may make its way to the stream through groundwater circulation. Water may also reach a stream as *surface runoff*. *Tributary* streams contribute water to a main river. As the sources of water vary in amount, the *discharge* (volume of water passing a given point in a given length of time) and the elevation of the stream surface will vary accordingly. Also, the rate of increase or decrease in discharge and the maximum and minimum discharge achieved depend upon variations in the rate of supply.

Stream levels decline during periods of minimum precipitation due to lack of surface runoff and gradual decrease in the influx of groundwater. During a drought, levels decline radically, and prolonged drought may cause streams to go dry as the water table sinks below the elevation of the

bottom of the channel. On the other hand, during rainy periods, stream levels rise relatively rapidly as water that is unable to infiltrate the groundwater system flows over the surface into the channel. The amount of surface runoff depends on the rate of precipitation compared to the rate of infiltration into the groundwater system. *Infiltration capacity* varies according to the permeability of the rock, sediment, and soil underlying the drainage basin; the slope of the land; and the kind and degree of vegetation. Heavy rainfall is likely to saturate the surface quickly, preventing infiltration and resulting in abundant surface runoff and a rapid rise in stream level. Gentle rainfall, even if prolonged, may not exceed infiltration capacity, and results in little or no surface runoff; thus, stream discharge and stream level will increase gradually.

The rate of surface runoff from snow or ice will depend upon the rate of melting and the degree of saturation of the ground. Rapid melting quickly saturates the surface, resulting in a high rate of runoff. Stream discharge and level are also affected by dams, lakes, and reservoirs. Flow may be blocked by vegetation or ice, or by dams made by animals or humans.

The extent to which a stream will flood depends not only upon fluctuations in discharge, but also upon factors such as the cross-sectional shape and area of the channel, its gradient and its straightness. These factors help to control the stream's effectiveness in transmitting water, and may vary considerably along its length. Thus, one section of a stream may be able to transmit an increased discharge without overflowing, while another section of the same stream may top its banks and flood low-lying regions.

The areal extent of flooding and the depth of water covering an area will be affected both by the amount of stream discharge and the configuration of local topography. Fig. 10.2 illustrates some typical river-valley cross sections. Streams flowing in narrow, steep-sided valleys increase considerably in

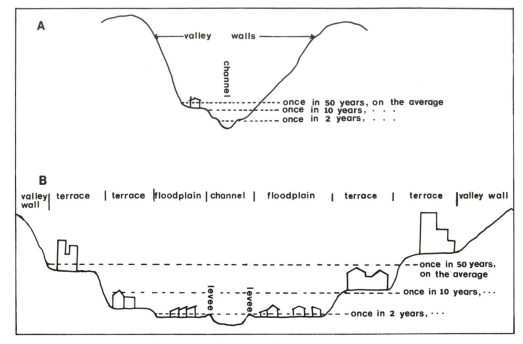

10.2 Schematic cross-section of stream valleys showing heights of
2-, 10-, and 50-year floods. (A) Narrow, V-shaped valley. (B)
Broad valley with levees, floodplain, and terraces.

depth during times of increased discharge, but will not cover materially larger areas. However, towns, highways, and railroads in narrow valley bottoms are almost always subject to flooding. Streams that flow on the floors of broad, flat valleys may cover a large area during flood. Flat areas commonly subject to flooding are called *floodplains,* and in a very real sense are the high-water channels of streams. Floodplains, because of the fertility of their soil, and their proximity to a source of water, an avenue of transport, and a medium for waste disposal, are a common site for human settlement. *River terraces* (flat, horizontal areas within a river valley at an elevation distinctly higher than the floodplain) offer relative freedom from flooding within reasonable distance from a river and the advantages it offers. Much of the central district of Wash-

ington, D.C., including the Capitol building, is built on terrace deposits. In arid regions of the country, *alluvial fans* (formed where streams bring sediment from mountainous regions during cloudbursts) are becoming increasingly urban. The intermittent streams that flow over these deposits characteristically shift their course from time to time, making such areas potentially hazardous. Parts of Salt Lake City and Los Angeles are built on alluvial fans. Figure 10.3 shows relative flood danger on a typical alluvial fan in the western United States. In cities of the Southwest, such as Las Vegas, Tucson, and Albuquerque, structures have been erected directly in dry stream channels in the mistaken belief that they have been permanently abandoned by the streams. Some of these structures have subsequently been destroyed by floods.

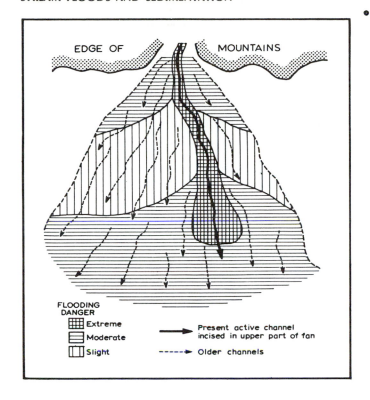

10.3 Map showing the relative flooding danger on a typical alluvial fan in the western United States.

Evaluating Flood Hazards

A multiplicity of information is needed to evaluate flood hazards, including frequency and magnitude of flooding; rate of discharge; area, depth, and duration of inundation; floodwater velocity; sediment load; and time of the year when flooding is most likely.

The frequency and magnitude of floods may be estimated from past records of stream behavior. The U.S. Geological Survey publishes flood-information atlases that include hydrologic data concerning the extent, depth, and frequency of flooding. In 1967, there were more than 8000 USGS gaging stations operating continuously in the conterminous United States, and 225 in Alaska and Hawaii. The Army Corps of Engineers and the Tennessee Valley Authority

also provide information relevant to floods.

If records of stream behavior are unavailable, flood frequency may be estimated from the general configuration and climate of the drainage basin. *Discharge-frequency* or *flood-frequency* curves, like the one shown in Figure 10.4 may be constructed by plotting recurrence intervals of peak flows of individual streams. Such plots suggest the likelihood of occurrence of a flood of given magnitude within a given time period. For instance, in the example shown, a stream discharge of 5000 cubic feet per second may occur on an average of once every six years; that is, the likelihood of a discharge of that amount within any given year is one chance in six, or 16.6 percent. This does not mean that such a flood will occur within the stated interval; rather it suggests that over a very long time

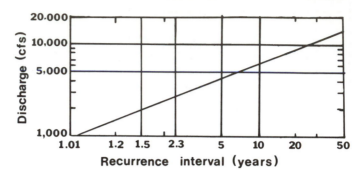

10.4 Graph showing the recurrence interval of floods of different magnitudes.

period, six years will be the average interval between floods involving a discharge of that amount of water.

The *average annual flood* is determined by calculating the arithmetic mean of the largest flow occurring each year for the length of time that records have been kept for a given stream. Studies of stream channels reveal that they are constructed and maintained (by the stream) so that they transmit, without overflowing, discharges just slightly less than those equal to the average annual flood. "Flooding" in the ordinary sense, therefore, involves discharges equal to or in excess of average annual floods. Most streams "flood" once every 1.5–2 years.

Another useful concept involves the maximum expectable height that a stream may reach within a given length of time. Referring to Figures 10.5 and 10.6 it may be seen that in the Lake Street Basin along Salt Creek, a flood rising to 672.3 feet may be expected on an average of once every 25 years. Such a flood is referred to as a "25-year flood." Similarly, elevations of 10-year, 50-year, 100-year, and N-year floods may be estimated. The probability that a 25-year flood will occur is 10 percent; that a 50-year flood will occur is 2 percent; that an N-year flood will occur is $1/N \times 100$ percent. Such information is valuable in estimating flood hazard at a particular locality.

Using flood-frequency curves and calculations of the areal extent of floods, the probability and depth of flooding at points away from the stream channel may be estimated. Hypothetical calculations such as this along with observations of actual floods may be used to construct flood-hazard maps.

Flood-Hazard Maps

An extensive flood-hazard mapping program in the metropolitan Chicago area was initiated in 1961. Figure 10.5 is a topographic map of part of the Elmhurst quadrangle, just west of the city. Consider the problem of estimating flood hazard at a particular point 23.5 miles above the mouth of Salt Creek (the major stream). Figure 10.6 is a flood-frequency curve for the Lake Street Bridge. The point in question lies downstream of the bridge, and an adjustment must be made for the water-surface slope between the two points. From the profiles or high-water elevations of floods along Salt Creek (Fig. 10.7), it may be seen that at the bridge (river mile 24) the 1954 flood crested at 671.5 feet, while at river mile 23.5 (the point in question), the crest was 671 feet. Figure 10.6 shows that the 1954 flood has an 8-year "recurrence interval"; thus, at river mile 23.5, flood waters may be expected to reach an elevation of 671 feet on an average of once every 8 years. The extent of inundation perpendicular to the stream at river mile 23.5 may be determined by examining the topographic map (Fig. 10.5) to see where the land lies

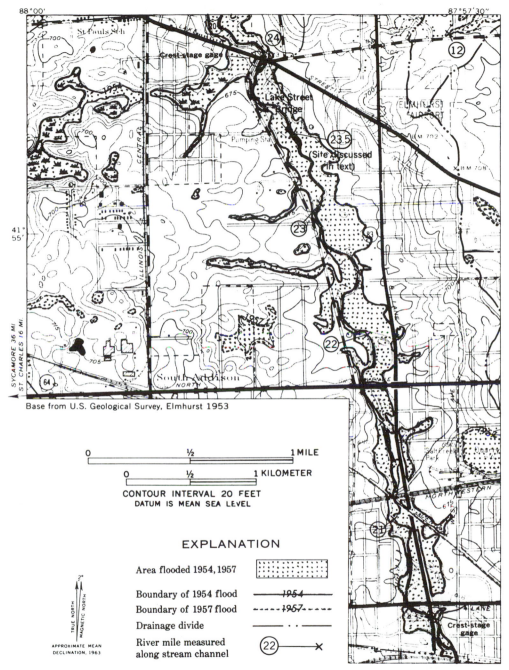

10.5 Flood-hazard map of part of the Elmhurst, (Illinois) quadrangle.

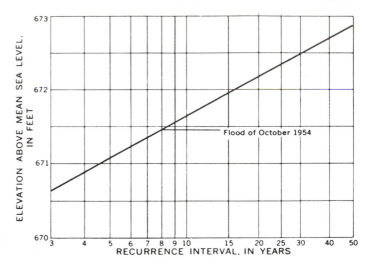

10.6 Frequency of floods on Salt Creek at Addison (Lake Street).

below 671 feet. (On the map, the area inundated by 8-year floods is dotted, because the 1954 flood was an 8-year flood.) For floods of different recurrence intervals, the flood-frequency curve and the flood-profile graph (Figs. 10.6 and 10.7) may be consulted. For instance, the flood-frequency curve for a 25-year flood indicates that at the Lake Street Bridge, high water will reach 672.3 feet. If this elevation is plotted at river mile 24 on the graph, and a line is drawn through the plotted point parallel to the 1954 profile, it will be seen that at river mile 23.5 the high-water level for a 25-year flood would be 671.8 feet (assuming the slope of the water during the 25-year flood is the same as that during the 1954 flood). Locating that point (671.8 feet) along the line perpendicular to the stream at river mile 23.5 will reveal the expectable extent of inundation for a 25-year flood. Similar calculations may be made for other points along the stream for floods of differing recurrence intervals.

From such calculations, together with field investigations of areas flooded in the past, maps permitting estimates of flood-hazard may be prepared, and the advantages of a given land use may be weighed against the probability of flood damage within a given time interval.

Fig. 10.8 illustrates the probable boundaries of areas that would be inundated at Boulder, Colorado, by hypothetical floods having recurrence intervals of 25, 50, and 100 years. All the estimates are based on the condition of Boulder Creek Valley in the fall of 1959. The depth of the 50- and 100-year floods may be estimated by computing the difference between the elevation of the water surface and the ground. Figure 10.9 is a flood-frequency curve for a crest-stage gaging site on Boulder Creek. A broader view of the areas subject to inundation in the event of a 100-year flood within the city limits is shown in Figure 10.10.

Flood-hazard maps thus indicate *flood zones,* defined as bands within which floods occur with comparable frequency. Proper land use within each zone would reflect frequency of flooding in that zone. One suggestion for appropriate land use in a flood zone is that the 1.5-year zone should correspond to the channel itself, and no obstructions should interfere with the free flow of water. The 1.5- to 10-year zone should also be kept free of obstacles and be reserved for agriculture, parks, and roads. In the 10- to 100-year zone, buildings might be permitted, either with the first floor higher than the 100-year level, or flood-proofed (Bue, 1967).

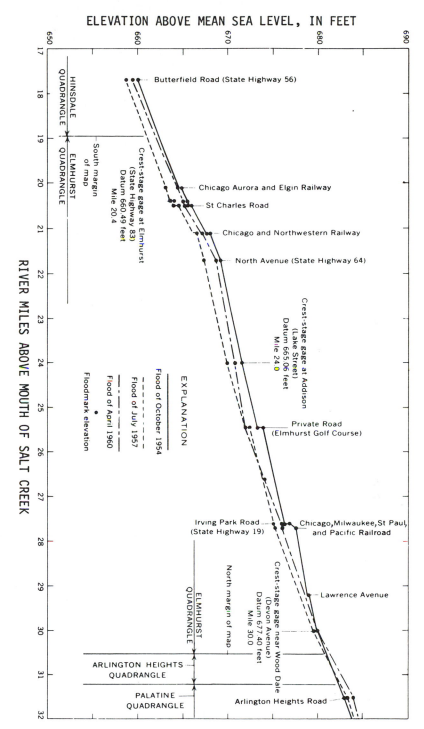

ELEVATION ABOVE MEAN SEA LEVEL, IN FEET

RIVER MILES ABOVE MOUTH OF SALT CREEK

Butterfield Road (State Highway 56)

HINSDALE QUADRANGLE
ELMHURST QUADRANGLE

South margin of map

Crest-stage gage at Elmhurst
(State Highway 83)
Datum 660.49 feet
Mile 20.4

Chicago Aurora and Elgin Railway

St Charles Road

Chicago and Northwestern Railway

North Avenue (State Highway 64)

Crest-stage gage at Addison
(Lake Street)
Datum 665.06 feet
Mile 24.0

EXPLANATION

Flood of October 1954

Flood of July 1957

Flood of April 1960

Floodmark elevation

Private Road
(Elmhurst Golf Course)

Irving Park Road
(State Highway 19)

Chicago, Milwaukee, St Paul,
and Pacific Railroad

North margin of map

ELMHURST QUADRANGLE

Crest-stage gage near Wood Dale
(Devon Avenue)
Datum 677 40 feet
Mile 30.0

Lawrence Avenue

ARLINGTON HEIGHTS QUADRANGLE

PALATINE QUADRANGLE

Arlington Heights Road

10.7 A graph showing profiles (high water elevations) of 3 major floods along Salt Creek.

195

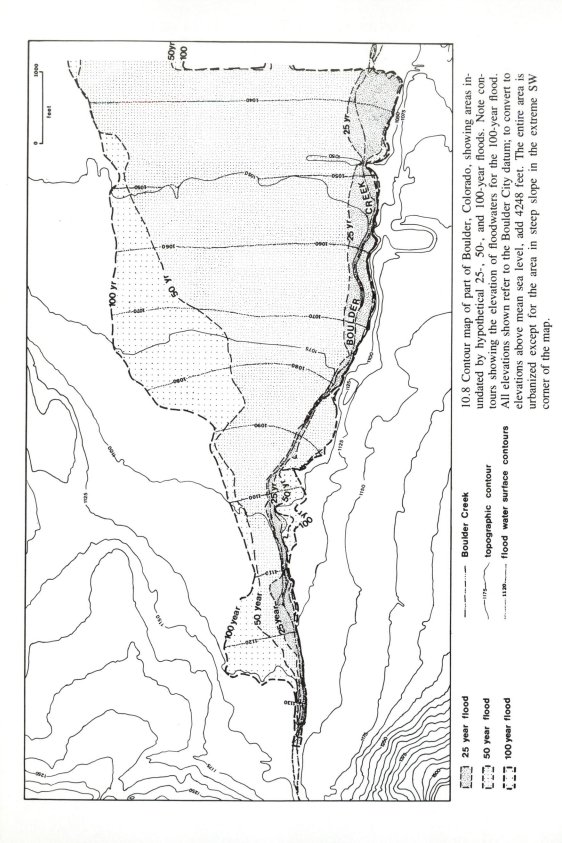

10.8 Contour map of part of Boulder, Colorado, showing areas inundated by hypothetical 25-, 50-, and 100-year floods. Note contours showing the elevation of floodwaters for the 100-year flood. All elevations shown refer to the Boulder City datum; to convert to elevations above mean sea level, add 4248 feet. The entire area is urbanized except for the area in steep slope in the extreme SW corner of the map.

Boulder Creek

1175 topographic contour

1120 flood water surface contours

25 year flood

50 year flood

100 year flood

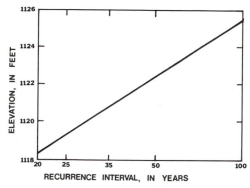

10.9 Frequency of floods reaching different elevations above 1118 feet at the Sixth Street crest-stage gaging site on Boulder Creek, Boulder, Colorado.

Floodplains within cities present dramatic possibilities for parks. In Fort Worth, Texas, the 8-mile stretch of the Trinity River floodplain is envisioned as a continuous corridor containing pedestrian, equestrian, and bicycle trails. In Dallas, the same Trinity River and its floodplain form a semi-circle around two sides of the central city, offering Dallas "the chance for a greenbelt more spacious than in any comparable city and a park system unsurpassed in its many uses and its close proximity to the central core . . ." (Heckscher, 1977, p. 226).

The need for flood-hazard information is particularly acute in metropolitan Chicago and other topographically similar regions of flat terrain and poorly developed drainage where floodplains are not readily perceptible to the human eye (Sheaffer *et al,* 1970).

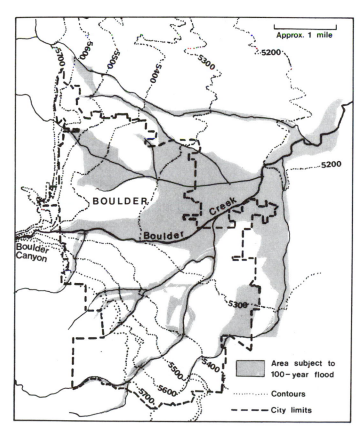

10.10 Map showing areas in Boulder, Colorado, subject to inundation in the event of a 100-year flood.

The first two phases of Chicago's flood-hazard mapping program were completed in 1969. Supplemental contours were added to existing topographic maps covering approximately 3700 square miles at a scale of 1:24,000; the boundaries of historical floods were outlined on inundation maps; and 394 crest-stage gages were installed. The cost was $474,460. Future plans call for the continued operation of the gage network. Thus, as urbanization continues, hydrologic data will be continually updated, flood-hazard maps periodically revised, the program extended to unmapped areas. Furthermore, the mapping of historical floods together with the boundaries of projected N-year floods will provide a sound basis for planning and decision-making. Boundary estimation of 100-year floods would be especially useful in determining premium rates under the National Flood Insurance Act of 1968 and the Federal Flood Disaster Protection Act of 1973, for it has been agreed that areas inundated by 100-year floods should define the regulatory areas of these acts. (See section on floodplain regulation).

In summary, the proper use of flood-hazard maps will help to: (1) Prevent improper land development in floodplains, (2) restrict uses hazardous to health and welfare and which would lead to undue claims on public agencies for remedy, (3) encourage adequate stream-channel maintenance, (4) protect prospective home-buyers from locating in flood-prone areas, (5) preserve potential for natural groundwater recharge during floods, (6) guide the purchase of public open space, (7) avoid water pollution resulting from flooding of sewage treatment plants and solid-waste disposal sites, (8) enable banks or private lenders to consider flood hazard in writing mortgages (the availability of loans usually controls construction), (9) permit premium rates for flood insurance to reflect the degree of risk more accurately, and (10) allow specific flood warnings to be given in areas likely to be inundated (Bue, 1967; Schaeffer *et al*, 1970).

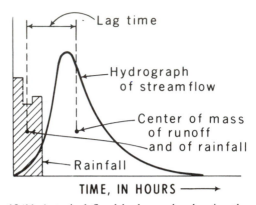

10.11 A typical flood hydrograph, showing the relationship between rainfall and magnitude of stream flow with time. The vertical axis indicates amount of rainfall or magnitude of stream discharge.

Flood Hydrographs

Flood hydrographs are also important in estimating flood hazard and in preparing adequate response to flood dangers. A typical hydrograph is shown in Figure 10.11, and illustrates the change of discharge during a particular flood at a single gaging station. The discharge-time curve reveals several important flood characteristics: The height of the curve equals *peak flow*. The steepness of the two limbs of the curve indicate the rate of increase and decline of discharge. The horizontal width of the curve at any given discharge shows the length of time that particular discharge was equaled or exceeded. The area under the curve indicates the amount of total runoff. From this information, changes in the extent and depth of inundation with time can be calculated. If flooding is caused by a rainstorm, and if the storm is plotted on the same graph as discharge, then lag time and flood-to-peak interval can be determined. *Lag time* is the lapse in time between the center of mass of precipitation (the midpoint of total precipitation during a storm) and the center of mass of associated runoff (the midpoint of total runoff flow). *Flood-to-peak interval* is the time-lapse between the moment a predetermined discharge rate (*floodstage*) is exceeded and the moment flood crest is reached.

The Effect of Urbanization

Flood frequency, magnitude, and hazard are affected by natural variables such as thawing of snow or ice, heavy precipitation, and soil moisture; by characteristics of drainage basins and stream channels; and by the presence of water-storage areas. An additional significant factor is the extent of urbanization of a drainage basin.

Urbanization, through the construction of buildings, roads, and paving, decreases the infiltration capacity of a region by making much of it impervious. Also, storm sewers increase the rate at which surface runoff is transmitted to stream channels. A useful measure of degree of urbanization, as far as it affects the flow regimen of streams is, therefore, the percentage of an area made impervious together with the percentage of an area served by storm sewers.

Figure 10.12 compares for varying degrees of urban development the peak discharge of the mean annual flood before and after urbanization as measured by percent impervious and percent served by storm sewers. In completely impervious and fully sewered areas, peak discharge increases to more than 6 times that in non-urbanized areas. A study of the Houston, Texas, metropolitan area indicates that urbanization has increased the magnitude of 2-year flood peaks by a factor of nine, and 50-year peaks by a factor of five (Johnson and Sayre, 1973). Suburbanization of a rural area increases surface runoff by more than 100 times during most summer thunderstorms (Cherkauer, 1976).

Figure 10.13 compares typical hydrographs before and after urbanization of an area. The fast runoff of water from roofs and paved areas and its transmission to streams by sewers or other artificial conduits decreases lag time for urban as com-

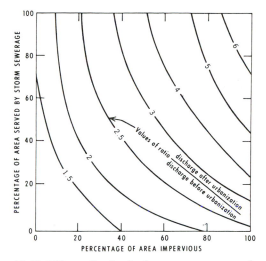

10.12 Effect of urbanization on mean annual flood for a one-square-mile drainage area.

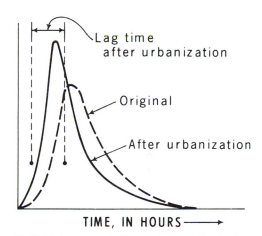

10.13 Hydrographs before and after urbanization of a region. The vertical axis indicates amount of rainfall or magnitude of stream discharge.

pared to non-urban areas. Also, a greater percentage of the storm water enters the stream as surface runoff rather than as groundwater. Decreased lag time and increased surface runoff increase peak discharge because a greater amount of water enters a stream in a shorter time. Similarly, the flood-to-peak interval is shortened, and the rates of rise and decline of discharge are increased.

The increase in peak discharge implies an increase in frequency or discharges great enough to overflow stream banks. Figure 10.14 illustrates this effect by comparing flood-frequency curves for an area in various stages of urbanization. Figure 10.15 compares the ratio of overbank flows with degrees of urbanization.

Beyond increasing the magnitude and frequency of flooding, urbanization affects the erosion of and amount of sediment transported by streams. As noted earlier, a stream can transmit just slightly less than the mean annual flood without overflowing its banks. One effect of urbanization is to increase the magnitude of the mean annual flood, which tends to enlarge the stream channel. Such erosion can produce as much as five years' production of sediment from an non-urbanized area of the same size.

Erosion in urban areas is also greatly increased after vegetation is removed and when sites are excavated and dirt is piled up without cover near the sites. Depending upon many factors, sediment yield for urban or developing areas may be up to hundreds of times greater than for non-urbanized areas.

The problems created by flooding in urban areas are complex, and not easily solved. In an attempt to carry away increased runoff produced by the urban development of two watersheds near Binghamton, New York, local creeks were straightened and lined to increase their efficiency. However, as a result of the "improvement," an increase in erosion, sedimentation, and flooding took place downstream (Morisawa, 1976).

Urbanization also diminishes stream discharge during dry periods. As the amount of water reaching the groundwater system is decreased, the water table is lowered and the flow of groundwater into stream channels is reduced. Also, between floods average stream depth will be reduced because less water flows in a larger channel.

Stream depth will also be affected by higher rates of deposition caused by increased sediment load and decreased carrying capacity during times of low discharge. Such changes may seriously affect the navigability of a stream and its recreational and aesthetic value.

Efforts to improve navigability through construction designed to prevent bank erosion often reduces the area of a stream channel, and flood crests are forced to higher levels. Also, construction of levees to contain high discharge causes sediment that formerly would have been spread out over the floodplain to be deposited within the channel. Modifications to the channel of the Mississippi since about 1837 have caused it to lose about a third of its volume and flood crests for given discharges have become significantly higher (Belt, Jr., 1975).

Prediction and Warning

Adequate response to the dangers of flooding in a given area require familiarity with the hydrologic characteristics of the entire drainage basin in which that area is located. With a knowledge of past stream behavior, climate of the region, and parameters of the drainage basin, the general character of floods within a basin may be described, and estimates made of the likely character and timing of specific floods may be made. National Weather Service graphs show the probability of occurrence of different degrees of high water for each month of the year for major U.S. river systems. The maximum likelihood of flooding for many rivers is the result of coincidence of rainfall and snow melt in the spring. Summer floods are common in drainage basins where summer rains are torrential. Some areas have wet winters and dry summers, and flooding is most likely during winter months. Floods in late summer and fall are common in hurricane areas. In some regions, a combination of factors may produce two flood seasons each year.

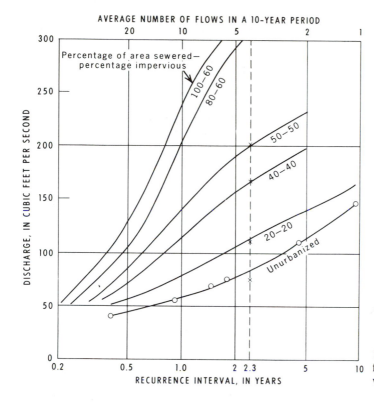

10.14 Flood-frequency curves for a one-square-mile basin in various states of urbanization.

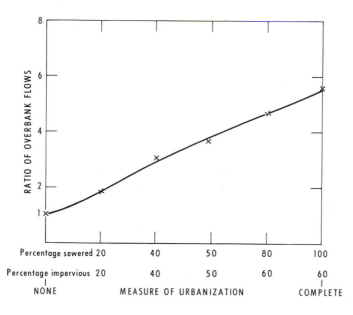

10.15 Graph showing the increase in number of floods as an area becomes urbanized.

Forecasts of specific flood danger are made by the River and Flood Forecasting Service of the National Weather Service, based upon monitoring of rainfall and of temperatures capable of causing significant snow melt. Such information, together with knowledge of past floods, permits estimates of rates of increase in stream height and floodcrest-movement and area, depth, and duration of inundation.

FLOOD CONTROL

The concept of flood control tends to be misleading, for it implies the possibility of complete control, an accomplishment rarely sought and even more rarely accomplished. As a rule, flood-control measures are only undertaken when the cost of control is less than the cost of damage avoided. Complete control of water movement within a drainage basin or even along a single river is usually prohibitively expensive, and the point of diminishing economic returns is a decisive factor in determining the extent of efforts. As has been seen, rational land use becomes one of the best ways to diminish flood hazard.

Methods of control or protection include construction designed to (1) confine water within a stream channel, (2) increase the capability of the channel to transmit water, (3) provide alternate routes for excess water, and (4) create reservoirs for storage and controlled release of water. Also important are land conservation practices that increase the retention of water by soil and decrease the rate of discharge into stream channels.

In the United States, the Department of Agriculture has primary authority in implementing flood-control measures in upstream areas; the Army Corps of Engineers has primary authority in downstream areas. Unfortunately, disputes between the two agencies have, on occasion, adversely affected efforts to control floods (Leopold and Maddock, Jr., 1954).

Land Conservation Practices   In forested or otherwise vegetated areas, more time is required for surface runoff to reach streams than in areas of exposed soil or rock. Thus, if a large part of a drainage basin is kept in forests or if sound agricultural practices such as contour plowing are employed to minimize surface runoff, fluctuations in stream discharge will be reduced. Lessening surface runoff will also reduce the rate of erosion, thereby helping to maintain stream channel quality and prolonging reservoir life through minimizing sedimentation.

Dams   Three sizes of dams may be used to retain and release water. (1) Numerous small dams may be placed across gullies to reduce erosion and to prevent high velocity runoff. (2) Larger dams with reservoirs of considerable capacity may be built across tributaries to the main stream. Such structures may prevent the entire flood from reaching the major stream at the same time. (3) Even larger dams may be constructed across a main stream. Dams and reservoirs may aid in supplying water during dry periods, and may also be used to generate electricity and to provide recreation facilities. Yet the construction of dams may be expensive and difficult, and where reservoir siltation is rapid, their useful life may be short. The potential threat to downstream communities in case of dam failure is always present, and, of course, valuable land may be lost to the area occupied by the reservoir.

In 1941, a survey by the Department of Agriculture revealed that 39 percent of the reservoirs in the United States had a useful life of less than 50 years, and only 36 percent a useful life of more than 100 years. These short life-spans are caused by the reservoirs filling in with alluvial sediment brought by the streams that feed them. Siltation is most acute in small reservoirs; most major reservoirs have an expected life-span of several centuries.

The catastrophic release of water from reservoirs may be caused by a variety of factors. A horrendous flood was caused by a landslide that displaced the water in the Vaiont Reservoir in Italy in 1963 (see

Chap. 8). Flooding caused by volcanic mudflows into reservoirs in the Cascade Range is discussed in Chapter 9. The San Fernando earthquake of 1971 caused the near failure of the Upper and Lower Van Norman dams, which threatened 80,000 people in Los Angeles County.

In the narrow valleys of southern West Virginia and eastern Kentucky, waste from mines often impounds rivers or is bulldozed to form crudely engineered dams for the purpose of creating settling ponds. In February 1972, a series of such poorly designed and maintained dams across Buffalo Creek, West Virginia gave way, killing 125 people and causing $50 million damage.

The infamous Johnstown, Pennsylvania, flood was due to failure of an earth-fill dam built in 1853 to supply water for the Pennsylvania Canal. In 1857, the dam was no longer needed and lay neglected. Twenty years later, the reservoir was bought to serve as a private resort. To increase the water level, the dam outlets were plugged, and, to permit a roadway to cross the dam, its height was cut down by two feet. In 1889 after a rainstorm, water began to pour over the top of the dam. After three hours, the dam had been worn so thin that it could no longer stand the pressure of the water behind it and gave way. The ensuing flood killed 2100 people in the downstream valleys.

On June 5, 1976, a 300-foot-high earth-fill dam being erected on the Teton River in Idaho gave way just before its completion. The wall of water that surged through the breach in the dam left 14 people dead, 30,000 homeless and caused almost half a billion dollars property damage. At least three-quarters of Rexburg, a town of 8000 people, was under water, and a torrent of mud, trees, debris, and water poured into low-lying commercial areas of Idaho Falls, the state's third-largest city. An investigative panel concluded that the dam failed because of inadequate design.

In 1972, a federal law was passed whose purpose was the protection of human life and property from the collapse of the es-

timated 28,000 dams in the United States. Excluded from the provisions of the law, however, are the several hundred huge dams operated by the Bureau of Reclamation, which provides its own safety-inspection program. The Teton Dam was one of the dams operated by the Bureau.

Altering Stream Channel Structure Flood-protection measures include straightening, enlarging, and smoothing stream channels (Fig. 10.16), and the construction of levees and diversionary channels. Straightening a channel has the effect of steepening its gradient and hence its ability to transmit water. For instance, if a meandering stream drops 10 feet in 10 miles, eliminating the meander by constructing a "cutoff," or "short-cut," may permit it to drop the same 10 feet in only 2 miles, thus quintupling the gradient. From 1933 to 1936, the channel of a 331-mile stretch of the Mississippi River was shortened by 116 miles, resulting in a lowering of flood levels from 2 to 12 feet. Channel enlargment through deepening, widening, or removing obstacles increases the efficiency of a stream and permits greater discharge without flooding. A similar result may be obtained by raising the stream banks through the construction of *levees*. *Dikes* are constructed at a distance from the stream channel to protect low-lying areas from inundation.

Despite efforts to improve the capacities of stream channels, disastrous floods may still occur. In September 1977, twelve inches of rain fell over Kansas City, Missouri, in a two-day period. Worst hit was the area near Brush Creek, where water in the concrete-lined drainage ditch rose five feet to its 500-year recurrence flood level and became a raging torrent that destroyed numerous houses, shops, and cars.

When dikes or levees are breached, the artificially raised stream levels may produce even more catastrophic flooding. Vanport City, Oregon, was completely destroyed in 1948 when the flooding Columbia River broke through railroad fill that was serving as a dike. In Kansas, during the period July

10.16 Channel improvements along the Conemaugh River at Johnstown, Pa.

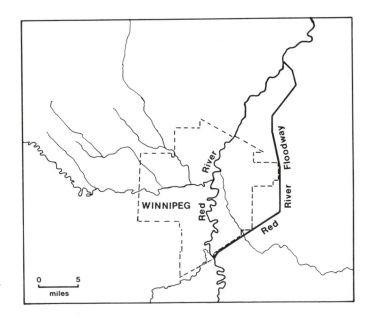

10.17 Map of Winnipeg, Manitoba, showing the Red River Floodway.

9–13, 1951, a storm dumped more than 16 inches of rain onto the already saturated Kansas and Neosho river basins. Levees, at Topeka and North Topeka failed, and large portions of the city were floodswept. Lawrence, Kansas, was similarly affected. In addition, the central industrial sections of Kansas City suffered $140 million damage when dikes and levees were overtopped.

During the last century, the channel of the Rio Grande above Albuquerque, New Mexico, has become shallower as sediment brought to it by tributary streams is deposited. At the same time, irrigation has saturated adjacent low-lying lands. The flood-carrying capacity of the river has been significantly decreased, and parts of Albuquerque are now below the level of the self-elevated river bed, in constant danger of inundation.

In Italy, aggradation of the Po River has raised it well above the level of the surrounding floodplain, and the levees are, in places, higher than the roofs of nearby houses. Similarly, parts of the Hwang Ho and Yangtze Kiang in China flow well above the level of the surrounding heavily populated land.

Another serious consequence of interfering with the natural structure of a channel is that, although a particular area may be protected from floodwaters, the danger of downstream flooding is increased. Water that would previously have spread out over the upstream floodplain is now transmitted downstream, adding to the volume of normal floodwaters. Channel improvement and levee construction must be integrated along the entire length of a stream. Along the Mississippi, levees extend for 2500 miles.

An effective flood-control measure is the creation of diversionary channels (*floodways*) through which floodwaters may bypass specific areas that need protection. In 1961–65 a floodway was constructed to protect Winnipeg, Canada, from the floodwaters of the Red River (Fig. 10.17). A deleterious effect, however, was that seepage into the floodway when it was empty lowered the level of the water table in adjacent regions. The construction of floodways has been of particular importance along the lower Sacramento River in California and along the lower Mississippi (to protect such towns as Cairo, Illinois, and New Orleans). When these rivers reach a critical stage, they are diverted to portions of their natural floodplains defined by pairs of levees.

New Orleans is built entirely on river-deposited sediment, and much of the city is below flood level of the Mississippi. Between its founding in 1717 and the construction of an adequate levee system in 1849, New Orleans was subjected to repeated inundation. A single break in the system today could prove disastrous. Figure 10.18 shows the Bonnet Carré Spillway which in times of flood diverts the Mississippi water to Lake Ponchartrain.

Floodplain Regulation

Floodplain regulation has become increasingly important in recent years. However, as of 1971, only about one in six of the significant-sized towns and cities in the United States located partially or wholly on floodplains had adopted appropriate regulations for use of flood-prone areas (Goddard, 1971). In an attempt to remedy this situation, the Federal Flood Disaster Protection Act (1973) initiated a program to (1) provide flood insurance at reasonable rates (through subsidies) to property owners in areas of normal flooding, and (2) reduce flood damage by encouraging communities to develop rational land-use practices on floodplains. (Normal flooding was defined as areas affected by 100-year floods.) To qualify for federal assistance and federally insured loans or mortgages, communities must strictly regulate building in flood-hazard areas. Furthermore, once the U.S. Department of Housing and Urban Development (HUD) provides the community with flood-hazard maps and flood data, the community must prevent any development that

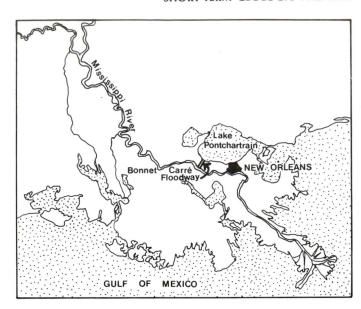

10.18 The Mississippi Delta region, showing the Bonnet Carré Floodway, which was constructed to protect the city of New Orleans against Mississippi flooding.

could interfere with the flow of water, require flood-proofing or elevation of new structures outside areas commonly flooded but within the floodplain, and prepare plans for comprehensive floodplain management.

The U.S. Water Resources Council (1971) has outlined what constitutes rational floodplain management (Fig. 10.19). For a given region, an estimate should be made of the magnitude of the maximum flood likely to occur within a designated period—the *regulatory flood*. For instance, it may be decided that it is reasonable to try to prevent hazard in the event of a 50-, 100-, or 500-year flood. Once the regulatory flood is established, a *regulatory floodway* is designated, encompassing the stream channel and whatever adjacent land is required to permit the passage of waters without increasing flood heights more than a designated amount above natural levels. This definition suggests that if the pathway is too narrowly defined, and if areas just outside it are overly obstructed, floodwaters will be forced to higher elevations in order to pass (Fig. 10.20). Adjacent areas that may be covered by water in times of flood but

which are not vital to the passage of floodwaters are called *floodway fringes*. Structures that will not be affected by inundation may be built in this zone. Figure 10.21 indicates one way in which an area may be zoned for a regulatory floodway and floodway fringes.

Relocation of Buildings Buildings in hazardous areas of floodplains, wherever possible, should be relocated. Prairie du Chien, Wisconsin, is situated on the Mississippi at a point where the river valley is 8000 feet wide and bounded by high cliffs. Part of the town is on a stream terrace some 25 feet above the usual level of the river, and part is along the river at elevations of only 10–20 feet above the water. Periodic spring flooding of lower parts of the town have resulted in proposals to evacuate these areas, relocating the buildings at higher levels. In 1974, Congress approved funds to initiate planning for these changes.

Four Case Studies

Whether communities will choose to defend themselves against flood hazard is uncertain. The study of Boulder, Colorado, il-

RIVERINE FLOOD HAZARD AREAS

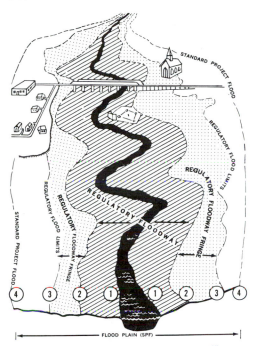

1. REGULATORY FLOODWAY—Kept open to carry floodwater—no building or fill.
2. REGULATORY FLOODWAY FRINGE—Use permitted if protected by fill, flood proofed or otherwise protected.
3. REGULATORY FLOOD LIMIT—Based on technical study—outer limit of the floodway fringe.
4. STANDARD PROJECT FLOOD (SPF) LIMIT—Area subject to possible flooding by very large floods.

VALLEY CROSS SECTION

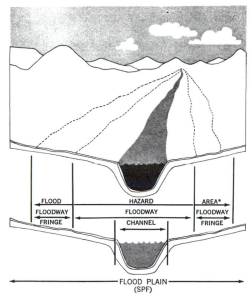

* Designated flood.

10.19 Diagrams illustrating concepts and terminology of rational floodplain management.

lustrates some of the difficulties involved in good floodplain management. The study of Toronto reveals more positive community attitudes. A multi-faceted engineering approach to flood control has been undertaken in Los Angeles. A major part of Rapid City, South Dakota, has been literally removed from the hazard of floods.

Boulder, Colorado

The city of Boulder is situated along Boulder Creek at the foot of the Rocky Mountains, just east of the mouth of Boulder Canyon (Fig. 10.10). Serious floods in 1864, 1876, and 1894 affected industrial and commercial structures that occupied part of the 100-year floodplain. Following the floods, suggestions for

protection and control were made, but never implemented. Between 1900 and 1920, six more floods occurred. An engineering survey (1912) designed to prod the adoption of flood-control measures and land-use management had failed due to lack of funds and a general lack of interest. Between 1940 and 1974, the town's population jumped from 12,000 to more than 60,000, and was accompanied by considerable building on the 100-year floodplain. From 1945 to 1973, more than 20 floodplain surveys were carried out, but only rarely were proposals adopted and funded. "In 1945, the Corps of Engineers submitted to the municipal authorities recommendations for protective construction works, but envisaged costs and widespread skepticism with regard to the very existence of the hazard prevented these

FLOODPLAIN ENCROACHMENTS INCREASE FLOOD HEIGHTS

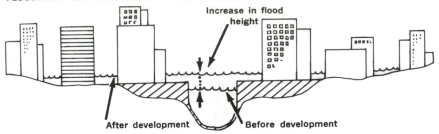

For the purposes of this report, the regulatory floodway is defined as the calculated unobstructed portion of a flood plain consisting of the stream channel and overbank areas necessary to convey flood flows for a selected flood discharge without increasing flood levels more than a selected increment above natural levels.

THE REGULATORY FLOODWAY DEPENDS UPON THE SIZE OF FLOOD CHOSEN AS A BASIS FOR REGULATION

Natural floodway limits for a flood which on the average would occur:
- (A) Once every 25 years.
- (B) Once every 50 years.
- (C) Once every 100 years.
- (D) Once every 500 years.

THE WIDTH OF THE REGULATORY FLOODWAY FOR THE SAME SIZE FLOOD WILL VARY DEPENDING UPON PERMISSIBLE BACKWATER EFFECTS

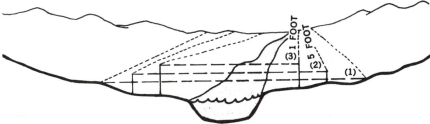

- (1) Natural floodway boundaries for a flood which on the average would occur once every 100 years.
- (2) Regulatory floodway for 0.5 foot of acceptable increase in flood heights for the same flood.
- (3) Regulatory floodway for 1 foot acceptable increase in flood heights for the same flood.

10.20 Diagrams illustrating the principle of a "regulatory floodway."

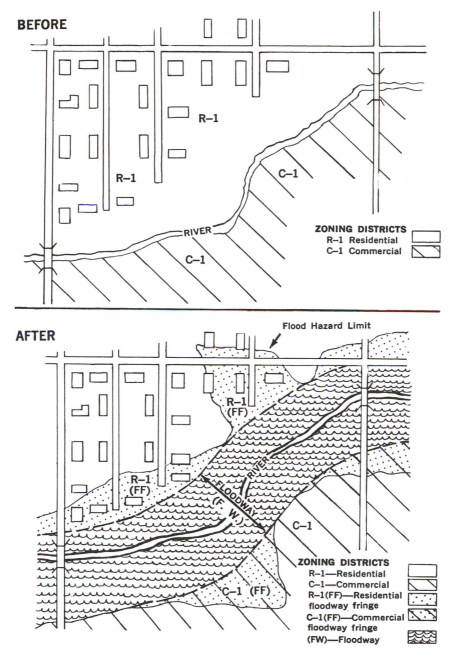

BEFORE

R–1

R–1

C–1

RIVER

C–1

ZONING DISTRICTS
R–1 Residential
C–1 Commercial

AFTER

Flood Hazard Limit

R–1
(FF)

R–1
(FF)

FLOODWAY

(F W)

RIVER

C–1

C–1 (FF)

ZONING DISTRICTS
R–1—Residential
C–1—Commercial
R–1(FF)—Residential
floodway fringe
C–1(FF)—Commercial
floodway fringe
(FW)—Floodway

10.21 Typical zoning maps before and after addition of flood regulations.

proposals from being implemented. Not only had the perception of the flood hazard been dulled, but a general sense of security prevailed since it was widely believed that the flood hazard was a problem of the past that no longer existed. . . .'' (White and Haas, 1975, p. 39). In 1956, efforts to create a flood control district for Boulder were defeated. Finally, after severe damage was inflicted by floods in 1965 and 1969, floodplain management and engineering planning began to receive serious attention. In 1973, the City Council passed an ordinance that created a storm drainage and flood-control utility. The floodplain is still occupied, however, and serious potential for catastrophe remains in the event of severe storms (White and Haas, 1975).

Toronto

On October 14–15, 1954, after an unusually wet autumn that had already saturated the ground, Hurricane Hazel dumped 9 inches of rain on northwestern Toronto, causing a flood along the Humber River that took 81 lives, left 1868 families homeless, and caused millions of dollars of property damage. This disaster spurred recognition that proper control of a river system requires treating the entire drainage basin as a single unit, that a regional approach to conservation is essential, and that an appropriate tax base must be established. The Metropolitan Toronto and Region Conservation Authority (MTRCA) was created, embracing the 6 municipalities of Toronto and 22 adjoining municipalities. Among the aims of the MTRCA are flood control, a reserve water supply in case of emergency, a minimum year-round stream flow, and recreation areas. Plans were made for extensive land acquisition in floodplain areas; removal of houses from hazardous regions; the construction of 13 major dams; stream-channel improvement; a flood-warning and forecasting system that involves constant monitoring of rainfall, snowfall, and river flow; and careful control of land use in flood-prone

areas. Measures were also taken to prevent slumping and erosion of valley slopes caused by regrading for apartment houses. Sediment produced by such erosion could silt up local reservoirs and reduce the effectiveness of dams in flood retention. It could also block up Toronto Bay, requiring expensive dredging to keep it open for navigation. The MTRCA views the valleys and rivers that traverse the Toronto region as one of the city's greatest assets. Poor land-use practices not only increase flood hazard, they destroy the beauty and potential of these natural corridors. The agency's ultimate goal is to preserve and restore where necessary the aesthetic qualities and pristine amenities of these areas while reducing through conservation practices the flood threats they pose to Toronto's inhabitants.

Los Angeles

Los Angeles and neighboring communities occupy the floor and lower slopes of a bowl-like amphitheater surrounded on three sides by mountains and on the fourth side by the ocean (Fig. 10.22). Under natural conditions, rain that used to fall on the mountains was funneled along stream networks onto the floor of the amphitheater, where it normally soaked into the thick accumulation of sediments underlying the basin (see Fig. 3.25). When rainfall was heavy, however, the runoff roared through stream channels that were, in most cases, dry. Frequently, these torrents which brought with them masses of loose debris washed down from the mountains, overflowed the stream banks and spread out over adjacent flat areas. (A more complete description of the geography, geology, and climate of the Los Angeles region is given in Chap. 3.)

Floods of sufficient magnitude to inundate the entire floor of the amphitheater can be expected on an average of once every 100 years. The last such flood occurred in March 1938, taking 59 lives and causing $62,000,000 damage. Large floods that

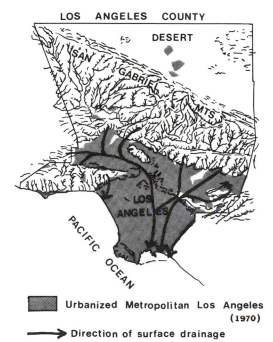

LOS   ANGELES   COUNTY

DESERT

PACIFIC OCEAN

▓ **Urbanized Metropolitan Los Angeles (1970)**

➤ **Direction of surface drainage**

10.22 Los Angeles County, showing the major landforms, the extent of urbanization, and the direction of major paths of surface drainage.

cover all low-lying valleys and sections of the coastal plain adjacent to stream channels may be expected six times a century. To diminish flooding, the L.A. County Flood Control District and the U.S. Army Corps of Engineers have undertaken a number of projects (Fig. 10.23). Twenty flood-regulating dams with a combined reservoir capacity of 237,972 acre-feet have been built. Six hundred and forty-two miles of stream channel have been designated as permanent flood channels, and are being straightened, cleared, and lined to increase their efficiency. Thirty areas, covering 2225 acres are being set aside as *spreading grounds* (places to which floodwaters are diverted and allowed to sink into the ground). A total of 105 *debris basins* will be constructed to catch sediment washed down from the mountains and to prevent it from silting up reservoirs and stream channels. In

addition, 1700 miles of storm drains are being installed and 41 pumping plants are being built to redistribute water. The U.S. Department of Agriculture has undertaken upstream flood control and conservation works to control erosion and surface runoff. Despite these projects, however, the danger of flooding persists. Particularly hazardous areas are shown in Figure 10.24. The Regional Planning Commission notes that where new urbanization is taking place, flood-hazard zones must be avoided. However, land values are high, and often the practice is to "flood-proof" areas by replacing natural stream channels with concrete channels or storm drains—eliminating in the process part of the aesthetic and recreational value of an area. If development were restricted to safe, high ground, then natural stream channels and adjacent areas could be preserved and devoted to parks, golf courses, or farming.

Rapid City, South Dakota

After the disastrous flood of 1972 in Rapid City, South Dakota, nearly all the homes and businesses along a seven-mile stretch of the Rapid Creek floodplain have been relocated. In their place, a 1025 acre floodway has been created, with parks, playing fields, and a golf course. On adjacent higher ground, a $10 million highschool, an $8.5 million civic center, and an industrial park have been created. To achieve these changes in land-use, federal aid to the amount of $400 million was provided (the equivalent of $10,000 for each resident of Rapid City in 1972). Unfortunately, because of the expense involved, it is unlikely that other flood-stricken communities will be rebuilt in such a creative and generous way.

SEDIMENTATION

During each year of recent geologic times, before people were present in significant numbers, approximately 10 billion tons of

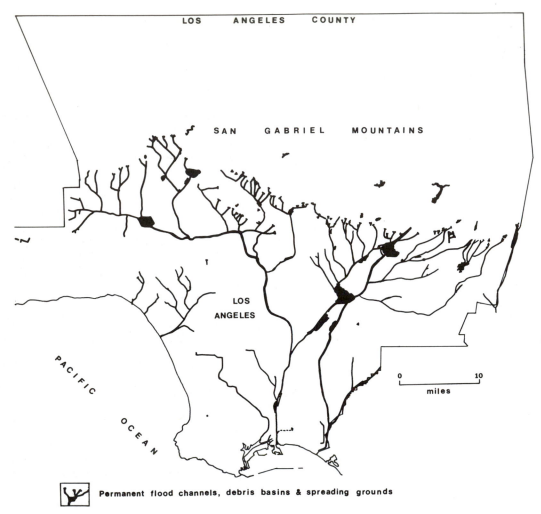

10.23 Los Angeles County, showing location of engineering projects designed to reduce flooding.

rock, sediment, and soil were eroded from the land masses of the earth and transported to the oceans (Judson, 1968). As population and the importance of humans as agents of erosion grew, the annual mass of material moved from land to sea rose to approximately 25 billion tons. This increased rate was brought about at first by the spread of agriculture and by poor agriculture practices and destruction of forests and grasslands.

The growth of mining and quarrying and later, highway construction and urbanization accelerated the process.

Wherever the ground is disturbed or laid bare, rocky materials are subject to being dislodged and transported. Before it reaches the ocean, this eroded material may lodge for varying lengths of time in lakes, reservoirs, streams, drainage ditches, pipes, conduits, estuaries, or on floodplains. The

FLOOD HAZARD AREAS

10.24 Los Angeles County, showing areas threatened by floods.

harmful effects are manifold. Sediment deposited on floodplains may cover fertile soils and reduce their productivity (although some annual floods actually renew soil fertility). The carrying capacities of streams may be reduced as their channels are clogged by sediment, causing increased frequency and magnitude of flooding. When flooding does occur, the damage to structures is increased if the floodwaters are sediment laden. Sediment deposited behind dams decreases the storage capacity of reservoirs; in the United States, about 40 billion cubic feet are lost each year. Similarly, sediment accumulating in rivers, harbors, or other bodies of water necessitates dredging to keep shipping channels open. Sediment suspended in water reduces its aesthetic quality and recreational value; sediment suspended in water-supply systems requires treatment to clarify the water. Where sediment is introduced into aquatic environments, animal and plant life may be adversely affected. Also, it may transport chemical and biological pollutants.

Erosion and sedimentation are urban problems both in direct and indirect ways. If cities are primarily dependent for their continued existence upon a successful agricultural hinterland, erosion and sedimentation that adversely affect agriculture adversely affect the cities. The abandonment of Mayan cities in the Petén District of Guatamala has been attributed to such causes. The Petén District consists of hilly areas underlain by limestone and covered by a thin layer of black soil; and low flat areas underlain by tough, black, carbonaceous clay. It is thought that in the past, before the area was occupied, the hilly areas were covered by a thick layer of fertile soil and that the flat, lowland areas were lakes. As the region was settled, the uplands became the site of productive, intensive agriculture, and the lakes and connecting streams provided the basis for an excellent transportation network. Sufficient surplus food was produced to support a non-agrarian population in cities. However, as the primeval forests were cut to permit agriculture, the cultivated soil, exposed to torrential rains, began to erode rapidly. With the passage of time, the fertility of the land declined and the eroded soil was washed down into the lakes, filling them in and converting them to swamps. Thus, the food surplus diminished, the transport network was disrupted, water became scarce in the dry season, and, with the growth of swamps, came an infestation of malarial mosquitoes. Eventually the population and prosperity of the region dwindled and the cities died (Cooke, 1931).

In Mesopotamia, the site of the world's earliest cities, success of agriculture depended upon an intricate network of irrigation canals. Inability to deal with siltation of the canals and increasing salinization of the soil resulted in a chain of events that was a major factor in the decline and destruction of the cities (Jacobsen and Adams 1958). The deposition of dissolved salts from evaporating irrigation waters gradually reduced the fertility of the soil, and as agricultural production declined, the ability to support large urban populations also declined. With the decline of the urban centers, the strong central authority necessary for maintaining the canals was weakened, and the canals became clogged with silt. Agricultural production diminished further, accelerating the demise of the cities.

In modern times, the prosperity of urban centers that serve agricultural hinterlands are also affected by changes in agricultural productivity. However, erosion and sedimentation affect urban areas more directly, having an impact upon public health, topography, water supply, waste disposal, flooding, and transportation. (The effects of coastal erosion and sedimentation are discussed in Chapter 11.)

Geologist Harold P. Guy has listed urban problems caused by erosion and sedimentation. Clogged drainage channels may encourage mosquito breeding. Harmful bacteria, toxic chemicals, and radionuclides tend to be absorbed onto sediment particles and may be transported into water-supply systems. Erosion and deposition at construction sites makes construction more difficult and expensive. Erosion of or deposition in stream channels can cause bridge or culvert failure. In the Los Angeles area, there are numerous "debris" basins designed to trap sediment so that small streams draining the steep foothills will not clog drains when they enter developed urban areas. In Chicago, more than 70 percent of the street-litter sweepings are sediment and rock.

As has been noted, in urbanized areas stream-flow during dry periods is apt to be considerably lower than before urbanization, resulting in sedimentation that may seriously affect the navigability and recreational value of the stream. In addition, increased flooding caused by urbanization erodes the banks and bed of a stream and may greatly increase sediment production.

During periods of construction in urban areas, sediment from erosion of exposed land may be increased by a factor of thousands (Leopold, 1968). Highway construction which denudes the natural cover and exposes the soil can increase sediment production locally by 20,000 to 40,000 times that expectable from farms and woodlands in an equivalent period (Wolman, 1964).

Erosion and sedimentation may be reduced through replanting of denuded areas, proper agricultural practices (such as strip cropping and contour plowing), proper mining practices, maintenance of adequate drainage, sediment-retarding structures and sedimentation basins, and minimizing the time-span during which soils are left exposed during construction.

Losses from erosion and sedimentation in California between 1970 and 2000 are estimated at $565 million. In urban areas, the major costs are in removing sediment from private and public drainage systems. It is estimated that two-thirds of the projected losses could be reduced by proper engineering design and construction practices (Alfors et al, 1973). Whether such measures will be taken remains questionable. As of 1969, although sediment was described as "our greatest pollutant" (Robinson, 1970), not one state had established specific criteria on suspended solids with respect to water quality. Only as the public is made aware of the extent to which the environment is being degraded by avoidable erosion and sedimentation and of the costs of such degradation, will much-needed programs of prevention and control be developed. The first steps in this direction have been encouraged through the passage of the National Environmental Policy Act (1969) and the passage by most individual states of their own legislation requiring environmental impact statements (EIS). These statements force consideration of the effect on the environment of major governmental (and in some cases private) projects before the projects are initiated.

11. Coastal Hazards

Coasts have long been a major focus of human attention. The constant surge and crash of waves, the flood and ebb of tides, the broad expanse of water reflecting sky fascinate their observers, suggesting a sense of power and dimension beyond their own. The oceans have always been both comfort and threat, nourisher and destroyer. In earliest times, protected coves provided a convenient and abundant source of food in the form of fish, shellfish, and seaweed. As the arts of shipbuilding and navigation were mastered, the oceans became avenues of commerce and conquest and the lands at the water's edge grew in importance. A large number of the world's great cities originated as ports and expanded about flourishing harbors. Ideal sites were those where navigable streams emptied into the sea and which were protected from the open ocean by islands, sandy bars, or complex irregularities in the configuration of the coast. In such places, the rivers satisfied thirst and provided water for irrigation or industry and an avenue of communication with the interior of the country; the ocean provided both connection with the rest of the world and a seemingly endless self-cleansing reservoir into which wastes could be poured and from which food could be extracted. Today, with the extraction of oil and gas from beneath the floors of the continental shelves, and the

increasing likelihood of large-scale exploitation of other natural resources that lie on or under the bottom of the sea, coastal regions and coastal cities continue to grow in importance.

But if humans have learned the advantages of living next to the sea, they have also learned that the join between water and land is an uncertain place of dynamic process, where security and prosperity may be consumed by inconvenience, economic decline, or even physical destruction and death.

FORMS, MATERIALS, AND PROCESSES

The processes and changes along a particular length of coast depend upon numerous factors: configuration of the coastline; topography of land and sea floor; weather and climate; the nature of bedrock and surficial materials; and the effects of artificial structures and human activities.

The *coast* (Fig. 11.1) is that strip of land adjacent to the sea and affected by the sea. The *beach* is the accumulation of loose material extending from the upper (landward) limit of wave action to the zone where waves approaching from deep water first cause appreciable movement of bottom material on the sea floor. The *shore* is that strip

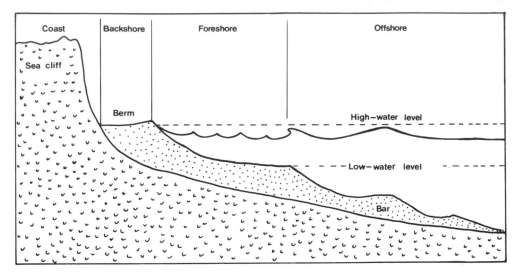

11.1 Coastal terminology.

of ground alternately covered and un-covered by tides and waves, and may or may not consist of a beach. (That is, the shore in places may be bedrock rather than loose surficial material.) It is convenient to divide the shore region into the backshore, foreshore, and offshore. The *backshore* lies above the limit of the swash of normal high-est tides, and may include landward-tilted backbeach deposits (the *berm*), parts of cliffs, sand dunes, and salt marshes. The *foreshore* is the area regularly covered and uncovered by tides. The *offshore* extends seaward from the low-water line to the depth where waves first "feel bottom" (the seaward limit of the beach). Continuously submerged ridges or mounds of sand or gravel, called *submarine bars,* are often present at the mouths of rivers or estuaries, and are sometimes present a short distance from and usually parallel to beaches.

Many shorelines may be classified as ei-ther irregular or simple. Where ocean water laps against topographically complex land, the shoreline is highly irregular, character-ized by numerous inlets, bays, promon-tories, and islands. In places, the land de-scends gently to the water; in others, the

contact is precipitous (cliffed) or steeply in-clined. Where river valleys meet the sea, deep inlets called *estuaries* are found. Sandy bars and *spits* (bars with curved ends) may extend across indentations in the shoreline (Fig. 11.2).

Where the coast is topographically regu-lar and the land descends beneath the water as a gently inclined, more or less planar sur-face, the shoreline is simple: either straight or gradually curved. Such shorelines may be characterized by *barrier islands* or *off-shore bars,* narrow sandy islands that paral-lel the mainland. There may be bars and spits connected to the mainland. Shallow bodies of protected seawater, called lagoons separate the barrier islands, bars, or spits from the mainland (Fig. 11.3).

Other shorelines of special interest are those of fiords and deltas. In many moun-tainous coastal regions, glaciers carved deep coastal valleys. As the ice retreated, sea-water advanced into the valleys, forming lengthy arms called *fiords.* Fiord walls usually rise steeply from the coast to a mountainous interior (Fig. 11.4).

Where sediment-laden rivers enter the sea, deposition at the river's mouth may

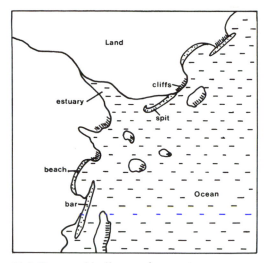

11.2 Topographically complex coast.

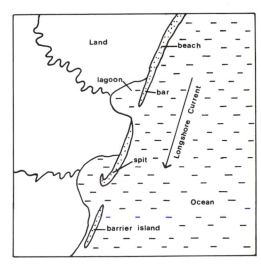

11.3 Typical coast where the land descends beneath the water as a gently inclined planar surface. The straight shoreline is characterized by beaches, bars, lagoons, spits, and barrier islands.

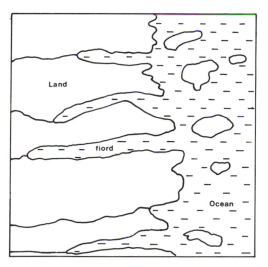

11.4 Coast characterized by fiords.

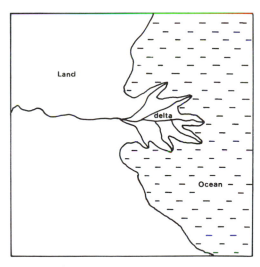

11.5 Deltaic coast.

result in the formation of a *delta* and a *deltaic coast,* if there are no oceanic currents to disperse the sediment (Fig. 11.5).

A dynamic and complex inter-relationship exists between the configuration of a coastline, the materials of which it is composed, and the dominant types of coastline processes. There is a direct correlation between the slope of a beach, the width of the foreshore, and the size of sediment.

Beaches composed of coarse materials (sand, gravel, shingle, cobble) are found along coasts exposed to open ocean where the action of large waves has removed finer materials. Beaches composed of finer materials (silt, mud, clay) are found in protected areas such as bays, lagoons, or marshes. Coarse shingle or pebble beaches are typically steep and narrow; moderate- to fine-sized sand beaches are flat and broad. Shorelines that are particularly exposed to the open ocean, such as promontories, may have little or no cover of beach materials; instead, rocky cliffs and benches meet the water directly.

The principal agents acting upon the shore are *waves* and *currents*. Waves are generated by wind moving across the ocean surface. The stronger the wind, the greater the length of time it blows in a given direction, and the longer the stretch of water over which it blows, the larger the waves will be. Waves disturb the ocean only to a depth of about half the distance between successive *wave crests*. Thus, waves only begin to "feel bottom" and to be affected by the ocean floor in the shallow depths, perhaps only several hundred feet. As their movement is impeded and their velocity diminished, some of the energy of their forward momentum is converted into increased *wave height*. If waves approach a coast at an angle (Fig. 11.6), their direction will be altered as the nearshore part of the wave encounters the ocean floor and slows down, while the offshore part advance's unimpeded through deep water. Along an irregular coastline (Fig. 11.7), this bending, or *refraction,* concentrates the wave energy upon promontories or headlands and attenuates the energy imposed upon recessed or embayed areas. As a result, the coast tends to become less irregular as headlands are worn back and the eroded debris is deposited in protected embayments.

The material that forms beaches is derived from erosion along coasts, but most important, from sediment delivered to the

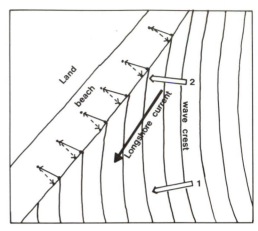

11.6 Change of direction of advance of waves as they approach a coast at an angle. Arrow 1 shows the wave direction in deep water; arrow 2, in shallow water. Arrows on the beach indicate the movement pattern of sediment. Net movement of sediment (littoral drift) is parallel to the longshore current.

oceans by streams. Longshore currents transport sediment parallel to a coast: as waves wash over a beach they move loose sediment alternately shoreward and seaward. If the waves move into the shore at an angle, the landward transport of the sediment tends to be parallel to the shore (Fig. 11.6), while the seaward transport has little or no parallel component. The result is a constant rhythmic movement of water and sediment parallel to the shore. The net movement of water is known as a *longshore current;* that of the sediment as *littoral transport.* Such currents affect not only the foreshore, but also the permanently submerged offshore zone, and their action may create shoals or bars and spits across coastal indentations (Fig. 11.3). Where longshore currents are interrupted by promontories or are funneled into submarine canyons, coasts further downcurrent will lack or have poorly nourished beaches.

Waves also shift materials back and forth. Typically, during storms sediment is

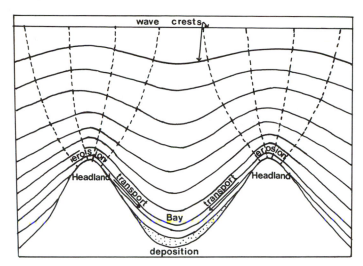

11.7 Refraction of waves along an irregular coast. The dotted lines show the direction of wave advance, and the solid lines show the position of individual wave crests. Note how the energy of lengths of wave crest that are equal in deep water are concentrated on headlands and attenuated in bays. Note also the transport of sediment from headlands to bays due to the development of longshore currents.

moved away from the land, from the foreshore to the offshore, thus diminishing the visible portion of the beach. Small waves then shift the sediment back toward the land, making the visible portion of the beach wider again. Corresponding to these changes in the visible portion of the beach are simultaneous changes in the distribution of offshore sediment. Thus, as the beach narrows and widens, submarine bars and troughs are constantly growing, diminishing, and shifting.

Where there is a constantly replenished supply of foreshore sand and a prevailing onshore wind, *sand dunes* adjacent to the backshore are a common coastal feature.

Storms accompanied by huge waves, especially when they coincide with high tides, may cause extensive erosion, deposition, and transport. Waves pounding against a cliff can result in its collapse and retreat. Acting on loose material, they can throw coarse sediment far up onto a beach, or they can scour and drag sediment seaward from the beach, creating submarine bars and depositing sand in deeper water offshore. Exceptionally large waves may wash over or break through barrier islands, depositing

sand in the usually protected waters of the lagoon. Where low coastal regions are not protected by barrier islands, wide beaches, or dunes, extensive coastal flooding may take place.

As the rise and fall of tides change the level of the ocean, *tidal currents* transfer water between adjacent portions of the oceans whose surfaces are at different elevations. Such currents attain particularly high velocities at the mouths of restricted bays and narrow inlets, and are capable of deeply scouring narrow marine channels and of transporting considerable quantities of sediment.

From this brief description it may be seen that coasts are dynamic environments, continually changing. Short-term changes are produced by waves and tides. Long-term changes result from the cumulative effect of the short term-changes, and may result in erosion, deposition, or the establishment of a dynamic equilibrium in which erosion and deposition cancel each other out. The long-term direction of coastal change may be affected by changes in climate and sea level, by crustal elevation, depression or tilting, or by other major geologic events.

11.8 The harbor at Rio de Janeiro. Note the islands and the hilly coastline.

Sea Level Changes

The general world-wide rise in sea level of 400–600 feet that has taken place within the last 15,000 years, due to the melting of the Pleistocene ice sheets, has resulted in a general advance of sea water over the land and the common occurrence of irregular shorelines, deep estuaries and fiords. Without that rise harbors would have been few and far between. A classic example of a harbor situated along a "drowned" hilly coast is Rio de Janeiro (Fig. 11.8).

In places, local crustal movements have added to or subtracted from the general sea-level rise. Scandinavia, relieved of the burden of glacial ice some 8000–11,000 years ago, has risen in places up to 900 feet, and

it is estimated that a further rise of 700 feet may occur before isostatic equilibrium is restored.

Along the Massachusetts coast, the post-glacial sea-level rise drowned the irregular hilly topography and produced the bay and sheltering islands that led to the establishment of the port city of Boston. However, as in Scandinavia, the direction of sea-level change in the region of New England may now be reversed by local post-glacial crustal upwarping (Legget, 1973).

Many major ports along the East Coast south of New York City are located on estuaries formed when the post-glacial rise in sea level drowned pre-existing river valleys. Subsequent minor crustal upwarp has in places modified but not cancelled this effect. Examples of such ports are Norfolk, Washington, Baltimore, Wilmington, and Philadelphia, located on the shores of the Chesapeake, Potomac, and Delaware estuaries.

The importance of New York City as a port stems, in part, from the fact that the floor of the Hudson River remains below sea level for 150 miles north to Troy, providing sufficient depth for navigation more than 100 miles inland, and permitting easy access to the interior of the country.

In England, in Roman times, the section of the Thames River affected by tides extended only to the present-day location of London Bridge; today, the river is tidal to Teddington, about 18 miles further upstream. This change has been brought about by subsidence of southeast England that has amounted to about 15 feet in the last 2000 years, and that continues at a rate of about one foot per century (see case study of London later in this chapter).

Changes in sea level in the Mediterranean have resulted in the stranding and drowning of ancient port cities. South of Haifa on the coast of Israel, the foundations of the Roman port of Dor now lie barely visible beneath the waves. In Italy, the ruins of the Temple of Serapis in the ancient city of Puzzuoli reveal a complicated story of changes in sea level. Today, the ruins lie partly beneath water. The temple columns, however, display borings of marine clams at heights up to 20 feet above the present level of the sea. These facts indicate that after the temple was constructed, the sea rose well above its present level and then declined to its present height. Fluctuations in the level of the Mediterranean continue. A rise of about 15 centimeters per century in the vicinity of Venice has contributed to the problems of coastal flooding faced by that city.

Figure 11.9 illustrates projected past and future positions of the coast along the mid-Atlantic shore of the United States. The assumption is that the location and shape of the coast are the result of rising sea level and active coastal processes.

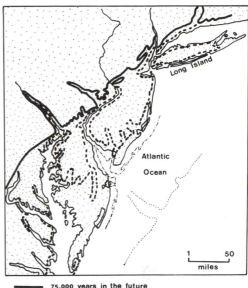

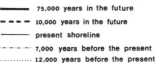

——— 75,000 years in the future
– – – 10,000 years in the future
——— present shoreline
–··–··– 7,000 years before the present
············ 12,000 years before the present

11.9 Projected past and future positions of the mid-Atlantic coast of the United States.

Coastal Erosion

Substantive changes in the location and configuration of coastlines are brought about not only by changes in sea level, but also by coastal erosion and deposition.

The cliffed Holderness coast of southeast Yorkshire in England has retreated 2.5–3 miles since Roman times, resulting in the loss of more than 30 towns in the last 2000 years. The severity of retreat is attributable in large part to the soft, easily erodable glacial sands, gravels, and boulder clays of which the Yorkshire cliffs are composed. On the Suffolk coast, during a major storm in 1953, a cliff made of glacial sand retreated 35 feet overnight. Rates of erosion of bedrock cliffs are considerably slower, but may be as much as 15–30 feet a century.

With time, the retreat of cliffs may be accompanied by the formation of a wide rocky platform over which storm waves must pass to reach the cliffs, thus diminishing the energy with which they can attack the coast. A rise in sea level, however, will mitigate this effect and re-establish dynamic contact between storm waves and cliffs.

A major factor affecting the rate of retreat of cliffs is the presence or absence of a protective beach. A wide, high beach is capable of absorbing much of the energy of storm waves, thus providing protection against coastal erosion. Beach materials may be shifted offshore during storms, but much of it will be brought back by normal wave action during clement weather. If there is a longshore current, re-establishment of the beach will depend upon whether the current is supplying fresh sediment from updrift regions as fast as it is removing and transporting it downdrift. Along the Holderness coast, one of the places being most rapidly eroded lies just downdrift of an area where shore protection structures have been erected to stop cliff erosion. The protected cliffs no longer provide the material that formerly helped maintain beaches downdrift of the cliffs.

Where cliffs are undercut by the attack of waves and collapse along the shore, fallen debris may form an effective defense against further undercutting and collapse. The longevity of this natural barrier depends upon the ease with which waves and currents are able to disperse it. Large blocks of bedrock are less easily reduced in size and removed than are unconsolidated small fragments.

Low-lying inland areas not separated from the ocean by cliffs depend upon the presence of a natural barrier for protection from the sea. Dunes, beaches, barrier islands, or the separation provided by lagoons and marshes serve this purpose well. In some places, a dense growth of mangroves or substantial coral reefs protect inland areas. However, all such environments are exceedingly fragile and subject to rapid change if an equilibrium with coastal processes has not been established or is interfered with.

Storm Surges

When high winds blow for protracted periods over vast stretches of the ocean, they can build up high waves capable of causing major erosion, flooding, and destruction along low-lying coasts. Especially dangerous conditions arise when high waves coincide with high tide, heavy rains, and *storm surges* (also called *storm tides*). A storm surge is a local rise of sea level caused by high winds of violent oceanic storms pushing water in an on-shore direction and by the drop in barometric pressure associated with such storms. (That is, the low barometric pressure acts as a partial vacuum that "sucks" up the general level of the sea in that area.) Hurricanes moving over shallow water are particularly effective in creating storm surges. If the ocean basin has the right shape, an additional "resonance" effect may develop. Resonance refers to the way in which the storm surge may oscillate, or "slop about." Coasts along broad, shallow continental shelves or narrow, shallow embayments are most vulnerable to storm surges.

New York

The most recent large hurricane to strike the coast of the New York City area was Hurricane Donna. On September 12, 1960, Donna passed over eastern Long Island with gusts up to 125 miles per hour. An associated storm surge struck New York City coincident with astronomical high tide, causing a record high tide of 8.4 feet. Luckily, the duration of the storm surge was short, and flood damage was less than might have been expected. The U.S. Army Corps of Engineers estimated that from Manasquan Inlet, New Jersey to the eastern end of Long Island, flood damage amounted to $48 million.

Galveston-Houston

Coasts along the Gulf of Mexico are particularly subject to hurricanes and storm surges (Fig. 11.10). Under the aegis of the Texas Bureau of Economic Geology, detailed investigations of the Texas coast are being compiled for an environmental geology atlas. Part of the impetus for the study has been the increasing development and population of the coastal zone in recent years, its susceptibility to geologic hazards, and a history of not-infrequent disasters. The land is low, gently inclined seaward, and where it meets the Gulf, is characterized by a complex of barrier islands, peninsulas, marshes, lagoons, bays, estuaries, deltas, and dunes.

Along 60 percent of the Texas Gulf shoreline the most active geologic process is erosion. Coastal retreat takes place at a rate that locally is up to 80 feet per year. Shoreline erosion at eastern Matagorda Island during the period 1856–1957 may have been as much as 2100 feet (McGowan *in* Wermund, 1974). The most dramatic short-term changes are produced by the frequent hurricanes that hit the coast. During the few hours of a hurricane, as much coastal erosion and deposition may take place as during months or years of normal coastal activity.

Most significant, with respect to urban hazard, a total of 5787 square miles of the Texas coastal plain are less than 20 feet above mean sea level. Since storm surges may rise as much as 25 feet above sea level in the narrow, funnel-like bays, the danger is readily appreciated. Even along the straight barrier-island shorelines, storm surges may push sea level to dangerous heights. The city of Galveston is situated on a low barrier island two miles off the mainland (Fig. 11.11). In 1900, the city was struck by a hurricane with winds of 110 mph. At that time, the highest point on the island was only 8 feet above sea level, and the storm surge inundated much of the is-

land to a depth of 4 feet. More than 6000 people were killed and 8000 left homeless. Since then, a 17-foot-high seawall has been constructed to protect the city, and the land elevation has been raised to the level of the seawall on the Gulf side of the island, sloping gently down to the lagoon on the other side.

More recently, in 1961, 694 square miles of lowland in the Galveston-Houston area were flooded by the storm surge of Hurricane Carla. Figure 11.12 shows the wind velocities of that storm. Note that if the center of the storm had passed over Galveston, winds there, instead of being about 75 mph, would have exceeded 175 mph. Since 1961, urbanization of areas subject to storm surge has increased. Figure 11.12 shows the area inundated during Hurricane Carla, and areas urbanized by 1971. In the period 1900–72, 27 hurricanes with velocities greater than 74 mph struck the Texas coast. In the Galveston region, between 1886–1971, there were three hurricanes with velocities in excess of 125 mph.

With increasing urbanization, the potential for catastrophe grows alarmingly. During a future great hurricane centered on Galveston Bay (one with a magnitude which may be expected every 50 or 100 years), more than 1000 square miles could be flooded if the associated surge reached 25 feet above mean sea level (Fisher *et al,* 1972). "The entire Smith Point Peninsula and all of Bolivar Peninsula, Galveston Island, and Follets Island, except perhaps for a small area of made-land in downtown Galveston, have been and will again be entirely inundated by a severe hurricane." (Fisher *et al,* 1972, p. 21)

Heavy rains associated with hurricanes commonly cause flooding along streams and poorly drained areas. Dunes may be eroded and barrier islands breached. On the positive side, however, hurricanes nourish beaches by transporting offshore sediment to the shore. They also flush sediment and pollutants from bays.

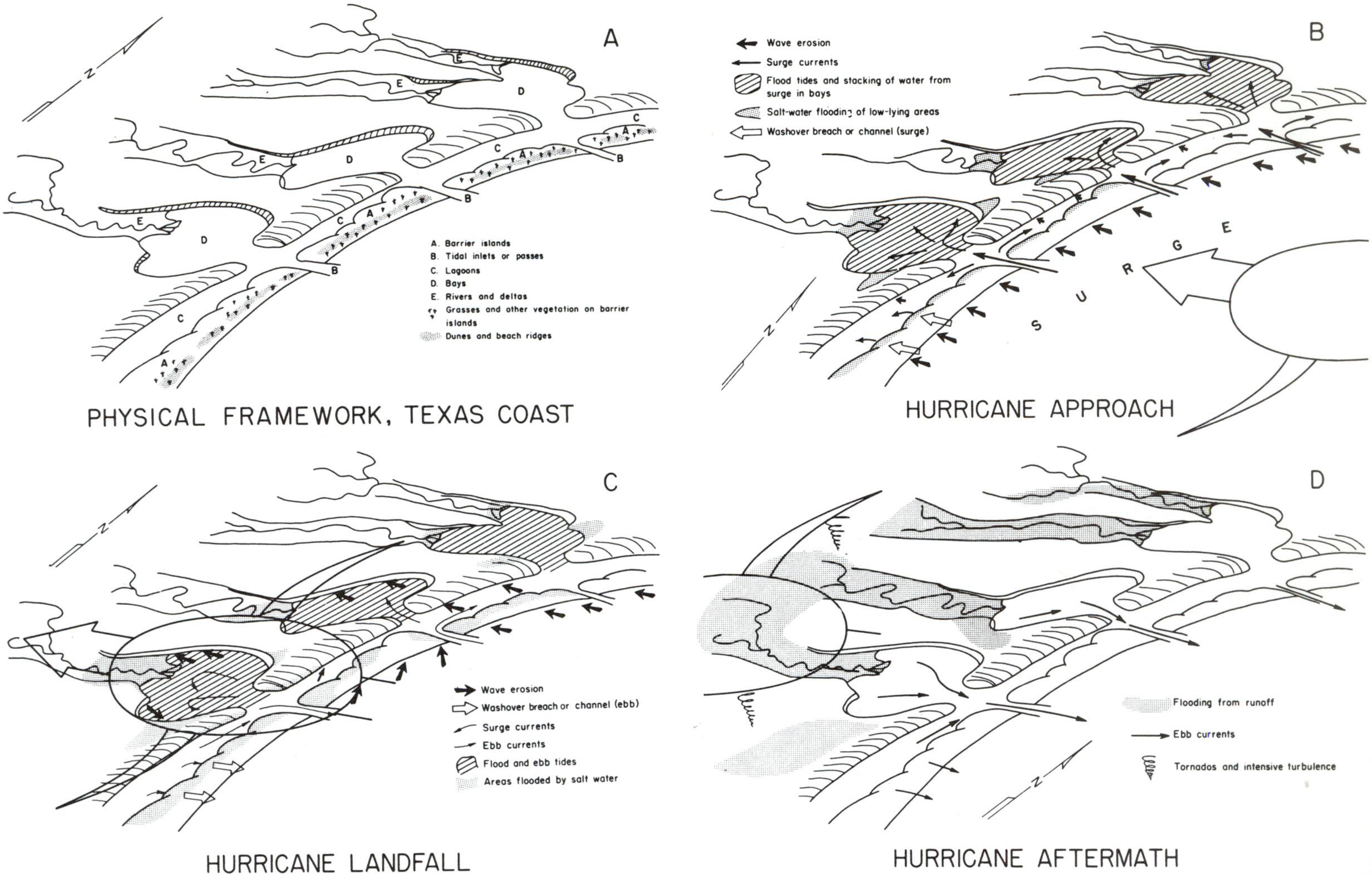

PHYSICAL FRAMEWORK, TEXAS COAST

A

A. Barrier islands
B. Tidal inlets or passes
C. Lagoons
D. Bays
E. Rivers and deltas
☆ Grasses and other vegetation on barrier
   islands
▪ Dunes and beach ridges

HURRICANE APPROACH

B

→ Wave erosion
⇒ Surge currents
▨ Flood tides and stacking of water from
   surge in bays
▨ Salt-water flooding of low-lying areas
⇨ Washover breach or channel (surge)

HURRICANE LANDFALL

C

⇒ Wave erosion
⇨ Washover breach or channel (ebb)
⇒ Surge currents
↗ Ebb currents
↗ Flood and ebb tides
▨ Areas flooded by salt water

HURRICANE AFTERMATH

D

░ Flooding from runoff
→ Ebb currents
〰 Tornados and intensive turbulence

11.10 Schematic model of hurricane effects on the Texas Coastal Zone. (A) Physical features characterizing the Texas coast. (B) Effect of an approaching hurricane. (C) Effect of a hurricane's impact on the coast. (D) Aftermath of a hurricane.

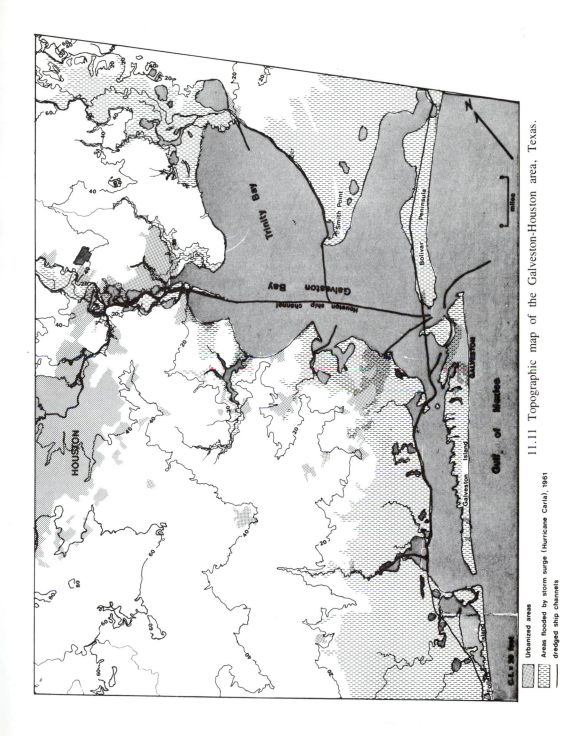

Gulf of Mexico

Galveston Island

Follets Island

GALVESTON

Bolivar Peninsula

Galveston Bay

Houston ship channel

Smith Point

Trinity Bay

HOUSTON

N

miles

C.I. = 20 feet

Urbanized areas

Areas flooded by storm surge (Hurricane Carla), 1961

dredged ship channels

11.11 Topographic map of the Galveston-Houston area, Texas.

225

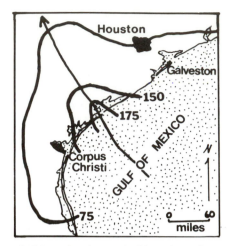

11.12 Map showing velocities, in miles per hour, of winds associated with Hurricane Carla, 1961. The arrow shows the track of the hurricane across parts of the Gulf of Mexico and the Texas coastal plain.

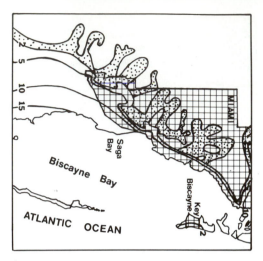

11.13 Map showing depths of inundation that may be expected during severe hurricane-associated storm surges in the Miami metropolitan region. Numbers show depth of inundation in feet. Cross-hatch pattern shows urbanized areas. Dot pattern shows areas subject to two feet inundation due to the combined effect of storm surge and 10 inches of rain.

Certain human activities in the Galveston-Houston area are increasing the potential for damage during future hurricanes. Pumping of groundwater and oil has resulted in land subsidence on the order of two to six feet in many places. Ultimate future subsidence is estimated at about ten feet, which will effectively double the amount of land subject to hurricane-surge flooding (Fisher *et al,* 1972). Furthermore, devegetation of barrier island dunes and of marshes and grass flats along the margins of the bays, renders the coast even more susceptible to erosion. Also, when artificial waterways are cut through barrier islands, the bays behind them become more vulnerable to the effects of storm surges.

Miami

Coastal regions of heavily populated south Dade County, Florida, which includes most of the metropolitan Miami region, are affected by frequent tropical storms and hurri-

canes. On the average, hurricanes with velocities of 74–125 mph may be expected every 7 years; those with velocities greater than 125 mph may be expected every 22 years. Storm surges up to 14 feet have been recorded. Figure 11.13 shows urbanized areas; areas that may be flooded by storm surges; and depths of inundation that may be expected during storm surges associated with hurricanes. Storm surges and flooding produced by heavy rainfall may result in close to a billion dollars damage for a single storm.

Behaviorial scientists White and Haas have constructed a scenario of events that might occur if a hurricane and storm surge equivalent to hurricanes Donna (1960), Carla (1961), and Betsy (1965) were to strike the Miami region in the near future. (Note that such a hurricane would be much less severe than the Keys hurricane of 1935, which drowned 750 people in an area which at the time had a relatively low population density.) One particularly vulnerable area within metropolitan Miami includes Key Biscayne and Virginia Key (combined population 10,000), whose elevations range from 2 to 10 feet above mean sea level. The islands are connected to the mainland by a two-mile causeway which is bisected by a drawbridge. Under ideal circumstances, 9 or 10 hours would be needed to evacuate the population. As much as 6 hours before the hurricane strikes, a rising tide produced by the approaching storm surge starts to flood roads and to interrupt traffic. However, according to the scenario, even though the National Hurricane Center at Coral Gables issues a warning at least 12 daylight hours before the predicted landfall of the hurricane, more than 50 percent of the population do not respond to the warning because they are not aware of the dangers of coastal storms. As a result, when danger is imminent, massive traffic tie-ups, intensified when drawbridges are opened to permit small craft to seek shelter, prevent large numbers of people from escaping the expected 10-to-15 foot storm surge waves.

Another vulnerable area of metropolitan Miami is Saga Bay, which may serve as an example of how mainland coastal development has exacerbated hurricane disaster potential. Saga Bay is expected to house more than 100,000 people initially. Its natural elevation is from zero to five feet above mean sea level; developers are required by federal regulation to place houses on fill built up to at least five feet above mean sea level. However, the developers have torn out the protective mangroves along the coast, replacing them with smooth beaches. With the mangroves removed, which formerly provided one of the most effective protections against storm surge, there remains little to deter the storm surge from sweeping across the entire area. As at Key Biscayne, inadequate evacuation routes and tardy response to warnings will prevent much of the popuation from escaping.

Atlantic City

Atlantic City, has received considerable attention recently because of the introduction of legalized gambling. There is little doubt that with the advent of gambling, population and capital investment in the area will increase. It is therefore appropriate to review the history of storm surges on this vulnerable coast.

Absecon Island, on which Atlantic City, Ventnor City, Margate City, and the Borough of Longport are located, is a low-lying barrier island with maximum elevations of only slightly more than ten feet. In March 1962, an extreme storm surge was superimposed upon regular tides at their monthly high, and most of the island was covered by water (Fig. 11.14). Wind-driven waves overtopped seawalls and other protective works along the open Atlantic coast, while rising tidal waters flowed through Absecon and Great Egg Harbor inlets and into the waterways on the northwest side of the island, Flooding progressed inland from all sides. (The tidal marshes northwest of the island were also affected, but flooding there was not investigated.) Water levels on Absecon Island rose 7.2 feet above mean sea level at the Steel Pier gage on the Atlantic coast, and 8.3 feet at the powerplant gage on the Beach Thorofare coast. The depth of inundation at any point may be estimated by subtracting the ground surface elevation, estimated from contours, from water surface elevation, obtained by interpolating between the maximum tide elevations shown on the map. Statistical evaluation of tidal records permits estimation of the frequency of high storm-tides. The relation of recurrence interval to elevation of high tides at Atlantic City is shown in Figure 11.15. It may be seen that oceanfront tides equal in elevation to the storm tide of March 1962 may be expected on an average of once every 34 years. Flooding as severe as that which occurred on the northwest (Beach Thorofare) side of the island may be expected once every 47 years.

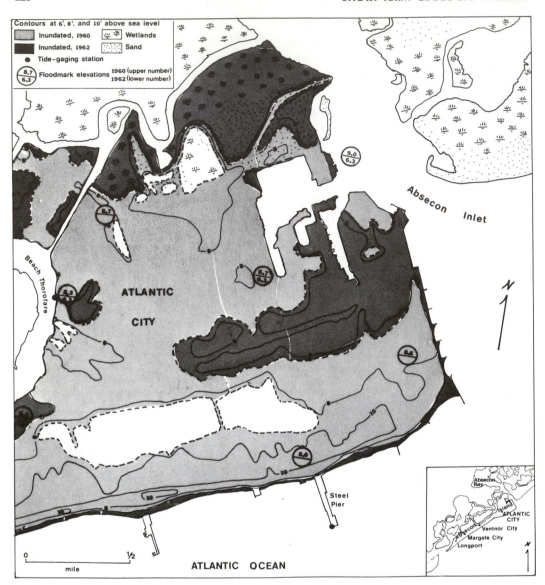

11.14 Map of part of northeast Absecon Island, New Jersey, where Atlantic City is located, showing inundation from storm surges in 1960 and 1962.

England and the Netherlands

From January 31 to February 1, 1953, a severe storm and accompanying surge produced extensive flooding along the southeast coast of England and even greater damage along the dike-protected coast of the Netherlands. Along the east coast of Britain, the surge moved from north to south, sweeping into inlets such as The Wash and the Thames and Humber estuaries (Steers, 1971). Approximately 350 square

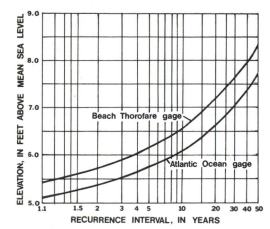

11.15 Graph showing recurrence interval of high storm tides at two locations in Atlantic City, New Jersey.

miles of low-lying coastal areas were flooded and 307 people lost their lives. At the village of King's Lynn, the surge added 8.1 feet to the predicted 22.9 foot tide, pushing the water level to 31 feet. Luckily, the surge did not coincide with high tide, and normal high tides were not at their spring high. Otherwise, damage would have been much greater. Damage was least where beaches were wide and in areas of well-developed dunes. Along narrow beaches, dunes and seawalls were severely battered and in places were destroyed. The worst damage occurred where structures were located below the high-tide level. Such low-lying areas, which include reclaimed marshes or tidal flats, depend upon seawalls for protection. Where the seawalls were breached or overtopped, flooding was extensive. In addition, rapid erosion took place along cliffed coasts where soft materials were exposed.

Along the North Sea coast in southwest Holland, the same storm produced onshore wind gusts of up to 90 mph. Sea level rose 9–11 feet higher than theoretical high tide, and the main dikes were overtopped and destroyed. About 700 square miles of low-lying land were flooded, 1835 people drowned, 47,300 houses were damaged (9215 of them badly or irreparably), and the lives of three-quarters of a million people were affected. Holland is particularly susceptible to coastal flooding caused by intensive use of land reclaimed from the sea. Storm surges in the years 1099, 1421, and 1446 each took the lives of more than 100,000 people in England and the Netherlands.

Venice

Short- and long-term sea-level changes in the northern Adriatic have periodically inundated Venice, threatening its continued existence. Drops of atmospheric pressure on occasion cause a sea-level rise of more than 12 inches in this region, and southeast winds can raise the water level in the lagoon of Venice by an additional 3 feet. These effects, together with heavy precipitation, Adriatic seiches, and land subsidence, combine to produce the catastrophic *aqua alta* (high water). More detailed discussions of flooding in Venice are found in Chapters 2 and 12.

Coastal Accretion

Seaward advances (accretion) of coasts rarely threaten life and limb, but can fill in or block harbors, affect the navigability of estuarine streams, and can even destroy or alter the economy of coastal cities by separating them from the coast. Accretion occurs where the rate of deposition exceeds the rate of erosion. Sediment may be brought to a region by waves, tides, longshore currents, rivers, wind, and living organisms, especially humans. Accumulation in the form of a delta is likely at river mouths where there are no strong currents to remove and disperse alluvium. Longshore currents may form bars and spits across bay mouths. Storm waves and tidal currents can wash over barrier islands, dunes, or beaches and fill in lagoons, marshes, and tidal flats.

Some of the most rapid accretionary coastal changes have occurred where deltas of major rivers have been built out into the sea. The Persian Gulf once extended northwest of present-day Baghdad, but sediment carried by the Tigris and Euphrates rivers has since advanced the shoreline about 300 miles. The site of the ancient Sumerian city of Ur, which was an important port, now lies more than 100 miles from the head of the Gulf. The advance of the Tigris-Euphrates delta has been estimated to be about two miles a century, and was most probably accelerated by the intensive cultivation of the Mesopotamian lowland that began about 4000 B.C.

In the Adriatic, the advance of the Po delta in the last 1850 years has put the sea some 14 miles from the Roman port of Adria. Ostia, another seaport of ancient Rome on the Tiber now lies four miles inland from the Tyrrhenian Sea.

Longshore currents are capable of transporting considerable quantities of sediment along coasts. Typical rates of littoral drift in the United States, in cubic yards per year, range from 30,000 to 500,000 on the Atlantic coast; 50,000 to 440,000 on the Gulf Coast; 30,000 to 1,000,000 on the California coast, and 8000 to 50,000 along the shores of the Great Lakes (Wiegel, 1964). Shoreline changes at East Rockaway Inlet, New York (Fig. 11.16) are largely the result of such longshore current transport of sediment westward along Long Island's south shore, and have been rapid and complex.

On the south coast of England, accumulation of shingle (flattish pebbles) in the Dungeness area has separated the old ports of Winchelsea and Rye from the English Channel by two and four miles. From 1600 to 1800, the rate of extension of the coast seaward may have been more than 15 feet a year. Longshore currents carry the shingle to the vicinity where it is then thrown up above sea level by storm waves.

Short-term, seasonal changes in beach width and profile are common. In one summer, the berm along the beach north of La

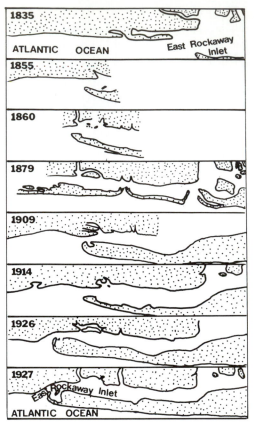

11.16 Changes in the configuration of the shoreline, East Rockaway Inlet, New York, due to westward transport of sediment by longshore currents.

Jolla, California, grew by several hundred feet. Small summer waves transport sand onshore, and the gentle backwash is ineffective in removing it. During winter storms, the beach is narrowed as the violent waves stir the sand up and the backwash carries the suspended sand offshore. In places where the summer movement of sediment is consistently greater than the seaward movement during winter the berm becomes increasingly wide. Eventually, the inner part of the berm may be converted to dunes, which, if stabilized by dune grass, will become a part of the land.

Fine sediment can accumulate only in

protected areas, such as estuaries and the sheltered waters behind spits, bars, and barrier islands. Sediment is transported to such areas by tides and rivers. Entrapment of the sediment by vegetation, such as marsh grasses, hastens the filling in and conversion of such areas to salt marshes. Dune sand blown onto the developing marshes aids in the process. In the tropics, mangroves are similarly effective in trapping fine sediment.

ARTIFICIALLY INDUCED COASTAL CHANGES

Human beings are among the most effective agents initiating or accelerating coastal change. The purpose of human interference in the coastal regime is usually to reduce or stop erosion, to preserve beaches, to maintain or improve harbors and their approaches, or to reclaim land from the sea. However, the changes wrought, whether purposeful or incidental, often achieve a magnitude or direction that is neither foreseen nor desired.

About 42 percent of the 37,000-mile shoreline of the United States, excluding Alaska, is undergoing significant erosion. The U.S. Army Corps of Engineers estimates that along 2700 miles of shoreline, erosion is critical, and in 1973 recommended the expenditure of $1.8 billion to alleviate the situation. The major types of engineering works designed to change the distribution or character of coastal materials, or to modify coastal processes are described below.

Sand Replenishment

Beach erosion may be temporarily remedied by sand replenishment. The sand used must be sufficiently coarse, otherwise it will rapidly wash away. Very often, obtaining coarse sand is very costly, and locally available fine sand is used despite its short-term residence on the beach. In sand replenishment, care should be taken that the beach profile is not steepened: the steeper the pro-

file, the faster the rate of erosion until the beach once again establishes equilibrium. For reasons of cost, sand replenishment is usually restricted to the visible portion of a beach. The offshore beach, however, should also be replenished; if not, both the foreshore and backshore zones will lose material to the offshore, and more frequent replenishment will be necessary.

Dune Erosion

Erosion of dunes may be retarded by encouraging the growth of vegetation that tends to hold the dunes in place. Fences, car bodies, or other objects which help trap wind-blown sand are also effective. (Efforts to halt erosion at Smith Point County Park on Long Island included stacking 150,000 unsold Christmas trees along the nearly eleven-mile-long beach.) Dune buggies, motorcycles, or excessive trampling injure fragile dune plants and should be discouraged. Passageways cut through dunes will be widened and scoured when storm waters wash through them.

Ironically, attempts to protect barrier-island shorelines through dune stabilization and dune construction may affect beach systems adversely. Under natural conditions, if sea level rises or the supply of sediment nourishing the system is reduced, a beach will migrate landward, with areas of backshore becoming foreshore, and areas of dunes becoming backshore (Fig. 11.17). Artificially stabilized dunes will restrict the beach, which becomes narrower and steeper—and beach steepening results in increased erosion. Fine beach sands are most vulnerable to removal and are washed offshore. Since it is these sands that normally nourish the oceanward side of the dunes, beach narrowing is accompanied by dune shrinkage. Figure 11.18 illustrates the evolution of natural and artificially controlled barrier-island shorelines.

Groins   A groin (Fig. 11.19) is a narrow, elongate structure usually built perpendic-

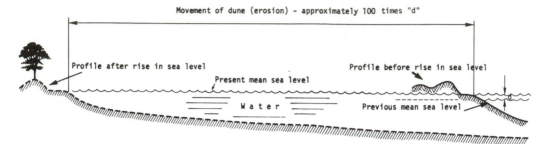

Movement of dune (erosion) - approximately 100 times "d"

Profile after rise in sea level

Profile before rise in sea level

Present mean sea level

Water

Previous mean sea level

11.17 Response of a sand dune to rise in sea level (not to scale).

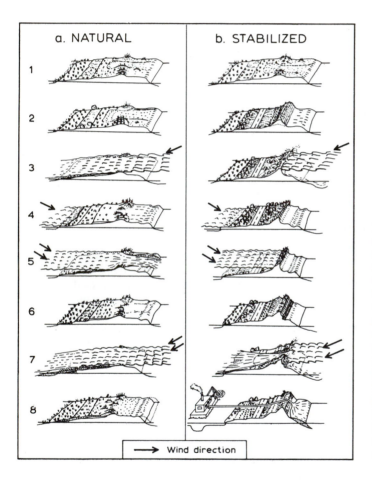

a. NATURAL   b. STABILIZED

1
2
3
4
5
6
7
8

Wind direction

11.18 Block diagrams showing changes through time of (**a**) natural barrier-island shorelines, and (**b**) stabilized barrier-island shorelines. (From Godfrey and Godfrey, 1973) To begin with (stage 1), both (a) and (b) shorelines are alike. At stage 2, an artificial dune is constructed to protect a road (diagram 2 b). Stages 3 to 8 illustrate the effects of several storms. Note that the natural barrier-island system recovers from each storm; the artificial system is badly damaged by each storm and requires increasingly expensive repair.

ular to the shore, whose purpose is to trap sediment moving parallel to the shore or to retard erosion. Unfortunately, although a groin will trap sediment on the updrift side and widen the beach there, areas for some distance downdrift of the structure, deprived of the sediment that previously nourished them, will erode. Response to such erosion

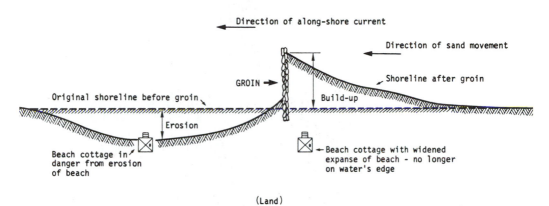

11.19 Schematic map showing a groin and its effect upon a shoreline.

usually is the construction of another groin, which in turn causes erosion downdrift of it.

Jetties   A jetty is a structure extending into a body of open water, and is designed to prevent channel silting. This purpose is accomplished by confining and directing tidal or stream currents so that they scour the bottom and maintain a navigable channel and also, in some cases, by blocking littoral drift (Fig. 11.20). Where littoral drift is operative, accretion takes place on the updrift side of the jetty and erosion on the downdrift side. If too much sediment accumulates on the updrift side, however, the excess sediment will begin to pass around the end of the structure and may actually block the channel. The accumulating sediment must then be moved to downdrift of the jetty. Dredging or pumping are the methods commonly employed.

At Palm Beach, Florida, an inlet was dredged and jetties were built in 1918–25. The jetties almost completely blocked the southward littoral drift, and serious erosion took place on the south side of the inlet (Bruun *in* Steers, 1971). Later, attempts were made to combat erosion by the construction of almost 100 groins. However, since the littoral drift was blocked and there was no source of sediment, the groins had no effect. Eventually, artificial beach nourishment and a sand-bypassing operation capable of pumping 200,000 to 250,000 cubic yards of sand per year across the inlet remedied the situation.

Breakwaters   Breakwaters are designed to protect a shore area, harbor, or anchorage from waves. They may be connected to the shoreline or may be located offshore. *Shore-connected breakwaters,* like other structures projecting from the land, can cause coastal accretion and erosion if they intercept littoral drift (Fig. 11.21). Sediment may not only accrete on the updrift side of the breakwater, but may also be deposited in the protected waters behind it.

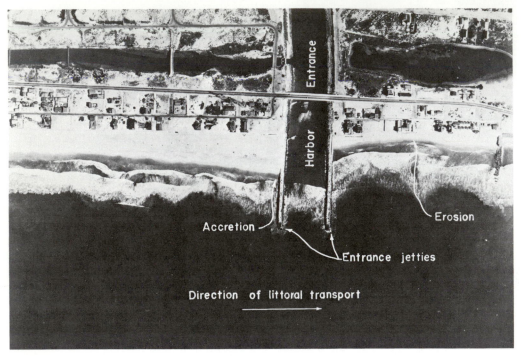

Entrance

Harbor

Accretion

Erosion

Entrance jetties

Direction of littoral transport

11.20 Aerial photo of the jetties at the entrance to the harbor at Ballona Creek, California, showing their effect upon the shoreline.

Silting may be prevented by dredging the shoaled sediment and piping it (*sand bypassing*) to downdrift areas where it can nourish beaches and prevent erosion.

Offshore breakwaters act as artificial offshore islands, creating a calm lagoon between the breakwater and the mainland. Littoral drift is effectively trapped in such areas, and causes the shoreline to accrete outward toward the breakwater (Fig. 11.22A & B). If the breakwater is of sufficient length with respect to its distance from the shore, deposition of littoral drift in the lagoon may eventually connect the breakwater to the mainland. Such accretion destroys the usefulness of the area as a harbor.

Piers   Piers serve as landing places or recreational facilities rather than as devices for coastal protection. The piles supporting

them can interfere with littoral drift and cause accretion and erosion of shorelines.

Seawalls   Seawalls separate land and water areas, and are primarily designed to prevent erosion and other wave damage. However, when waves encounter seawalls, they are reflected back onto the beach, causing steepening and erosion. Where dunes are present, seawalls hinder the exchange of sand between dunes and beach, causing both to erode. Figure 11.23 illustrates the effect of a seawall on a beach profile. Extensive seawalls have been built in Massachusetts, Florida, Mississippi, Texas, and California. Cape May in New Jersey and Miami Beach, our oldest seashore resorts, have few beaches today because of seawalls built there many years ago (Pilkey, Jr., 1975). Figure 11.24 reveals the threat that receding beaches pose to hotels along the

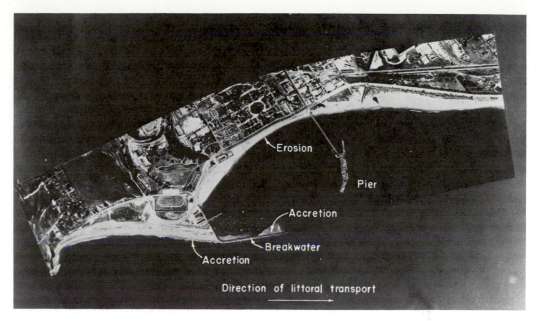

Erosion

Pier

Accretion

Breakwater

Accretion

Direction of littoral transport

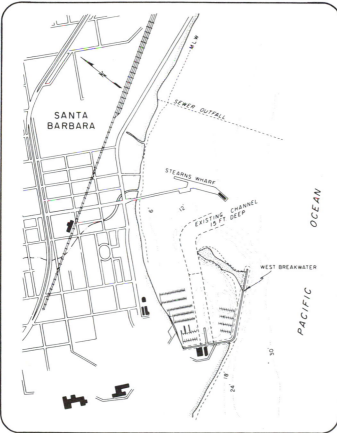

SANTA
BARBARA

MLW

SEWER OUTFALL

STEARNS WHARF

EXISTING CHANNEL
15 FT DEEP

6'

12'

WEST BREAKWATER

18'

24'

30'

PACIFIC OCEAN

11.21 Aerial photo and map of
the breakwater at Santa Barbara,
California, illustrating the effect
of the breakwater (accretion and
erosion) upon the natural regime. Sand is dredged from inside the breakwater and pumped
to the downdrift beach.

235

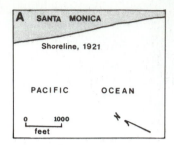

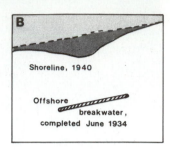

11.22 The configuration of the shoreline at Santa Monica, California. (A) In 1921, before construction of the offshore breakwater. (B) In 1940, six years after construction.

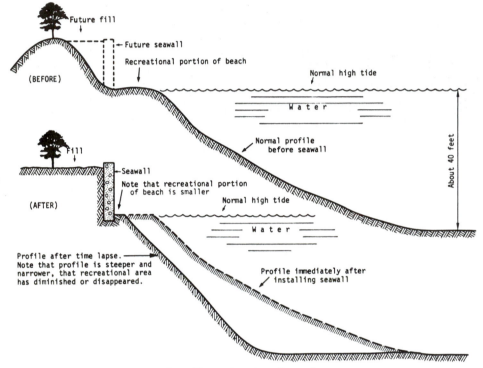

11.23 Two diagrammatic cross sections illustrating the effect of a seawall on the profile of a beach.

Miami shore. It is estimated that only 15 percent of visitors to Miami Beach swim in the ocean; most of the visitors prefer the numerous swimming pools. "The natural conclusion seems to be that Miami Beach is not a very attractive beach for ocean bathing. . . . It has probably cost several millions of dollars to build up coastal protection at Miami Beach, mainly based on groynes and vertical sea walls, and the result is that little beach is left. If a source of suitable material had been located in the bay and this material had been dumped on the beach, we would still have had, and could still maintain, a beach at Miami Beach instead of great amounts of coastal protection junk. . . ." (Bruun *in* Steers, 1972, p. 211).

11.24 Aerial photos illustrating how receding beaches increase the likelihood of structural damage to hotels along Miami's beaches. The pictures show the most and least eroded beaches.

The presence of seawalls and other defenses against the sea often encourage a false sense of security. In many coastal areas, residential and commercial development occurs in times of low storm frequency and minimal shoreline retreat. Buildings are often constructed on "stabilized" or altered dunes or on fill emplaced behind seawalls. During a major storm, seawalls may be overtopped or fail, and the dunes and the fill behind them will be scoured and removed. In September 1975, in the vicinity of Panama City Beach, Florida, Hurricane Eloise was accompanied by a storm surge and waves that caused extensive damage to building foundations when seawalls failed (Morton, 1976). If they are not adequately protected by grass, asphalt, or concrete, seawalls themselves may break when water flows over them, eroding supporting soils. Inadequate protection caused seawalls to fail during the North

Sea Storm of 1953 that took such a great toll of lives in the Netherlands.

The U.S. Army Corps of Engineers concludes that "beach structures, when properly used, have a place in shore protection. But research has shown that the best protection is afforded by using methods as similar as possible to natural ones. In other words, a greater degree of effectiveness is obtained by the type of protection provided by nature, which permits the natural processes to continue unhampered. To simulate natural protection, dunes and beaches are rebuilt artificially. . . . Coastal engineers can now determine required dune and beach dimensions to protect against storms of any given intensity. . . ." (*National Shoreline Study*, 1973, vol. I, p. 111).

Sand, however, is a rapidly diminishing resource. Much sand that once reached the coasts is trapped in reservoirs behind river dams. Sand may be obtained from bays, lagoons, estuaries, and offshore areas, but care must be taken that the mining process does not upset natural equilibria and trigger unwanted changes. Mining of beach and dune sand for commercial uses must be held to a minimum. In California, where large volumes of sand are lost naturally through littoral drift into near-shore submarine canyons, the use of traps and transport mechanisms to bypass the sand around the entrances to the canyons is being considered.

Land Reclamation

Population pressure in urban areas commonly results in efforts to reclaim land from the sea. Land reclamation also occurs in densely populated agricultural regions, such as the Netherlands and the Fen district in England, along coasts that are desirable for recreational purposes, and on the peripheries of harbors where port facilities are constructed. In New York City, a survey made in 1862 estimated that since 1688 the average width of reclaimed land along the waterfront amounted to 626 feet (Griffin, 1959). Infilling of San Francisco Bay and

adjacent areas since the end of the nineteenth century has reduced the area of the Bay by 11 percent and the area of the marshes by 60 percent (Nichols and Wright, 1971). Much of Copenhagen lies on land reclaimed from shallow sea floor.

Land reclamation is most feasible in areas where shallow, calm water is the rule. Unfortunately, reclamation of such areas removes important natural coastal protection and eliminates or reduces special environments in which abundant marine, amphibious and bird life flourish. Furthermore, interference with coastal regimes often triggers natural responses that place development on such reclaimed land in frequent or constant danger.

Figures 11.25 and 11.26 show how the coastlines of Manhattan and Brooklyn in New York City have changed since these areas were first settled by Europeans. Figure 11.27 shows the erosion control and hurricane protection project proposed by the U.S. Army Corps of Engineers for East Rockaway Inlet to Rockaway Inlet and Jamaica Bay, New York City. The plan provides for a gated surge-control barrier across the entrance to Jamaica Bay having an elevation of 18 feet above sea level, together with floodwalls, levees, dikes, and a program of beach nourishment.

Besides taking action to protect already settled areas, the Corps of Engineers is also attempting to prevent reclamation of some unique, delicate, or hazardous coastal regions.

Marco Island, situated almost due west of Miami on the opposite side of the Florida Peninsula, "has been long recognized as one of the most promising resort properties any real estate developer has ever come by. The wide Marco Beach, made up of fine white sand and stretching for some 5 miles along the Gulf of Mexico, is one of Florida's best. Little imagination has been needed to see this magnificent strand lined by posh high-rise condominiums and resort hotels. . . ." (Carter, 1976, p. 641). Development, however, would involve destruction of mangrove swamps, which pro-

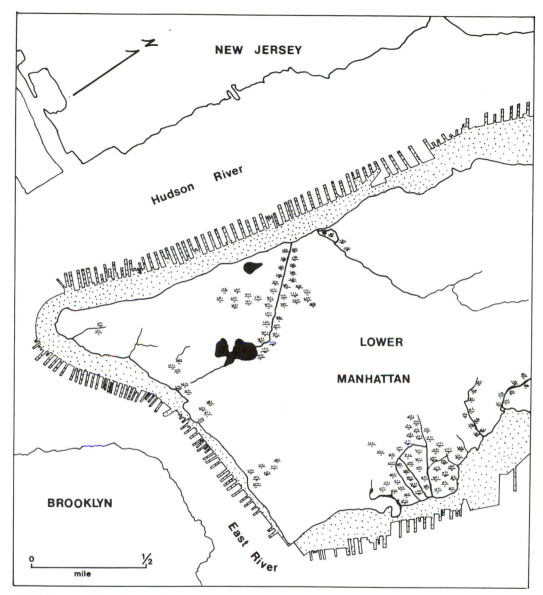

11.25 Lower Manhattan in the seventeenth century, showing the positions of the coastline at the time of its discovery.

vide an important habitat for marine fauna, form a vital buffer against storms, and help keep coastal waters free of excessive sediment. As a result, the Corps of Engineers has denied dredge-and-fill permits for a proposed 18.2-million-cubic-yard operation.

London

London is situated on both sides of the River Thames, which is tidal (estuarine) to a point about 18 miles upstream of London Bridge. More than 30 square miles of the

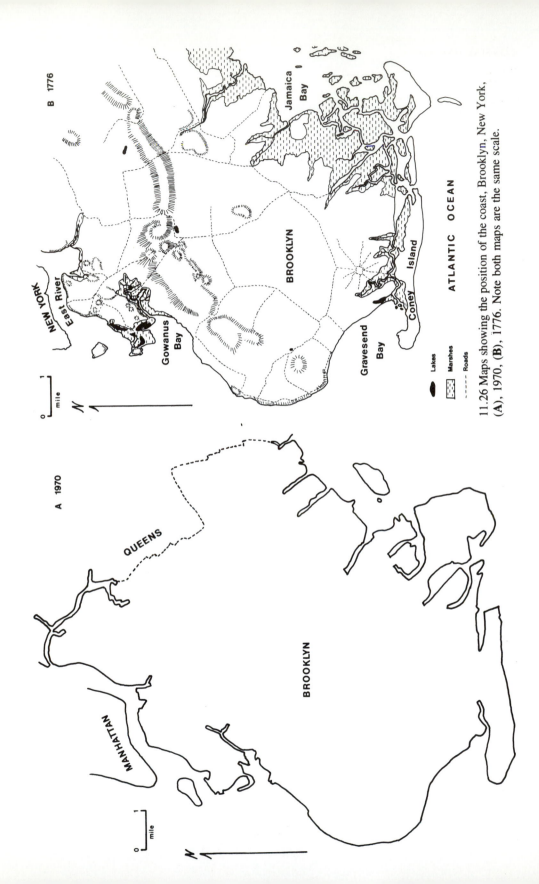

11.26 Maps showing the position of the coast, Brooklyn, New York, (**A**), 1970, (**B**), 1776. Note both maps are the same scale.

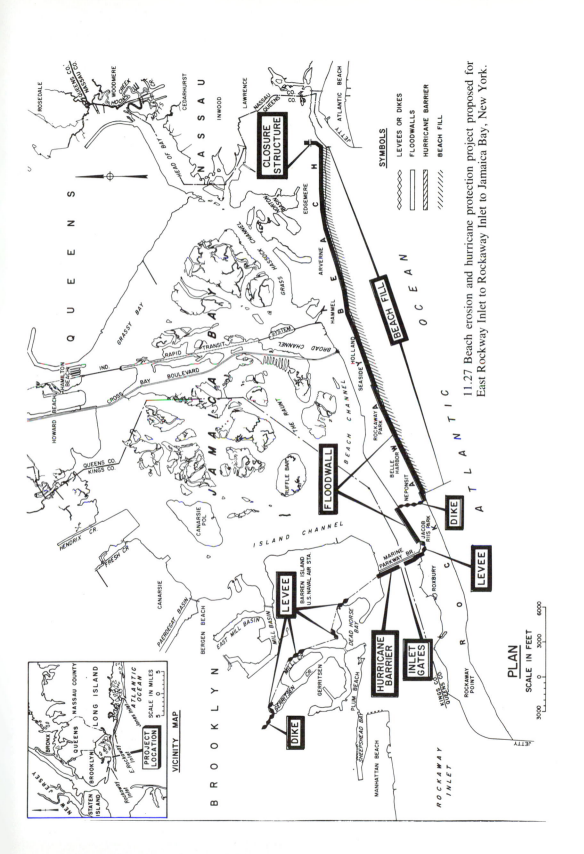

11.27 Beach erosion and hurricane protection project proposed for East Rockaway Inlet to Jamaica Bay, New York.

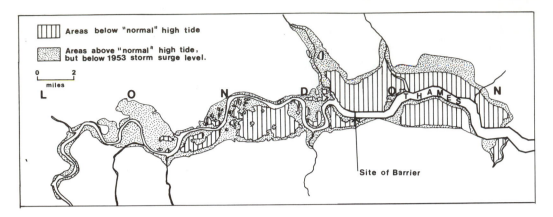

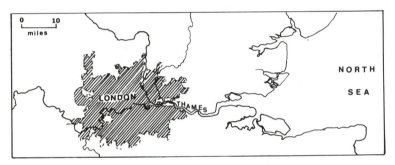

11.28 *Above* London, showing the site of the Thames Barrier and areas below ''normal'' high tide and additional areas below the 1953 storm-surge level. *Below* the location of London with respect to the River Thames and the North Sea.

land occupied by the city was once tidal marshland subject to flooding at high tide (Fig. 11.28). Because tradition held that anyone who reclaimed land from tidal areas should have rent-free use of that land, from time immemorial, river walls and embankments were constructed to drain and protect the rich fields of the lower Thames Valley. However, as might be expected, breaks in these defenses were frequent and flooding was a common occurrence. The Romans were the first to build an organized system of walls and embankments. Unfortunately, it was not sufficient simply to keep the Roman works in good repair because, since about A.D. 200, southeast England has been sinking at a rate of about one foot per cen-

tury, necessitating constant rebuilding and heightening of the sea defenses. After the departure of the Romans, it was not until the thirteenth century that a central authority exercised some control over the scattered efforts to keep water out of low-lying areas. Nevertheless, exceptionally high tides continued to break through and cause extensive flooding on an average of once every ten years. As London grew larger and occupied more of the lowland, the consequence of floods became more serious. In 1736, for instance, Westminster Hall was inundated to a depth of two feet (Hitheman, 1973). The greatest times of danger were those when storm surges swept up the Thames from the North Sea, causing river levels to rise well

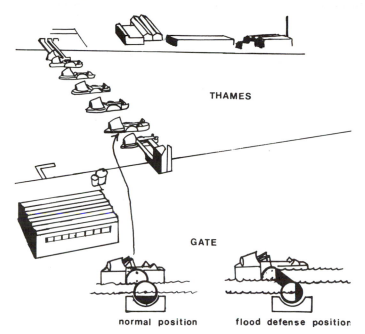

THAMES

GATE

normal position   flood defense position

11.29 Diagrammatic sketch of the Thames Barrier. The barrier consists of a series of moveable gates which, when open, permit the passage of river traffic and which, when closed, exclude floodwaters from upstream areas.

above normal high tides. In 1928, a tide more than six feet higher than normal broke through the river wall at Lambeth, drowning many, and inundating considerable areas of central London. A quarter-century later, the same area was saved from the threat of serious flooding when the extraordinary storm surge of 1953 was diverted elsewhere by the failure of flood defenses downstream of London.

Thus, throughout the 2000-year history of the city, the reclaimed lands have frequently been "claimed back" by the sea. In modern London, the situation is especially serious. Forty-five square miles of the metropolitan region (Fig. 11.28), with a population of 1,200,000, are below the maximum height reached by the 1953 storm surge. If the defenses had given way, flood damage on the order of 2–3 billion dollars would have been inflicted upon industrial facilities. Fifteen major power stations, several large hospitals and gas, sewage, and water works would have been hit. Seventy stations and 46 miles of the London Underground and the Houses

of Parliament and many other important administrative buildings would have been flooded as well. Moreover, southeast England, is continuing to sink, and that, together with the problem of compacting clays underlying London, increase the chances of serious flooding with the passage of time.

To reduce the risk of flooding, the Greater London Council and other bodies decided to build a barrier across the Thames (besides continuing the traditional approach of heightening and strengthening the river embankments and walls). The Thames barrier, which is to be completed about 1980, consists of a series of giant, moveable gates constructed side-by-side across the 520-meter width of the river (Fig. 11.29). During normal times, the gates will be left open to permit the usual flow of the water and traffic. In times of danger, the gates can be closed within 15 minutes. Despite its cost of about $300 million, the barrier will only be effective for 60 years. During the first years of its operation, it will probably have to be closed once a year. By the year 2030, due to the general subsidence of the area, the frequency of flood threat will necessitate closing the barrier about 10 times a year. After that, new methods will have to be sought to keep London above water.

Estuaries

Estuaries, the indented portions of the coast where rivers meet the sea and feel the influence of oceanic tides, are of special significance to humans. They provide protected harbors and connect inland water routes with the sea. They are rich in sea life and their continual flushing by tides and currents disperses and dilutes wastes. Seven of the 10 largest metropolitan areas in the world and 22 of the world's 32 largest cities are located on estuaries. These bodies of water have been profoundly changed by human activity. The dumping of sewage and industrial wastes and the flow of polluted rivers into estuarine waters have altered their chemistry and temperature, producing radical alterations in the abundance and diversity of their flora and fauna. Accelerated erosion in a watershed may contribute abnormal amounts of silt to an estuary, resulting in changes in estuarine volume, configuration, depth, and channel location, and have affected the ability of estuarine waters to support life. The accumulation of silt within estuaries is also affected by shoreline development, land reclamation, and dredging.

Where rivers flowing into estuaries have been diverted or reduced in volume, estuarine processes may be significantly affected. Low tidal ranges and reduced river flow in Galveston and Trinity bays, Texas, have made the discharge of waste materials into the estuaries a critical problem. Dams built across the mouths of bays or estuaries to protect them against storm surges inhibit the flushing out of silt and polluted waters during hurricanes. Pollution of estuaries is discussed in Chapter 4.

Harbors

Many of the greatest cities of the world are port cities. The Latin *portus* means gateway, and port cities are gateways between the worlds of land and sea. An essential part of a port is an adequate harbor. A harbor must provide shelter from the open ocean; have sufficient area and depth for maneuvering and anchoring large ships; have good holding ground for anchors; and be free of strong tidal currents, ice, and fog.

The U.S. Navy has classified harbor types into eight groups. *Coastal* harbors include:

() Natural harbors. Those sheltered from the wind and sea by virtue of their location within a natural coastal indentation or in the protective lee of an island, cape, reef, or other natural barrier.

(2) Breakwater harbors. Those lying behind a breakwater.

(3) Tide-gate harbors. Those whose waters are constrained by locks or other mechanical devices in order to provide sufficient water to float vessels at all stages of the tide.

(4) Open roadstead harbors. Those that have no natural or artificial protection.

Another classification of harbors is based upon coastal characteristics and upon artificial coastal modifications (Morgan, 1952). An example of each type is shown in Figure 11.30.

Harbors on irregular coasts, formed by coastal drowning after the retreat of the Pleistocene ice sheets, include Portsmouth and Southampton (England), Piraeus, the Golden Horn, Portland (Maine), New York, Baltimore, Newport News, Norfolk, Portsmouth (Virginia), Boston, San Francisco, Seattle, Tacoma, Halifax, Victoria, Vancouver, Sydney, Nagasaki, and Rio de Janeiro. The last city is perhaps the finest example of a harbor on a submerged coast. Rio is located on a bay 30 miles in circumference, up to 85 feet deep, and only one mile across at its entrance.

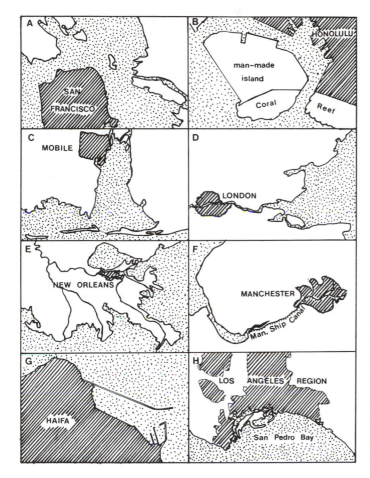

11.30 Sketch map of harbors classified according to coastal characteristics and artificial coastal modifications (see text). (A) On an irregular, drowned coast. (B) Protected by a coral reef and an artificial island. (C) Separated from the ocean by a lagoon and barrier islands. (D) On an estuarine river. (E) On a delta arm. (F) Connected to the ocean by a canal. (G) Protected by a breakwater. (H) Extended seaward to deeper water.

Harbors protected by *coral reefs* include Honolulu and Pearl Harbor. Entrances to these harbors usually are created or improved by dredging through the protective reefs.

Harbors protected by *barrier islands* or *spits* include Venice (Italy), Galveston, Mobile, and Durban (South Africa). The protection offered by barrier islands and spits is adequate except during storms of great intensity when these low-lying landforms are apt to be breached. Sufficient depth must be maintained or created by dredging. The port of Houston is connected to the Gulf of Mexico by a channel dredged in the extensive shallow lagoon behind Galveston (Fig. 11.11). Similarly, Mobile is situated behind a sandbar and lagoon, and depends upon a channel dredged through the lagoon for its connection to the Gulf.

Harbors located on *estuarine river reaches* include Québec, Hull, Liverpool, London, Glasgow, Lisbon, Bordeaux, Le Havre, Antwerp, Rotterdam, Bremen, Hamburg, Philadelphia, Melbourne, and Brisbane. These harbors are to varying degrees dependent upon the level of the tide for access. Sediment transported by tidal and longshore currents and inflowing rivers commonly form shoals and bars. Tidal scour may help in keeping channels open, but dredging is a common necessity.

Harbors on *delta arms* include Calcutta on the Ganges Delta, Danzig on the Vistula Delta, and New Orleans on the Mississippi Delta. New Orleans is kept open by dredging a 114-mile approach to a depth of 35 feet.

Artificial harbors fall into several categories. The city of Manchester, England, was made a port by cutting the Manchester Ship Canal to connect it to the sea. Amsterdam, located on the Zuiderzee, became important as a port in 1300 when a good channel was found between the Zuiderzee and the North Sea. As far back as 1400, however, a submarine bar developed at the port entrance which, by 1544, had reduced the depth of the channel so that only ships drawing less than twelve feet could pass. By the seventeenth century, the channel depth was further reduced, and only ships drawing about 9–10 feet could traverse it. This impediment to traffic was a major reason why, in the eighteenth century, Amsterdam gave way to London as a great trading center. In 1824, a canal to the North Sea was completed and used until 1876. Since then, a shorter, deeper canal has provided the vital link. The canal lock at IJmuiden allows the passage of ships of 150,000 tons with drafts up to 50 feet. The approach to Rotterdam, located on the estuary of the Maas, had been silting badly, and in 1866–72 a direct approach to the North Sea was established by cutting a canal (the Rotterdam Waterway) through the dunes at the Hook of Holland. Since then, Rotterdam has become one of the major ports of the world. Utrecht, built on the main mouth of the Rhine River, has been silted up since about the year 1900. A canal had to be dug to a new branch of the river to re-establish connection with the sea. The city of Bruges, in Belgium, originally was an important port on the Zwyn estuary into which the Ree River flowed. By the fourteenth century, the Zwyn had silted up, severely damaging the economy of Bruges. That hardship, together

with political troubles of the sixteenth century, brought prosperity to an end. Today Bruges is eight miles inland; however in 1903, a canal was cut to Zeebrugge on the coast, allowing the city to flourish as a port once again.

Harbors protected by large *breakwaters* include Haifa, Valparaiso, Barcelona, Casablanca, Madras, Le Havre, Boulogne, Marseilles, Genoa, Naples, Osaka, Yokohama, and Corpus Christi.

Where harbor depths are not very great, extension of the harbor seaward to deeper water may be feasible. In the port of Los Angeles, an enormous artificial harbor has been advanced about four miles into San Pedro Bay. At Cape Town, South Africa, a similar extension to deeper water has taken place.

Lakefront Floods

In the United States and Canada, lakefront flooding is concentrated in regions adjacent to the Great Lakes. The level of these lakes is controlled by stream discharge, tidal changes, weather, and artificial diversion of water. Fluctuations of 10 feet and more have been recorded along the shore of Lake Erie at Buffalo, New York. Fluctuations in the other lakes, which are deeper, average 2–3 feet. Changes are also produced by slow deformation of the earth's crust. The shores of Lakes Ontario and Erie, most of Lake Michigan, and the southern part of Lake Superior are, in general, sinking relative to their outlets, and levels are rising. The shores of Lake Huron, northeastern Lake Michigan, and northern Lake Superior are rising relative to their outlets, and levels are falling at the rate of one foot per century.

Flood hazard has increased due to development of lake shores during decades of relatively low lake-levels. Locations particularly affected include areas around the Duluth-Superior harbor in Minnesota; Green Bay, Wisconsin; the Saginaw Bay area of Lake Huron; the 170-mile stretch of Lake

Erie shoreline from Detroit to Sandusky, Ohio; and along the Lake Ontario shore west and east of Rochester, New York (Hoyt and Langbein, 1955).

Conclusion Human contact with coastlines is bound to intensify. Annual attendance at beaches in and near New York City in recent years was 20 million at Coney Island, 15 million at Rockaway Beach, and 13 million at Jones Beach. Other beaches in the area were visited by an additional 9 million people. Greater and greater lengths of coastline are being used for residences and for recreation and industry. Nearly half of the population of the United States lives in counties that border on the sea or the Great Lakes. Furthermore, between 1960–70, 90 percent of the country's population growth took place in coastal states, which already have 75 percent of the nation's population and 12 of the 13 largest cities. As a result, a vital and fragile environment is being radically altered, and natural protection against coastal hazards is being impinged upon or destroyed. Wetlands are being reclaimed; beaches and dunes overused, or eliminated; and lagoons, bays, and estuaries are dredged, filled-in, or polluted. The development of areas dangerously close to coastal cliffs accelerates. Not only do problems connected with the disruption of coastal systems proliferate, but questions concerning land use, ownership, public access, transportation, insurance and regulation of waterways become of increasing importance. As human use of the coast continues to intensify, the need for intelligent planning becomes paramount. The benefits and drawbacks of alternative approaches must be considered and must include estimates of natural and social costs as well as purely short-term economic costs.

The U.S. Army Corps of Engineers (1973) has suggested guidelines for a program to improve the use and management of the shore. Decisions must be made regarding possible uses of the shore, which include (1) recreation; (2) the extraction of fish, sand, gravel, and minerals; (3) waste disposal; (4) transportation; (5) residential, commercial, and industrial development; (6) leaving the shore in an undisturbed natural state. When decisions have been made, then engineering and managerial techniques may be developed.

12. Subsidence and Collapse

When the earth's surface sinks, as little as a few square yards or as much as hundreds of thousands of square miles may be involved. At two o'clock in the afternoon on December 2, 1973, part of the forest floor near Montevallo, Alabama, measuring 425 by 350 feet, suddenly collapsed and dropped downward 150 feet. In England, in September 1892, a steam locomotive was shunting wagons in a freight yard. Suddenly the ground opened up and the engine disappeared into the hole. After the Alaska earthquake of 1964, it was found that tens of thousands of square miles had subsided by as much as 7.5 feet.

Many instances of lowering of the earth's surface take place slowly. Five thousand square miles of the San Joaquin Valley, California, subsided up to 28 feet from 1925 to 1970. The land around Houston, Texas, has gradually subsided up to 10 feet since World War II. Just as sinking of the earth's surface may be slow (*subsidence*) or rapid (*collapse*), the causes may be short- or long-lived. Broad regions of the earth's crust involved in isostatic adjustment may undergo vertical movement that continues for thousands or millions of years. Similarly, vertical adjustment caused by compression or extension of the crust may be of long duration and affect large areas. Such movement, together with the apparent uplift

or subsidence of land surfaces that result from world-wide changes in sea level, are beyond human control. The hazards stemming from such movements are discussed in Chapters 11 and 13.

Other types of sinking are more local, and are limited in duration and modest in cause: withdrawal of solids or fluids from beneath the earth's surface; loading of areas capable of settlement, compression, or plastic flowage; hydrocompaction.

Subsidence rarely results in loss of life, but annually causes many millions of dollars damage. It is of particular interest when it occurs in built-up areas—especially if the sinking is uneven or is accompanied by lateral movement. Subsidence has on occasion seriously disrupted drainage patterns. If it occurs adjacent to the ocean serious flooding and erosion may result.

Many instances of subsidence are caused by humans, and, although rarely reversible, may be halted. Damage caused by natural subsidence may be held to a minimum if processes are understood and their likelihood and place of occurrence are recognized.

The problems associated with surface loading, swelling clays, and creep are discussed in Chapter 6. Subsidence triggered by earthquake vibrations is considered in Chapter 7.

EXTRACTION OF FLUIDS

The withdrawal of water or oil from the ground is a major cause of subsidence; withdrawal of gas may also be important. As fluids are extracted from porous materials, the fluid pressure within the material is reduced, thereby increasing the *effective stress* (stress transmitted from grain to grain). An increase in effective stress increases pressure on the material's solid components and may reduce its open or pore space. The rate and amount of subsidence will depend upon the amount of effective stress, and the presence or absence of overlying rigid layers that are able to withstand loss of support without collapse or deformation.

Withdrawal of fluids from coarse sediments results in immediate compaction; if fluids are reintroduced, expansion is possible. When fluids are withdrawn from highly compressible, fine-grained materials, a somewhat slower but permanent rearrangement of the grains takes place, resulting in irreversible subsidence.

Documentation of subsidence caused by withdrawal of fluids is relatively recent (Poland and Davis 1969). Subsidence resulting from withdrawal of groundwater was first recorded in California's Santa Clara Valley in 1933; subsidence over the Goose Creek oil field in Texas was noted in 1925. Since World War II, the phenomenon has become increasingly significant. Its origin, no doubt, lies in the accelerating demand for such fluids caused by rapidly increasing population and industrialization. Furthermore, with the growth of cities and the increasing extraction of fluids from natural reservoirs beneath urbanized areas, the effects of subsidence in terms of disruption of services and damage to structures has become correspondingly more noticeable and widespread.

Subsidence due to fluid removal usually may be halted by stopping the process or by providing artificial or natural recharge. Damage may be avoided through the use of appropriate foundations or special structural design (see Chapter 6).

Examples of cities in which subsidence has been a significant problem are described below.

Houston

Within the last 25 years, subsidence of two to four feet has been recorded in Houston, Texas, and up to six feet in the nearby areas of Baytown and Texas City (Fig. 12.1). The sinking is attributed to extensive withdrawal of artesian groundwater: as water is extracted from the sand aquifers, associated water-saturated clay beds gradually dehydrate and compact. Maximum subsidence closely coincides with areas of intensive pumping. Future subsidence up to about 10.5 feet has been predicted, nearly all of it occurring as a result of declines already produced by present rates of withdrawal. Ninety percent of the ultimate subsidence will take place even if the amount of groundwater withdrawn does not increase (Fisher *et al*, 1972, p. 64). There have been few problems of differential settlement around Houston. However, since the area is almost at sea level, subsidence has exacerbated the problem of flooding caused by storm surges (see Chapter 11).

Faults in the Houston area have also been affected by groundwater withdrawal. The buoyancy of the sediments is reduced, activating movement along the faults. Such movement has damaged roads, buildings, airport runways, sewers, and other utilities (Clanton and Amsbury, 1976). The extraction of oil and sulfur, and salt mining have also caused some local subsidence up to 10 feet.

California

California has experienced greater problems from subsidence than any other state (Fig. 12.2). It is estimated that if no remedial measures are taken, subsidence will cause

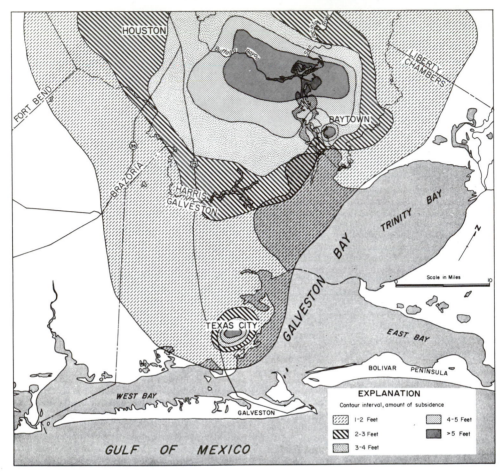

12.1 Land-surface subsidence in the Houston area (1964).

$26 million damage in the period 1970–2000 (Alfors *et al*, 1973).

In the Los Angeles coastal plain the withdrawal of oil, water, and gas from the Wilmington and Inglewood oilfields has caused significant subsidence. Between 1928 and 1962, 1397 billion gallons of liquids were extracted from the Wilmington field, which over the years developed an elliptical, funnel-shaped depression that by 1967 had subsided 29 feet at its center in the Long Beach harbor (Fig. 12.3). The subsidence was caused mainly by compaction of the oil reservoir sands. Particularly

alarming was that much of the area was originally only 5–10 feet above sea level. By 1960, an area of 20 square miles had subsided, and more than 3000 acres of land had settled well below sea level. Remedial measures to protect port and industrial facilities, a major naval shipyard, and many other threatened structures included the construction of levees and seawalls, emplacement of fill, and the elevation of some structures. The vertical subsidence also resulted in horizontal movements of up to 9 feet that sheared pipelines, oil well casings, and utility lines. Buildings were damaged,

12.2 Areas of land subsidence in California. Areas where major subsidence is caused by withdrawal of fluids are shown in black. Subsidence in the San Joaquin Delta area (striped) has been caused by oxidation of peat.

12.3 Aerial view of Long Beach, California, showing total subsidence contours (in feet), 1928–68.

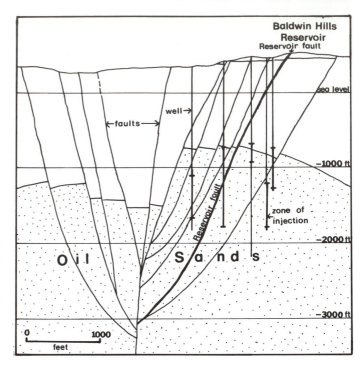

12.4 Cross section of a faulted anticline in the Inglewood Oilfield, California. Note the Reservoir Fault, which intersects the ground surface under the Baldwin Hills Reservoir. Oil wells and sections of wells where fluid injection is employed are shown.

and the cost was more than $100 million. Eventually the movement was stopped or retarded (and in some places reversed) by injecting salt water into the oil-bearing formations to restore fluid pressure.

In the northwest part of the Los Angeles Basin, subsidence in the Inglewood field has been causally linked with the failure of the Baldwin Hills Reservoir just east of Santa Monica (Hamilton and Meehan, 1971). On the 14th of December, 1963, water broke through the dam and poured onto downstream communities, damaging or destroying 277 homes, killing 5 people, and causing $12 million property damage. Examination of the emptied reservoir revealed that the protective clay lining had been ruptured by a fault along which six inches of vertical displacement had taken place. This rupture had allowed water to work its way under the dam, gradually eroding a larger and larger passageway. Investigators assembled the following infor-

mation: the oilfield, adjacent to the reservoir, drew upon oil-bearing formations that occupied an anticline traversed by numerous faults (Fig. 12.4). After the inception of pumping in 1924, a bowl-like subsidence developed that amounted to more than six feet at its maximum. In 1951, the Baldwin Hills Reservoir was opened despite knowledge that ground surface elevation changes were taking place and that it was underlain by a fault (known as the Reservoir Fault). Six years later, in 1957, surface cracking and faulting southeast of the reservoir attracted attention. The rupturing was coincident with large-scale injection of water into the oilfield designed to increase oil recovery.

From these facts an explanation of the dam failure was constructed. Intensive withdrawal of fluids from the faulted anticline resulted in compaction of the oil-bearing strata. Not only did the surface subside, but a shearing stress was exerted on the faults.

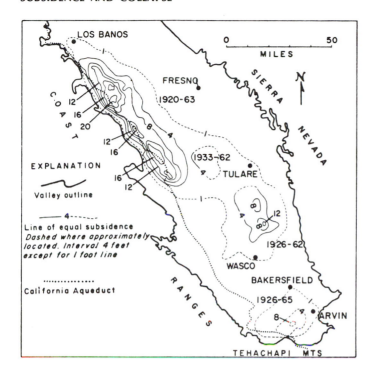

12.5 Map of the southern part of the San Joaquin Valley, California, showing the magnitude and areal extent of subsidence.

The fault surfaces, however, were able to withstand the stress because there was sufficient friction to inhibit movement between them. However, when water under high pressure was injected, it lubricated and "pushed apart" the fault faces, allowing slippage to occur. One of the moving faults intersected and cracked the lining of the dam, and gradually eroded and and enlarged the opening until the dam burst.

In the San Joaquin Valley thousands of square miles have subsided from 1 to 20 feet as a result of extensive withdrawal of groundwater for irrigation, and the structural integrity of the California Aqueduct (Fig. 12.5) has been threatened. Cessation of groundwater withdrawal and the use of imported water for irrigation are now permitting groundwater levels to rise, and the subsiding land surfaces are now becoming stable (Poland *et al*, 1975). The Aqueduct was also threatened by the fact that, in dry regions of the San Joaquin Valley, it crosses 70 miles of clay-rich alluvial fan deposits that tend to compact and shrink when wet. To avoid subsidence, these clays were pre-wet so that hydrocompaction would take place before construction of the Aqueduct (Poland, 1969).

Around the southern margin of San Francisco Bay, in the Santa Clara Valley between Palo Alto and southern San Jose, parts of which are heavily populated, groundwater withdrawal has caused considerable subsidence—up to 12.7 feet from 1960 to 1967 (Fig. 12.6). A serious side effect has been an increase in flood hazard from the waters of the Bay and from streams that traverse the area. About $9 million of public funds, it is estimated, have been spent on the construction of levees (Poland, 1971). Also, compaction of the sediments has ruptured several hundred well-casings at a cost of about $4 million. Subsidence in the area was brought to a halt in 1971 when water was imported, thus diminishing the drain on local groundwater supplies.

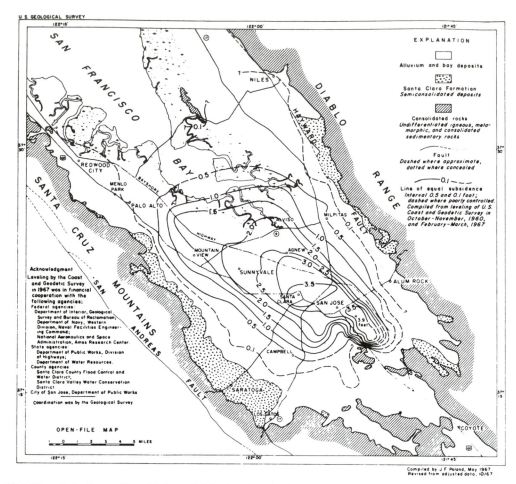

12.6 Map of the Santa Clara Valley, California, showing land subsidence from 1960 to 1967.

In the Sacramento–San Joaquin Delta drainage of areas underlain by peat deposits has resulted in subsidence to elevations well below sea level. The sinking has been attributed to the decay and shrinkage of the dried peat, and to wind erosion, burning, and compaction of peat by farm machinery.

Mexico City

Mexico City occupies a closed basin about 7500 feet above sea level surrounded by high mountains. Many small rivers flow into the basin and, over the course of time,

have deposited great thicknesses of alluvial fill. Occasionally, lakes have occupied parts of the valley floor, so that lake deposits are interlayered with stream deposits. Volcanic eruptions deposited ash layers, now altered to clays. Modern Mexico City was built on a site that, until it was drained, was occupied by a lake. The area is underlain by water-saturated sand, gravel, silt, fine-graned volcanic ash, and clay (Legget, 1973). The city grew rapidly. Its population in 1895 was a half a million, in 1922 one million, and by 1974 more than 8 million. Water was withdrawn for urban use at a rate

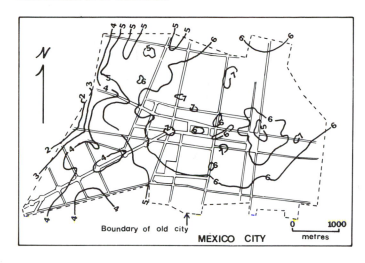

12.7 Map showing subsidence in Mexico City. Heavy lines are lines of equal subsidence, in meters.

far exceeding natural recharge, and extensive compaction of the silts and clays took place, with corresponding subsidence up to 25 feet (Fig. 12.7). At times, the rate was almost 2 feet per year. Efforts to reduce or halt the sinking have been undertaken, and include projects to import water into the city and the construction of recharge wells through which flood waters may be injected into the underlying aquifers (Poland and Davis, 1969). For further discussion, see Chapter 6.

Venice

Subsidence in the vicinity of Venice has been in progress for thousands of years. Since prehistoric times, on the order of 20 feet is indicated, ten feet of which has taken place since Roman times. In recent years, however, the rate has accelerated, from 0.04 inches yearly in the period 1908–25, to 0.02 inches per year from 1953–61 (Berghinz, 1971). The early, slow subsidence has been attributed to natural settling of the loose lagoonal sediment underlying the area. Accelerated subsidence coincides with the industrial development and urbanization of adjacent Marghera and Mestre, where extensive building has placed a considerable load on the sediments. More important, a greatly increased withdrawal of water from

underlying aquifers has led to compaction (Bolt et al, 1975). As a result, parts of Venice are submerged at high tide (Fig. 12.8). In 1966, a storm surge inundated 80 percent of the city and caused irreparable damage to its architecture and treasures of art. Happily, cessation of groundwater withdrawal seems to have halted subsidence. The Venice Geological Research Laboratory has stated that sinking is unlikely to resume, and that natural recharge of the groundwater system had resulted in a rise of several millimeters since 1972 (*The New York Times*, Aug. 30, 1975, p. 21).

Japan

In Japan, many large cities are built on low, alluvial plains underlain by unconsolidated sediments, from which there has been extensive extraction of groundwater for industrial and residential purposes (Poland, 1972). In Tokyo, 30 square miles of land bordering Tokyo Bay, on which 2,000,000 people live, have subsided up to 7 feet below sea level. Massive dikes have been built around the entire area, and drainage pumps have been installed. The pumping of groundwater has been restricted, and alternate water supplies for East Tokyo are being developed, but they will take many years to complete. Meanwhile, the area is

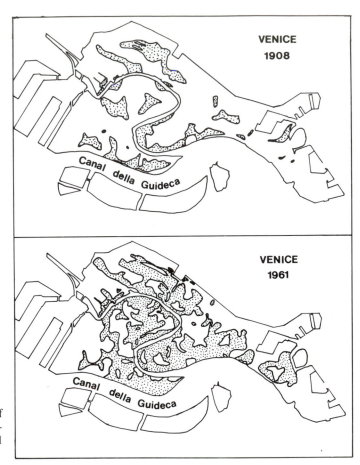

**VENICE
1908**

Canal della Guideca

**VENICE
1961**

Canal della Guideca

12.8 Two maps of the center of
Venice, showing areas inundated by sea-level rises of 1.1
meters, 1908 and 1961.

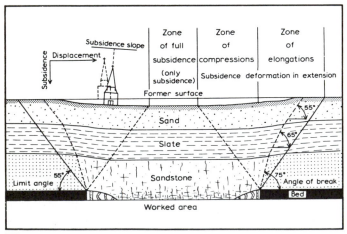

Subsidence		Zone of full subsidence (only subsidence)	Zone of compressions	Zone of elongations

Subsidence slope

Displacement

Subsidence deformation in extension

Former surface

Sand — 55°

Slate — 65°

Limit angle — 55°

Sandstone — 75°

Angle of break

Bed

Worked area

12.9 Diagrammatic cross section
showing surface sinking caused
by collapse of an underground
mined area. The "limit angle"
is defined by the line joining the
edge of the collapsed area underground to the edge of the
area of surface sinking. The
"angles of break" will vary depending upon the geological
characteristics of the rock formations.

threatened by typhoons and by the possible failure of the dikes and drainage pumps in the event of earthquakes. Furthermore, sewage has to be pumped above sea level in order to be disposed of. It has been suggested that as land becomes available, it should be filled in and the general grade-level gradually raised (Poland, 1972).

In Osaka, 75 square miles have subsided, 20 of which, those in the vicinity of the waterfront, have fallen to as much as six feet below sea level. Almost 375,000 people occupy this area. Reduction of groundwater extraction, however, had slowed subsidence to 2 centimeters per year by 1968.

Other Cities

Numerous other cases of subsidence in urban areas caused by fluid withdrawal have been documented. In Shanghai, China, sinking of up to 8 feet has caused waterfront flooding (Bolt et al, 1975). Groundwater withdrawal around Phoenix has caused subsidence of as much as 7 feet, and the development of open fissures one inch across and as much as a mile long. Drainage of surface water into these fissures has widened some of them to as much as 30 feet (Schumann, 1974). Large areas of New Orleans have settled to as much as 13 feet below sea level. As a result, storm waters must be pumped up and out of the city at considerable expense. Even greater costs are incurred by the continual need to repair sewer and water pipes (Spangle et al, 1974).

EXTRACTION OF SOLIDS

The extraction of solids from beneath the earth's surface may cause subsidence or collapse if the overlying layers are not strong enough to withstand the loss of support. Material may be removed through the natural or artificial solution of soluble materials such as limestone, dolomite, gypsum, sulfur, or salt, or through the mining of solids such as metallic ores, coal, and gypsum.

Where a horizontal layer of solid material is removed, the amount of sinking will be equal to two-thirds the thickness of the ex-

tracted layer. The surface area affected may extend laterally beyond the section removed by an amount equal to about half the depth of the removed material (Fig. 12.9). Subsidence or collapse caused by mining or tunneling may be minimized or prevented by leaving sufficient supporting material in place or by filling no longer needed voids with rubble, concrete, or other material.

Seams of coal that extend beneath Pittsburgh have been mined extensively, and where adequate support was not provided, collapse has occurred, damaging buildings, streets, and utilities. In 1968, subsidence caused considerable damage over areas mined for coal near Wilkes-Barre, Pennsylvania. Partial collapse of roads is common in coal-mining districts of England and Scotland.

Paris   One-tenth of the surface of Paris, some 3000 acres, is underlain by abandoned gypsum quarries. These quarries provided the original "plaster of paris." As the city expanded, the quarries were filled in and built over. However, with the passage of time, groundwater has dissolved part of the gypsum, and continual slippage adjustment of the fill has resulted in subsidence and cave-ins that have caused serious damage to buildings and roads. Response to the problem is now new. Just before the French Revolution, Louis XVI organized an inspection of the subsoil of the city, motivated in part by the occasional disappearance of pedestrians who fell into underground pits. In recent years, subterranean cameras and television have been employed in an attempt to map the labyrinthine meanderings of the underground passageways so that they may be pumped full of concrete and stabilized. In the interim, construction has been halted in certain areas roughly north and east of the Sacre Coeur pending more accurate determination of subsidence hazards.

Sinkholes

Areas underlain by soluble limestone may collapse when underground passageways or

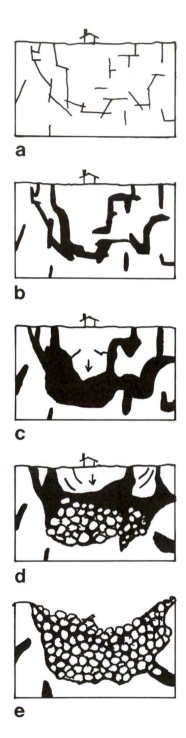

a

b

c

d

e

caverns form. Groundwater moving along fractures may gradually dissolve the limestone until a "swiss cheese" or "honeycomb" texture is developed. As the openings enlarge, the mechanical strength of the remaining rock structure is gradually diminished, and eventually it caves in. If the collapse is deep underground, sinking of the surface may not occur until the collapse works its way to the surface (Fig. 12.10). Surface depressions resulting from such collapse are known as *sinkholes*. Sinkholes may also form where insoluble materials collapse due to solution and removal of underlying limestone or other soluble rocks. Lowering of the groundwater table or other changes that affect the distribution and flow of groundwater may also initiate or accelerate the formation of sinkholes.

Sinkholes are common throughout the world. In one 10-square-mile area in southern Alabama, more than 1000 sinkhole collapses occurred in less than 20 years, from 1958 to 1973. One crater was 425 feet long, 350 feet wide and 150 feet deep. Houses in a number of communities in Florida and Alabama have been damaged or destroyed during such cave-ins. In Akron, Ohio, the roof of a department store collapsed and killed one person when part of the building's foundation sank into an unsuspected underground cavern. Other areas subject to hazard due to the presence of limestone or other soluble rocks include Kentucky, Tennessee, New Mexico, Pennsylvania, and parts of Yugoslavia, South Africa, France, Cuba, and Puerto Rico.

12.10 Schematic cross sections showing the development of a sinkhole. (a) fractured limestone, (b) fractures enlarged by solution. (c) continuing enlargement of fractures, resulting in underground caves and passageways. Cave roof weakened and about to collapse. (d) collapse of cave roof; new roof weakened and about to fall. (e) cave roof falls, involving all materials up to the surface, resulting in a *sinkhole*.

Long-term Geologic Hazards

Human occupancy of the earth is threatened by certain dangers whose advent lies an uncertain number of decades, centuries, or millenia in the future. Some of these threats are so remote or unlikely that their consideration long will remain, no doubt, within the realm of scientific speculation and science fiction: the gradual drift of continents to less benign latitudes; the slowing rotation of the earth and the accompanying amplification of the differences between daytime and night-time temperatures; reversals and diminutions in the magnetic field of the earth that may intermittently expose its surface to greatly increased radiation from outer space, and so forth. Other problems, however, are relatively immediate when measured against the duration of civilizations, and may be exacerbated by the presence and activities of humans. These *long-term hazards* include (1) detrimental environmental change and (2) shortages of raw materials and energy. It must be noted that this twofold division is arbitrary and proposed only for convenience of discussion: environmental change results in shortages; efforts to alleviate shortages can produce profound environmental change. The topics discussed are climatic change (glaciation and the spread of deserts), soil erosion, and shortages of water, minerals, and energy.

These hazards (some of which are not so long term) and their implications constitute a large part of what has come to be known as the "environmental crisis." Their effect upon urban inhabitants is often the result of the interdependency of the urban and non-urban aspects of existence. The purpose of this and the next chapter is to sketch out the general nature of these hazards and to highlight their influence upon the urban environment.

13. Environmental Change

CLIMATE

Temperature, humidity, wind velocity and direction, the degree of cloudiness, barometric pressure, and the amount of precipitation are the major ingredients of *weather*. The general long-term weather pattern for any given place over a period of years (perhaps 40 years or more) constitutes its *climate*. In terms of human life, climate usually changes very slowly. It seems unlikely that the climate of New York City, characterized by highly variable weather and strong seasonal contrasts, would suddenly become like that of Seattle, typified by clouds, frequent rain, and a small annual temperature range. If such rapid climatic changes did occur, the world would be a much more difficult place in which to live. Natural vegetation would be altered, and agriculture would be severely affected. Housing styles, insulation, and modes of heating or cooling might become quite unsuitable; water supply, and sewers inadequate; waste-disposal techniques inefficient. Subsidence, landslide, flood, erosion, or sedimentation might occur. The economic ramifications could be catastrophic, and whole lifestyles would have to be readjusted.

In areas that are climatically marginal in terms of successful human occupation, vari-

ations in the direction of more extreme climate would be especially traumatic. Consider, for example, the loss of life and great suffering caused by the recent (1968–1975) drought in the arid, relatively sparsely populated lands of the Sahel just south of the Sahara. Imagine the consequences if the life-giving monsoon rains of crowded India and Pakistan were to cease, or if the area affected by the harsh Russian winter were to expand, shifting the agricultural belt of the USSR south of its border. Neither modern nor primitive agricultural systems would escape severe disruption if there was any abrupt change in the length of the growing season, annual rainfall, or mean annual temperature (Hammond, 1974).

Some insight into the likelihood and the consequences of climatic change may be gained by examining recent meteorological records and historical, archeological, and geological evidence. Results that are both interesting and disturbing emerge from such studies. Climates that we are used to thinking of as "normal" and to which our society is adjusted are *not,* evidently, normal. This may be true in several senses. First, from 1955 to 1970, climate was remarkably uniform and favorable, and should not be regarded as typical. Second, it is likely that temperatures that have existed since the dawn of civilization, some

8000 years ago, have been considerably warmer than those prevailing on earth during perhaps 90–95 percent of the last 2 million years. Third, during the period 1880–1940, when much of the urban environment we inhabit was constructed, and the image that many people today have of the world was conceived, the mean annual temperature of most of the Northern and Southern hemispheres was unusually high (by half a degree C) compared to the previous several centuries. It might be thought that such a small temperature change is insignificant, but during this abnormally warm period glaciers shrank, floating sea ice diminished considerably, shallow lakes in arid regions of the western United States dried up, crops improved, and the distribution of animals and plants was materially affected. On the other hand, when the temperatures in central England during the sixteenth to eighteenth centuries dropped by less than two degrees C, the shift from warm to cold was accompanied by such radical changes that the period has been dubbed the "Little Ice Age." Winds blew more strongly; western Europe became substantially wetter and snowier; the Gulf Stream shifted south; and the oceanic area characterized by floating ice and icebergs enlarged and glaciers expanded. During one winter, the Baltic Sea froze over and wheeled vehicles were able to travel directly from Germany to Sweden over the ice. In Iceland and Switzerland, glaciers overrode farms and villages.

If climatic variations are viewed on a somewhat longer time scale, the significance of small changes in mean annual temperature becomes even more evident. In recent geologic history (approximately the past 2 million years), slight cooling and warming trends have triggered the advance and retreat of glacial ice sheets over vast areas of the earth's surface. From about 25,000 to perhaps only 10,000 years ago, masses of ice, in places more than 10,000 feet thick, extended thousands of miles from the polar regions toward the equator

and spread outward from high mountain ranges (Fig. 13.1). If the continent of Antarctica is excluded, 13 times as much land area was covered by ice during the last great Ice Age compared to today. However, mean annual temperatures were only 5–8 degrees C lower than today in mid-latitude coastal areas. Thus, variations of fractions of a degree in just a few years or decades take on added meaning, especially when it is realized that during the last 700,000 years, eight major advances and retreats of ice have taken place. In other words, during recent geologic time, frequent advances and retreats of ice sheets have been the rule rather than the exception.

The effects of a major advance or retreat of glacial ice would be numerous. Obviously, as large areas are covered by ice, human activities would be displaced. Other effects are more subtle. As glaciers advance over the land, they excavate and transport enormous quantities of loose soil and sediment and even solid bedrock. When the ice melts, this material is deposited by the ice or redistributed by streams. As a result, many glaciated areas have little or no soil cover or are covered by great masses of boulder-laden earth. The agricultural potential of such lands is usually low. Many glaciated areas are characterized by poor drainage, as is evidenced by numerous swamps and lakes. These features developed from uneven gouging of the land by the glacial ice and the blockage or destruction of previous drainage systems. Also, glacial ice as well as glacial deposits may divert or dam river channels, forcing streams to find new routes or creating temporary lakes. In the New York City region, large lakes collected in the vincinity of the glacial margin and lasted thousands of years (Fig. 13.2).

Radical changes in climate accompany glacial advances. During the peak of the last Ice Age, about 18,000 years ago, the Gulf Stream shifted south and flowed toward Spain instead of England, and the Asian monsoon was weaker and located so that the rain fell south of the Indian subcontinent. In

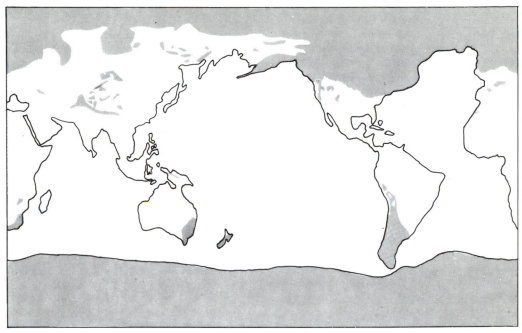

13.1 World map showing land areas and oceans during a time of maximum glaciation. Shaded areas covered by ice. Note change in shape and size of land areas.

northern Africa, Mediterranean-type trees and plants at times spread 1000 miles further to the south across what today is extreme desert. In Nevada, Utah, and southeastern California (Fig. 13.3) extensive ancient lake deposits and the remnants of once much larger (*pluvial*) lakes suggest a former climate that was wetter and had lower rates of evaporation. During the period 37,000–13,000 years ago, south-central Florida appears to have been much drier than it is now, suggesting a northward extension of an equatorial arid zone (Moran, 1975).

In places adjacent to or underlying glaciers, extensive, thick permafrost is likely to develop and to persist thousands of years after the ice has melted away. Permafrost considerably complicates human usage of such regions.

A major accompaniment to glacial ad-

vances and retreats are worldwide changes in sea level. Water that collects as ice accumulates at the expense of water subtracted from the oceans through evaporation. It is estimated that during times of maximum glacial advance during the Ice Age, sea level was perhaps as much as 325 feet lower than today. If a similar glacial advance and sea-level drop were to recur, the consequences would be cataclysmic. Alaska and the Soviet Union would be joined across the Bering Strait; England would be connected to France; the East Indies would be absorbed by Australia and Asia (Fig. 13.1). Many of the world's great coastal cities (those not covered by ice) would be stranded as much as 100 miles or more inland. Some of these cities, if located on rivers, might survive as ports if the rivers were able to extend themselves to the retreating oceans. For example, during

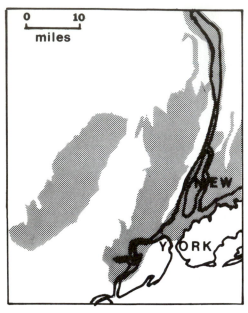

13.2 Map of the New York City region showing areas covered by lakes (shaded) at the end of the Ice Age. (After Schuberth, 1968)

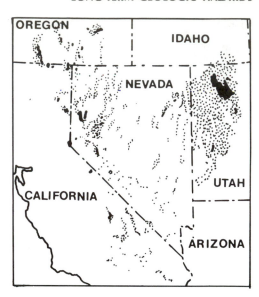

13.3 The southwest United States, showing distribution of modern lakes (black) and pluvial lakes (dotted areas)

the last Ice Age, the Hudson River flowed in a deep channel across the exposed continental shelf to the distant Atlantic. Another significant effect of reduced ocean area would be reduced evaporation, resulting in lowered precipitation and the spread of grasslands, steppes, and deserts at the expense of forests.

The effects of a glacial retreat and accompanying sea-level rise would, perhaps, be even more catastrophic. If the Antarctic and Greenland ice caps were to melt, sea level would rise to about 200 feet above its present elevation. Cities such as Houston, New Orleans, Tampa, Miami, Savannah, Charleston, Norfolk, Amsterdam, Rotterdam, Copenhagen, Stockholm, Buenos Aires, Tel Aviv, Leningrad, Calcutta, and Shanghai, all of which lie on flat coastal plains, would be completely drowned. Other coastal cities in areas of greater topographic relief would be partially preserved as a series of islands and peninsulas (Fig.

13.4). Furthermore, enormous areas of rich agricultural land, would be inundated (Fig. 13.5). An interesting side effect of the glacial melting would be that the crust of the earth in Greenland and Antarctica relieved of the weight of huge masses of ice, would gradually rise by as much as 2000–3000 feet. Thus, contrary to the loss of land in most other regions of the globe, these areas would increase considerably.

To evaluate whether the advance or retreat of glacial ice poses a real threat to humanity, questions such as how fast such changes can occur and the likelihood of their happening in the near future must be answered.

Glaciers form and grow when the amount of snow that accumulates in the winter consistently exceeds the amount of melting that takes place during the summer. Thus, glacial growth may be fostered by cooler summers or increased snowfall in winter. It has been calculated that for many regions of

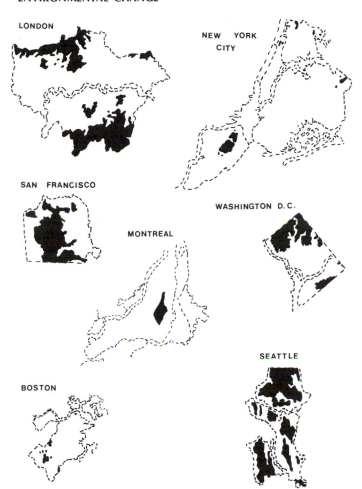

13.4 Seven coastal cities, showing areas (black) that are 200 or more feet above present sea level. These areas would remain as land in the event of a 200-foot sea-level rise due to the melting of glacial ice.

high latitude or high elevation, a drop of less than 5 degrees in average summer air temperature or a doubling of the amount of snowfall would initiate a new ice age. Numerous suggestions have been made regarding natural mechanisms that might bring about such changes (Lindholm, 1976): variations in the energy output of the sun; periodic alterations in the tilt of the earth's axis and the shape of the earth's orbit; shifts in patterns of oceanic circulation; and changes in the ability of the earth's atmosphere to transmit and retain heat are but a few.

The rate at which such changes induce or terminate an ice age is highly speculative. Estimates range from a couple of centuries to several thousand years. More frightening is the possibility of an *ice surge:* the essentially instantaneous slippage of an unstable portion of a continental ice sheet into the ocean. If, for example, the entire Marie Byrd Land ice sheet were to break off from the main Antarctic glacier and slide into the ocean, sea level all over the world could rise by as much as 30 feet, bringing massive destruction and loss of life to coastal regions. There is no clear evidence that

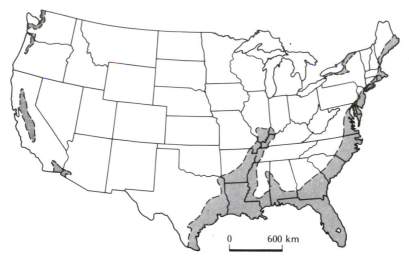

13.5 Areas of the eastern United States that would be inundated by ocean water in the event of a rise in sea level due to the melting of glacial ice.

such an ice surge is possible or has ever happened in the past, but the Ross Ice Shelf Project, an international effort with ten co-operating nations, is investigating this and other ice-related phenomena.

Since the last 2 million years or so has been characterized by a succession of glacial and interglacial ages, it is highly likely that this pattern of climatic change will continue into the future. The earth now seems to be in an interglacial age, which in the past have each lasted about 10,000 years. Since the last major glaciation ended about 10,000 years ago, it would seem that the time is ripe for the onset of another glacial age (Hays *et al*, 1976). However, predicting such an event is difficult because the mechanisms causing the climatic changes are not well understood. The global climate reached a thermal maximum 7000 years ago, and, except for short-lived reversals such as the world-wide warming between 1880 and 1940, has generally been decreasing. Ironically, there is no general agreement as to whether the immediate global climate is warming or cooling. The well-publicized cooling of the Northern Hemisphere since

the 1940s may be more than offset by warming trends in the Southern Hemisphere (Damon and Kunen, 1976). Thus it is quite possible that further melting of glacial ice and consequent rises in sea level may precede the arrival of a new glacial age.

A significant question is whether human activities can influence climatic trends. The ability of the atmosphere to transmit solar energy and to retain heat radiated by the earth's surface is affected markedly by the presence of small quantities of water vapor, carbon dioxide, ozone, trace gases, and tiny airborne particles called *aerosols*. Since humans have begun to burn fossil fuels in large quantities, the carbon dioxide content of the atmosphere has increased considerably. It is estimated that atmospheric carbon dioxide may double in amount by A.D. 2040, leading to a substantial global warming. Aerosols, such as the dust produced by burning fossil fuels or unwanted vegetation, may produce either warming or cooling effects. Propellants used in aerosol (spray) cans, the oxides of nitrogen released into the upper atmosphere by the jet engines of supersonic planes and by nuclear explosions can also affect the thermal structure of the atmosphere. Extensive use of chemical fertilizers can significantly increase the amounts of trace gases in the atmosphere, leading to temperature increases (Wang *et al*, 1976). Similarly, *thermal pollution* (heat produced during the generation of energy, industrial operations, or through burning fuels) may become an important factor contributing to global warming (Cole, 1969). If oil spills occur in the Arctic, darkening the pack ice that covers most of the Arctic Ocean, they may cause the ice to melt and prevent it from reforming. The presence or absence of pack ice in that ocean may play a major role in the triggering of glacial or interglacial ages.

Land-use practices have an important effect upon climate. Areas within or near cities commonly have higher temperatures and precipitation than surrounding regions. Thus, as urbanization spreads, it may have an increasing influence upon world climate. The growth of deserts along the former Fertile Crescent of the eastern Mediterranean may have been caused in part by overgrazing by goats (Kellogg and Schneider, 1974). Irrigation of deserts, the damming of rivers, and the cutting of forests change the reflectivity of the land surface and affect regional atmospheric temperatures and moisture content.

A number of suggestions have been made on how climatic conditions might be changed artificially. One such imaginative (and potentially catastrophic scheme) is melting the Arctic pack ice to produce warmer winters in northern regions. Melting could be accomplished in several ways: covering it with soot so that it will absorb heat; diverting rivers that flow into the Arctic Ocean to increase its salinity and thus lower its freezing point; or damming the Bering Strait and drawing warm Atlantic waters into the north polar region. It is quite likely, however, that if the ice pack were melted, the open Arctic Ocean would provide sufficient moisture for an increase in snowfall that could trigger the onset of glaciation in northern Canada and Europe (Kellogg and Schneider, 1974).

Whether current human activities will add to or subtract from natural global atmospheric trends is unknown. Clearly, increased knowledge of climatic mechanisms and trends is essential if climatic changes are to be predicted and before over-ambitious climate-altering projects are undertaken. An institute of climatology should be established to assess the global effects of human production of energy (Weinberg, 1974), and a more intensive and coordinated international "world weather watch" undertaken to monitor climatic trends that may vitally affect human welfare (Damon and Kunen, 1976).

Even if radical climatic changes do not occur, any drift toward lower temperatures will have increasing economic impact as the cost of energy used for heating becomes greater. Also, as the world's population continues to expand, the effect of colder, longer winters upon food production will become more critical. On the other hand, less energy may be required for refrigeration and air-conditioning, and it may well be that increased rainfall—(if such is the trend)—may make some agriculturally marginal areas more productive. However, the very fact of change always involves expense and disruption.

DESERTS AND EROSION

The spread of desert conditions and the loss of arable land are sources of concern more immediate than problems associated with glaciation. Deserts may be loosely defined as those regions in which the amount of water available for the support of living organisms is minimal. The scarcity of "useful" water may be due to low rainfall, high evaporation rates, extreme cold (so that water is usually only present as ice), or an infiltration capacity that is so high that little or no water remains at or near the ground. The more usual concept of deserts, and the

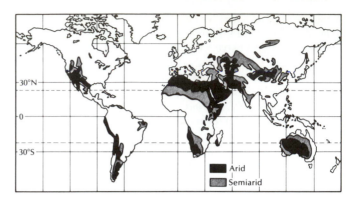

13.6 World map showing the location of deserts and semiarid regions (areas of low precipitation and high rates of evaporation).

one which will be adhered to here, refers to those areas, that are dry due to low rainfall (less than ten inches each year) and high evaporation rates. Figure 13.6 illustrates the occurrence and distribution of such deserts and associated semiarid regions. There is abundant evidence that the margins of deserts are not stationary. Remains of abandoned cities in parts of North Africa and the near East that now are extreme desert evoke earlier times when milder conditions prevailed. Elsewhere, fossilized desert sand dunes underlie areas now characterized by luxuriant vegetation and frequent rainfall.

As mentioned earlier, the conversion of non-desert regions into desert may be brought about by world-wide shifts of climatic zones. At present, however, an alarmingly rapid spread of deserts and deterioration of semiarid areas is taking place in Africa, Asia, and Latin America, caused in large part by misuse of the land. According to the Worldwatch Institute, an environmental research organization, there is no firm evidence of a decline in rainfall in North Africa over the last century. It attributes the "desertification" to erosion caused by the destruction of the natural vegetative cover through overcultivation, overgrazing, and deforestation. A United Nations Study has revealed that in this manner arable areas equal to almost 7 percent of the land surface of the earth have been turned into desert in the last 50 years.

Moreover, once the vegetative cover is lost, reflection of sunlight increases, changing the local climate in the direction of greater aridity. Thus, once started deserts tend to enlarge themselves (Hammond, 1974).

Misuse of land and erosional loss of topsoil is not restricted to the developing countries. In Iowa, about an inch of topsoil is being lost every decade because the land is inadequately protected against water and wind erosion. The significance of this loss becomes evident when it is realized that in many parts of Iowa only 6–8 inches are left of a topsoil cover that 100 years ago was 12–16 inches deep. For the entire United States, it is estimated that during the last 200 years, at least a third of the topsoil in cropland areas has been lost (Pimental *et al,* 1976). In a world of rapidly increasing population, such losses of arable land and irreplacable topsoil invite disaster.

URBANIZATION AND ARABLE LAND

Decreases in arable land are not only caused by climatic change and erosion, but also by the spread of cities and the construction of highways. In the United States, more than 2.5 million acres of arable cropland are lost each year to urbanization, roads, airports, etc. (Pimental *et al,* 1976). For example, in arid Arizona, Phoenix is spreading out over valuable agricultural land in Maricopa

County. In New Jersey, more than 650,000 acres of rich farmland were urbanized from 1950 to 1975, leaving only 1,000,000 acres left in cultivation. Until shortly after World War II the borough of Queens in New York City and adjacent Nassau County on Long Island were major centers of dairy farming; now farms have vanished from Queens and are nearly extinct in Nassau County. In Connecticut, during the same period, farmland decreased from 1.6 million to 0.48 million acres. These losses are partially offset by the development of 1.25 million acres of new cropland through irrigation and drainage each year, thus reducing the net loss within the United States each year to 1.25 million acres. Since 380 million acres (about 81 percent of all arable land) are now cultivated and 740 million are in pasture and rangeland, the loss of land through urbanization does not pose an immediate threat to agricultural production. However, since urban development tends to take place preferentially in areas of high agricultural potential (flat well-drained land near rivers),

and the supply of potentially productive agricultural land is finite, the threat will become increasingly real as population continues to concentrate in urban areas and the world-wide demand for food becomes more desperate.

In other countries less well-endowed with arable land, the spread of cities at the expense of farmland has already become a major problem. In Egypt, for example, where only the narrow strip along the Nile and part of the Mediterranean coast are cultivated, urban expansion to accomodate a population increase of one million a year is causing the country's arable land to shrink despite large-scale reclamation projects.

It will be particularly ironic if the flight from the land to urban areas results in there not being enough agricultural land left to feed the world's population. To avoid or stave off this possibility, the character of the land and the use to which it is put must be carefully matched *before* the land is irrevocably devoted to less than its highest most valuable function.

14. Shortages of Natural Resources

Throughout history most individuals have been engaged in a more or less continual, arduous struggle to secure the necessities of life. However, what the individual has conceived of as necessities has varied considerably. Necessities have always included the basic physiologic requirements: food, drink, warmth, shelter, but have gradually expanded through time to encompass almost innumerable other amenities: knives and forks to eat with, clothes that are "presentable," houses that are spacious and satisfactorily furnished, labor-saving devices, mean of transport, entertainment, education. Indeed, for much of the affluent world, each generation's luxuries have a way of becoming the next generation's necessities. If these "necessities" become unduly expensive, shortages are said to exist, and shortages, almost by definition, are regarded as something to be overcome. The overcoming of shortages is usually interpreted in terms of increasing supply. Only on rare occasions is the existence of a shortage seen as a challenge to reduce demand.

Because the planet earth is a finite body with fixed material resources, an ever-growing human population may eventually face shortages that cannot be overcome through traditional means. Well before the point of literal exhausion of raw materials, the so-

cial, economic, and environmental costs of their extraction, processing, and distribution are likely to become unacceptable. For some vital substances, this point is already being reached. Humanity must, therefore, pursue nontraditional ways of increasing supply, and also seriously examine the merits of the major alternative *reduced demand*.

For those large segments of the human population that live in poverty, reduced demand can only be achieved through stabilizing human numbers, not by diminishing the meager portions of most individuals. Indeed, if population growth can be stemmed, then consumption by the individual can and should be increased. It is those who inhabit the affluent world who must reconsider the nature of "necessities" and "shortages." It may well be that as some necessities are recognized as dispensable and inefficient, the feeling of affluence will be enhanced as shortage is transmuted into adequacy or even abundance.

WATER

Lack of sufficient water already hampers the continued expansion of existing cities and the founding of new cities in many parts of the world. The mechanics of water supply, the statistics of water usage, and the role water has played in the founding and development of cities are discussed in some detail in Chapters 2 and 3. In summary, water shortages may be attributed to (1) the rapid increase in world population, (2) increasing per capita use, (3) increasing demands for water for agriculture especially as more and more arid regions are irrigated, and (4) pollution of water reserves. Shortages are likely to be exacerbated in the future as energy and mineral shortages become acute. If the large-scale recovery of oil from oil shale is undertaken, large quantities of water will be required for processing; extraction of coal may interrupt flow of water through underground aquifers; water passing through mineral or coal waste piles becomes polluted; coal gasification and transport can require abundant water. Last, and perhaps most pertinent, accelerated urbanization of arid areas, such as southern California and Arizona, threatens to bring the problem of adequate urban water supply to a crisis point in the near future.

Throughout history, the classic solution to local shortages has been to bring in water from elsewhere (Warnick, 1969). From as early as 2500 B.C., great engineering works have been constructed for water transfer (see Chap. 2). Today in the United States hundreds of miles of aqueducts supply New York, (see Fig. 3.35), Los Angeles, San Diego, San Francisco (see Fig. 3.28), and Denver. Figure 14.1 shows the location and status of present and future water-transfer networks in the western United States.

Impressive as these systems are, they pale in comparison to proposals for future regional water transfer. One facet of the North American Water and Power Alliance (NAWAPA) plan (Fig. 14.2) developed by the Ralph M. Parsons Company, would be to collect water from Alaska, British Columbia, and the Northwest Territories, and store it in a 500-mile-long reservoir in the Rocky Mountain Trench in the Canadian Rockies at 3000 feet above sea level. From this reservoir, the water would be transferred to the water-deficient areas of Utah,

Nevada, southern California, Arizona, New Mexico, and Mexico. A Canadian plan, the Central North American Water Project (CeNAWP) (Fig. 14.2), envisions bringing water to the Great Plains, the southwestern states, and Mexico from the rivers and lakes of northern Canada. Other proposals (Fig. 14.1) include diverting water southward from the Columbia River into California and the southwestern states; feeding water from the Yellowstone and Snake Rivers into the Green and Colorado rivers; and conducting water from the Mississippi to western Texas and eastern New Mexico. Similarly ambitious plans have been proposed for other countries.

The benefits of large-scale, long-distance water transfer are considerable, permitting increased irrigation and agricultural production, urban and industrial growth, and the generation of larger amounts of hydroelectric power. Whether the benefits outweigh the costs is controversial. Building the system can be enormously expensive; for example, estimates of the costs of the NAWAPA project are around $100 billion. Legal and administrative problems involved in transfer of water across international and state boundaries are complex but not insoluble (Weinberg, 1969). It may be noted, however, that controversies between water-exporting and importing regions, and disagreements over sharing water have always been the source of much tension, and occasionally violence. Friction between the residents of Owen's Valley and Los Angeles over diversion of water into the Los Angeles Aqueduct has become almost legendary (see Chap. 3). In 1934, Arizona almost went to war with California over withdrawal of water from the Colorado River. Governor Moeur called out the Arizona National Guard and requisitioned a river ferry to prevent Californians from starting construction of Parker Dam. States within the Columbia River Basin, fearful of plans to divert water into the Colorado River Basin for the benefit of California and the Southwest, forced the passage of a law

14.1 Map of the western United States showing proposals for regional water transfer. The long arrows indicate directions of water movement. Dashed lines are aqueducts, canals, and tunnels that already exist, are under construction, or whose construction is likely in the near future.

prohibiting even reconnaissance studies for such diversion during the period 1968–78. International disputes over water rights have often been bitter. Plans to divert the waters of the Jordan River have added fuel to the controversy between Israel and her neighbors Syria and Jordan.

Assuming that the money required to build water-transfer systems is allocated and that legal and political difficulties are ironed out, other problems remain. Regional transfer usually involves the temporary storage of water in reservoirs, during which time evaporative losses increase concentra-

14.2 Map of North America showing two proposals for regional water transfer: the North American Power and Water Alliance (NAWAPA); and the Central North American Water Project or CeNAWP. RMT = the proposed Rocky Mountain Trench reservoir.

tions of dissolved minerals. Similarly, as water is transferred through surface canals, evaporative losses and mineral buildup continues. An increase in salinity is particularly accelerated by irrigation. For instance, as the Colorado River flows from its source in the Rocky Mountains to the Mexican border, its salinity increases from 50 parts per million (ppm) to 1100 ppm. A salinity of 1100 ppm makes the water only marginally useful, even for irrigation; the maximum allowable salinity for drinking water is often set at 500 ppm. (It should be noted that about half the increase in salinity of the Colorado is caused by the natural seepage of salt springs and the passage of the river over salt formations. Furthermore, the Colorado is perhaps unusual because it flows through extremely arid areas.) However, whenever water is transported and stored in open conduits or reservoirs and is used by humans en route to its destination—especially for irrigation—deterioration of quality may be expected.

Changes in water distribution can have marked effects upon wildlife. Flooding of land to form reservoirs and the construction of canals may eliminate wildlife habitats and interfere with migration routes. Changes in water volume, salinity, temperature, and turbidity in lakes, streams, and estuarine areas can affect fish and other aquatic life. For instance, diversion of water from the Mississippi might cause saltwater intrusion into the Delta. Also, as suggested in Chapter 13, streams that empty into the oceans could trigger large-scale climatic changes as patterns of oceanic salinity and temperature are altered.

Thus, the answer to the question of whether the benefits of large-scale regional water transfer outweigh the costs is not at all clear. Sanitary engineer P. H. McGauhey notes that "It is characteristic of most every effort man has made to shape his environment . . . that he has viewed his objective more as an isolated task rather than as one facet of a complex system existing in a dynamic equilibrium. Consequently he is continually surprised to find that the evil he set out to overcome was in reality the device that held a whole set of other evils in balance; and that by his well-intentioned action he has triggered a scramble for a new equilibrium in nature. This new balance may be either more or less desirable than the old in relation to the original objective of the action. . . ." (1969, p. 358). One would hope therefore that before future schemes are undertaken, careful analyses will be made of all the possible ramifications. However, a review of water-transfer projects on five continents could not point to a single example of good advance planning involving the entire scientific community (Thomas and Box, 1969).

The pressure for grandiose water transfer schemes is bound to grow as the world's population multiplies and the demand for food and new living space increases. Urban expansion in arid regions has been rapid in recent years. In the United States, cities of the Southwest continue to attract people seeking milder climates. In other parts of the world, cities in dry areas grow as people from the countryside try to escape rural poverty and the threat of starvation. Between about 1955 and 1969, for example, Lima, Karachi, and Alexandria increased in population by 5 to 11 percent each year. Tijuana, Mexicali, and Kuwait have also expanded dramatically (Meigs, 1969). Water shortages also threaten cities in what seem to be well-watered regions. By the year 2000, the New York metropolitan area may experience severe shortages if solutions to the problem are not found. Southern England suffered serious drought in 1976.

Since it is highly unlikely that those who stand to benefit directly from large-scale regional projects can pay for them, the cost must probably be met by the taxation of entire nations (Howe, 1969). Thus, it behooves the general public to demand investigation of feasible alternatives, a number of which do exist. Wasteful usage should be discouraged. Life styles appropriate to moderate water availability should be adopted. (Lawns, for instance, are out of place in cities like Los Angeles, Phoenix, or Tucson.) Polluted rivers should be cleaned up so that their waters become available for urban use. (It is preposterous that New York City faces water shortages while the Hudson flows past its shores, unusable because of urban and industrial effluents poured into it locally and upstream.) Government and private funds should be directed to encourage expansion of population and industry where water is plentiful rather than where it is in short supply.

In the developing countries, agricultural production could be increased through regional development and management of irrigation systems. Canadian writer Clark Blaise describes how failure to enforce land-reform measures in parts of India prevents modernization of agriculture and increased production: ". . . While the Bihar Tenancy Act entitles the landlord to no more than 25 percent of the yield, any sharecropper not turning over at least 50 percent would simply be evicted. . . . At that level of nonincentive, no tenant farmer would add the necessary inputs, nor would he bother to plant a second crop. India is a vast land with more soil and water than it needs to feed its people and even to become a net exporter; it is the feudal structure of land ownership that underutilizes land and water, keeps the entire country on the brink of starvation, and floods the cities, especially Calcutta, with millions of illiterate, unhealthy, and unemployable beggars." (1977, p. 107)

In some areas, desalinization of sea water may become of increasing importance. The port of Eilat in Israel, which occupies a desert coast on the Red Sea, obtains more than 60 percent of its water supply through the distillation of about 7000 cubic meters of sea water each day. If the cost of desalting sea water becomes competitive with other sources, then coastal cities in less arid regions which face water shortages, such as Los Angeles, San Diego, San Francisco, Houston, and conceivably New Orleans, Boston, New York, Philadelphia, Baltimore, and Washington may turn to desalinization to supplement other sources

(Cargo and Mallory, 1977). Whether desalinization becomes widespread will depend in large part upon the extent to which the inexpensive energy is available.

MINERAL AND ENERGY RESOURCES

Of the 103 chemical elements known at present, about 90 occur naturally in the crust of the earth. Eight elements (oxygen, silicon, aluminum, iron, calcium, sodium, potassium, and magnesium) make up more than 98 percent of the crust. The remaining elements vary from uncommon to exceedingly rare. A few, such as gold, silver, or carbon, may be found physically mixed with but chemically uncombined with other elements. Most elements are chemically bound to other elements to form *compounds*. Both the uncombined and combined elements of the earth's crust are known as *minerals*, the building blocks out of which rocks are made. Minerals, like elements, vary tremendously in abundance. Of the approximately 2500 known minerals, perhaps two dozen make up the bulk of crustal rocks and another two hundred are relatively common. Not only do elements and minerals vary in general abundance, but their relative abundance varies enormously from place to place. For instance, feldspars are the most abundant minerals in the earth's crust, but they may be totally absent within a coal seam, a quartz sandstone, a limestone, or a salt bed. Similarly, copper constitutes about 0.006 percent of the earth's crust, but within a chunk of native copper, the copper content approaches 100 percent, within the mineral chalcocite (copper sulfide) 80 percent, and within the mineral chalcopyrite (copper iron sulfide), 35 percent. Within any given body of rock, the copper content will depend upon which (if any) copper-bearing minerals are present, and what percent of the total rock consists of these minerals.

Certain minerals are considered particularly useful to humans; some indeed, vital to our type of civilization. The minerals that constitute building stone are useful collectively, as rock. Some minerals may be useful in themselves: quartz for making glass, coal for fuel, diamonds as ornaments. Others are useful in that they contain valuable chemical elements. The chalcocite and chalcopyrite mentioned previously are potentially valuable because they contain copper and copper is considered useful to humans.

Geologic, Technologic, and Economic Factors   Broadly speaking, a mineral deposit traditionally has been considered valuable if the materials sought can be extracted, processed, and sold at a profit. Such a deposit is called an *ore,* the valuable minerals within it *ore minerals,* and the associated non-valuable minerals *gangue.* (These terms are usually reserved for deposits containing valuable metals; it will serve our purpose to apply them to all valuable deposits.) The concentration of an element necessary to form a "workable" ore varies from as low as 2.2 times the average crustal abundance for aluminum, to 11,200 times for mercury (Table 14.1). Natural modes of concentration take place in a great variety of ways, most of them requiring enormous lengths of time, sometimes up to many millions of years. Thus, once extracted and used, they are effectively gone forever as far as human beings are concerned.

Some economically valuable materials

Table 14.1. The degree of natural concentration of selected crustal elements necessary to make a deposit economically valuable. (After Cook, 1976, p. 678, Table 1.)

Element	Concentration Factor	Element	Concentration Factor
Mercury	11,200	Uranium	350
Lead	3,300	Carbon	310
Chromium	2,100	Nickel	100
Tin	2,000	Copper	56
Silver	1,330	Iron	3.4
Gold	1,000	Aluminum	2.2

are the results of common geologic processes. Building materials, for instance, are common rocks and sediment, and are widespread. Valuable salts are found around the shores of shrinking salt lakes or isolated, evaporating bodies of sea water. Coal forms through the accumulation and alteration of decaying vegetation, and is not uncommon in layered sedimentary rocks. Particles of dense substances such as gold may be concentrated where rushing water sweeps away all less-dense substances. Sometimes groundwater dissolves and removes non-valuable substances, leaving behind and thus concentrating those of value. At other times, groundwater selectively dissolves and transports valuable materials, which may then be precipitated in rock fractures or in pore spaces. Groundwater sometimes effects an exchange, expelling non-valuable substances and replacing them with valuable ones. Similarly, hot solutions expelled from magmas, or migrating chemicals impelled by the processes of metamorphism, may selectively deposit valuable materials in joints or pore spaces, or replace susceptible rocks with which they come in contact. When magma begins to solidify and crystallize, particularly dense minerals rich in iron or chromium may sink rapidly to the bottom of the magma chamber and be concentrated there.

After minerals are located, methods of extraction and processing must be determined. Geologic factors include the size and shape of the deposit, the degree and manner of concentration of the ore mineral, and the depth of the deposit beneath the surface. For instance, a large simply shaped ore body at or near the surface with a high percentage of a useful material is likely to be valuable and an *ore*. On the other hand, a small or complexly shaped deposit at considerable depth, in which ore minerals are not highly concentrated is less likely to be considered an ore.

Varying amounts of gangue minerals may be extracted along with the ore and must be separated from it. In order to do so, it may

be necessary to break the chemical bonds within the ore. The ease of such separation may be a crucial factor in determining whether a given mineral is valuable. Aluminum, for instance, is the third most abundant element in the earth's crust, but usually occurs bound to silicon, oxygen, and other metals (as in feldspar) and is exceedingly expensive to isolate. However, aluminum bound only to oxygen and hydrogen (as in the mineral *bauxite*) is relatively easy and inexpensive to isolate.

Once a mineral has been extracted, it must be transported for processing or use. If a substance has a high-value per unit volume or weight (platinum, gold, or radium, for example), it may be economically feasible to transport it great distances. Coal mining in Antarctica, however, is not worthwhile because the transport costs are too high. Another major factor in determining the worth of a mineral deposit is market price. Prices fluctuate constantly, and deposits of marginal value may be worth working at times and not worth working at other times. In a deposit containing several minerals, the high value of only a few of them may make the entire deposit profitable (minor amounts of gold and silver in lead or zinc deposits, for example).

Social and Environmental Factors Very often the evaluation of a mineral deposit neglects social or environmental considerations that may, in fact, outweigh more simply conceived monetary gains. Putting it another way, social and environmental considerations may not have been assigned monetary values, and were therefore left out of the economic analysis.

Examples of the detrimental aspects of mineral production are numerous. Underground mining is inherently dangerous, given chances of explosion, collapse, flooding, and dust inhalation. *Strip mining* (surface excavation) may disrupt the landscape, removing valuable farmland from production, increasing rates of erosion and sedimentation, and interfering with drainage.

Waste piles of excavated *overburden* (the materials lying between a mineral deposit and the land surface) or of separated gangue can cause landslides. Also, water filtering through gangue may become contaminated and pollute supply systems. Oil spills contaminate coastal regions and kill marine life. If extraction or mineral processing takes place in inhabited regions, noise, air, and water pollution may be the unwelcome accompaniments of the operations.

As the demand rises to modify the detrimental aspects of mineral production, the economic cost will necessarily reflect social and environmental costs, and some mining will cease to be profitable. On the other hand, as will be seen, increasing shortages of some minerals will cause prices to rise sufficiently to offset increases.

Some social and environmental problems attendant upon mineral production are not easily solved. Discovery of a deposit may cause a sudden influx of population into an area, disrupting established patterns of life and heavily taxing existing facilities. Similarly, it may well be that the working life of a newly discovered deposit is relatively short, and when it is abandoned, a second disruption of local life may take place. The people of Crandon, Wisconsin, have been upset by the recent discovery of a huge zinc deposit that may be worth more than $6 billion, and anticipate radical changes in the population of the town and its quiet way of life. In the Rockies of Montana and Wyoming, coal boom towns are appearing that are typified by crowded and unsanitary living conditions, lack of basic community services and recreational outlets, absence of community identity, and abundant drunkeness, depression, delinquency, and divorce (Christiansen and Clark, Jr., 1976). Such towns need substantial help from either state of federal sources to manage their growth properly. In Canada, the prospect of pipelines designed to carry natural gas from arctic regions to the inhabited south has stirred resentment among native Indians and Eskimos, who feel that the construction of such

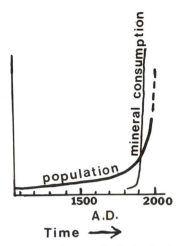

14.3 Graph showing qualitatively the increases in mineral consumption and world population with time.

lines would further undermine traditional lifestyles and increase their dependence on outside help (Panitch, 1977). Objections have been made to proposals for copper mining in Puerto Rico because of the cultural changes that would be imposed on the region (Brooks and Andrews, 1974).

Some towns have been able to weather the start and stop of mineral production. Bancroft, Ontario, was the site of a uranium boom in the mid-1950s. When the market evaporated in the 1960s, the mines closed. The town, however, was able to survive because of a broad-based economy dependent upon tourism, lumbering, and government and educational services. Due to a recent increase in the price of uranium the Bancroft mines reopened in 1977 and should remain open at least until 1985. Many of the inhabitants welcome this addition to the town's economy, even if it is temporary.

Mineral Supply and Demand   As human population has increased exponentially in recent years, so has mineral consumption (Fig. 14.3), especially in industrialized nations (Table 14.2).

Table 14.2. Per capita consumption of some common minerals in the United States (From U.S. Bureau of Mines, 1975.)

Mineral	lbs	Mineral	lbs
Stone	9250	Iron and steel	1300
Sand and gravel	8500	Aluminum	65
Cement	800	Copper	25
Clays	550	Zinc	15
Salt	450	Lead	15

Since earth resources are finite, a disturbing question arises: how long will mineral deposits be able to furnish the materials necessary for the life and well-being of humankind? Answers to this question are not easy. Estimates of future demand must be compared to probable supply. Demand will depend upon rate of population increase and the rate and direction of industrialization, neither of which can be determined with great accuracy. Calculation of probable supply is equally elusive.

At the start it must be recalled that the natural concentration of elements and minerals involves processes that may take thousands to millions of years. Thus, humans cannot afford to entertain the hope that natural ores they draw upon are being regenerated at a commensurate rate. If the sources are depleted, they are, in terms of the length of human life, depleted forever. That is, most valuable mineral deposits are *non-renewable resources,* in contradistinction to such *renewable resources* as timber or fish which, if not abused, can replenish themselves at rates similar in magnitude to their consumption.

Also, valuable mineral deposits are not distributed evenly throughout the world. Figure 14.4 shows known oil locations. Such non-uniform distributions are geologically real, and do not merely reflect differences in exploration efforts (Cook, 1976). It becomes apparent, therefore, that world supply must be distinguished from national supplies. In times of emnity between nations, import-export links may be

severed. Table 14.3 suggests the current dependence of the United States upon imported mineral products.

Setting aside geographic and political considerations, determining actual quantities of available minerals is a difficult task. It was seen earlier that whether a particular mineral deposit is worth exploiting depends upon numerous factors. As demand and prices increase, deposits that were previously thought to be too "low grade" to work may become valuable. Thus it would appear that increasing demand "creates" new supplies. Also, technological advances in extraction and processing allow the profitable exploitation of deposits of lower grade. For example, in 1900, only those

Table 14.3. Percentage of U.S. mineral requirements imported in 1977. (*Statistical Abstract of the United States, 1978*)

Mineral	Percentage Imported	Major Sources
Sheet Mica	100	India, Brazil, Malagasy Republic
Manganese	98	Brazil, Gabon, South Africa
Aluminum (oxides)	91	Jamaica, Australia, Surinam, Guinea
Chromium	89	South Africa, U.S.S.R., Turkey
Tin	86	Malaysia, Thailand, Bolivia, Indonesia
Nickel	70	Canada, Norway, New Caledonia, Dominican Republic
Zinc	58	Canada, Mexico, Australia, Peru
Mercury	46	Spain, Algeria, Mexico, Yugoslavia
Oil (includes natural gas liquids)	46	Saudia Arabia, Nigeria, Libya, Venezuela
Vanadium	37	South Africa, Chile, U.S.S.R.
Iron Ore	33	Canada, Venezuela, Brazil, Liberia

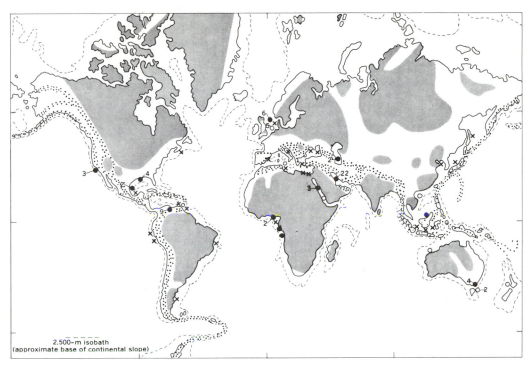

14.4 World map showing the location of major oil fields (solid circles) and gas fields (open circles); also shown are less important areas and areas under development (X). Figures indicate the number of fields in a specified area. Note the coincidence between field locations and areas that (1) are now tectonically active (stippled), (2) have not been active since Paleozoic and Mesozoic times (unpatterned), or (3) have not been active since Precambrian time (shaded).

copper deposits with 3 percent copper were considered workable; today deposits with as low as 0.35 percent are workable.

Next it must be seen how the use of lower-grade ores affects the potential amount of material available. The metals of most interest to industry—aluminum, iron, magnesium, titanium, and manganese—are found in most rocks. A graph of abundance plotted against grade (the potential tonnage available at each level of concentration) is a simple bell-shaped curve (Fig. 14.5). That is, well into the future, as more and more lower-grade deposits are worked, increasingly large quantities of these metals may

be tapped. For the host of other metals that are rare but of considerable importance, the plot is quite different (Fig. 14.5). These scarce metals may be locally concentrated by nature; they may also be present in common rocks, but only in minute quantities that are exceedingly difficult to extract. It is likely that a large percentage of the concentrated scarce minerals have already been mined. Once such deposits are exhausted, the increase in energy required to extract them from common rocks will be about 100–1000 times greater (Skinner, 1976). For instance, at the Cuajone copper mine in Peru, the energy required to mine and mill

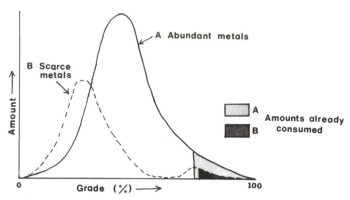

14.5 Graph showing how the amounts of metals in the earth's crust vary according to the grade of the ore, for abundant metals, and scarce metals. Note that the highest-grade ores (shaded) have already been extracted from the earth. Note also the bimodal distribution of scarce metals.

rock containing less than 0.20 percent copper is more than 16,000 times that necessary for containing 1.32 percent copper (Cook, 1976). Since energy shortages are likely to be at least as acute as metal shortages (unless technological breakthroughs take place), such demands will be unacceptable (Fig. 14.6). Also, as lower grade ores are used, the amount of rock that must be excavated increases exponentially, causing environmental problems, such as those connected with the disposal of waste materials, to become greater and greater. (For each ton of copper obtained from an ore containing 0.35 percent of the metal, 600 tons of rock may have to be excavated and 300 tons pro-

cessed.) Similar analyses of non-metallic mineral deposits result in parallel conclusions: the quantities available to humans at reasonable cost (social, environmental, economic) are limited.

In comparing abundance of minerals to rate of consumption, several commonly used terms should be defined: *Mineral reserves* are deposits from which materials can be extracted profitably at current prices using existing technology. *Mineral resources* encompass reserves and (1) known deposits that cannot at present be mined profitably and (2) deposits that may be inferred to exist on the basis of geological reasoning but that have not yet been discovered. Typically, world reserves of most minerals have been relatively small compared to rates of consumption. However, in the past as reserves were consumed, new deposits were discovered and technology improved adequately to compensate for consumption. That is to say, the transfer of mineral resources into the realm of mineral reserves has for the most part kept pace with demand. To judge whether this transfer can continue successfully requires comparison between estimated future rates of extraction and the total amount of material that can be extracted profitably but in a socially and environmentally acceptable way. Any conclusions must necessarily be tentative. Nevertheless, it has been argued convincingly that on a world basis, scarce metals will have

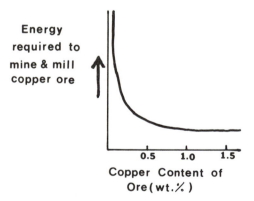

14.6 Graph showing the way in which the energy required to mine and mill copper ore increases as the percent copper in the ore decreases.

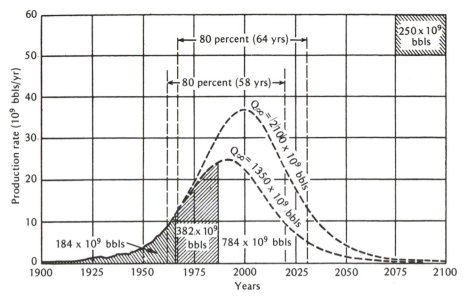

14.7 Graph showing the complete cycle of world crude-oil production for 2 estimates of total recoverable oil ($Q\infty$) made by M. King Hubbert in 1969.

been essentially "mined out" within 100 years (Skinner, 1976).

If the prospects of the United States, for example, are examined, similar conclusions may be reached. A summary of the nation's mineral resources (excluding coal, oil, and natural gas) distinguishes between identified and hypothetical resources. *Identified resources* are mineral reserves plus known resources that may be exploitable in the future; *hypothetical resources* are undiscovered but geologically predictable deposits; that is, resources waiting to be discovered. The identified and hypothetical resources of 26 major commodities are compared to the minimum anticipated cumulative demand (MACD) for the period 1968–2000 in Table 14.4. At best, hypothetical resources only double the amounts available. "Only a few commodities are readily available to the United States in quantities adequate to last for hundreds of years . . . our dependence on mineral resources places in jeopardy not merely afflu-

ence, but world civilization." (Brobst and Pratt, 1973, p. 7).

Energy Supply and Demand

Research geophysicist M. King Hubbert has recently reviewed world energy resources, concluding that production of crude oil, which began in 1857, will reach its peak between 1990 and 2000, and that recoverable supplies will be 90 percent exhausted by about 2075 (Fig. 14.7). In the United States, production peaked in 1970 and is now declining. (The recent Prudhoe Bay discovery in Alaska represents less than a three-year supply for the United States.) The peak for natural gas production was probably reached about 1975, and the pattern of future production most likely will parallel that of crude oil. The outlook for coal is more optimistic, although estimates vary considerably. Peak world production of coal may be reached between 2100–2200, and the complete cycle of pro-

Table 14.4. Potential U.S. resources of some important mineral commodities, in relation to minimum anticipated cumulative demand to year 2000 A.D. (From Brobst and Pratt, 1973)

ST = short tons.   LT = long tons.   TR oz = troy ounces.

  I   Domestic resources (of the category shown) are greater than 10 times the minimum anticipated cumulative demand 1968–2000.
  II   Domestic resources are 2 to 10 times the MACD.
  III   Domestic resources are approximately 75 percent to 2 times the MACD.
  IV   Domestic resources are approximately 35–75 percent the MACD.
  V   Domestic resources are approximately 10–35 percent the MACD.
  VI   Domestic resources are less than 10 percent of the MACD.

Commodity	Minimum Anticipated Cumulative Demand, 1968–2000 [1]	Identified Resources	Hypothetical Resources
Aluminum	290,000,000 ST	II	Not estimated.
Asbestos	32,700,000 ST	V	VI
Barite	25,300,000 ST	II	II
Chromium	20,100,000 ST	VI	VI
Clay	2,813,500,000 ST	III	II
Copper	96,400,000 ST	III	III
Fluorine	37,600,000 ST	V	V
Gold	372,000,000 Tr oz	III	Not estimated.
Gypsum	719,800,000 ST	I	I
Iron	3,280,000,000 ST	II	I
Lead	37,000,000 ST	III	IV
Manganese	47,000,000 ST	III	Not estimated.
Mercury	2,600,000 flasks	V	Not estimated.
Mica, scrap	6,000,000 ST	II	I
Molybdenum	3,100,000,000 lbs	I	I
Nickel	16,200,000,000 lbs	III	Not estimated.
Phosphate	190,000,000 ST	II	I
Sand and gravel	56,800,000,000 ST	III	Not estimated.
Silver	3,700,000,000 Tr oz	III	III
Sulfur	473,000,000 LT	I	I
Thorium	27,500 ST [2]	II	Not estimated.
Titanium (TiO$_2$)	38,000,000 ST	II	II
Tungsten	1,100,000,000 lbs	IV	IV
Uranium	1,190,000 ST	II	III
Vanadium	420,000 ST	II	Not estimated.
Zinc	57,000,000 ST	II	II

[1] As estimated by U.S. Bureau of Mines, 1970.
[2] For thorium, *maximum* anticipated cumulative demand 1968–2000, which assumes commercial development of economically attractive thorium reactors by 1980.

duction may be finished sometime between 2375–2700 (von Engelhardt *et al*, 1976). Unfortunately, in the United States, much of the coal in established fields in the East and Midwest is high in sulfur (Osborn, 1974). Burning sulfur-rich coal pollutes the atmosphere unless expensive "cleaning" techniques are employed. Western coal is low in sulfur, but its increased extraction will deplete water supplies in areas already searching for more water.

Oil and natural gas form from the accumulation and alteration of organic matter that has been incorporated in a sedimentary sequence. Because these substances are of low density compared to rock or water, they

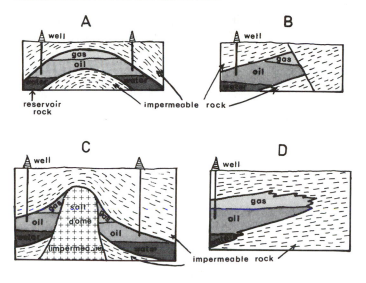

14.8 Cross sections showing four major types of oil and gas traps: (A) An *anticlinal trap,* in which the oil and gas migrate upward toward the crest of the fold. (B) A *fault trap,* in which the oil and gas migrate up a permeable bed until stopped at the fault by contact with an impermeable rock. (C) A *salt-dome trap,* in which oil and gas migrate up the inclined reservoir rock until stopped by the impermeable salt. (D) A *stratigraphic trap,* in which the oil and gas migrate up the inclined reservoir rock until it becomes impermeable.

gradually work their way upward, and, if nothing stops them, may reach the earth's surface and be quickly dissipated and lost. However, if they encounter an impenetrable layer of rock, they may be trapped and concentrated in the rock pores or fractures under the impenetrable layer (Fig. 14.8). Layers in which oil and gas accumulate are known as *reservoir rocks* or *"oil pools,"* and the impenetrable rock which stops their upward migration, the *cap rock.* Certain rock configurations aid in trapping and concentrating oil and gas, and are shown in Fig. 14.8. If the openings in the reservoir rock are interconnected, the oil may be extracted with relative ease. Oil may spurt out of a drill hole spontaneously, driven by the pressure of the natural gas. Usually, however, it must be pumped or flushed out of the ground with water. Much oil and gas occurs in sedimentary layers whose openings are not efficiently interconnected, and ways of extracting the minerals from such formations are being investigated. Proposals include fracturing rocks with atomic or conventional explosives, or crushing or chemically treating quarried rock to free the oil or gas.

Similar treatment is proposed for the recovery of petroleum or petroleum-like substances from *oil shales* and *tar sands*. Large quantities of heavy petroleum occur within the pore spaces of certain sediments and sedimentary rocks collectively called *tar sands*. Because the petroleum is too viscous to be pumped out of the host rocks, they are excavated and then washed with hot water to isolate the oil. Economic and environmental considerations have limited large-scale exploitation of tar sands to the Athabaska region of Alberta, Canada. Certain *oil shales* contain solid organic materials known as *kerogen,* which, if distilled, yields usable petroleum. However, with present technology, for each barrel of oil recovered, almost 3 tons of rock must be excavated and 3 barrels of water consumed. Methods are being sought whereby the shale can be heated underground to convert the kerogen to oil. The oil could then be pumped to the surface and recovery accomplished with little harm to the environment. If clean extraction techniques are not perfected, the exploitation of tar sands and oil shales will be extremely costly to the natural environment.

Production of electricity using nuclear power may be accomplished in two distinct ways: through *nuclear fission* or *nuclear fusion*. One type of fission reactor requires as its raw material uranium-235, a rare form of uranium. It is sufficiently rare that without the use of *breeder reactors,* world supplies of uranium would be exhausted in less than a century. Breeder reactors are unique in that, starting off with small quantities of uranium-235, they can convert the more common uranium-238, and thorium-232 into the fissionable materials plutonium-239 or uranium-233. These materials can be substituted for the rare uranium-235. If breeder reactors are employed, the uranium within just 25 square miles of a uranium-bearing formation such as the Chattanooga Shale could produce an amount of energy equivalent to that available from all the coal, oil, and natural gas in the United States. However, grave drawbacks hinder the development of breeder reactors. Plutonium-239 is extraordinarily poisonous. It has been estimated that a grapefruit-sized lump of the material could, if appropriately distributed, kill the entire human race. It can also be used to manufacture atomic bombs. Problems of reactor safety, disposal of radioactive wastes, and the prevention of the diversion of plutonium for the manufacture of atomic weapons have, in the eyes of many, made breeder reactors an undesirable source of energy.

The production of power through nuclear fusion employs *deuterium,* an unusual form of the common element hydrogen occurring in sea water in the ratio of one atom of deuterium for every 6700 atoms of ordinary hydrogen. Energy released through the fusion of deuterium in one quart of sea water is equivalent to that produced through the combustion of about 50 gallons of oil. Unfortunately, controlled fusion has not yet been achieved. If and when it can be, ordinary sea water will provide an essentially inexhaustible supply of power.

Numerous other sources of power are actually used or proposed. Power from falling water (*hydroelectric power*) provides about 15 percent of the electricity in the United States—roughly one-third of the ultimate potential capacity for hydroelectric production in this country (Hubbert 1973). On a world-wide basis, about 8.5 percent of potential hydroelectric capacity is now being utilized. In a few localities, *tidal power* is used to generate electricity, capitalizing upon the flow of ocean tides in and out of narrow inlets. With present technology, tidal power could produce electricity equivalent to about 2 percent of the world's hydroelectric capacity. Hot spots within the earth's crust present the possibility for developing *geothermal power.* Geothermal power depends either upon the natural emission of hot water or steam by the earth, or pumping water into the earth where hot spots exist and then recovering it at an elevated temperature as hot water or steam. The production is miniscule at present, but if the potential is fully developed, geothermal power may equal 2 to 20 percent of the earth's hydroelectric capacity. However, it is estimated that most of the hot spots would be cooled within a century or so due to the withdrawal of heat (Hubbert, 1973). Direct use of sunlight (*solar power*) to generate heat or electricity shows promise of becoming an important, environmentally "clean" source of energy.

In summary, it becomes clear that traditional sources of energy are dwindling. Indeed, in the United States and many other countries, the existence of an energy crisis is generally recognized. Similarly, recovery of a number of metals and other mineral-derived substances that our civilization depends upon heavily is becoming prohibitively costly in terms of the energy required to extract and process them.

Handling Shortages

Shortages may be handled in three ways: (1) reducing demand through substitution of other minerals, reduction of waste, or elimination of some uses; (2) recycling scrap and used materials; (3) increasing reserves through discovery of new deposits and through the development of technology which will permit the working of low grade deposits (Pratt and Brobst, 1974).

Substitution

If inexhaustible, non-polluting sources of energy can be found, there are no insurmountable technological or envirionmental obstacles to prevent the substitution of abundant materials for scarce materials. Future societies could be largely based upon the use of glass, plastic, wood, cement, iron, aluminum, and magnesium (Goeller and Weinberg, 1976). However, to avoid war and other societal disruptions during the transition period, unprecedented foresight and planning would be needed.

Recycling

Cities may play a large role in recycling and may be anxious to do so because they stand to benefit in several ways. The collection and disposal of refuse cost well over $6 billion in 1975, and such expenditures are expected to rise rapidly as wages and per capita generation of refuse continues to increase (Blum, 1976). Landfill areas are becoming difficult to obtain in most large cities. Burning refuse is becoming more expensive as incinerators have to be upgraded or replaced to meet clean-air requirements. Studies by the National League of Cities indicate that half of the cities in the United States will be running out of ways to dispose of refuse within 1 to 5 years. Thus, recycling may help solve a rapidly mounting urban crisis.

In 1976, only about 7 percent of discarded material was recycled; 93 percent of municipal solid wastes was disposed of in landfills, dumped in oceans, or burned. Such unrecycled material can potentially represent an *urban ore* (Blum 1976). Techniques for the recovery of ferrous metals, aluminum, paper, and plastics exist or are in an experimental stage. By 1990, iron from municipal solid waste (MSW) could equal 6 percent and aluminum 15 percent of U.S. domestic mine production. Moreover, generation of energy from MSW could supply 7 percent of the fuel needs of the electric utilities. From a narrow point of view, some recycled products cannot at this time compete with some other sources. However, if "total community benefit" is considered, recycling may well be worth the effort.

District Heating

Cities can contribute significantly to energy conservation through the use of *district heating* (Karkheck *et al,* 1977). Large quantities of waste heat are produced by electric generating plants and industry. Disposal of this heat has been a matter of environmental concern because water taken from lakes and streams for cooling purposes is unacceptably warm when it is discharged back into them. In many parts of the world, however, this heat is distributed as hot water through a grid of transmission pipes used to heat residential and commercial buildings and to provide hot water. Such heating is most economic where population densities are high. In Sweden, one quarter of the population, including those who live in the cities of Västeras and Malmö, are already served by district heating, and within 10 years, Stockholm will also be served by central heat-distribution systems. In West Germany, the needs of 6 percent of the population are met by district heating, and a study is being conducted of the possibilities of creating a super-grid which will supply heat to all cities with populations of 40,000 or more. In the Soviet Union, 70 percent of urban heat demand is met through such systems. Extensive heating networks exist in Moscow, Leningrad, Kharkov, Kiev, Minsk, Rostov, and other cities. In Finland, half a million people in Greater Helsinki by 1987 will utilize waste heat from nuclear plants. France, Switzerland, and Denmark have similar plans.

District heating has not caught on in the United States for both technical and eco-

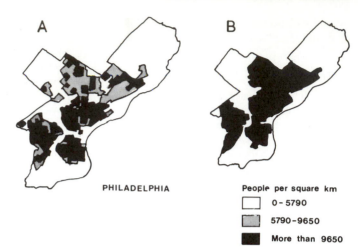

14.9 (A) Map of Philadelphia, showing population density. (B) Areas (in black) suitable for district heating.

PHILADELPHIA

People per square km

☐ 0 - 5790

▨ 5790 - 9650

■ More than 9650

nomic reasons. Steam rather than hot water is generally used as a medium of heat transfer, and steam is not well-suited for long-distance transfer. Perhaps more important, the initial cost of installing distribution grids is very expensive, and the incentive for private investment is low because initially, profits would be absent. However, conservation of scarce energy resources and reductions in imports of fuel would benefit the whole nation; thus, government involvement would be logical. Financing and administration of district-heating installations could be similar to those of water and sewage networks.

An evaluation of nine urban areas in different parts of the United States concludes that district heating would be economically advantageous for cities in the colder parts of the country and also for some densely populated cities in areas of milder climate. Figure 14.9 shows population density in Philadelphia and those areas that could be served by district heating. It is estimated that 50 to 55 percent of the U.S. population could be served by district heating at costs equal to or less than conventional methods. Also, costs would tend to be more stable. The resulting conservation of oil would be 1.1 billion barrels per year—equivalent to about 33 percent of current oil imports. The re-

duction in foreign payments would be more than $15 billion per year. The district-heating scheme would pay for itself in 14 years or less, if implemented maximally. Furthermore, removing heat from electric generating plants improves their efficiency. Thus, district heating, which permits better cooling of generators, makes electricity production more efficient. In this way, the equivalent of a billion barrels of oil a year could be saved, in the generation of electricity. If solar heating becomes a major energy source, district heating will provide efficient supplementary heat during times when solar energy is not sufficient (cloudy periods, cold spells, short winter days). Lastly, district heating is a proved technology that requires simple hardware and is reliable and easy to operate.

Cities and Shortages

The physical effects upon cities of mineral and energy shortages may be manifest in a number of ways. If energy shortages become critical, densely populated cities with efficient mass transportation will have an advantage over more sparsely populated areas. In this sense, places such as New York, Boston, or Chicago, which became

14.10 Adobe-style architecture, Santa Fe, New Mexico. Note the
soft flowing lines of the buildings.

large cities before the age of the automobile, may gain an advantage over more
recent, sprawling urban areas such as Los
Angeles, Houston, Phoenix or Albuquerque. Indeed, increasing cost of commuting
may result in a migration toward urban centers, and urban design that fosters bicycle
and foot traffic and makes extensive use of
underground facilities (see Chap. 6) may
supplant design predicated upon car ownership.

An energy crisis may have an effect upon
building design: Buildings will have to be
functional and efficient rather than purely
personal aesthetic statements. The high cost
of transport may cause a return to the use of
local building materials and to architecture
with a ''local flavor'' (Fig. 14.10). Building
design will have to take into account climate and topography in order to minimize
heating and cooling costs.

Increases in population density may be
encouraged by the advantages of district
heating; thus, attached houses and apartment houses may be favored over free-
standing, single-family houses. (Already,
due to lesser dependence upon automobiles
and to abundant use of multiple dwellings,
the average resident of the New York metropolitan region in 1977 used about one-
third less energy than the average U.S. citizen. Those within New York City itself
used about 45 percent less energy than the
average.)

As recycling becomes increasingly profitable, the problems of disposing of municipal solid wastes may be alleviated. Mineral
and energy shortages may help reduce the

per-capita generation of garbage and aid in the maintence of clean cities. For instance, a growing number of states require deposits on many bottles or cans to reduce litter and save energy.

If humans fail to solve the problems posed by mineral and energy shortages, civilization as we conceive of it will collapse. Moreover, the collapse might be forever, for never again will future generations have the advantages of easily discoverable, easily workable natural mineral deposits (Brown, 1954). Cities, the original hearths of civilization, if they are frugal in consumption, rational in operation, and creative in design can play a key role in determining that this challenge to the future will be met successfully.

IV

Geology and the Human Potential of the City

The accelerating growth of human population and the accompanying worldwide movement of people to urban areas will necessitate rapid expansion of existing urban areas and the creation of new urban nuclei. Within the next 25 years the amount of building that must take place will effectively double the current number of structures. In perhaps a century, the human environment will be, for most people an urban environment. The expenditure of energy involved in this planetary urbanization will be enormous, and the potential for improving or degrading the human condition correspondingly large. As has been seen, proper understanding of the variable character of the earth will be vital in assuring that physical necessities are provided and hazards avoided. However, to improve the quality of life, cities of the future must be successful not only in the material sense but also in the human sense. Here too, the earth has a vital role to play. Cities that forge strong visual and sensual links with the land work aesthetically; they nourish psychological and social stability by providing individuals with a continuing sense of a natural world that is greater than themselves and than humankind. Chapter 15 explores the nature and importance of aesthetic aspects of urban environment and how they are related to the earth.

To assure the material and spiritual success of future cities, methods of urban and regional planning must be developed that draw upon all the diverse genius of humankind. Communication must be established between the public and experts in various fields. Goals must be defined and rational ways of attaining them found. Only as the relationship between people and the earth is understood and accepted will the human potential of the city become fully realized. Chapter 16 considers the history and current status of planning, sketches visions of future cities, and illustrates their dependence upon the earth.

15. Geology and the Urban Aesthetic

Cityscape, the out-of-doors visual environment of the urban dweller, is a complex mélange of artificial and natural elements. Larger architectural units, such as houses, churches, sports arenas, factories, bridges, gas tanks, and skyscrapers, vie with what may be called the "furniture" of the street—hydrants, street lights, statues, fountains, telephone poles, advertisements, merchandise displays, fences, garbage cans—for the attention of the passer-by. The "natural" world is suggested by the presence of tree-lined streets, parks, gardens, and waterfront features, and by glimpses of the ocean or countryside that lie beyond the limits of the city. Little of the natural world, especially in the vicinity of cities, has been unaffected by human presence (Mikesell, 1968). "Natural," therefore, is to be taken as a relative term.

The arrangements in space of the material objects of cityscape are as important as the objects themselves. To quote townscape consultant Gordon Cullen, "One building standing alone in the countryside is experienced as a work of architecture, but bring half a dozen buildings together and an art other than architecture is possible . . . the art of relationship" (1971, p. 7). The dimensions, gradient, geometry, and arrangement of streets, plazas, and parks play a major role in the placement of buildings. Reciprocally, it may be that the location of buildings, property lines, and natural features have controlled the location of thoroughfares and marketplaces (See Chap. 2). Whatever the origin of the city plan, it plays a vital part in determining the character of the paths of movement through and around a city, another crucial element of urban landscape.

Awareness of the urban environment is not only visual. Smell, sound, touch, the sense of motion (kinesthetics) all interweave to create the substance of the urban world. What humans experience, however, depends equally upon the interior baggage with which they are inevitably freighted: their genetic inheritance, their cultural attitudes, their age, their biases, their hopes. The degree to which urban environment is pleasing or beautiful depends upon the psychic distillation of the inseparable meld between what is "out there" and what the individual brings to it. However, aesthetic success cannot be dismissed as a matter of taste. Certain cities or parts of cities are generally agreed to possess qualities that make them beautiful. That is, somehow they "work"; they are pleasing to most people. Moreover, there is strong evidence that the aesthetic success of an environment

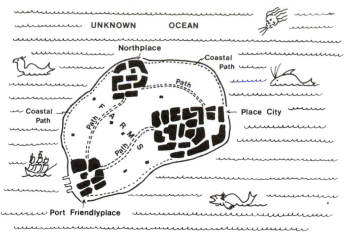

15.1 Existential space consists of known places, paths, and domains.

THE ISLAND OF EXISTENTIAL SPACE

is a subtle but significant factor in determining whether human life itself has meaning and is pleasing.

The purpose of this chapter is to investigate what determines the aesthetic success of the physical aspects of cityscape, what it means to urban inhabitants, and the role that geology plays in achieving pleasing urban environments.

Other aspects of this discussion are found in Chapters 2 and 16.

AESTHETIC SUCCESS OF CITYSCAPE

To be successful in any sense, urban environment must satisfy the basic human needs that result in the formation of cities: the desire to be in close contact with other people and the wish to create surroundings that are orderly and comforting in contrast to the apparent chaos of the outer world. The city becomes an extension of the sensory and psychological filters that screen the almost infinite amount of information that the universe provides. The city becomes "sacred space," a symbol of cosmic wholeness, a microcosmos of beneficial influence (Tuan, 1974). The city, in short, must be a place in which one feels at home.

Feeling at home, according to art histo-

rian Norberg-Schulz, arises when where one is coincides with *existential space,* the center of a "stable system of three-dimensional relationships between meaningful objects . . ." (Fig. 15.1) (Norberg-Schulz, 1971, p. 11). The construction of a city, then, may be thought of as a way of creating satisfactory existential space, in which people know where they are and may learn what they are. In order to do this, humans both change the environment and accommodate themselves to the conditions it offers. Space is organized—it becomes known and individuals are able to orient themselves within it—into *places, paths,* and *domains*. A place, such as a house, neighborhood, or city, is what is best known within a world largely unknown and often frightening. It is inherently concentrated and enclosed. From this concept, it may be inferred that a city should be densely populated and sharply differentiated from that which is not a city. *Paths* connect places and are characterized by continuity. A path may symbolize human life, progress from birth to death, movement through time, organization of events, and is always tinged with the tension between the known and the unknown. Paths divide the rest of the world into *domains*: oceans, deserts, mountains, lakes, as well as political or economic realms. Thus, if a city is to be satisfactory existential space, the cityscape must provide means of location and orientation, knowledge of where "this" is with respect to "that," and be distinct from and yet related to the surrounding landscape. How these requirements are most properly achieved depends partly upon the nature of landscape. That is, landscape should influence urban form, urban form should influence architecture, architecture should influence interior furniture and decor. In such an integrated environment, everything "works," everything fits together, and humans are most at home.

But will what "works" be the same for everyone? How people are affected by and respond to their environment is the subject of several disciplines: human geography, environmental perception, and environmental psychology. Geographer Yi-Fu Tuan defines and elaborates *topophilia:* the affective (emotional) bond between people and place or setting. According to two other geographers, Paul English and Robert Mayfield, since almost all landscape is to some extent shaped by humans, it "provides insight into human value systems . . . the aesthetic landscape is a symbolic creation . . . whose form reflects a set of human attitudes . . . the landscape is a document to be read as an intellectual, moral, and aesthetic statement of man as a human and humane being" (1972, p. 7). Aesthetics has been defined as the "feeling" of a space; as has been suggested, how people "feel," or emotionally respond to their environment may vary considerably (Walker, 1971).

Several examples will elucidate these points. In western cultures, objects are perceived, whereas in Japan, the spaces between objects are of major importance. G. A. Jellicoe, an authority on landscape design, notes that "Christianity is one of the few religions, if not the only one, from which the beauty of the landscape has been excluded" (1966, p. 36). He attributes this exclusion to a reaction against the pagan Greek vision of divinity inhabiting the whole environment, and also to the hostile character of the Palestinian landscape in which the New Testament was conceived. During the Renaissance, humankind conceived of itself at the center of the universe, and nature and landscape was viewed in relation to self and as a means of personal development. In China, it was accepted that landscape dominates humans; harmony with rather than dominance over nature was sought, a view symbolized by the receptive character of the concave-upward design of Chinese roofs—as compared to the assertive character of convex upward roofs (Bacon, 1974). To a child, the world consists of immediate surroundings; distant objects or panoramas are of no special interest (Tuan, 1974). This is so because "seeing" the landscape requires the ability to make sharp distinctions between self and non-self, an ability that develops only with time. Whereas desert to many is indeed deserted, useless, and even threatening, to others it represents an escape from voluptuous luxury and is infinitely enticing (Lawrence, 1926; Doughty, 1931). Adjectives used at various times to describe mountains are numerous: awe-inspiring, remote, towering, desolate, dangerous, sacred, sublime, unchanging, aloof, hostile, wild, stately, grand, glorious, healthful (Tuan, 1970). Ecologist Paul Shepard reviews the evolution through geologic time of the structure of the human eye and its effect upon human interpretation of landscape.

A question that must arise is whether there is a common thread linking these reactions to spatial environment. Are there some aspects of response to landscape and cityscape common to all people? G.A. Jellicoe concludes that irrespective of cultural differences, there are elements of abstract design in the realm of landscape that have universal appeal (1966). In *The Experience of Landscape,* geographer Jay Appleton offers a theory of the underlying rationale to aesthetic response to landscape. It has not been very long, he states, in terms of the history of the human race, "since a keen sensitivity

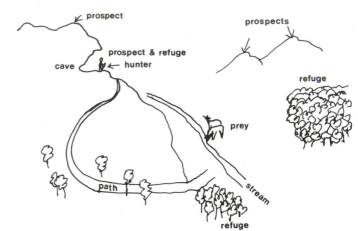

15.2 A landscape rich in prospects and refuges. The hunter in the cave is in the ideal position as he can see his prey drinking from the stream below without being seen himself. Moreover, there is a good way of getting to the prey along the path.

to environment was a prerequisite of physical survival" (1975, p. 69). Thus, the aesthetic satisfaction experienced in contemplation of landscape may be attributed to "spontaneous perception of landscape features which, in their shapes, colours, spatial arrangements and other visible attributes, act as sign-stimuli indicative of environmental conditions favorable to survival, whether they really *are* favorable or not. This proposition we can call *habitat theory*" (1975, p. 69). Habitat theory asserts that asthetic satisfaction "arises from a spontaneous reaction to . . . environment as habitat, that is to say as a place which affords the opportunity for achieving our simple biological needs." When this appraisal is no longer needed, the mechanisms do not immediately die out in the species. Instead, they afford us the "satisfaction which results from the perception of a biologically favorable environment without uncomfortably exposing ourselves to the hazards against which this sensitivity to our surroundings would protect us in a 'state of nature'" (1975, p. 70). As to what constitutes a biologically favorable environment, for creatures who hunt and are hunted, it is one in which the organism can "see without being seen."

Having established this premise, Appleton then classifies the components of land-

scape according to whether they are conducive to seeing or hiding (Fig. 15.2). Places which afford unimpeded opportunity to see are called *prospects*. Places that provide the opportunity to hide are called *refuges*. Interpreting landscape in the light of prospect-refuge theory in order to identify aesthetic potential involves one further element: *hazard*. If there is no hazard, no hunting or being hunted (real or symbolic), then prospect and refuge are deprived of their roles. What is needed, therefore, for keen aesthetic appreciation of landscape is a feeling of exposure to the power of nature, a sense of the infinite, experienced from a safe vantage-point. The observer must also feel that the landscape provides opportunity for successful movement between various key positions in the prospect-refuge complex; that is, in the terminology of Norberg-Schulz, the landscape must be clearly structured into *places, paths* and *domains,* the components of satisfactory existential space.)

Enjoyment of landscape, according to habitat theory, implies involvement of the observer with the landscape. However, humans have gradually gained control over their environment, remolding it to suit their needs: wilderness has given way to a tamed countryside and cities. Within this new environment, the natural prospect-refuge symbols are absent, thus frustrating part of the human biological makeup—the ability to hunt without becoming another hunter's quarry—and removing stimuli important to living a full life. Thus, humans constantly hanker after a visible environment where sign-stimuli can be recognized (Appleton, 1975). From this stems "the common preference for architectural concessions to naturalism such as thatched roofs and local stone and timber, which blend into the landscape. . . . Thus masonry surfaces [of quarried or reconstituted local stone] are suggestive of cliffs or rock surfaces as might occur naturally in that particular environment." That is, humans seek to reconcile the artificial with the natural to preserve the sign-stimuli that activate our aesthetic responses. At the same time that we rejoice in our release from the toil and danger that our ancesters experienced in their habitat, we seek assurance that we can still have a relationship with the natural habitat. A partial solution to this dilemma is building into the urban environment "counterparts which resemble the sign-stimuli of the prospect and refuge of nature closely enough to resucitate our aesthetic responses" (1975, p. 174). This does not imply a slavish imitation of natural forms but rather that buildings should be "so designed and so positioned as to provide effective symbolic substitution for those environmental features which, in their natural forms, suggest an opportunity for seeing without being seen" (1975, p. 201). Also, the "aesthetic potential of places derives from the rocks which underlie them, the presence or absence of water and the form in which it occurs, the cover of vegetation, the climatic conditions. . . ." (1975, p. 238).

It becomes clear from this exposition that preserving a sense of the land, of natural environment within or near urbanized areas is not a matter of luxury, but is of importance to our psychological well-being. To achieve effective land-use planning, Appleton concludes, "more penetrating methods of understanding our scenic resources and

more effective ways of evaluating them" are desperately needed. This is especially true because haphazard preservation of "bits" of natural environment is of little value. Individual elements of landscape do not have significant intrinsic qualities. Beauty is not an inalienable quality of itself. "If a mountain is beautiful, its beauty is not to be sought in its mass, its outline or its mineralogical composition, but in its relationship to other landscape components . . . it is only in the total environmental context that we can assess the aesthetic qualities of a *particular* place, a *particular* view, *a particular* landscape" (1975, p. 243).

Landscape architect R. B. Litton and colleagues join the consensus that the aesthetic experience of landscape is dependent upon the interplay between the observer's state of mind and environmental stimuli. They do, however, develop objective aesthetic criteria to be applied to landscape: unity, variety, and vividness. In applying these criteria, they examine three different scales of landscape environment. Since their principal interest is the role of water in the landscape, the smallest environmental unit is the *waterscape unit,* which consists of bodies of water and their shores. Each waterscape unit lies within a *setting unit,* or "container"—"a visual corridor or envelope of space which is set by enclosure of land forms or forest edges. . . ." (Litton *et al*, 1974, p. 43). The *landscape unit* consists of a series of similar or visually related setting units, and achieves cohesion in a regional sense. It is stressed that the aesthetic quality of these units depends upon the sense of the unit being clear and complete—although diffuse, less well-defined units can link more positive units and acts as foils for them. Human development of the landscape, such as urbanization, can disastrously affect the scenic quality of units unless such development is carefully planned.

An interesting way to evaluate the interaction between urbanized areas and their

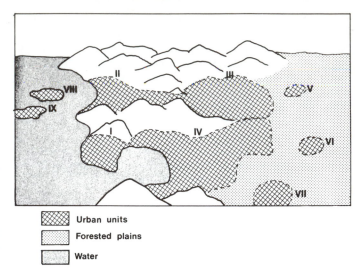

15.3 Urban units occupy setting units I–IX, visually bounded by ocean, mountains, and/or forest. The setting units form three distinct landscape units: linked valley floors (I–II–III–IV), forested plains (V–VI–VII), and islands (VIII–IX).

Urban units

Forested plains

Water

large-scale natural surroundings is to define *urban units* in a manner analogous to waterscape units, and then to consider them in terms of setting units, and finally landscape units (Fig. 15.3). The importance of large-scale consideration of environment has been emphasized: the experiential quality of the environment must be planned for at a regional scale because people live their lives at that scale (Lynch, 1976).

The importance of knowing where one is, of being able to orient oneself, is returned to frequently by many writers. One relates spatial orientation to survival and sanity: in an emergency, one must be able to act instinctively. Without knowledge of the relation between self and surrounding, the chance of correct, instinctive reaction is lessened (Hall, 1969). In Appleton's prospect-refuge theory, lack of orientation means that the environment lacks obvious or available refuges, prospects, and movement corridors. Norberg-Schulz's existential space is space in which one can locate oneself. Edmund Bacon, a renowned city planner, notes that architectural design, and by implication, cityscape, should provide a sense of connection with a system greater than humans: in Savannah, Georgia, city

squares produce a ''sense of being within a complete organism: a kind of simultaneity that is most satisfying.'' (Bacon, 1974, p. 221). According to Tuan, ''the city dweller seems to have a psychological need to possess an image of the total environment. . . .'' (1974, p. 172). Within the Sufi tradition of Persian architecture, the traditional human need for structured space ''is most often attained through the interaction of man's cities with prominent sites, an interaction that creates a definite, regional sense of place. . . . . Outstanding examples of this space definition are found in the plateau regions of Iran where the cities are situated on the apron of majestic mountain ranges. These ranges act as macroscale walls which define a regional space within which the positive shape of the city evolves. The city becomes the centripetal node within a regional space that often relates centrifugally to a geographic space of vast dimensions.'' (Ardalan, et al, 1973, p. 13) Figure 15.4 illustrates such relationships. Note their similarity to setting units. The city-landscape relation may be just one manifestation of the desire to locate oneself in the universe. Another mode of orientation is derived from the heavens and the

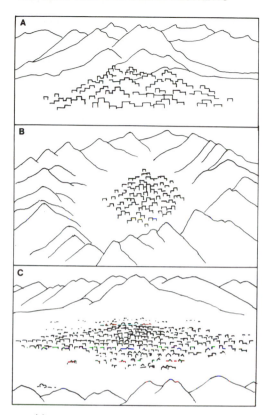

15.4 The relationship between cities and nearby mountain ranges. (**A**) a city next to a wall. (**B**) a village in a bowl. (**C**) a city between two parallel walls.

Kevin Lynch has investigated what he calls the clarity, legibility, or *imageability* of cityscape. Without such imageability, surroundings are chaotic, and the individual may become disoriented, anxious, even terror-stricken. On the other hand, where orientation is facilitated, a sense of well-being and balance is induced; a harmonious relation between the individual and the outside world is achieved; the depth and intensity of experience is heightened. A highly imageable city would have a "pattern of high continuity with many distinctive parts clearly interconnected" (1960, p. 10). In such a city, new sensual impact would not disrupt the basic image, but would relate to it. Parts of the whole must be distinct in themselves and yet suggest the nature of the whole. Furthermore, when there is a strong image of the city held by its inhabitants, it helps to bind the community together socially.

Topography, Lynch suggests, can play an important role in reinforcing the elements of the urban landscape, thereby providing strong imageability: sharply rising hills can define regions; rivers and beaches make strong edges; the focal points of the city can be placed at key places in the terrain. Several examples illustrate this concept: To the inhabitants of Boston, certain topographic features such as Beacon Hill, the Charles River, Boston Harbor, aside from their inherent interest help to furnish the city with an understandable structure.

Los Angeles is described by those who live there as spread-out, spacious, formless, without centers, and hard to conceptualize as a whole. However, on a regional scale, especially on freeways, a traveler can gain a sense of the major topographic features—the ocean, mountains, hills and valleys—as well as large developments and a concentric age gradient of condition and style.

Jersey City, New Jersey, is Lynch's example of a city that has no imageability. To those who live there, it is "a place to pass through rather than to live in . . . a place on the edge of something else." (1960, p.

motions of the planet. In the sacred landscape of Jerusalem (see case study at end of chapter), the Dome of the Rock, (a mosque which is the visual center of the Temple Mount in the Old City, the heart of Jerusalem) is aligned symmetrically with the path of the equinoctial sun (Kutcher, 1973). The human desire to be cosmically oriented may originally stem, in part, from the need to establish a calendar so as to increase the chances of planting at the correct time of year (Reyman, 1976). If this is so, it is another example of a biological imperative being translated into metaphysical and aesthetic expression.

In *The Image of the City,* urban planner

25; 29) Its major features are overhead rail-roads and highways, the cliffs of the Palisades overlooking the Hudson River and the New York City skyline, and the Pulaski Skyway leading to Newark. It is a drab, dirty city and cut up into isolated fragments. Considering its location and topography, declares Lynch, Jersey City could be a highly dramatic and imageable place to live in if it were torn down and built completely anew.

Manhattan permits ease of orientation be-cause it has well-defined districts set in an ordered frame of rivers and streets.

In Tehran, the east-west line of the El-borz Mountains, on whose southern slopes the city is built is visible from everywhere and provides a frame of reference. Even at night, the ubiquitous tilt of the land fur-nishes a sense of the region and the ability to orient onself.

Florence, Italy, often cited as one of the world's most beautiful cities, is highly visi-ble. It lies in a bowl of hills along the Arno River. Hills and the city are always inter-visible. To the south, open country pene-trates almost to the heart of the city, provid-ing clear contrast to what is inside and what is outside. To the north, small villages perched on hills are clearly visible. The Arno cuts through the city and connects it to a larger landscape. The Duomo (Cathedral) and the nearby campanile in the city center are visible from every section of the city. "Every scene is instantly recognizable, and brings to mind a flood of associations. Part fits into part. The visual environment be-comes an integral piece of the inhabitants' lives" (Lynch, 1960, p. 93).

Unfortunately, such beautiful city envi-ronment is rare, especially in the United States. The photographer George A. Tice describes how he chose Paterson, New Jer-sey, as the subject of a visual essay: Garret Mountain, Passaic Falls, and the setting of the city (Fig. 15.5) attracted him. The en-during mountain, the sense that the valley, the falls had been there long before: "if I lived in Paterson, I would look to the moun-tain as a sanctuary . . . and hear the falls . . . [as] a voice of elemental power, a source of wonder and awe. . . . But even from Garret Mountain it is possible to see that the City of Paterson does not match the magnificence of its natural setting. There is a clear deterioration here. Greed and indif-ference have tarnished the noble promises of the site" (Tice, 1972).

Lynch considers that nowhere in the world is there a metropolitan area with strong visual character or evident structure. Cities deteriorate to faceless sprawl at their peripheries. But "the metropolitan region is now the functional unit of our environment . . . and we must somehow make the 'jump' in awareness and ability so as to learn how to properly structure urban areas. . . . A clear and comprehensive image of the entire metropolitan region is a fun-damental requirement for the future. . . ." (1960, pp. 112–20).

Bacon discusses the roles of movement and topography in determining the character of cities. "Movement systems must be re-lated to natural or manmade topography: they must take into account the nature of terrain and the natural features or structures that are part of it" (1974 p. 35). In Rome, straight, major streets interconnect key buildings across the famous seven hills. "The movement system acts uncompromis-ingly across the countryside, tense and organic, moving directly to its goal but dis-turbing only what is necessary for the achievement of its purpose." The rising and falling of straight avenues creates a rhyth-mic experience: "it is the very purity of this counterpoint, the tense network of ways overlaid on the soft, rounded contours of the land, that contributes so greatly to the quality of Rome. . . . The quality of the land, made articulate by movement sys-tems, is or should be a generating force in all architecture" (p. 159). On the flat, mo-notonous terrain of the Netherlands, the Dutch, "with rare artistry, have set about remedying the defect by rearing city sky-lines that are total works of art" (p. 164).

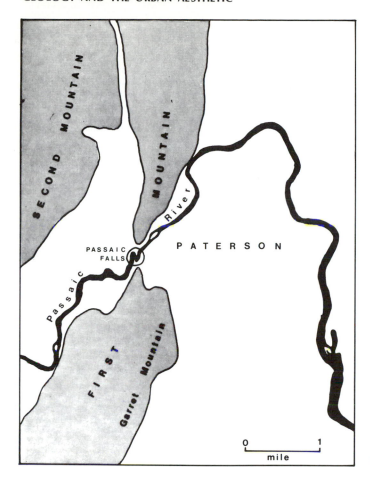

15.5 The topographic setting of Paterson, New Jersey.

Moving around the city, one experiences an exciting kinetic sensation as the relative positions of the spires shift due to the parallax effect.

Gordon Cullen also emphasizes the importance of movement in experiencing surroundings: "from the point of view of the moving person . . . the whole city becomes a plastic experience, a journey through pressures and vacuums, a sequence of exposures and enclosures, of constraint and relief" (1971, p. 10). The body has a continuous, instinctive habit of relating itself to its environment; it develops a sense of position that cannot be ignored. "Arising out of this sense of identity or sympathy with the environment . . . we discover that no sooner do we postulate a HERE than automatically we must create a THERE, for you cannot have one without the other" (p. 10). In order to create and preserve the sense of here and there, the major landscape categories—metropolis, town, arcadia, park, industrial, arable, wild nature—must be maintained. If the distinction between those or other categories is not preserved, "all we get is a form of porridge which will maintain life only if one can refrain from vomiting it up" (p. 57). From this can be gathered the importance of a city having a distinct boundary, an edge that increases the feeling of enclosure, of refuge.

Urbanist Hans Blumenfeld has under-

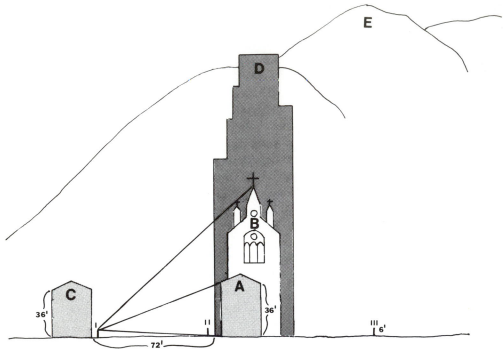

15.6 To person I, person II is just recognizable, but person III is not recognizable. To person I, building A may be seen at a glance and is at human scale. Buildings B and D and mountain E cannot be taken in at a glance and belong, respectively, to superhuman, inhuman, and extrahuman scales. Buildings A and C are separated by a distance twice that of their height and border a street of human-scale width.

taken a visual and psychological analysis of the size of objects compared with that of humans. Experience of scale depends upon other senses than the visual, but visual experience is perhaps paramount. The apparent size of an object depends upon the visual angle it subtends (Fig. 15.6). An object cannot be discerned if it occupies an angle of less than one minute; to see a whole object at a glance, it must not occupy a vertical angle of more than 27 degrees; that is, the ratio of its height to its distance from the viewer must not be less than 1:2. To people, other human beings are the most significant objects to fall within their visual field. A motionless person cannot be distinguished from a non-human object such as a tree trunk of similar size and shape beyond

a distance of 70–80 feet because facial features at such distances subtend less than one minute, and cannot be discerned. From these facts, Blumenfeld has set up a series of scales which describe the psychological impact of structures based upon both actual and apparent size. A maximum street width of 72 feet assures that the facial features of persons on the opposite side of the street can be discerned. Buildings lining such a street can be seen at a single glance if they are no higher than about three stories (about 36 feet). Such a street may be characterized as fitting into a *human scale* and forming an urban landscape in which one can feel very comfortable. Objects are neither too large at human scale, nor too small. It is especially suited to residential neighborhoods. Objects which loom large because of great height or close viewing distance belong to *superhuman scale*. They cannot be taken in at a glance; the neck must be craned to see the top; they fill the field of vision; they create feelings of awe and exultation. Superhuman scale is appropriate to political, cultural, and religious centers. If it is overdone, it may become *inhuman scale*—alien and threatening, the scale of the gigantic or colossal. However, the gigantic or colossal are acceptable for structures other than those designed to shelter man, such as bridges, dams, power stations, cloverleafs, and blast furnaces. Skyscrapers whose windows are not visible as such and are thus not intuitively associated with human presence may be included in this category. These objects are constructed according to the scale appropriate to the exigencies of the machine: an *extra-human scale*. It is also the scale of nature, of rivers, lakes, valleys, mountains.

In a successful city, the human, superhuman, and extrahuman scales are all present, each applied to appropriate structures. The human and superhuman scales must contrast with and reinforce each other. The extrahuman must avoid devaluating the superhuman. Lastly, to work properly, structures built on an extrahuman scale must have a scale commensurate with that of the surrounding natural landscape. Thus, the total urban landscape, by implication, becomes inextricably bound up with the natural landscape.

The natural landscape, especially its rocky features, also plays a significant role in providing urban dwellers with a sense of temporal continuity in a world of increasingly rapid change. The importance of a sense of continuity, of the feeling that some things are permanent is a current that runs throughout history. Megalithic man in Brittany, circa 2000 B.C., erected huge stones which have an overwhelming personality, seeming "to form a link between ourselves and our origins" (Jellicoe, 1966, pl. 67). Similarly, in the presence of the stone circle

at Avebury, England (Fig. 15.7), "one feels in the presence of a form venerable beyond imagination and bearing all the marks of the processes of nature spread over almost infinite time" (1966, p. 61). The rock and sand garden at Ryoanji, Japan, created in A.D. 1499, consists of fifteen rocks placed in five groups in raked sand (Fig. 15.8). "They at once hold the attention by their relationship to one another. Their position, sequence of number, and shape seem to be inevitable . . ." The sand represents timelessness; the rocks are tangible and time is visible upon them. Thus, the rocks "act as an intermediary between our own short-lived selves and the infinite. . . ." (1966, p. 95). The creation of such structures may be an echoing of natural surroundings which, for primitive people, stands for continuity and certainty in an uncertain world (Lynch, 1960).

Lynch also stresses the social role of the landscape: it provides common memories and symbols that bind a group together. In rapidly changing American cities, even structures such as freeways, which persist through the demolition and reconstruction of neighborhoods, become important in that they provide a link with the past. In Los Angeles, residents cling to anything that survives radical upheaval of urban surroundings. Protection and renovation of historic brownstone neighborhoods in large cities of the eastern United States stems in part from similar needs. It has been noted that wherever a mountain dominates the site of a city, it bestows on the city its continuing identity (Blumenfeld, 1967). In Japan, far-away Mount Fuji dominates Tokyo and symbolizes its continuity. Mount Rainier performs the same function for Seattle. In Montréal, efforts are being made to try to preserve Mount Royal from being obscured by skyscrapers.

ROLE OF THE EARTH

The earth is often invoked as a significant factor in the aesthetic success of urban land-

15.7 Part of the prehistoric stone circle at Avebury, England.

scape and, indeed, as having the potential to fulfill other human and social needs. These functions may now be recapitulated:

1. For those cities that have developed without an overall, preconceived plan, the topography of the land has been important in determining the arrangement and configuration of streets. Roads tend to zigzag up hills, wind around steep bluffs, follow the edges of watercourses, circumvent large boulders or otherwise difficult ground. That is, routes were determined in part by ease of travel, which often meant *not* proceeding along straight lines. Cities with such organic street plans are praised as exciting, intimate, human. To the inhabitants, knowledge of the intricacies and idiosyncracies of

15.8 The rock and sand garden at Ryoanji, Japan. (Japanese Consulate, New York)

15.9 A typical steep street on Russian Hill, San Francisco.

the streets and their relation to one another increases feelings of possessing the city. Of course, to an outsider trying to find his or her way, they may become frustrating rather than charming. Planned cities sometimes mimic organic patterns of growth, usually, however, only in thinly populated suburban areas. It is interesting to compare a proposed exception to this generality, Daniel Burnham's never-implemented plan for San Francisco, with the actual arrangement of streets. Instead of the rectangular grid system that is ruthlessly imposed upon most of San Francisco's hilly terrain, the streets would have curved gradually up and around the hills. Nevertheless, to many, the breathtaking steepness of San Francisco's streets as they exist today is exhilarating (Fig. 15.9). It is clear that whether the street configuration is organic or rectangular, the topography of such terrain must impress itself upon the consciousness of those who confront it.

2. Landscape features such as mountains, cliffs, or bodies of water that can be seen from many points within a city act as beacons, providing physical orientation and location. Such information is important in achieving a sense of place and feelings of stability and assurance.

3. In a similar way, the presence of highly visible and relatively unchanging landscape features creates reassuring feelings of continuity. Rock itself, with its aura of great age and timelessness, acts as an intermediary between humans and the infinite.

4. Views of natural landscape or other types of awareness of the earth create spatial and temporal links between humans and the larger enduring universe. Cityscape, in the form of city plan and architecture, should interact with and strengthen these links.

5. Natural landscape visible from points within the city, helps to create a clear sense of what is inside and outside the city, of the here and there that creates a sense of location, enclosure, protection. It also helps ensure the diversity necessary for a rich exciting environment. Thus, the importance of parks within cities and nearby wilderness areas becomes explicit.

6. The use of local stone in building creates a material connection with the surrounding natural world. Also, it mimics the natural textures of cliff, terrace, and cave. In older cities where local stone has been widely used, it helps to unify the city architecturally and provides it with a unique identity. Aberdeen, Scotland, is known as the "granite city." Images of Jerusalem cannot be separated from the gold, pink, and tan limestones from which it is largely constructed. The cities of Bath in England and Québec in Canada gain much of their character and beauty from the use of local limestones as building materials. The older buildings of Tiberias, Israel, are of distinct, dark basalt. The "brownstone" buildings of Brooklyn and Manhattan make use of micaceous, iron-oxide-stained sandstones. Even where the use of local stone is not widespread, it may play a notable architectural and aesthetic role in establishing the significance of public buildings. Consider, for example, the white Pentelic marble, the blue Hymettus marble, and the grey Piraeus limestone used to construct the famous buildings of ancient Athens (MacKendrick, 1962). The aesthetic value or spiritual significance of certain stones is attested to by the distance they are transported. In England, prehistoric sandstone boulders, some of which weighed several tons, were dragged many miles to form the stone circles of Avebury and Stonehenge. Rome imported Greek Pentelic marble. Most thirteenth- and fourteenth-century English churches have some architectural details in Purbeck marble which comes from the Isle of Purbeck in southern England (Davey, 1976). Granite from Aberdeen, Scotland, has been used in San Francisco.

7. Until recently, the architectural character of cities was in part determined by the na-

ture of the underlying foundation. The early development of skyscrapers in Manhattan was facilitated by the presence of strong metamorphic bedrock at reachable depths. The low profile that once characterized London was influenced by the presence of the soft London clay that until the development of modern technology, would not readily support high buildings.

8. The presence of fossils in building stones provides the perspective of a sense of a past without humans.

9. Prominent landscape features within or near a city may be inseparable from the image of the city: the Acropolis of Athens; Telegraph, Nob, and Russian hills and the Bay in San Francisco; Sugarloaf Mountain in the harbor of Rio de Janeiro; the snow-covered Coast Ranges that flank Vancouver, British Columbia; Vesuvius and Naples; the Thames of London; Paris and the Seine.

10. Rivers and lakes in urban areas are aesthetically important and should be treated as continuous elements that will serve to strongly define and interconnect an open-space system. Development should reinforce the unity and continuity of the natural drainage (Litton *et al*, 1974).

ROLE OF GEOLOGY

I would like to suggest here that the science of geology can add to and enhance aesthetic appreciation of urban environment. Understanding something of the way the earth works, what it is made of, how it is put together, and how it has come to be what it is today provides considerable potential for greater consciousness and appreciation of the natural world. Geology, like the other natural sciences, attempts to find order and logic within the universe. With a knowledge of geology, whatever sense of the earth is present in urban areas can be fitted into a larger framework in space and time. Geology thus permits an additional way of locat-

ing and orienting oneself, of connecting with things bigger and more durable than humans and their physical creations. From my window in Brooklyn, I can see, to the left, hills underlain by glacial debris brought there during the Great Ice Age. In front of me is the flat expanse of the outwash plain, built up of sediment deposited by rivers carrying away the waters of melting glaciers. In the distance to my right, just visible on the horizon, are the Watchung Mountains of New Jersey, remnants of lava flows that erupted during the Triassic, over 200 million years ago. If I look down at the limestone window sill on which I am leaning, I can see tiny fossil shells that accumulated on the floor of an ancient ocean. The city begins to fit into and occupy an understandable niche in the natural world. It is no longer an isolated, artificial phenomenon. Geology helps to make the city *imageable*. It has different, recognizable, distinguishable parts; parts that join together to form a comprehensive whole.

Perhaps the branch of geology most relevant to appreciating cityscape is *geomorphology:* the description and study of the origin of landforms. The city itself rests on and is surrounded by landforms. They are the framework, the body of all landscape. The understanding of landforms, like the understanding of anything else of value, increases awareness—both of the outside world and of self. Understanding helps one see and feel, and these in turn provide understanding. If, as landscape architect Ian McHarg puts it, humans must learn to "design with nature," they must understand nature. Only in this way will human life and human works become rationally and fruitfully integrated with the natural framework of which they are a part and in which they must exist.

Three case studies illustrate the relations between geologic setting and aesthetic aspects of urban environment. In Jerusalem, the land is an integral part of the holy character of the city. New York's vast conurbation is deciphered in terms of its topogra-

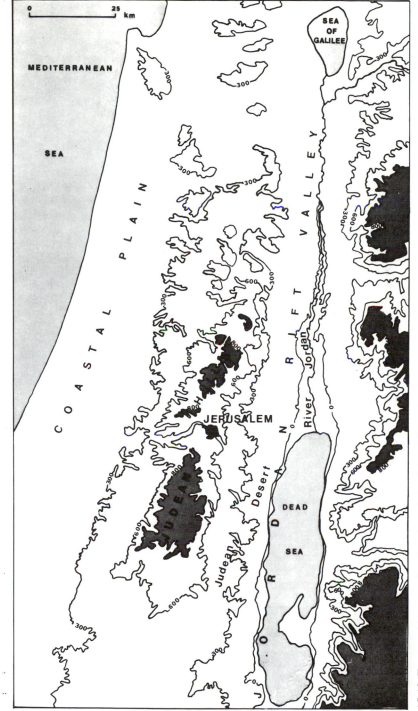

15.10 Topographic map showing the relationship of Jerusalem to regional landforms. Contours at 0, 300, 600, and 800 meters above sea level. Dark shaded areas are higher than 800 meters.

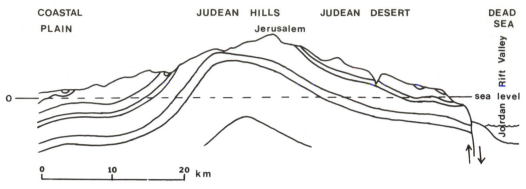

15.11 Diagrammatic cross section showing the geologic structure from the Mediterranean Coastal Plain to the Dead Sea in the vicinity of Jerusalem.

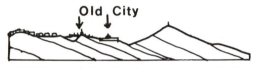

15.12 Cross section showing the relationship between structure and the topography of Jerusalem.

phy and geology. Vancouver provides an example of a metropolitan region of intermediate size that is imageable.

Jerusalem—Sacred Space

A well-known analysis of the aesthetic interplay between an urban area and its natural surroundings is found in architect Arthur Kutcher's evaluation of proposed future development of the city of Jerusalem. Jerusalem, traditionally considered the center of the world, spiritual focus of three of the world's major religions, has a history that stretches back four thousand years to its origin in the Bronze Age. Until 1967, when it was united under Israeli rule, Jersualem largely escaped the processes of "westernization" and retained its provincial, mideastern character, one that had achieved delicate harmony and balance with the particular beauty of the surrounding landscape. Since 1967, massive infusions of

Western culture and technology have begun to effect radical changes in the size and appearance of the city. The question posed here is whether this rapid growth will take place in a way that will enhance or destroy the sacred aura of the city.

Jerusalem, at 2500 feet above sea level, occupies an oval, hilly plateau that forms a pass midway along the backbone of the north-south trending Judean Mountains (Fig. 15.10). The plateau, which forms the city's immediate setting, consists of softly domed hills and shallow valleys. These give way abruptly at the edge of the plateau to lower, steep hills and twisting valleys that fall away to the west toward the Mediterranean coastal plain and to the east towards the Jordan Rift Valley. Within the Valley lie the harsh Judean desert and the Dead Sea, 1310 feet below sea level, the lowest place on the earth's surface. Jerusalem itself has a semi-arid climate: short, mild, rainy Mediterranean winters and summers of blazing sun. The climate and location create an atmosphere of extreme clarity and brilliance in which "distances are hard to judge: near and far often appear juxtaposed, seemingly on the same plane" (Kutcher, 1973, p. 11). Geologically, the plateau is underlain by eastward dipping limestones of the east limb of the anticline that forms the substance of the Judean Mountains (Fig.

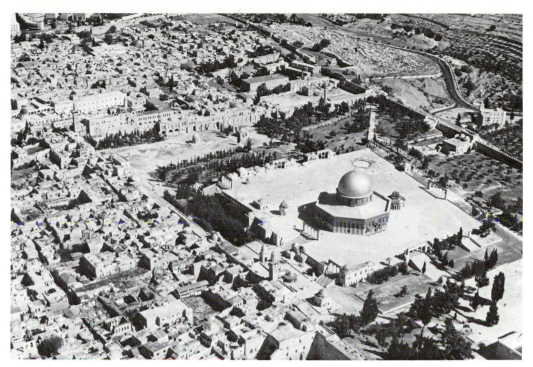

15.13 The octagonal Dome of the Rock dominates the rectangular space of the Temple Mount in the heart of Jerusalem's Old City. Part of the wall of the Old City may be seen running from center right to center top of the photograph.

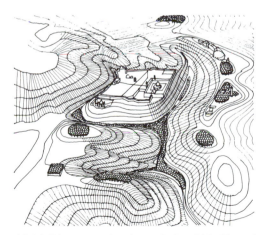

15.14 Diagrammatic view of the Old City of Jerusalem's visual space as seen from the south.

15.11). Differential erosion of these limestones has controlled the dimensions and rhythms of the gentle, rolling topography of the plateau, producing a repetition of hilltops at about 800-meter intervals (Fig. 15.12).

The heart of Jerusalem is the walled Old City, in which lie the holy Temple Mount and its visual center, the mosque Dome of the Rock (Fig. 15.13). The Old City occupies a southward jutting spur of the plateau, an undulating platform that protrudes from the center of a bowl-shaped valley surrounded by hills (Fig. 15.14). Until the rapid changes initiated in 1967, most of the rural and urban elements of the landscape were clearly related to the natural surroundings. They "produced a simple, yet ex-

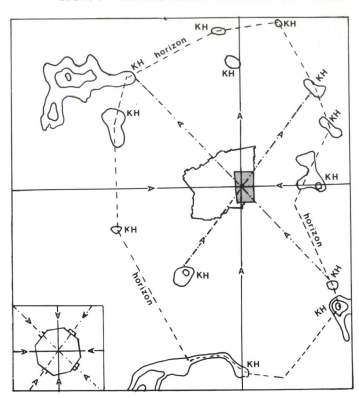

15.15 Most key hilltops (KH) on or near the horizon (H) as seen from the Temple Mount (shaded) lie along the axes (A) of the octagonal Dome of the Rock. The Dome of the Rock is within the Temple Mount at the intersection of the axes. See enlargement in inset.

tremely powerful man-made counterpoint to the starkness and intricacy of the natural landscape, to the massive domes of its ancient hills, its faceted slopes, and the delicate texture of its vegetation'' (Kutcher, 1973, p. 13). Dark groves of pine emphasized hilltops; religious monuments and public institutions respected the scale and essence of the topography; the use of the local limestones as building materials ensured a blend between edifice and earth. The wall of the Old City ''follows the line of the hills gracefully, its precise geometry clarifying rather than overpowering the topography'' (1973, p. 16). The principles of organization of the Temple Mount ''are totally interlocked with the structure and rhythms of the landscape which encloses it. . . . One sees and senses in an immediate and in a completely physical way the dialectical unity of the place: the overwhelming

sky, the dazzling crystal clarity of the architecture, the sensuous lines of the distant hills'' (1973, p. 19).

In an attempt to define more precisely what produces the Temple Mount's particular serenity, Kutcher has proposed a geometric-architectural-topographic explanation. When the visual space of the Temple Mount (that part of the landscape visible from it) is plotted on a topographic map, it may be seen that the axes of the octagonal Dome of the Rock intersect key hilltops on the periphery of the visual space (Fig. 15.15). Thus, a powerful tie is created, one that binds the Temple Mount and its buildings to the surrounding hills. Reciprocally, when the Temple Mount is viewed from the hills, it is clearly seen as the focus of a bowl-like space. On the hilltops, groves of pine and well-scaled towers of public or religious buildings have emphasized these rela-

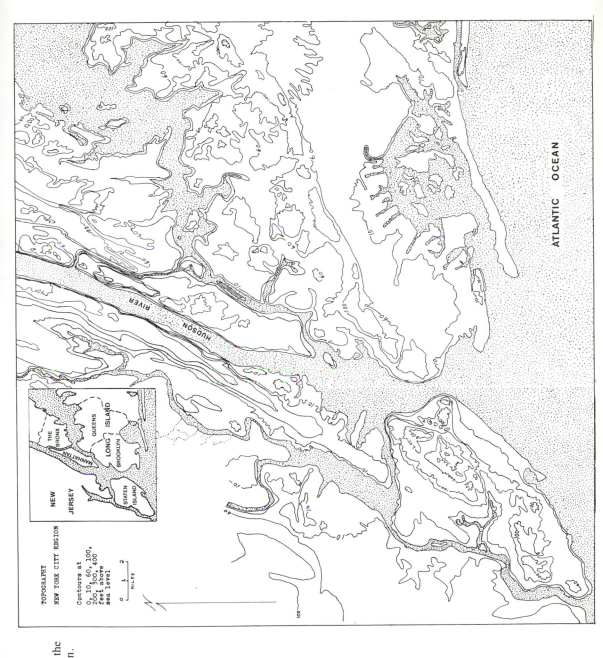

15.16 Topography of the New York City region.

TOPOGRAPHY
NEW YORK CITY REGION

Contours at
0, 10, 60, 100,
200, 300, 400
feet above
sea level

NEW JERSEY

THE BRONX

QUEENS

MANHATTAN

LONG ISLAND

BROOKLYN

STATEN ISLAND

0   1   2
MILES

HUDSON RIVER

ATLANTIC OCEAN

tionships, reinforcing the Temple Mount as
"the place where all the 'visual lines of
force' of the landscape come to rest"
(1973, p. 25).

Although the visual space of the Temple
Mount appears to the viewer as vast, it is in
fact quite small, measuring about two to
three miles from horizon to horizon. The
dominant buildings are, by Western standards, miniatures. This is a vital point, for
the delicacy of the landscape of the Old
City and of its buildings "would be crushed
by the presence of ordinary, medium sized
contemporary buildings and roads, and the
ambiguity and impressiveness of its scale
would be erased" (1973, p. 26). With the
erection of high-rise hotels and apartment
houses and the bulldozing of broad highways, precisely this "crushing of the landscape" has begun. It is hoped that analysis
and understanding of what creates the
uniqueness and vitality of the Jerusalem
landscape will help to stop its destruction.
Indeed, waves of protest have halted some
particularly damaging construction projects.

In the Semitic East, Kutcher notes,
sacred buildings were placed at key points
within the landscape, thus activating the
space of the landscape and giving it a specific scale. This was done not to impose
order upon nature, but rather to create a
spatial dialogue between artificial forms and
the landscape. From this concept he concludes:

The feeling shared over thousands of years that
Jerusalem is a sacred site comes, then, not only
from the religiously significant events which
have occurred there, but also from the fundamental physical nature of the place. To the ancient Hebrews particularly, the site must have
seemed an appropriate place to worship and
communicate with a deity who was both im-
manent and transcendent, a deity with whom
men could speak. The site does not present infinite perspectives. Its limited vistas, its sense of
definition and enclosure tie the place to the earth.
The shrines and altars are not arrogantly above,
they are part of and within the tangible world.
On the other hand only a place which physically
embodied perfection was suitable as the site of

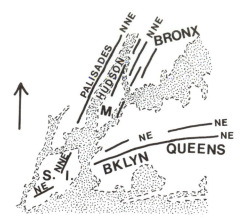

15.17 Topographic trends in the New York City
region.

God's House, and in that respect as well, Mount
Moriah [the site of the Temple Mount], central
and serene in the landscape, was ideal (1973, p.
38).

The Geomorphic Framework of New York

In detail, the New York City region is
highly varied topographically (Fig. 15.16).
However, two linear topographic trends pre-
dominate: one that runs north-northeast, the
other northeast (Fig. 15.17). The north-
northeast trend is manifest in Manhattan and
the Bronx by a series of more or less parallel, elongate ridges and valleys. Also, for
much of their length, the Hudson, Harlem,
and East rivers, the Palisades cliffs along
the west shore of the Hudson, and Todt
Hill, the central, high spine of Staten Island, follow this trend. The other, northeast
trend is formed by an abrupt junction between the hilly sections of northern Brooklyn and Queens and the gently sloping, almost flat areas to the southeast. It is also
present, but less clearly, in the southeast
margin of the hills of southeast Staten Island.

The *north-northeast trend* is, for the most
part, the result of differential erosion of
tilted or folded rocks whose general orienta-

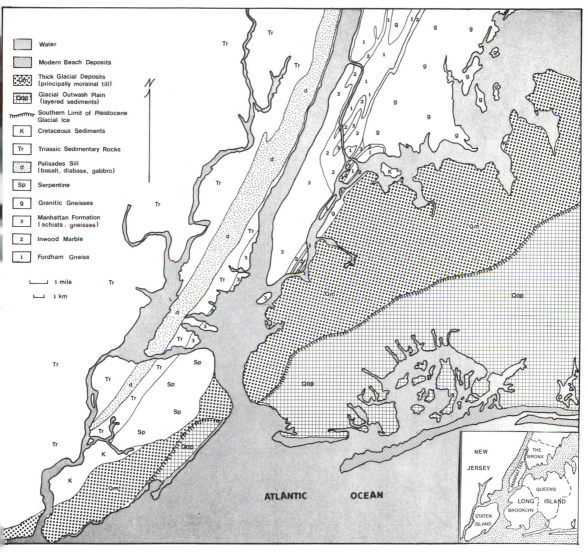

Water

Modern Beach Deposits

Thick Glacial Deposits (principally morainal till)

Glacial Outwash Plain (layered sediments) Qop

Southern Limit of Pleistocene Glacial Ice

K   **Cretaceous Sediments**

Tr **Triassic Sedimentary Rocks**

d   **Palisades Sill** (basalt, diabase, gabbro)

Sp **Serpentine**

g   **Granitic Gneisses**

3   **Manhattan Formation** (schists , gneisses)

2   **Inwood Marble**

1   **Fordham Gneiss**

1 mile

1 km

ATLANTIC OCEAN

NEW JERSEY

MANHATTAN

THE BRONX

QUEENS

LONG ISLAND

BROOKLYN

STATEN ISLAND

5.18 Geologic map of the New York City region.

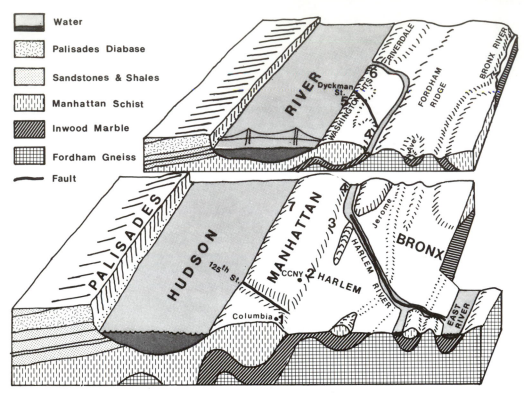

15.19 Block diagram showing the relationship between topography and geologic structure and materials in parts of Manhattan, the Bronx, and adjacent New Jersey. (1) Morningside Park. (2) St. Nicholas Park. (3) Colonial Park. (4) High Bridge Park. (5) Fort Tryon Park. (6) Inwood Park. (7) Riverside Park.

tion parallels that of the Appalachian Mountains and whose configuration is the result of the deforming stresses that created the Appalachians over hundreds of millions of years (Fig. 15.18). Gently plunging folds composed of gneisses, schists, and marble underlie Manhattan and the Bronx (Fig. 15.19). The marble is much less resistant to erosion than the gneisses and schists, and underlies valleys, lowlands, and river channels (the Jerome Avenue Valley, the low area of Harlem, the East and Harlem rivers). The gneisses and schists form highlands or ridges: the main spine of Manhattan, Washington Heights, Riverdale, and Fordham Heights. The Palisades are the re-

sult of differential erosion of tilted diabase, a tough, dark, igneous rock that forms the cliffs, and less resistant shales and sandstones above and beneath the diabase. The serpentine which composes Todt Hill, the highest point on Staten Island, is similarly tougher and more resistant to erosion than are adjacent sedimentary rocks.

In several places in Manhattan and the Bronx, valleys and portions of river channels that run north to northwest interrupt the trend. These features follow differentially eroded fault zones. In fault zones, the rock is highly fractured, and thus much more accessible to weathering and erosion than nearby, unfaulted rocks. Examples (Fig.

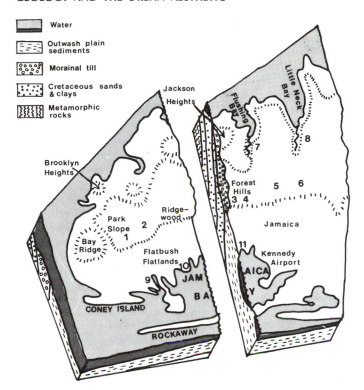

Water

Outwash plain sediments

Morainal till

Cretaceous sands & clays

Metamorphic rocks

15.20 Block diagram showing the relationship between topography and geologic structure and materials in Brooklyn and Queens. (1) Greenwood Cemetery. (2) Prospect Park and Brooklyn Botanic Gardens. (3) Cypress Hills Cemetery. (4) Forest Park. (5) Cunningham Park. (6) Alley Pond Park. (7) Flushing Creek. (8) Alley Creek. (9) Marine Park. (10) Canarsie Park. (11) Spring Creek Park.

15.19) include the Dyckman Street fault valley in northern Manhattan, which cuts through Washington Heights; the 125th Street fault, which underlies the center of the valley between Columbia University on Morningside Heights and the College of the City of New York on Saint Nicholas Heights; the north-south portion of the channel of the Harlem River; and the channel which separates Randalls Island from the Bronx.

The *northeast trend* roughly parallels the orientation of the length of Long Island and the strike of the sedimentary layers and the glacial moraines that compose the island. Brooklyn and Queens at the western end of Long Island are underlain by sedimentary layers that strike northeast and are inclined gently to the southeast (Figs. 15.18 and 15.20). These layers appear at or near the surface in the vicinity of Long Island Sound, where differential erosion has left

relatively tough sands and clays at elevations of more than 60 feet above sea level. Streams flowing northward into the Sound carved a series of short, steep valleys which, subsequently widened and deepened by glacial erosion and flooded by rising sea level, formed a series of embayments (Flushing Bay, Little Neck Bay). Resting on top of these sands and clays and forming the highest elevations is a belt of glacially deposited debris composed of an unsorted, unstratified mixture of boulders, sand, silt, and clay. This debris was deposited in the interval between 75,000 and 17,000 years ago when the area was covered by a massive sheet of glacial ice. In the vicinity of New York, the ice was moving in a generally southerly direction, bringing with it a huge load of detached bedrock, sediment, and soil that it had scoured from more northerly regions. This rocky debris was dumped as the periphery of the glacier mel-

ted, forming a belt of hills known as a terminal moraine. Localities such as Forest
Hills, Kew Gardens Hills, Park Slope, Prospect Park, Ridgewood and Bay Ridge rest
on the terminal moraine. A continuation of
the moraine and the underlying inclined
sedimentary layers forms the southernmost
hills of Staten Island.

Sloping gently southeastward from the
edge of the terminal moraine in Brooklyn
and Queens is an apron of sediment (outwash plain) that slopes very gently toward
the Atlantic Ocean. This rests on the underlying inclined sedimentary layers, and
was formed through the accumulation of
sand, silt, and mud deposited by streams
carrying away meltwaters from the glacial
ice. The sharp edge between terminal
moraine and outwash plain constitutes the
major element of the northeast trend.

Along the Atlantic shore, loose sediment
has been thrown shoreward by waves and
carried westward by longshore currents to
form a series of barrier islands and spits,
most notably Rockaway Peninsula and
Coney Island. These sandy bars protect
bodies of quiet, lagoonal water such as Jamaica Bay.

An understanding of the broad geomorphic framework upon which New York is
built—the comparative resistance to erosion
of the different rock and sediment types,
their structural (geometric) configuration,
the processes which operate on them, the
general sequence of geologic events—
provides the observer with a new sense of
environment, another means of "finding
one's way around." Rocky outcrops are not
necessary as signposts: the slope of the land
penetrates consciousness through the thick-
est layers of concrete, bricks, and asphalt.
A walk or drive "uptown" (north) or
"downtown" (south) in Manhattan or the
Bronx is almost inevitably along or across
ridges and valleys. Where the drop of the
ground is pronounced, as at the 125th Street
fault-valley, the subway lines, seeking to
remain level, emerge from underground and
proceed along trestles. In Brooklyn, the "F"

train's elevated route is interrupted as it
plunges into a tunnel that burrows through
the terminal moraine. Many parks and cemeteries are located where the land was too
steep for easy farming or subsequent urbanization. Morningside, St. Nicholas, Colonial, High Bridge, Fort Tryon, and part of
Inwood parks occupy steep ground where
the schists of the Manhattan Formation rise
above the weak Inwood Marble (Fig.
15.19). In Brooklyn and Queens, Greenwood Cemetery, the northern parts of Prospect Park and the Brooklyn Botanic Gardens, Cypress Hills and adjacent
cemeteries, Forest Park, and the southern
parts of Cunningham and Alley parks all lie
along the crest of the terminal moraine (Fig.
15.20). Natural creeks, subsequently much
modified, have also become the sites of
parks (Flushing Creek, Alley Creek, Bronx
River) as have outlying marshy areas reclaimed through sanitary landfill: for example, Marine, Canarsie, and Spring Creek
parks around the edge of Jamaica Bay.

The precipitous cliffs of the Palisades
across the Hudson River are highly visible
from many places in Manhattan and the
Bronx: when looking westward down cross-
town (east-west) streets; from Riverside
Park; from tall buildings; when driving
along highways on the east side of the Hudson River (Fig. 15.19).

Topographic barriers result in departures
from the grid pattern of streets. Note how
Dyckman Street, 125th Street, and Broadway are adjusted to the exigencies of the
terrain (Fig. 15.21).

A host of small details of New York's
geological landscape are ubiquitous, especially in the city's numerous parks. Glacial
erratics (large boulders deposited by glaciers)
suggest the enormous power of moving ice
(Fig. 15.22A). Glacial striations and
grooves and lopsided, glacially carved bedrock hills indicate the direction of glacial
movement (Fig. 15.22B). In Pelham Bay
Park in the Bronx is found the southernmost
example in eastern North America of a
"rockbound" coast, replete with storm-

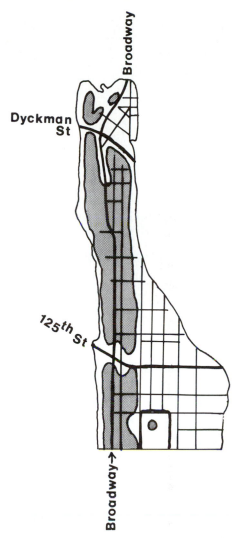

15.21 Map showing generalized street grid of northern Manhattan. Note how Dyckman Street, 125th Street, and Broadway follow the topography.

eroded headlands and tiny, sheltered bays. Sand dunes, beaches, and tidal inlets and flats at Plumb Beach in Brooklyn present another type of coastal expression.

The geologic and geomorphic setting of New York is clearly manifest in numerous ways: directly visible in parks and along many waterfronts; directly felt and seen in the changing slope of the land; indirectly experienced in land-use decisions and the geometry of the city plan. Knowledge of the geology of this area provides a constant stream of opportunities for identification with larger natural frameworks of space and time.

Vancouver—An Imageable City

The Vancouver metropolitan region in British Columbia is an example of an urbanized area that is, in terms of its natural setting, divided into distinct, highly imageable parts (Fig. 15.23). Visible throughout are the snow-capped Coast Ranges which rise abruptly from the waters of Burrard Inlet (Fig. 15.24). The communities of North Vancouver and West Vancouver rest on the lower slopes of the mountains. Vancouver itself, together with the suburbs of Burnaby and New Westminster occupy an east-west belt of gently rolling hills across the water to the south. The southern margin of the hills is approximately coincident with the North Arm of the Fraser River, beyond which lie the flat lands of the Fraser River delta and the towns of Richmond and Delta. Thus, looking north from the delta, the flat foreground gives way to the hilly middle-ground of Vancouver, silhouetted in turn against the bulk of the mountains in the farground. Looking to the south from the southern slopes of the mountains, Lions Gate Bridge and Second Narrows Bridge arch across Burrard Inlet to the undulating urban carpet of Vancouver, beyond which stretch the flat delta lands, leading, in the far distance, to the vague presence of the Cascade Mountains in northern Washington State (Fig. 15.23). A sense of nature, of wilderness, hovers about the periphery of the city. In addition to the ubiquitous presence of the mountains, there is constant encounter with water, beaches, sea cliffs, and the many islands of Howe Sound and the Strait of Georgia.

The topography of the Vancouver region

15.22 (Above) A large glacially transported boulder of diabase in the Brooklyn Botanic Gardens, Brooklyn, New York. (Below) A glacial groove carved into bedrock.

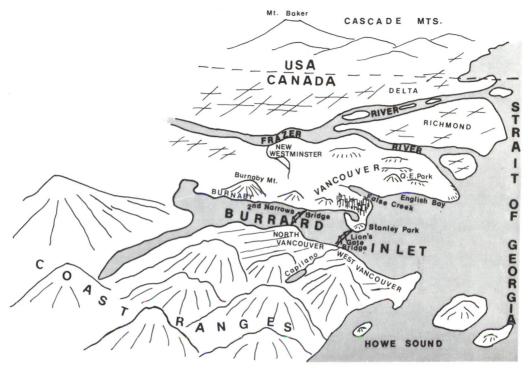

15.23 Sketch showing the major topographic features in the vicinity of Vancouver, British Columbia.

15.24 The natural setting of Vancouver, British Columbia. Looking across English Bay (foreground), the skyscrapers of downtown Vancouver are seen in the middle distance against the backdrop of the Coast Ranges.

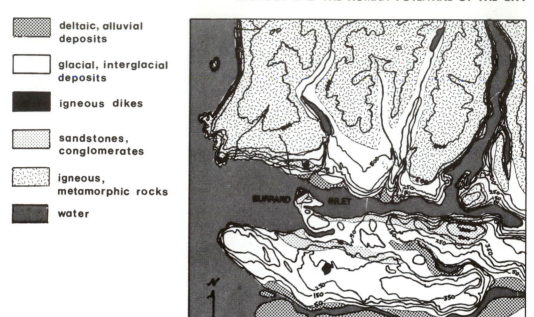

deltaic, alluvial
deposits

glacial, interglacial
deposits

igneous dikes

sandstones,
conglomerates

igneous,
metamorphic rocks

water

15.25 Geologic and topographic
map of Vancouver, British Columbia.

may be related succinctly to geologic materials, structure, and history (Figs. 15.25 and
15.26) (Eisbacher, 1973). The Coast
Ranges, which consist mainly of igneous
and metamorphic rocks, were elevated
about 80 million years ago. After they were
elevated, streams flowing south and west
toward the ocean spread out debris eroded
from the mountains in a vast sloping apron
of mud, sand, and gravel (Fig. 15.26),
which was gradually lithified to form mudstones, sandstones, and conglomerates.
These sedimentary rocks and the rocks of
the Coast Ranges were intermittently intruded by magma to form dikes and plugs
such as those found in Queen Elizabeth and
Stanley parks, and eruptions of volcanic
material (Mount Baker in Washington is
still active and Mount Garibaldi to the north
erupted frequently until just a few thousand
years ago). During the Ice Age, the Coast
Ranges and adjacent areas were covered by
glaciers up to an elevation of 6000 feet.

Only the highest peaks stood above the ice,
and its weight so depressed the crust of the
earth that areas not covered were inundated
by the waters of the Pacific. Glacial meltwaters spread sediment over the floor of the
ocean, and huge masses of till were deposited directly by the ice as it melted. With
the final retreat of the glaciers, the earth's
crust rose by as much as 500 feet, exposing
areas previously under ice or water and revealing marine sediments and glacial till.
Former river valleys deepened by moving
ice became fiords. Former beaches and
shorelines were lifted high above sea level.
The Fraser River then began to build its
delta into the Straits of Georgia; this westward deltaic advance continues today at
rates of 6–30 feet each year.

Thus, the deltaic lands upon which Richmond and Delta are built are underlain by
water-saturated alluvial sediments and lie
almost at sea level. Flood threats are
frequent. The hilly topography of Van-

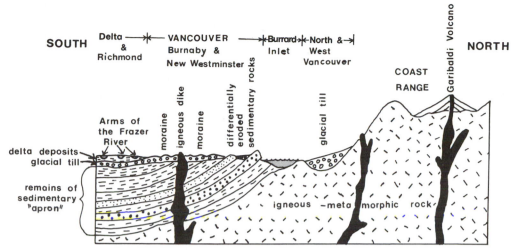

15.26 A generalized, north-south cross section from the Fraser River Delta to the Coast Ranges in the vicinity of Vancouver, British Columbia.

couver, Burnaby, and New Westminster is seen, upon closer examination, to consist of several east-west ridges and valleys. This configuration is due to differential erosion of the pre-glacial sedimentary rock "apron": resistant sandstones and conglomerates stand higher than adjacent less-resistant mudstones. The ridge-and-valley topography was later modified by a veneer of glacial till (Fig. 15.26). For example, the hilly south shore of Burrard Inlet, which includes Burnaby Mountain, is supported by a hogback of sandstone and conglomerate. The low area between Burnaby Lake and False Creek is underlain by less-resistant sedimentary material. Smaller topographic details, such as the hill which forms the center of Queen Elizabeth Park and the ridge between Prospect Point and Siwash Rock in Stanley Park, were formed by differential erosion of resistant igneous basalt and less-resistant sedimentary strata.

The northward spread of urbanization from the city of North Vancouver toward Capilano Lake and up the valleys of Lynn Creek and Seymour River has been aided in these areas by the relatively gentle slope of

the land compared to the generally steep rise of the mountain flanks. The flatness of these areas is mainly due to a filling-in of formerly steep valleys by glacial debris. After the sharp drop in sea level in post-glacial times, modern streams cut narrow, deep canyons into the glacial debris; these canyons interrupt the street grid and are the site of a number of parks. In western West Vancouver, where no such infilling and flattening of the topography has taken place, the urbanized belt is restricted to a narrow strip parallel to the shore of Burrard Inlet.

Vancouver is one of the most sought-after places in North America in which to live. Its magnetism may be successfully understood in terms of the analyses of aesthetic success presented in this chapter. The ring of mountains and water that surrounds the urbanized area provides a distinct sense of boundary, of inside and outside, a sharp limit beyond which human influence pales and is gone. Moreover, the varied nature of the topography within the city, together with the highly visible character of the natural surroundings (except when obscured by low-hanging clouds) permit continuous and accurate orientation. It is a city whose scale and articulation are particularly human and comprehensible. There are different, distinct parts, each small enough to explore comfortably, yet large enough to contain the unexpected. Also, the involuted configuration of the shorelines, together with the different levels of the city make the different parts frequently visible from one another.

In addition to the unique and splendid natural setting, the mild climate, the gracious character of the residential neighborhoods, the increasingly cosmopolitan population, and the general absence of social tensions add to the attractiveness of Vancouver. With the advent of the Greater Vancouver Regional District (GVRD) which binds together 17 communities in the metropolitan area to form a limited regional government, it is to be hoped that the further development of the area will be such that the natural advantages of Vancouver will be enhanced by architectural excellence and rational, exciting land-use planning rather than dissolved in undifferentiated endless urban sprawl.

16. Cities of the Future

By the year 2000, the earth's population is likely to reach 7 billion, and as many as 3.1 billion will live in cities. Less than 75 years from now, in the year 2050, approximately 90 percent will live in cities. That is—barring the unforseen—the earth's population will be entirely urbanized. Not everyone will live in cities, but essentially no one will escape urban influence (Jones, 1966). The process will be accomplished by expansion of existing cities, creation of new cities, and the reconstruction and renovation of parts of older cities. The forms that cities of the future will assume and the environment these forms will encompass and help to create will be of utmost importance to the quality of human life in the future. A challenge is posed. Can urbanization ameliorate the human condition and fulfill the promise of the word "city" (*civitas* 'civilization'), or will it be the final ensnaring of the bulk of humankind within a network of poverty, ugliness, and confusion from which there will be literally no escape? The construction of future cities will be, essentially, the construction of the future. The work may be approached casually, haphazardly, generating great hardship and trauma, or it may be enjoined with imagination, sensitivity, and purpose, drawing upon the most extensive array of skills and social understanding that humans can assemble.

There is, however, no general agreement as to what qualities ideal cities should possess, nor are there any simple prescriptions for achieving desired ends. The general direction of urban evolution is bounded by certain constraints inherent to humans and to the natural environment that surrounds them. Some constraints are relatively easily recognized and may be quantified: air, water, food, and shelter must be available in sufficient quantity; large-scale permanent construction must not take place where there is a strong likelihood of flood, earthquake, volcanic eruption, landslide, or subsidence; profligate use of limited resources must be avoided. Other constraints are less tangible: humans must feel at home within their surroundings and useful to themselves and society; a sense of orderliness and control must be maintained, but not at the expense of diversity, excitement, challenge; the press of the artificial world must be counterbalanced by the availability of a natural world.

A powerful tool to be employed in designing future cities is an understanding of the cities of today and how they came to be the way they are. The future evolution of cities cannot escape the past; their history is a history of the successes and failures of attempts to create satisfactory environments. Future cities will have to capitalize upon current urban achievement just as they will have to try to correct urban shortcomings. Moreover, just as most cities of today are an inheritance from the past, so for many years will the cities of the future incorporate the buildings and street patterns of today.

In some ways, however, the future development of cities promises to differ from their past development. The growing awareness of the necessity for guiding urban change has been accompanied by the development of methodology and technology appropriate to implementing such guidance. Within the last century, regional and city planning have become full-fledged, sophisticated disciplines. Second, deeper understanding of geologic and biologic processes offers the opportunity for a more beneficial relationship with the natural world. Third, the exponentially increasing ability of humans to manipulate their environment and to innovate in the fields of building, moving, and communicating may revolutionize the form and substance of future cities.

The future of cities will depend not only upon technological achievement, but just as largely upon how well institutions are able to cope with growth and change. Change will be best facilitated if those involved in its implementation are fully aware of the complex factors shaping its course. Thus, just as architects should be aware of social and geologic constraints, geologists who are called upon to contribute to the planning process will do well to have a general acquaintance with the social, economic, historic, and cultural forces that have shaped cities in the past and whose influence is bound to extend into the future.

This chapter will attempt to outline the physical evolution of cities; indicate the nature of and the trends in city planning, with emphasis on phases involving geologic opportunities and constraints; describe some innovative visions of future cities; and consider the role of societal institutions that affect the relation between the future development of cities and the earth.

URBAN FORM

The forms of cities may be described in terms of size, overall shape, street layout, and density of buildings. At any period in history, urban form will reflect cultural variation, the degree of technical skill attained, the purpose for which the city was built, and a variety of economic, military, and environmental factors. Thus, any account of urban form that falls short of exhaustive treatment must suffer greatly from the sins of simplification or omission. However, a brief sketch of the physical character of cities through time permits certain valid generalizations. The task is made somewhat easier if two categories are defined and treated separately: (1) cities that evolved spontaneously from rural beginnings and (2) those that were conceived of and constructed as new settlements. Many cities, of course, are the result of both accident and design and fit neatly into neither category; their placement in this discussion will be highly arbitrary.

Evolved or Spontaneous Cities

Whatever evidence remains of the oldest cities of the Sumerian and Indus civilizations (*ca* 3000 B.C.) suggests that they were walled, densely populated settlements, rectangular in shape, that housed tens of thousands of people (Fig. 16.1A). A set of several parallel north-south and east-west streets broke the cities into large rectangular blocks. Within each block were mazes of alleyways bounded by brick walls. Doorways in the walls led into courtyards onto which the houses faced. Monumental buildings, granaries, and fortresses were conspicuous structures.

In the New World after A.D. 300 but at a similar stage in the evolution from rural to urban life, cities of the Maya civilization developed that were quite different in character to those described above. Maya cities generally were without walls, diffuse, covered large areas, and may have contained as many as 200,000 people. The rural character of the peripheries gave way to intensely urban centers where pyramids, temples, colonnades, courtyards and observatories were clustered.

The city-states of classical Greece (Fifth century B.C.) were generally small, few perhaps, having had a population greater than 10,000. (Athens, however, may have had more than ten times that number.) Typically, the Greek cities were walled and centered about a natural defensive site, such as a hill-fortress *acropolis* and an *agora,* or marketplace, which was the social and political focus. The fabric of the city was an irregular, dense pattern of houses; the streets were the spaces left between the houses (Fig. 16.1B).

Ancient Rome, by contrast, was enormous. In the third century A.D., its population was between 800,000 and 1,200,000, and it covered an area of almost 5000 acres. Engineering feats commensurate in scale and ingenuity with the size of the city were undertaken to supply water, provide food, store goods, and entertain the populace. The grandeur appropriate to the capital of a great empire was expressed through the construction of monumental buildings rather than through the reconstruction of the basic street plan.

After the fall of Rome in the fifth century A.D., the commercial and military fabric of the Empire decayed, and urban life in Western Europe essentially collapsed. The self-sufficient agricultural hinterlands that had been in existence before the era of Roman force and Roman city-building reverted to insularity once the Roman presence was removed. Lacking function and nourishment, cities were either abandoned or destroyed, or persisted minimally as the sites of rural villages. Whatever remained of the spirit of civilization resided within the guarded confines of monastic communities. By the eleventh century, urban life began to revive. Medieval cities centered about the church and the marketplace developed. Most evolved from pre-existing villages and grew haphazardly, without plan, with streets whose width and direction varied according to the nature of the houses that bounded them. Some cities were nucleated on the remains of old Roman towns and inherited the geometric elements of the Roman street plan and the Roman wall. Generally populations numbered only in the thousands. Fifteenth-century London, with 40,000 people, was considered very large. Florence, which in the fourteenth century had 90,000 inhabitants, and fifteenth-century Venice, with 190,000 people, were commercial and manufacturing giants.

With the passage of time, power was transferred from cities to larger states. Commerce expanded and technological advances took place, and some few favored cities expanded rapidly as the sites of concentrated political machinery, wealth, and culture. The population of major cities of the sixteenth and seventeenth centuries numbered in the hundreds of thousands. To accommodate growth, city walls were periodically moved outward as military technology improved, and then eventually abandoned as obsolete. Long straight avenues that paid tribute to the magnificence of royalty and that also could facilitate troop movements were cut through the pre-existing city fabric, often in a radial pattern. In Paris, Louis XIV tore down old walls and constructed new boulevards and promenades. Great vistas were opened up. Later, impressive squares, triumphal arches, and columns were added. The climax of this trend was, perhaps, the network of broad boulevards that Baron Georges-Eugene Haussmann, under the aegis of Napoleon III, cut through the labyrinth of Paris in the nineteenth century (Fig. 16.1C).

Fundamental changes in size, in appearance, and in the quality of life came to cities with the advent of the Industrial Revolution. From the end of the eighteenth century to the beginning of the twentieth, massive urbanization took place, first in Britain, then across much of Europe and the United States. This rapid growth was facilitated by the development of rail networks, which

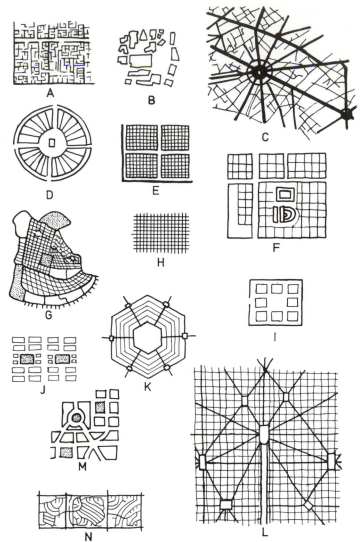

16.1 Examples of street plans: (A) A prehistoric city in the Middle East. (B) An ancient Greek city. (C) Mid-19th century Paris. (D) A circular, Persian city, *circa* A.D. eighth century. (E) Part of an ancient Chinese city. (F) A Roman colonial city. (G) A modern, "freeform" city. (H) An orthogonal grid. (I) A Spanish colonial city. (J) Savannah, Georgia. (K) radial-hexagonal grid. (L) Washington, D.C. (M) An English eighteenth-century planned city. (N) Suburban Phoenix.

permitted the import into cities of food and raw materials, and the export of manufactured goods. Equally important was the development of transport systems within cities—horse buses and trams, surface and underground railways—and later, automobiles, trucks and buses. Urban population began to be measured in large fractions or multiples of millions. Industrial cities, with their mills, gasworks, and factories,

were characterized by mile after mile of monotonous, unsanitary slums, polluted air and water, and a general degradation of the human spirit.

Due to the great value of land in core areas of cities, building density became extreme. With the advent of the elevator and steel-frame construction, skyscrapers displaced lower buildings. Simultaneously, with the development of a transport system that could carry commuters long distances in relatively short periods of time, and the use of septic tanks, which permitted suburban growth without expensive sewering, a major exodus took place toward the cleaner air and less-crowded surroundings of peripheral areas. Initially, decentralization took place in a tentacular fashion, along the major transport routes that radiated out from the city center. Later, by the 1940s, the wedge-shaped areas between major routes filled in as transport became more efficient. Inevitably the search for tranquil surroundings took people further and further into the countryside. This flight from the city rapidly became self-defeating as low-density urban sprawl spread inexorably in all directions over farmland, marsh, forest, prairie, desert, hillside, and valley. As an accompaniment to the rapid peripheral growth, there developed massive traffic problems as commuters and truckers fought their way to and from the urban centers. Highways constructed in response to transportation needs often cut across and destroyed the fabric of city neighborhoods, as did some attempts at slum clearance (urban renewal) in which run-down housing was demolished without providing for adequate replacement housing for the dispossessed.

In an effort to avoid the congestion and high costs of central areas of cities, a number of factories, office buildings, and shopping centers joined the flight of many of the middle and upper classes to the less expensive and more spacious urban fringes. Thus, especially in the United States, the central cities have become more and more exclusively the home of the poor, together with those few for whom the cultural and business amenities still outweigh other considerations. The core areas of older cities have deteriorated into checkerboards of juxtaposed affluence, social tension, and physical decay. On the other hand, the suburban areas suffer from the tedium of physical and social uniformity and a lack of human contact and exchange. In a similar way, some of the new cities whose principal growth took place in response to the automobile were from the beginning sprawling and diffuse, lacking any semblance of a dense core, and were characterized by many of the advantages and disadvantages of the suburbs of older cities.

Planned Cities

Cities whose major features were conceived in advance seem to have a history almost as venerable as that of "spontaneous" cities. For example, in the fifteenth century B.C., upon the command of the Pharaoh Akhenaten, the city of Akhetaten was built to replace Thebes as the capital of Egypt (Galantay, 1974). Planned cities are recognized by such features as regular external shape or geometric street plan, or by independent historic knowledge of planning. The reasons for building new settlements have varied widely: to provide a "fit" setting for the national capital, to create centers of colonization, to spur regional development, to decongest existing cities and provide a physical basis for social improvements (Galantay, 1975). The particular forms that such cities have assumed have depended upon functional and philosophic factors as well as the physical constraints and opportunities of the site. A brief survey of planned cities will illustrate these points.

Many planned cities have regular external shapes that are the expression of aesthetic, religious, or philosophic ideals or which may serve specific functional needs. Ancient Persian and Muslim cities were often ovals or circles (Fig. 16.1D). The Sassanian city of Gur (Firuzabad), built in A.D. 226, was a circular symbolic representation of the sundial. Baghdad, in the eighth century, was constructed as a perfect circle more than half a mile in diameter, and housed perhaps 30,000 people. Its central area of monumental buildings set in a garden was meant to represent paradise on earth. In ancient China (twelfth to third centuries B.C.), the layout and size of cities reflected cosmological speculation, Confucian ideals of so-

16.2 Nineteenth-century map of the City of New York by William Bridges (1807), showing the proposed northward extension of the gridiron street pattern in Manhattan. Note the absence of Central Park.

cial hierarchy, and the functional demands of irrigation and flood-control techniques. The result was square or rectangular cities built up through the addition or agglomeration of square semi-independent units (Fig. 16.1E). In this way Chinese cities were able to grow to enormous sizes and yet remain functional. Roman colonial cities, following religious principles and serving first military and then civic needs, were commonly rectangular (Fig. 16.1F). The external shapes of irregular or "freeform" planned cities are likely to be the result of primary attention given to topography or to functional variations within different parts of the city (Fig. 16.1G).

Street plans may spring from several motives: to provide movement channels, to separate different areas within a city, to create certain visual and psychological effects, to encourage certain specific activities. Perhaps the most common layout is the orthogonal grid: two parallel sets of streets at right angles to each other (Fig. 16.1H). The orthogonal grid seems to have arisen independently in the Mideast, China, and Pre-Columbian America. Its origin may stem from military and agricultural operations in which grid patterns facilitate order and efficiency. The earliest known examples have been found in the excavated remains of Chinese cities of the twelfth century B.C. and Mesopotamian cities of the eighth century B.C. Later, the grid spread throughout countries over the globe and has remained common throughout history. Orthogonal grids inherited from Roman colonial cities have persisted more or less intact in modern cities such as Chester, England, and Turin, Italy.

Orthogonal grids are easy to survey and subdivide, and record-keeping and finding one's way within the city are relatively simple. Unbroken, however, they are monoto-

nous and difficult to adapt to different uses of the land. In hilly areas or those traversed by irregularly shaped bodies of water there is a lack of harmony with the natural setting. Yet in some places, such as Priene, Greece (300 B.C.), and San Francisco, such grids have been imposed on rugged terrain with results that have been variously described as exhilarating, inconvenient, ridiculous, and incongruous (see Fig. 15.9).

The undifferentiated grid systems that characterize most cities in the United States are the result in large part of the Land Ordinance of 1785, which established a system of six-mile-square townships in the Northwest Territories. These rectangular limits strongly encouraged the use of orthogonal grids, and the practice spread across the country. Thus, in a sense, the grid systems of most American cities are not the result of planning, but of a *lack* of planning. They represent a facile approach to land division and land ownership that has often become, in the long run, impractical in terms of both movement and economic and social function. In New York, for example,

the irregular street pattern of the early Dutch settlement of New Amsterdam was soon abandoned, and a rigid gridiron pattern was proposed (1811) for the extension of the city north along the island of Manhattan. No concession to local topography was made, and there was little provision for open space or other functional differentiation (Fig. 16.2). Luckily, in 1856, 840 acres were purchased to form Central Park (Johnson, 1972). Chicago's street pattern is even more relentlessly unrelieved (Jones, 1966).

Grid patterns broken by squares or plazas are a pleasant deviation from undifferentiated grids. The Laws of the Indies (1593), prescribed the layout of colonial towns constructed during three centuries of Spanish conquest of the New World. The basic element was a central square surrounded by eight or more square blocks, depending upon the proposed population (Fig. 16.1I). Planned towns of New England, such as Cambridge, New Haven, and Hartford, had their central squares or "commons"; Savannah, Georgia, for the 120 years following 1773 was built up of a series of rectangular wards each of which contained central, public open space (Fig. 16.1J). William Penn's plan for Philadelphia (1683) consisted of an orthogonal grid broken into four quarters by two 100-foot-wide avenues. At their intersection was a ten-acre square, and each quadrant had a central, eight-acre square.

A few cities adopted radial-concentric grids: Baghdad (eighth century), Karlsruhe (eighteenth-century Germany) are examples (Fig. 16.1D). Seventeenth-century Amsterdam also has a radial-concentric plan, but with canals instead of streets. Grammichele (Sicily, 1693) and Canberra, Australia, begun in 1912, have street plans that are all or in part radial-hexagonal (Fig. 16.1K). Washington, D.C., has an orthogonal grid, upon which are superimposed a series of major avenues that radiate out from centers such as the Capitol and the White House (Fig. 16.1L). A number of state capitals, such as Indianapolis, Indiana, and Madison, Wisconsin, and at least one national capital, New Delhi, India, have developed along similar lines.

Grids of other planned cities lacked strict geometric regularity, but were often graced with squares, circles, ovals, and crescents as well as broad straight avenues. Bath, England, Edinburgh's New Town, and parts of London such as St. James, Mayfair, Marylebone, and Bloomsbury are good examples of this type of eighteenth-century planning (Fig. 16.1M). What particularly lent these plans power was that the architecture of the buildings that lined the streets and the placement of public structures integrated with the configuration of the streets. Some modern suburbs have imitated these street patterns (Fig. 16.1N), but the desired effect has not been achieved because the streets are lined with endless ordinary tract houses. As urban geographer Emrys Jones puts it, "the plan is an idle doodle in an uninspired builder's office; the radiating streets lead to nothing more than another pair of semidetached houses. . . ." (1966, p. 61).

San Francisco

The city of San Francisco originated in about 1835 as a small port known as Yerba Buena. In 1839, an approximately north-south, east-west orthogonal grid was laid out by Jean Vioget. The grid was appropriate for the flat land near the bay, but its extension would require cutting streets through dunes and lofty hills (Fig. 16.3). Subsequently a grid suited to the hilly terrain was proposed, but those who had an interest in real estate were well satisfied to extend the existing grid because of the ease of subdivision it provided. In 1865, the great landscape architect Frederick Law Olmsted, who along with Calvert Vaux created Central and Prospect parks in New York City, was authorized to prepare plans for a park. His proposal included a park system together with parkways, and a plan for the as-yet unbuilt western section of the city with streets that would ascend the hills diagonally to provide easy grades. The street-plan proposal was rejected. At the turn of the century, a committee which had been established to consider ways of beautifying and improving San Francisco received a plan from Daniel H. Burnham, an already famous American architect, which spelled out in detail how the next 50 years of San Francisco's growth should take place (Fig. 16.4). Burnham envisioned a grand outer boulevard encircling the city and a series of inner concentric rings tied together by major arteries. Diagonal streets were to unite the older and newer sections of the city. The most important avenues would radiate out from the civic center, leading to traffic circles from which further avenues would branch out. Chains of park-like squares would cross the flat residential sections. The hilly sections of the city would be crowned by parks and circled by roads following their contours. For the central business district he proposed one-way streets, and, to ease traffic, subways (Burnham, 1905; Scott, 1959; Hecksher, 1977). The Burnham Plan was completed in 1905 and deliv-

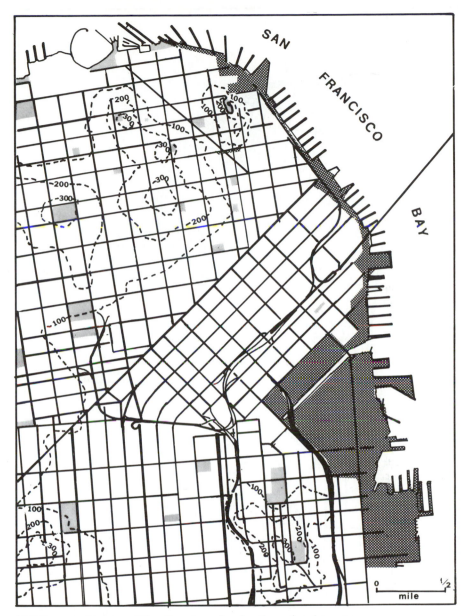

16.3 Topographic map of San Francisco showing the major elements of the street grid. The contour interval is 100 feet. Light shaded areas are parks. Darker areas are industrial areas and transportation and waterfront facilities.

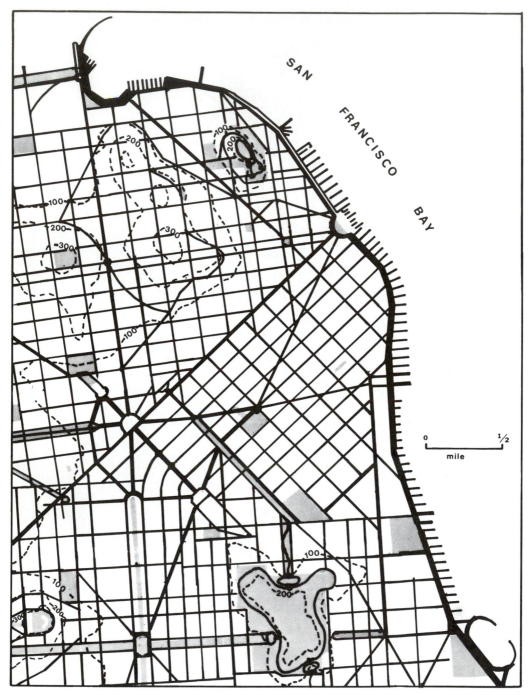

16.4 Diagrammatic sketch of part of the Burnham (1905) plan for San Francisco. The contour interval is 100 feet. Shaded areas are parks.

ered to City Hall in mid-April 1906. Within a few days almost all the copies of the plan were lost as the building and most of San Francisco were destroyed in the earthquake and fire of April 18, 1906.

As the task of reconstruction began, Burnham was sent for. It was hoped that he could help to build a new and better San Francisco. The decision whether to rebuild according to the old grid or according to Burnham's plan was put to a vote. Despite active opposition by Mayor Schmitz and the San Francisco Chronicle on the grounds that it was too expensive and that San Francisco needed business, not parks and boulevards, the plan actually received a majority of the votes cast. But the majority was not sufficient to authorize its implementation, and San Francisco's orthogonal grid was reconstructed. It is interesting to note that after the earthquake of 1964 in Anchorage, Alaska, a similar opportunity to reconstruct along lines differing from those antedating the catastrophe was successfully opposed.

Several critical tests may be applied to geometric plans. Do they readily accommodate to expansion of the city? Do they adequately provide for different activities in different parts of the city? Are they rational with respect to natural hazards and opportunities? Can they handle modern transport systems? Do they ease or exacerbate social and economic problems? No generalizations may be made. Roman colonial towns failed in that mechanisms for orderly expansion were never devised. On the other hand, these towns were built with a full complement of public buildings, aqueducts, baths, and theaters. The Laws of the Indies required enough open space around a town so that it could expand in accordance with the original plan. The cellular units of Savannah and of ancient Chinese cities also permitted orderly urban growth. The original plan for Washington, D.C., carefully took into account the topography of the site and the rivers that ran through it; later modifications of the plan somewhat violated the original intent (Bacon, 1974).

It rapidly becomes clear that although geometric plans may satisfy certain aesthetic urges and function well in serving some of the complex needs of modern cities, geometric regularity or symmetry are not profound criteria for the design of cities. If spatial relationships are to be considered, perhaps architect Amos Rapoport's comparison of traditional villages with new townships suggests the right direction in which thinking should proceed:

The unity of plan, site, and materials in traditional villages generates an enthusiastic response . . . evoked by [the] harmony with the landscape. . . . The flowing lines of the buildings sit on the natural contours, showing a flair for visually combining and relating groups of buildings with such natural features as rock outcrops, trees, and land forms. . . . In the new townships, the grid destroys both the intimate scale and the link with the land. The new visual elements no longer express the relation of the individual to the group and of the group to the land. . . . The new pattern makes the individual feel insignificant. Group unity is destroyed, and there is no clear relation of man to his surroundings through elements of increasing spatial scale and demarcation of domains in harmony with the land around. (1969, p. 77)

URBAN AND REGIONAL PLANNING

One of the responses to the rapid growth of the industrial city and its attendant problems was to relocate factories to the countryside and to build new communities around them to house the workforce. A number of these communities, constructed by industrialists with some philanthropic leanings, were social experiments in providing good, inexpensive housing in at least moderately pleasant surroundings: Pullman, Illinois, built (1880) by George Pullman of Pullman railway sleeping cars, and Bourneville, England (1879–95) built by George Cadbury of Cadbury chocolates are examples. These attempts to decongest the industrial cities gave rise to what is known as the *garden-city* or *new-town movement,* formalized by town planner Ebenezer Howard in England in 1898. The idea was that industry should be located either on the outskirts of or completely away from the congested centers of industrial cities. Around each new industrial plant complex, a new town would be built which would provide a healthy living and working environment. Such towns, separated from each other by rural areas (*green belts*), might be loosely grouped to form urban agglomerations housing as many as a quarter of a million people. Of particular importance was the idea that each new town was to have a definite maximum population; additional increments were to be accommodated in *new* new towns, always separated by green belts. From the start, the industrial base of each new town would ensure its economic viability. A later important development of the concept was the division of the towns into neighborhood units, centered about a school and shops, which would help to provide the inhabitants with a sense of identity with the community. Thus, sociological concepts started to blend with economic ideas in the theory of town planning.

In 1915, Patrick Geddes, a visionary Scots biologist who became a pioneer in town planning, elevated the focus of planning from local to regional, stressing the "intimate and subtle relationships which existed between human settlement and the land, through the nature of the local economy. . . ." (Hall, 1974, p. 64.) The basic framework for planning had to be the natural region, not the conventional town limits. This was so because in an age of easy and rapid transportation, cities soon spilled over town limits, and, through suburban growth tended to coalesce, forming giant urban agglomerations that Geddes dubbed *conurbations*. He devised a specific method of planning: survey the characteristics of and trends within a region, analyze the results, and then develop an actual plan. Within this framework, many philosophic variations arose as to the forms that future cities might have. Emrys Jones has summarized these forms as core, radial, linear, ring, dispersed, and dispersed with nodes (Fig.

16.5). Each form reflects different ideas on how best to handle traffic, maintain adequate open space, and achieve a desirable population density.

The *core city* is envisioned as an almost solid, compact three-dimensional block. New York most closely approaches this ideal. A *radial city* would be the result of outward growth from a central core along radial transportation routes, forming a starshape with open land between the arms of the star. *The Year 2000 Plan* for Washington, D.C., and vicinity, as proposed in 1961, adopts such a plan. Reston, Virginia, and Columbia, Maryland, were built by private developers in response to this plan. A major difficulty has been keeping the wedges of open land free of development. A plan for *linear* growth was proposed by Spanish transportation engineer Soria y Mata in 1882. The essence of the plan is a spinal road from which relatively short subsidiary roads spread. Urban density generally diminishes outward from the spine, and growth takes place by the addition of segments that extend the spine. A major objection is that the ends of the city eventually become too far apart. This problem is solved by bending the spine to make a *ring* with an open rural center. The Dutch cities of Haarlem, Amsterdam, Utrecht, Rotterdam, The Hague, and Leyden form a ring city. The *dispersed city,* as exemplified by Frank Lloyd Wright's "Broadacre City" consists of individual houses, each on an acre of land (enough for crops), tied together by a vast network of superhighways studded with shopping centers. A modification of this idea is the *dispersed city with nodes;* the nodes would be centers of government, cultural activity, and luxury shopping. Los Angeles and cities of North America that developed after World War II approach a realization of this concept, except that little food is grown, and Wright's concept of independence for each family based upon productive use of the land has been lost. A cross between the core-city and dispersed city concept is Le Corbusier's

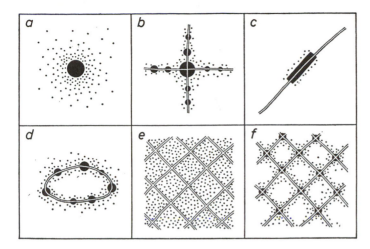

16.5 Six different city forms: (a) core city; (b) radial city; (c) linear city; (d) ring city; (e) dispersed city; (f) dispersed city with nodes.

"Radiant City"—a series of skyscrapers each separated by large areas of open space. In this way, high urban densities can be achieved while leaving most of the land open. Chandigarh in India is being built according to Le Corbusier's plans.

A major shortcoming of all of these plans is that they do not provide for changing needs and demands. Each is a static vision of the future and a blueprint for its achievement. There are no built-in mechanisms for flexibility. Present-day planning (*systems planning*) is much more concerned with identifying goals and devising alternate ways of reaching them. It attempts to monitor the complex interrelationships between social and physical aspects of urban existence, and modifies approaches as the stream of new information suggests or dictates. None of these aspects is simple. Goals are not easy to establish because there is a wide divergence as to what is and what is not desirable. Also different goals may not be compatible. For instance, placing a jetport close to the heart of a city is antithetical to attempts to reduce urban noise levels.

As a plan is implemented, unforeseen side effects may become apparent: for example, building highways to ease congestion may encourage greater use of the au-

tomobile at the expense of mass transit, thus increasing congestion and creating demands for yet more highways. External factors may intervene in the planning process: for instance, the growing energy crisis casts doubts upon the desirability of dispersed cities. In each case, values must be weighed and decisions arrived at through political or legal processes.

Land-Use Planning

A key part of urban and regional planning is deciding on how land is to be used. Most land use falls into the following categories; housing, industry, commerce, agriculture, institutions, transportation, conservation-recreation-open space, cultural and historic sites, and energy production and transmission. Decision-making should involve careful analysis of uses that are compatible both with the community goals and the natural environment. For example, high residential density is not compatible with aquifer recharge, heavy industry with recreation, floodplains with the construction of schools and hospitals. But floodplains are compatible with agriculture and aquifer recharge, steep slopes with forest or parkland, well-drained ground with the use of septic tanks. In this respect it is useful to define land capability and land suitability. *Land capability* refers to the capacity of the land to support particular uses in light of its natural properties: engineering properties of the soil, steepness of slope, earthquake hazard, and so forth. *Land suitability* refers to land capability, but also considers social and environmental factors and community objectives.

An eloquent exposition of how and why land capability and suitability should be made is presented by landscape architect and regional planner Ian McHarg in *Design with Nature* (1969). One of his case studies describes the process he used to choose a route for a proposed interstate highway (Richmond Parkway, Staten Island, N.Y.). McHarg's aim was to develop a route which would be minimally costly in social, ecologic, and economic terms. To do this he created a series of transparent overlay maps showing variations in slope; surface and subsurface drainage; foundation qualities; susceptibility to erosion and storm surge; historic, scenic, and recreation values; importance with respect to aquifer recharge; quality of the natural vegetation and wildlife habitat; and land and real estate values. On the maps, negative land suitability qualities are shown in dark tones, positive qualities in light tones. By superimposing the maps on each other and shining a light through them, the route with the fewest constraints becomes apparent: in McHarg's words, the "recommended minimum social-cost-alignment." Of course, such an analysis may still be considered arbitrary. Should a historic site, for example, preclude the choice of a particular area for high intensity use? What frequency of flooding is tolerable? In whose opinion is a landscape beautiful? But the value of a comprehensive approach is that at least questions are asked and data is amassed.

Psychologically, land-use proposals whose advantages can be stated quantitatively have a distinct edge over those whose values can only be suggested qualitatively. Suppose that a particular hill or river is threatened with destruction to make way for an industrial park or housing development, but objection is made on the grounds that the feature lends the area a unique scenic quality. The proponents can arm themselves with figures indicating the dollar value of increased tax revenues and employment opportunities, but the opponents may have to rely on the persuasive power of statements such as "I think it's very pretty," or "I enjoy going there to get away from it all."

In consequence, there have been attempts to quantify aesthetic, cultural, and recreational values; for example, geologist and conservationist Luna Leopold has quantitatively analyzed the social importance of Hells Canyon of the Snake River, which has been threatened by the possibility of a series of hydroelectric dams. Leopold assembled numerical data comparing the area with other canyons and rivers in the United States: dimensions of river and canyon, biologic and water-quality factors, and human use of the area. Thus, the uniqueness of Hells Canyon was demonstrated, allowing the cloak of rationality to adorn the decision-making process. *Landscape evaluation* is becoming of increasing interest to planners (see Mitchell, 1973; Robinson *et al.*, 1976; Litton *et al.*, 1974; Cooke and Doornkamp, 1974).

Once land-use decisions have been made, a map known as a *land-use master plan* may be drawn up (Fig. 16.6). Whether the plan is implemented depends upon many factors. In the United States, until recently, such plans have had no legal status. Land-use decisions traditionally have been implemented by city or county *zoning ordinances* that may be part of a comprehensive master plan or may lack any overall direction. Such ordinances designate how land may be used for residential, commercial, industrial, or agricultural development, and can spell out in greater detail, for example, building density, aspects of construction, or whether residences can be single- or multiple-family, attached or detached. It is important to note that zoning is not a policy in

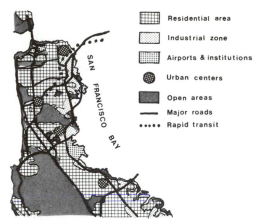

Residential area

Industrial zone

Airports & institutions

Urban centers

Open areas

Major roads

Rapid transit

16.6 Map of proposed major land uses and transportation facilities for the San Francisco region.

itself, but rather the legal tool by which overall land-use policy is enforced. Urbanization may also be governed by *subdivision regulations,* which prescribe such features as street improvement, lot size and layout, and procedures for setting land aside for public purposes. *Phased development ordinances* ensure that land development will take place only as adequate sewerage, drainage, parks, roads, water supply, and other community services become available in a community. Thus, it may be noted, allocating or withholding money for such community services is a powerful tool in controlling the pace of urbanization.

In close conjunction with the concept of phased development is proper *sequential use* of the land. For instance, proper sequential use of a parcel of land might be: (1) the quarrying of valuable minerals; (2) use of the exhausted quarry for land fill; (3) construction of buildings after the fill has subsided.

The power of local government to control urban growth is important within a democratic society. As indicated earlier, however, rational growth and planning must often be based upon natural regions that may cross the boundaries of small govern-

mental units. In Florida, Oregon, and California, it has now been decreed that local regulations and plans must be consistent with larger scale masterplans.

An alternate way to implement planning is to change the boundaries of local governmental units so that they are compatible with population distribution, communication and trade areas, and natural features. Such changes have occurred throughout history. Consider, for instance, the amalgamation of the five boroughs of New York City or the growth of Los Angeles described in Chapter 3. More recently, in 1953, to cope with an unprecedented population boom after World War II, the city of Toronto joined with twelve suburbs to become the Municipality of Metropolitan Toronto. London, England, has undergone a number of reorganizations to accommodate growth and to provide more responsive management and planning.

The development of environmental impact statements (EIS) as mandated by many state governments and the federal government for all significant federal projects (and in New York and California also mandated for private projects), conformity to the Water Pollution Control Amendments of 1972, the Safe Drinking Water Act of 1974, and the Clean Air Act of 1970 also help promote rational land use.

Environmental Impact Statements

The National Environmental Policy Act of 1969 and similar acts passed by state governments require the development of environmental impact statements for major governmental and many private projects. An EIS is a detailed assessment of the effect of a proposed development on the environment in terms of its ecological benefits and costs, and is separate from an analysis of monetary benefits and costs. A recommended sequence of steps to be followed in the development of an EIS is: (1) state major objective of the project; (2) analyze technological feasibility and alternate ways of achieving the objective; (3) describe the environment as it exists; and (4) assess the environmental impact of each of the proposed courses of action (Leopold *et al,* 1971). More specifically, the magnitude and importance of the impact must be determined. Magnitude of impact may be reduced to a more or less factual statement: "such and such will happen." Importance of impact is more judgmental, and refers to the consequences of changing one aspect of the environment upon other aspects of the environment. From this procedure should emerge a decision on a preferred course of action (Citizen's Advisory Committee on Environmental Quality, 1976).

ROLE OF GEOLOGY

Charles Yelverton, geologist of the Department of Building and Safety of Los Angeles states that "most master plans for cities have been devised for flat areas, with little or no attention paid to topographic diversity and the related problems of foundations, drainage, erosion, and utilities. . . ." (1971, p. 76). However, whether the presence of the earth is formally recognized in the planning and construction of cities, its presence will be felt—for better or for worse—in the resulting quality of the urban environment. Earth science information, therefore, should be made available and be made use of at all stages of urban development. If a new city is to be founded or an old city expanded, the geologic opportunities and constraints of proposed sites should be carefully evaluated. Questions regarding, for example, adequacy of water supply, waste disposal, the likelihood of natural hazards, or whether there is a better use for the land than urbanization, should be asked. Such questions should be asked *before* decisions are made. Once decisions are made, once construction has begun, it is exceedingly difficult to reverse or halt the flow of events. Thus, geologists should be involved in both the development of plans, the political and legal processes that control

decision-making, and the actual engineering and construction that create substance out of theory.

Effective communication between planners and geologists is of utmost importance. William Spangle and Associates, a group of city and regional planners who conducted an intensive study of the use of earth science information in land-use planning in the United States, found that "one of the more vexing obstacles to successful integration of earth science into land-use planning processes is the difficulty of achieving genuine communication between planners and earth scientists. The education and training of planners rarely includes basic background material from the earth sciences and . . . earth scientists, on the other hand, often find planning terminology confusing, partly because planners tend to use everyday words in specialized senses and partly because there is often lack of general agreement within the planning profession on the precise use of terms . . ." (1974, p. 9). Ideally, planners should have good backgrounds in earth science so that they can request and interpret appropriate geologic information, and geologists should be aware of the stages and complexities of the planning and implementation processes to assure that both plans and their achievement are compatible with the realities of the earth. Alternatively, geologists should learn how to present information in a form useful to planners, and planners should include a geologist as a member of the planning staff or consult regularly with outside geologists.

The consequences of the failure of scientists to communicate effectively with urban decision-makers is illustrated by the severity of landslide damage associated with the earthquake of 1964 in Anchorage, Alaska. "Information on the potential landslides that could occur on seismically unstable slopes, although presented in the technical reports, was not heeded in the planning and development of Anchorage. Some experts feel that if this information had been used to guide development, about $100 million of the $311 million loss could have been saved. . . .'' (Finger, 1971, p. 199).

The town of Portola Valley, California, south of San Francisco similarly faced with the threat of seismically triggered landslides successfully incorporated geologic factors into its planning program and zoning ordinances for a new residential development (Mader and Crowder, 1971). Under the plan, the spacing of houses was related to the average steepness of slope: the highest housing density reserved for flat land, the lowest for steep land. Also, wooded canyons and certain other areas were to remain undeveloped to protect slope stability and to retain their natural beauty. From topographic and geologic maps, an interpretive *relative stability map* was drawn up, indicating three main categories of land: stable, potentially moving, and moving (Fig. 16.7). Based on this information it was decided that house sites should be clustered together on the more stable ridge crests. Clustering allowed the number of housing sites to remain constant, and a decrease in the overall value of the land was avoided. No building was allowed within 100 feet of fault lines or near landslide scarps. The undeveloped land became open space shared by all. An earlier plan for the same area (Fig. 16.7), not based upon geologic information, proposed equal housing density over the entire area with little provision for open space. If it had been constructed, it is estimated that about 15 houses and several roads would have been damaged by earth movement every year. When urban development is adapted to the geologic environment by varying housing density and leaving hazardous areas as public open space, the geologic hazards ''may turn out to be assets to a community, because they can lead to diversity of landscape and variety in urban living. . . .'' (Mader and Crowder, 1971, p. 189).

A major problem preventing adequate use of geology in urban and regional planning is lack of sufficient information in the detail necessary for certain phases. Topographic maps at a scale of 1:24,000 are becoming the standard base for urban-planning activities throughout the United States, and thus are also the most appropriate base for general geologic mapping of urban areas. However, for some purposes, maps at a larger scale are necessary. Where landslides are common, maps at a scale of 1:4800 are needed. Detailed investigation for individual hillside subdivisions may require maps at a scale of 1:1200 to 1:480 (McGill, 1964).

Some cities, including Seattle, Omaha, Hartford, Anchorage, Salt Lake City, Denver, Boston, Los Angeles and San Francisco have benefited from mapping done by the U.S. Geological Survey (USGS). In the San Francisco Bay area, the Department of Housing and Urban Development (HUD) has joined with the USGS in a comprehensive study of the region. However, much more basic data is needed in these and other urban areas. In the area covered by the Metropolitan Washington Council of Governments, sound basic data is lacking on such natural features as topography, climate, groundwater recharge areas, and gravel resources (Spangle *et al,* 1974). Even the San Francisco Association of Bay Area Governments (ABAG) finds lack of data a problem. Hazard information is often presented at a regional scale (1:250,000) but decisions regarding land use are made at local levels. However, ABAG does regard the small-scale maps as useful in its regional planning and for alerting the public and their representatives to geologic hazards. The Northeastern Illinois Planning Commission, which focuses on metropolitan Chicago, also feels that its effectiveness has been limited by lack of data. On the other hand, the Southeastern Wisconsin Regional Planning Commission, which includes the Milwaukee, Racine, and Kenosha metropolitan areas, considers its efforts a success, attributable in part to ''the meticulous attention paid to the need for accurate data available at a large scale and suitable for use at the local as well as regional level. In addition the data is well integrated into all

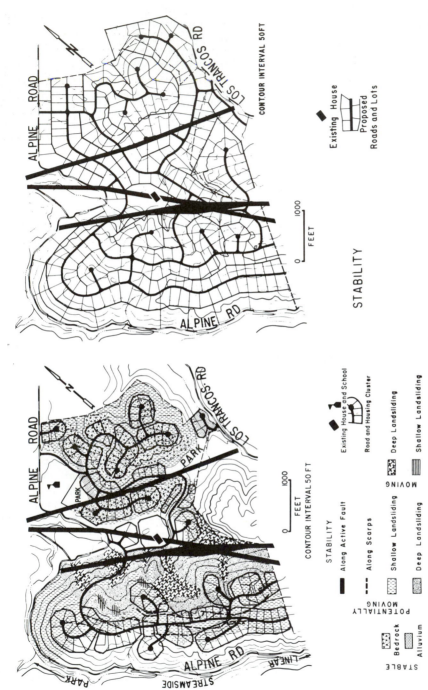

16.7 Two maps of the Bovet properties showing proposed development. (left) stability map, with houses clustered on ridges to avoid major unstable areas (1969). (right) earlier plan (1959) with about 15 houses and several roads on unstable land subject to frequent (yearly) movement.

phases of the planning process . . .'' (Spangle *et al,* 1974, p. 259).

The problem of interdisciplinary communication is aggravated by the difficulty of locating earth science information that already exists. In the United States, such information is generated by 14 federal agencies, hundreds of state, county, and city agencies, as well as by a host of private organizations. An urgent need exists for coordination of the work and for clearing houses that can simplify the task of obtaining data for a specific area. One example of an attempt to solve this problem is the *Urban Geology Master Plan for California,* prepared by the California Division of Mines and Geology, which identifies governmental and private sources of earth science information for urbanized and urbanizing areas within the state.

Two other major problems inhibiting proper use of geologic information are (1) lack of sufficient public funds to acquire open space in order to prevent its development, and (2) lack of power to implement good master plans where they exist. In the Washington, D.C. area for example, *The Year 2000 Plan* (1958), envisions outward radial growth along major transportation arteries, with wedges of open land left between the arms of the urban ''star.'' However, even though the natural features have been surveyed, inadequate funding for the open-space aquisition program and the powerlessness of the Metropolitan Washington Council of Governments to implement land-use regulations have been significant factors in allowing development to proceed in areas of aquifer recharge, expansive soils, landslides, shallow bedrock, and gravel resources. Only floodplains and slopes over 15 percent are hoped to be withheld from development.

REGIONAL PLANNING—SAN FRANCISCO

Regional planning in the San Francisco Bay area is directed by The Association of Bay Area Governments, a voluntary organization whose membership consists of the nine counties and 85 cities, covering 7000 square miles, geographically centered about San Francisco Bay. ABAG was created in 1961 ''in recognition of the fact that the physical, economic, and social well being of the entire region requires continuing, area-wide cooperation and coordination of policies, plans, and services. . . .'' (ABAG, 1966, p. 2). In developing a regional plan for the period 1970–90, ABAG strove to (1) understand the physical setting of the area; (2) postulate future population and economic growth; (3) define regional issues, goals, and policies; (4) develop an accurate picture of existing land use and current city and county zoning ordinances; (5) generate a series of possible future growth alternatives and (6) indicate the preferred direction of future growth.

The Physical Setting The complex topography and geology of the Bay Area is suggested by Figures 16.8 and 16.9. San Francisco Bay itself is generally shallow (mostly less than 18 feet deep), but contains a series of natural and artificial channels which, with regular dredging, are deep enough for ocean-going vessels. Thus, the Bay contains a number of important port facilities. Tidal flushing, together with the water brought to the Bay by the Sacramento River and other local streams help to dissipate municipal, industrial, and agricultural wastes. A flat fertile plain, underlain by considerable thicknesses of sediments, surrounds much of the Bay and extends northwest and southeast from it as a series of elogated valleys sandwiched between parallel segments of the Coast Ranges. This plain has been the site of most of the region's urban development, which has spread over its prime agricultural land. An important tideland or marshland area forms the boundary between the plain and the Bay. The marshes are underlain by hundreds of feet of water-saturated sediment which make it difficult to reclaim safely (by artificial fill) for building.

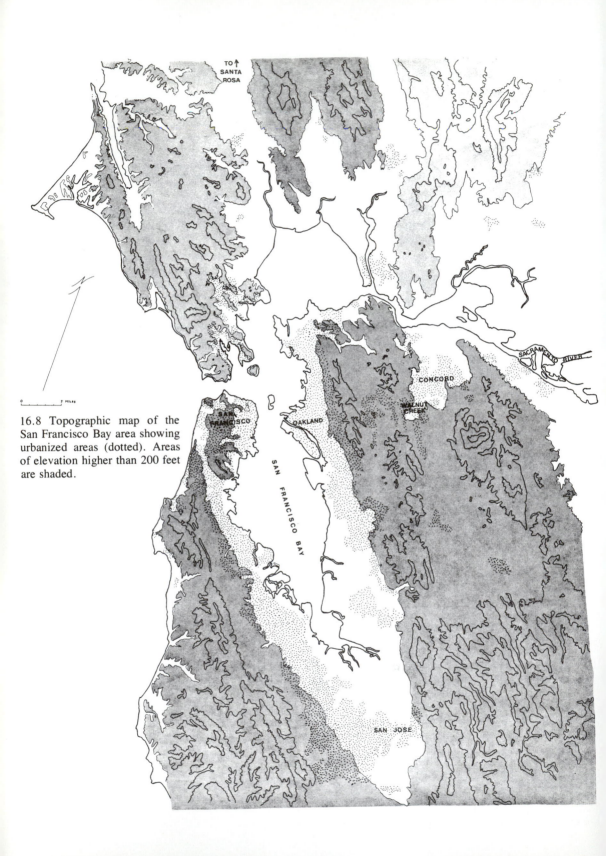

16.8 Topographic map of the San Francisco Bay area showing urbanized areas (dotted). Areas of elevation higher than 200 feet are shaded.

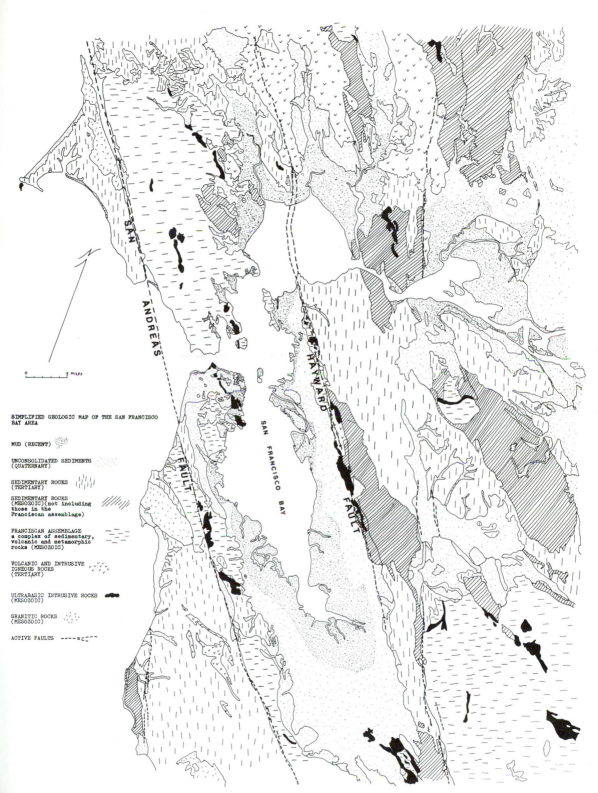

6.9 Simplified geologic map of the San Francisco Bay area.

During an earthquake, such reclaimed marshland is highly susceptible to liquefaction. Nevertheless, extensive building has taken place on reclaimed land and has helped reduce the area of the Bay from 680 square miles in the days of the Gold Rush to 400 square miles today. The coast ranges form a series of parallel, elongated, northwest-southeast trending ridges which in places attain elevations of over 5000 feet. The mountains and associated valleys provide natural northwest-southeast transportation routes, but at the same time form an almost continuous barrier to east-west travel, and separate the Bay region from the interior Central Valley. Where breaks (passes) do exist in the mountain barrier, transportation routes have been established. These routes have, in turn, influenced the location of urban centers. The steepness of the mountain slopes and the nature of the rocks of which they are composed make them extremely vulnerable to landslide. This tendency has been aggravated where vegetation has been destroyed and where slopes have been steepened and artificial fills created for construction. Flooding is common along the streams that flow down the mountains toward the Pacific. Two major, active fault zones (the San Andreas and the Hayward) run through the area, and catastrophic earthquakes and associated landsliding, liquefaction around the Bay margin, and tsunami flooding are likely to occur periodically. All in all it becomes clear that the diverse physical setting of the Bay area should play an important role in determining the pattern of urbanization and land use. However, as population and economic growth continue, there is great pressure to utilize physically unsafe or unsuitable areas. It is estimated that the population of the Bay area will increase from about 6 million in 1980 to about 7.2 million by 1990, and that the economy of the region will be such that growth will take place by expansion of urban centers at the expense of less-intensive land use, such as agriculture, mineral exploitation, and open space.

Land-Use and Zoning Existing land use and regulations governing land use are bound to play a major role in determining the form future development will take. Today's land-use patterns (Fig. 16.8) are strongly influenced by the region's main physical characteristics. Two major urban cores border the Bay: San Francisco-Oakland and San Jose. Suburban corridors spread out between and beyond these cores. The suburbs almost completely encircle the Bay, extend along the lengths of the valleys, penetrate the passes through the mountains, and culminate in two outlying cores: Santa Rosa and the Walnut Creek-Concord area. For the most part, high-density residential development has been concentrated next to major employment centers located on flat or nearly flat land and close to the major transportation facilities. In turn, their location has been determined largely by the topography. Open space consists of flat, cultivated agricultural land; grazing areas on hilly or gently rolling slopes; woods in hilly regions; evaporation ponds around the edge of the Bay (for the extraction of salts from sea water); and minor, scattered park and recreation lands.

Zoning in the Bay region is a complex and often conflicting assemblage of regulations that reflect the multiplicity of city and county jurisdictions in the area. Since zoning is a primary method of achieving land-use objectives, the development of a long-range, comprehensive regional plan to which local zoning ordinances can adhere becomes of paramount importance.

Growth Alternatives

Four alternative growth schemes are described by ABAG. Under the *Composite Plan,* development will take place according to local ordinances, with no adherence to a regional plan. The strength of the plan

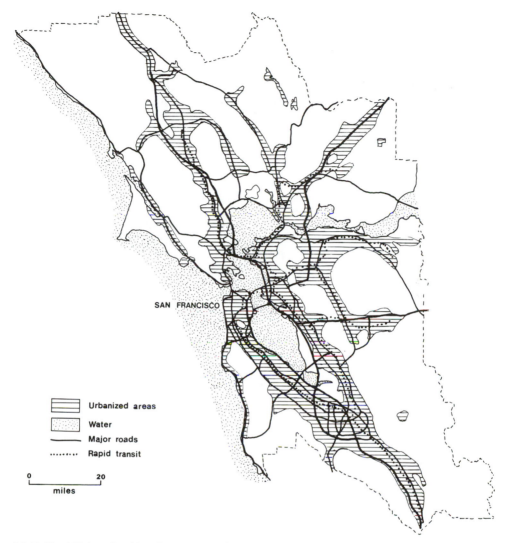

16.10 The "Urban Corridor Concept" for future urbanization of the
San Francisco Bay area.

is that it provides a strong sense of local involvement and identity. However, the lack of regional planning would produce a degree of economic stress and inadequate protection for natural resources and open space.

The *Urban Corridor Concept* (a linear, or ring city, plan) relates future land-use to the region's existing and proposed major transportation corridors (Fig. 16.10). New development is concentrated on flat valley floors and confined to narrow bands bordering superhighways and railroads. The trend toward urban sprawl is reduced and central cities develop higher population densities. Open space is preserved between urban cor-

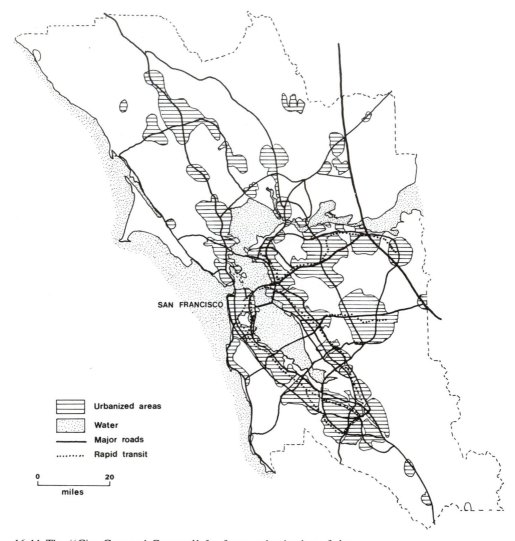

16.11 The "City Centered Concept" for future urbanization of the
San Francisco Bay area.

ridors, making rational use of the region's
long, narrow valleys and steep mountain
ridges. The concept makes more feasible
the development of a high-volume rapid
transit system. A strong identifiable regional
image, well-suited to the topography would
emerge. However, the sense of local identity might diminish as centers give way to
corridors. Substantial public investment is

required to construct the transportation facilities and to acquire or preserve the open
spaces between the corridors.

The *City Centered Concept* (a core-city
plan) envisions a series of densely settled,
specialized urban centers, ranging from
large metropolitan cores to small cities, separated by permanent open spaces and tied
together by road and rail networks (Fig.

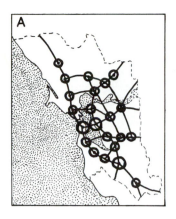
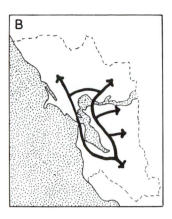

16.12 The approved plan for the urbanization of the San Francisco Bay region. (A) Schematic design of proposed urban centers and major metropolitan transportation corridors. (B) The general growth corridors.

16.11). The boundary between urban and rural areas is relatively sharp. Employment and commerce are concentrated in fewer but larger centers within planned urban areas. The economy and location of each planned city are carefully geared to the physical characteristics of the region. Cities will be self-contained and will foster feelings of community identity.

The last concept is that of *Suburban Dispersion* (a dispersed city plan), which pictures low-density development with an indefinite relationship between place of residence and place of work. Little reliance is placed on rail transit; an extensive highway network would be required. The preservation of open space is not a major factor in shaping the form of the region. Consumption of agricultural land for urbanization is maximal. Minimal planning and minimal changes in governmental structure will be required. The region develops an appearance of total urbanization. The Suburban Dispersion concept strongly resembles the Composite Plan and could represent the future if little or no regional planning is undertaken.

The 1970:1990 Regional Plan

The approved plan focuses on the City Centered Concept under which future urban growth through 1990 and beyond is accom-

modated within existing or new urban communities that are organized into a system that is in harmony with open space areas and nature (Fig. 16.12). The urban centers occupy "general growth corridors" that have a rational relationship to the physical characteristics of the region. Cities will be tied together by a multiple-mode transportation system (road, rail, water, and air; rapid and mass transit systems) designed to reduce reliance on the automobile. Careful attention is paid to water supply and conservation; disposal of sewage and solid wastes; reducing air and water pollution; and minimizing geologic hazards and soil erosion. To deal with these problems, a special three-year study entitled *The San Francisco Bay Region Environment and Resources Planning Study,* conducted jointly by the USGS and the U.S. Department of Housing and Urban Development, was made to evaluate the natural physical features, resources, and processes of the area in order to provide planners with the necessary earth science information.

Implementation of the Plan would be most easily achieved if a limited-function regional government vested with powers necessary for its realization could be established. Failing that, ABAG already has a powerful tool in its federal project review program. Since 1966, the association has reviewed applications made by local gov-

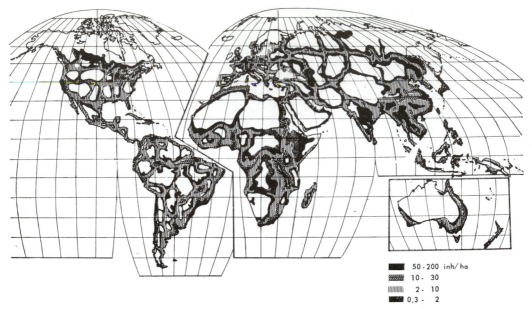

▰	50 - 200 inh/ ha
▨	10 - 30
▥	2 - 10
▰	0,3 - 2

16.13 World map showing estimated population density (inhabitants per hectare) by the end of the twenty-first century. The shaded areas constitute Doxiadis' *ecumenopolis* (worldwide city).

ernments for federal grants-in-aid for such projects as acquisition of open space, water development, and land conservation. The power to grant aid rests with the federal government, but the review program plays an important role in shaping federal decisions. ABAG also plays a major role in stimulating awareness of the benefits of regional cooperation and developing ways to foster such cooperation.

VISIONS OF THE FUTURE

That a battle against urban sprawl has been engaged is manifest in the rejection, by almost all professional planners, of the dispersed city concept, which would result in an earth randomly blotched by undistinguished, inefficient, energy- and land-consuming housing developments. Nevertheless, whether through urban sprawl or expanding networks of linear, ring, or core cities, the rising tide of humanity seems to

be on its way toward creating *ecumenopolis*. This universal city, as envisioned by Constantinos Doxiadis, an internationally recognized authority on town planning, will cover as much of the earth as can be built on, leaving only those scattered patches of farmland, forest, desert, and mountain that are necessary for human sustenance or whose environments are unacceptably hostile for human settlement (Fig. 16.13). As the numbers of humans continue to increase, the pressure to expand ecumenopolis into the remaining non-urbanized areas will grow until all "frivolous" uses of the land such as wilderness or parks are dispensed with, and the attempt is made to conquer and tame the remaining dangerous and inhospitable regions.

A number of ways in which this bleak future may be postponed or avoided have been proposed. Foremost among them is the control of human fertility. If the desirability of establishing population stability were universally accepted and the necessary measures immediately implemented, the world's population would still more than double to almost ten billion before leveling off. If, however, as is much more likely, delays of several decades occur in the starting of an effective equilibrium policy, within less than a century the number of people on earth might approach 20 billion. Assuming the problems of feeding such numbers of people were solved, accommodating them in conventional urban structures would more than exhaust the supply of habitable land. Moreover, the inordinate amount of energy and space that would have to be devoted to the movement of people and goods within ecumenopolis would be prohibitive. (Two-thirds of downtown Los Angeles is devoted to streets, freeways, and parking.) Thus, it seems likely that attempts to curb population growth will have to be accompanied by the development of unconventional urban structures.

Perhaps the most interesting proposals for unconventional urban structures are those that suggest the expansion of cities upward rather than outward. Planning experts G. B. Dantzig and T. L. Saaty's Compact City, designed to hold 2 million people, would consist of a huge shell 500 feet high that would enclose an area of about nine square miles. Within this climatically controlled enclosure, houses with gardens, apartments, shopping centers, office blocks, light industry, and plazas would occupy 16 levels, each 30 feet or more high. Horizontal and vertical movement would be accomplished by the use of walkways, bikeways, ramps, stairs, escalators, elevators, trams, and electric automobiles. Gardens on the roof of the shell could be reached from anywhere inside the city within one minute. The countryside could be reached by a maximum of 10 minutes' travel. To house an equivalent number of people in a conventional city would require an area of 178 square miles; that is, the conventional city would use up almost 20 times as much land. Moreover, the density of Compact City, in terms of the number of people per square mile of horizontal floor space would be much less than that of many conventional cities. Each family would have more usable living space. Also, the cost of building would be 25 percent less than that required for comparable conventional cities, and the amount of energy consumed by its population would be 15 percent lower. To curtail the increase in urban sprawl in the United States due to the expected population increase by 1995 would require the building of 15–25 Compact Cities, each at a cost of about $36 billion. Since hundreds of billions of dollars will have to be spent anyway on urban expansion, Dantzig and Saaty pose the question: why not spend the money on innovative, efficient and less costly Compact Cities?

A slightly earlier proponent of vertical cities is architect Paolo Soleri, whose proposals are part of his total philosophy on the long-term evolution of humans: a philosophy with a geologic perspective (1969; 1973). Soleri says if the quality of life is to improve and if humankind is to progress toward the spiritual sphere which is its proper evolutionary goal, human existence must become richer in its complexity, not complicatedness. Richness of complexity, in turn, depends upon miniaturization. The most obvious example is the way in which the enormous yet relatively limited computers of the 1950s have been replaced by the smaller, much more sophisticated computers of today. Likewise, the "flat gigantism" of our "pancake" cities, with all of their attendant ecologic and social evils, must be replaced by compact three-dimensional cities (Fig. 16.14). Soleri envisions today's urban areas with their noise, pollution, confusion, and inhumanity being replaced by "arcologies": bold one-structure cities that define a new cityscape in which are organized "the private and public institutions that go into making any urban center worthy of the term . . ." (1973, p. 46) and in which there is a new and more direct relation between urban and country life.

Arcologies emphasize the vertical dimen-

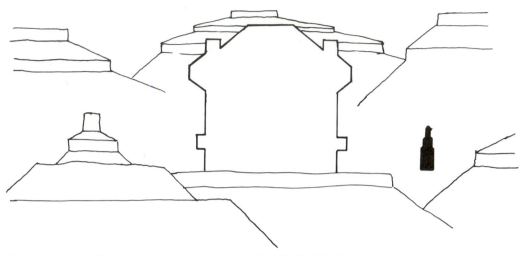

16.14 Sketch of a Soleri-type desert-country "arcology." The black building represents a conventional, 1000-foot-high skyscraper, shown for scale.

sion and exclude automobiles. (The ratio of height to breadth in a Compact City is about 1:35, in an arcology, about 1:2). Thus, compared to an arcology, Compact City is still somewhat of a "pancake" requiring roads and rail service. In an arcology, expenditures on goods, energy, waste disposal, maintenance, policing, and fire prevention could be drastically reduced. With no roads or railways, air quality would be good and the amount of usable space increased. Elevators and walkways would provide means of transport. Humans would be relieved of economic and environmental burdens and given the opportunity for a more creative and promising life. As in Compact City, people would be "constantly at the threshold between the city and countryside and [would] have the best of both . . ." (1973, p. 138).

The word *Arcology* itself is meant to suggest the proper dependence of architecture upon ecology. "That which does not belong to what surrounds it is lost to it . . ." (1973, p. 165). The design of each arcology varies according to the climate, topography, and geology of the area in which it is to be situated. Thus, for instance, cities in the desert should be like the cactus: dense, three-dimensional. Soleri, in *Arcology: The City in the Image of Man* illustrates arcologies appropriate for the open sea (floating arcologies), coastal regions, hills, plains, deserts, cold regions; arcologies that sit on dam sites, span ravines and canyons, occupy quarries, nestle against cliffs, rise from mesas; arcologies that orbit in space. In short, man must seek "the geology on which to root the structure of his universe. He must, not just metaphorically, become ecologically conscious and earthly relevant . . ." (1973, p. 181). The actual construction of an arcology, called "Arcosanti," has been underway in Arizona for several years.

Evaluation of proposals for Compact Cities or Arcologies or other visions of the urban future (Dahinden, 1972) is best accomplished if the philosophic attitudes of their proponents are separated from the technical, political, and sociologic fesibility of such cities. One may reject Soleri's view of the goal of human evolution and yet accept the idea of arcologies, or vice versa.

Dantzig and Saaty, forseeing objections to the absence of natural climate and vegetation within Compact City state that "plants need to be trimmed, watered, and weeded; and in the winter outdoor yards are bleak; at night and during hot summers outdoor areas may not be hospitable. . . ." (1973, p. 161). Yet trimming, watering and weeding plants is a source of great satisfaction for many people; the clamor or quiet of hot, perfumed summer nights may be the stuff of magic; and daily encounter with the at times harsh vagaries of the weather and the inexorable flux of the seasons may be invaluable contacts with and reminders of forces older and more powerful than humans. Soleri asserts that we must bid farewell to the romantic notion that "man and soil (man and asphalt really) must mingle in an inexhaustible embrace . . ." (1973, p. 204). But embracing the soil may be a psychological necessity rather than a romantic frivolity.

On the other hand, the rationality of three-dimensional cities cannot be denied. Clearly, such proposals warrant serious consideration, especially since the increasingly evident shortcomings of conventional alternatives become frightening if extropolated into the not very distant future.

If compact three-dimensional cities are to be constructed, capitalizing upon geologic opportunities and avoiding geologic hazards will become ever more important. Foundations of structures hundreds or thousands of feet high in which millions of people live and work must be of unquestionable stability. Only those areas of least susceptibility to seismic disturbance, volcanic eruption, or tsunami inundation should be considered. Dantzig and Saaty say that there is enough space in the 4000 square miles of San Diego County, California, to house 80 million people in 40 Compact Cities spaced 10 miles apart (1973, p. 174). But their statement reveals a disturbing disregard for the region's potential for catastrophic earthquakes. Furthermore, the problem of supplying water for close to 100 times the present population of an area that already must import almost all of its water is not even mentioned. Cities that are to float on the seas or be anchored to the sea floor (as have been proposed to ease congestion in Japan and Hawaii) should be restricted to seismically stable areas topographically protected from storm surges and tsunamis. Before large cities are built in arctic or antarctic regions, foundation problems and problems of water supply and waste disposal must be solved. The dangers of monolithic uniformity and loss of identity and orientation within one-structure cities must be avoided through appropriate design, perhaps incorporating or mimicking natural landforms, processes and materials within the body of the structure.

If cities of the future, whether conventional or fantastic, are to succeed they must, from conception to completion, be permeated and governed by a sense of the earth. Responsibility toward and appreciation of the earth become, ultimately, responsibility toward and appreciation of oneself and of humanity.

Glossary

abutment a mass of stone, concrete or masonry placed so as to counteract the lateral thrust of a bridge span or of a vault or an arch.

acre-foot the amount of water required to cover an area of land to a depth of one foot. Equivalent to 43,560 cubic feet, 1233 cubic meters, or 325,829 gallons.

adobe clayey and silty deposits used for making sun-dried bricks.

accelograph (strong motion accelograph) a device for recording the acceleration in velocity of earthquake vibrations.

acid mine drainage ground water or surface water that encounters sulfur-rich ores in mines or that filters through sulfur-rich waste piles and becomes highly acidic.

aeolian refers to the erosional, transportational, and depositional activities of the wind.

aftershock an earthquake of lesser magnitude that follows shortly upon and is genetically related to a larger earthquake that preceded it.

alluvial having to do with streams.

alluvial fan fan-shaped accumulation of sediment formed along a mountain front where a stream (typically intermittent) dumps sediment as it leaves the mountains and enters a flat plain; sediment deposition is caused by the reduction in water velocity.

alluvium stream-deposited sediment.

anticline an up-arched fold.

aqueduct an artificial channel or conduit for conveying water.

arable land which may be farmed by methods employing plowing.

assured capability the amount of water that may at all times be depended upon for withdrawal from a water-supply system.

basement rock (basement complex) the igneous-metamorphic rock complex that constitutes most of the crust of the earth and that at some depth underlies sediment and sedimentary rock.

bedding planes the planes that separate layers within a sequence of sedimentary or other stratified rocks.

bedrock any solid rock underlying soil or sediment.

boulder clay an unstratified, unsorted deposit of silt and clay in which are embedded particles ranging in size from sand to boulders; till.

brackish water slightly salty water.

breeder reactor a nuclear reactor that can create fissionable fuel, especially those reactors that create more fissionable fuel than they consume.

brine highly salty water.

brownstone a dark-brown sandstone, popular in the nineteenth century for building; most commonly obtained from Triassic deposits of the Connecticut River Valley.

building code a set of rules governing the construction, alteration, equipment, use, occupancy, location, maintenance, moving, and demolition of buildings.

cesspool a cavity in the ground, usually covered, into which drain household or stable wastes. The liquid usually escapes through an overflow pipe; solids are removed periodically by pumping or other means of extraction.

cistern   a water tank.

cleavage   the tendency of many minerals and some rocks to break along one or more sets of parallel planes.

coastal plain   flat areas that slope gently down to the coast, underlain by gently inclined sedimentary layers.

composting   creating, out of organic wastes, a mixture designed to act as a plant fertilizer or soil conditioner.

compound   a substance in which the chemical elements always occur in fixed proportions.

continental shelf   shallow, gently inclined part of the sea floor adjacent to the coast; a water-covered continuation of the coastal plain.

crystalline rocks   coarse-grained igneous and metamorphic rocks with granular textures.

cubit   a measure of length, roughly 18–22 inches.

differential erosion   the more rapid erosion of one part of the earth's surface as compared with another part.

dip   the acute angle an inclined plane makes with the horizontal.

drift   any rock material transported by a glacier and deposited directly by melting ice or by glacial meltwaters.

ecology   the branch of biology that considers the relationships between living organisms and their environment.

effluent   material that issues forth from an opening, such as sewage from a pipe or water from the ground.

element   a substance all of whose atoms have the same atomic number.

epoch   subdivision of a geologic period, the third largest division of the geologic time-scale.

era   the largest division of the geologic time-scale, defined on the basis of the type of fossil life found in the rocks that formed during the time-span in question.

estuary   the portion of a stream affected by oceanic tides; it contains a mixture of fresh and salt water.

evapotranspiration   the return of water to the atmosphere from the earth's surface by evaporation and transpiration. Transpiration is the process by which water escapes from a living plant and enters the atmosphere.

expansive soil   clay or shale that expands when wet and shrinks when dry.

fault   a fracture in the earth's brittle outer shell along which significant movement has taken place parallel to the fracture.

Fertile Crescent   a relatively well-watered semi-circular strip of land in the Middle East.

fission   the splitting of atomic nuclei and the accompanying release of energy.

floodplain   flat areas adjacent to a stream that are covered by water in times of flood.

foliation   rock layering developed during metamorphism.

footing   a projecting layer of stone, concrete, or masonry at the foot of a wall that transfers the weight of the wall to the ground.

formation (geologic formation)   an assemblage of rocks that have some character in common, such as origin, age or composition; the ordinary unit of geologic mapping.

fossil   remains or traces of prehistoric animal or plant life that have been preserved within rocks.

fossil fuels   fuels such as coal, oil, and natural gas that have formed through the alteration and decomposition of the remains of prehistoric living organisms.

geologic map   a map showing the distribution of the rocky materials of the earth's surface as they would appear if all obscuring non-rock substances were removed.

geothermal   refers to heat that exists within the earth.

glacial age   a time during which glacial ice covers relatively large portions of the land surface of the earth.

glacial debris   sediment transported and deposited by glacial ice or of predominantly glacial origin.

glacier   a thick mass of moving ice that flows generally downhill or outward away from a center of greatest thickness.

glaciofluviatile   pertaining to streams whose waters are derived principally from the melting of glacial ice, or to deposits made by such streams.

glowing avalanche   an incandescent mixture of hot gases and solids expelled during a volcanic eruption.

groundwater system   the complex network of water that exists in interconnected crevices, pore-spaces, and other openings underground, in the zone of saturation.

Gulf Stream   the Atlantic Ocean current that moves from the Gulf of Mexico toward Britain and Scandinavia, bringing with it the vast amounts of heat that make the climate of much of Northern Europe fairly moderate.

habitat   the environment in which the life needs of a particular plant or animal are met.

hardpan a hard, impervious layer of clay cemented by insoluble materials, that may require explosives to be shattered.

hogback a sharp-crested ridge formed by the more rapid erosion of layers adjacent to a steeply dipping bed.

hydraulic earthfill artificial accumulations of water-transported sediment that compacts as it dries.

hydrofracturing the fracturing of water underground by the forcible injection of fluids under high pressure.

hydrology the science that studies the surface and near-surface waters of the earth.

hydrostatic pressure pressure due to the weight of overlying water; more generally, pressure upon a point that is of equal magnitude from all directions.

Ice Age the Pleistocene epoch; the time during which great masses of glacial ice frequently covered large portions of the land surface of the earth, from about 2 million years ago to about 10,000 years ago.

ice cap a large glacier which flows radially outward from a center. An example is the ice cap that covers a large part of Greenland.

igneous rock rock formed through the solidification of molten rock.

isostasy the theory that the earth's crust "floats" on denser mantle rock material underneath and seeks an equilibrium, achieved through vertical movement of crustal segments, such that areas of the earth's surface underlain by dense or thin crust have lower elevations than areas underlain by less-dense or thick crust.

joints fractures in rocks, often occurring in parallel sets.

kerogen a solid, bituminous material formed from plant remains that is found in so-called oil-shale. When heated, kerogen yields a substitute crude oil similar to petroleum.

leach field a volume of soil or sediment, ideally within the zone of aeration, through which the effluent from a septic tank migrates and becomes partially or completely purified.

liquefaction the process whereby particles of sediment within water-saturated sand or silt are shaken into suspension, so that the entire mass temporarily loses its strength and enters a fluid-like state.

lithospheric plate a huge fragment of the earth's brittle outermost shell; slowly moves with respect to other plates; can be larger than a whole continent.

littoral drift the movement of sediment along the coast, within the littoral zone, due to the influence of waves and currents.

littoral zone the near-shore oceanic zone that lies between the limits of high and low tides.

magma molten rock that exists under the earth's surface, within the crust or mantle; does *not* refer to molten parts of the earth's core.

mangrove swamp a coastal marsh with abundant mangrove trees. Mangrove trees spread by means of aerial roots.

megalithic man prehistoric men who erected large, stone monuments, such as those at Carnac, Stonehenge, or Avebury.

megawatt one million watts. A watt is a unit of power equivalent to 14.34 calories per minute. A calorie is the amount of energy necessary to raise one gram of water one degree centigrade.

mesa a flat-topped hill or mountain bounded on one or more sides by steep cliffs.

metamorphic rock rock altered (but not melted) by high temperatures and/or pressures.

mid-oceanic ridge one of the linear, volcanic mountain ranges that rise from the floors of the oceans and which may extend for thousands of miles.

milling reducing rock to small particles by grinding or crushing.

minerals natural, inorganic compounds which in combination form rocks.

moraine a landform composed of glacially deposited sediment.

muskeg poorly drained, water-saturated areas of the north-central United States, Canada and Alaska, characterized by a semifloating mass of partially decayed vegetation.

Neolithic the New Stone Age, a stage in cultural evolution, lasting from about 10,000 to 5000 years ago in most places. Characterized by the use of ground and polished stone tools. Succeeded by the Age of Metals.

nodule a rounded, hard body within a rock that can be separated from the matrix in which it occurs. Examples are the flint bodies that occur in many chalks or other types of limestone.

non-renewable resource a resource that is regenerated so slowly that once used, it is not made available again within a time span useful to humans.

oceanic trench a very deep, elongate basin in the ocean floor that may attain a depth greater than twice the average depth of the ocean.

oil shale shale containing a solid, bituminous material (kerogen) which, upon heating, yields a substitute crude oil that may be refined and treated like petroleum.

orthogonal grid   in the context of this book, a street system composed of two mutually perpendicular sets of parallel streets.

outcrop   where bedrock is exposed at the earth's surface.

outwash plain   a flat plain formed peripheral to a glacier through the deposition of sediment by meltwater streams.

Paleolithic   the Old Stone Age, a stage in cultural evolution lasting from about 2 million to 10,000 years ago. Characterized by the production and use of chipped stone tools.

peat   partially decomposed plant material that accumulates in marshes and swamps. When dried, may be burned as a fuel.

percolation   the complex movement of a fluid through openings in rocks or sediment.

period   the second largest division of the geologic time-scale, defined as the time-span during which a particular aggregate of rock strata were deposited.

permafrost   permanently frozen ground.

permeability   a measure of the ease with which a fluid can flow through the open spaces within a solid such as rock or sediment.

pier   (1) vertical column that supports the span of a bridge or the weight of a building. (2) a structure built out into the sea.

pile   a strong vertical stake driven into the ground or bed of a river, etc., designed to support a building, bridge, or other structure.

plastic flow   the permanent deformation, without rupture (breaking), of a solid body subjected to a continuous force.

plate   see **lithospheric plate.**

Pleistocene   see the **Ice Age.**

plunging folds   rock folds whose axes are not horizontal.

porosity   measure of the volume of openings within the interior of a rock or mass of sediment compared to the total volume of the rock or sediment.

porphyry   an igneous rock with two distinct grain sizes: large phenocrysts in a finer matrix. Named according to matrix rock type; *e.g.*, granite porphyry, basalt porphyry.

precipitation   (1) any form of water, whether liquid or solid, that falls to the ground from the air: rain, snow, hail, sleet, drizzle. etc. (2) the deposition or crystallization of solids from a solution.

privy   a toilet. Often located in a small separate building set apart from living quarters.

pyroclastic   solid rock fragments expelled during volcanic eruptions.

radioactivity   the property shown by some chemical elements of changing spontaneously into other chemical elements by the emission of charged particles or rays from their nuclei.

Randstadt Holland   the complex "Ring City" of Holland composed of the major conurbations grouped around the cities of Rotterdam, The Hague, Amsterdam, and Utrecht.

raw sewage untreated sewage.

recurrence interval   the average length of time that elapses between successive events of magnitude equal to or greater than a stated value; *e.g.*, the average interval of time between floods of a certain magnitude.

recycling   the reuse of valuable materials reclaimed from wastes.

remote sensing   gaining information about something without coming into physical contact with it, through the use of recording instruments such as cameras, thermal infra-red devices, or radar.

renewable resource   a resource naturally or artificially regenerated within a short enough time to be useful to humans.

resonance   the increase in amplitude of vibration of a system when it is subjected to a stimulus of approximately the same frequency as its own natural frequency of vibration.

rift valley   an elongate depression formed by the downdropping of part of the earth's surface along two generally parallel faults.

rift zone (volcanic)   a narrow zone of fissures that extends down the flanks of a volcano. From these fissures, lava and pyroclastics may be erupted.

Sahel   the area characterized by grasslands with scattered trees and bushes located between the southern border of the Sahara and the forests of tropical Africa.

salt dome   a mass of salt (halite) that deforms plastically and migrates upward to form a vertical, cylindrically-shaped intrusive body that pierces overlying sedimentary layers. Oil and gas deposits often occur in the rocks that abut the flanks of the dome.

sand dune   a wind-deposited ridge or mound of sand.

scree   coarse rock debris on the sides or at the

base of a mountain slope or cliff. Approximately synonymous with "talus."

sediment loose rock fragments deposited by wind, water, glacial ice, or other agents of transport; also, salts precipitated from oceans or lakes.

sedimentary rock rock formed through the binding together of sediment by cementation, compaction, dehydration.

seismic pertaining to earth vibrations, usually those caused by earthquakes.

sewage sludge the solids that remain after wastes have undergone sewage treatment.

soft water water containing little or no dissolved calcium or magnesium salts. Relatively slow to leave a deposit in a kettle; soap lathers easily in it. The opposite of "hard water."

sorting a process whereby particles are separated according to size, shape, or density.

spring a place where a current of water issues naturally from rock or soil, either onto the surface of the land or into the bed of a stream, lake or ocean.

striations generally parallel scratches on glaciated rock surfaces, formed by the gouging action of rock fragments embedded in moving ice.

strike the compass direction or trend of a horizontal, linear feature.

strip mining mining coal or other materials from a shallow underground bed or seam by cutting and filling of parallel trenches.

structural basin a roughly circular, concave configuration of rock layers. There may or may not be a corresponding depression on the earth's surface.

syncline a down-arched or concave upward fold.

tar sands sands or sandstones in which the pore spaces between the sand grains are wholly or in part filled by a dense, sticky form of congealed petroleum known as bitumin.

tectonic referring to the structures that result from the deformation of rocks.

terminal moraine a belt of hills formed through the deposition of sediment from melting ice at the periphery of a glacier when the glacier attained its maximum extent.

thermal pollution raising the temperature of the atmosphere, groundwater, or surface water to a harmful extent, as a result of the production of energy or other industrial processes.

till sediment deposited by melting glacial ice, characteristically unsorted and unlayered.

topographic map a map that shows the configuration of the irregularities of the earth's surface.

trace gases gaseous elements that are present only in minor amounts.

turbidity the extent to which sediment is suspended in a liquid; "muddyness."

Uniform Building Code a building code drawn up by the International Conference of Building Officials in 1927, with revisions published at three-year intervals.

vesicle a small cavity in an extrusive igneous rock formed by the expansion of a bubble of gas during the solidification of the rock.

visual space the landscape that is visible from a given place.

volcanic ash fine (generally less than 4 mm in diameter) fragments of rock ejected during a volcanic eruption.

wadi in the Middle East, the bed of an intermittent stream.

wash (dry wash) the dry bed of an intermittent stream.

wave height the vertical distance between the crest and trough of a wave.

wave crest the highest part of a wave.

weathering processes whereby rock material at the earth's surface is broken down mechanically and chemically through contact with air, ice, watery solutions, and living organisms.

well field an area where there are a group of water-supply wells.

Bibliography

Abelson, P. H., 1976, A new window on our planet: Science, v. 194, p. 15.

Alberding et al, 1976, Wastewater renovation and use: virus removal by soil filtration: Science, v. 192, pp. 1004–5.

Alfors, J. T., Burnett, J. L., and Gay, T. E., Jr., 1973, Urban geology master plan for California: Bull. 198, Cal. Div. Mines and Geology.

Algermissen, S. T., Rinehart, W. A., and Stepp, J. C., 1973, A technique for seismic zoning: economic considerations: NOAA Technical Rept. ERL 267-ESL 30, pp. 82–94.

American Public Works Assc. Institute For Solid Wastes, 1970, Municipal refuse disposal, 3rd ed.,: Public Administration Service.

Amiran, R., 1975, The water supply of Israelite Jerusalem, *in* Jerusalem revealed, archeology in the holy city, 1968–1974: The Israel Exploration Society and Shikmona Pub. Co., pp. 75–78.

Anderson, J. R., Hardy, E. E., and Roach, J. T., 1972, A land-use classification system for use with remote-sensor data: USGS Circ. 671.

Appleton, Jay, 1975, The experience of landscape: John Wiley & Sons.

Ardalan, N., and Bakhtiar, L, 1973, The sense of unity, the Sufi tradition in Persian architecture: Univ. of Chicago Press.

Assoc. of Bay Area Governments, 1966, Preliminary regional plan for the San Francisco Bay Region.

————, 1970, Regional Plan 1970:1990, San Francisco Bay Region.

Aune, Q. A., 1966, Quick clays and California's clays: no quick solutions: Mineral Information Service, Calif. Div. of Mines and Geology, v. 19, no. 8, pp. 119–23.

Axtmann, R. C., 1975, Environmental impact of a geothermal power plant: Science, v. 187, pp. 795–802.

Bacon, E. N., 1974, Design of cities, revised edition: Viking.

Barker, F., and Jackson, P., 1974, London, 2000 years of a city and its people: Macmillan.

Barker, R. M., and Stone, C. S., 1972, Natural land slopes, Hartford North Quadrangle, Connecticut: USGS Folio Map I-7841.

Bateman, A. M., 1950, Economic mineral deposits, 2nd ed.: John Wiley & Sons.

Bellan, R. C., 1971, The evolving city: Copp Clark Pub. Co.

Belt, C. B., Jr., 1975, The 1973 flood and man's constriction of the Mississippi River: Science, v. 189, pp. 681–84.

Berg, G. V., 1973, Response of buildings in Anchorage *in* The Great Alaska Earthquake of 1964, Engineering: Nat. Acad. Sciences, pp. 247–82.

Berghinz, C., 1971, Venice is sinking into the sea: Civil Engineering, v. 41, pp. 67–71.

Bernstein, R., and Stierhoff, G. C., 1976, Precision processing of earth image data: American Scientist, v. 64, pp. 500–508.

Berry, B. J. L., 1968, Metropolitan area definition: a reevaluation of concept and statistical practice: Bureau of the Census Working Paper No. 28.

Berry, B. J. L., Goheen, P. G., and Goldstein, Harold, 1968, Chicago's commuting field and urbanized area: Bureau of the Census Working Paper No. 28.

Berryhill, Jr., H. L., 1974, The worldwide search for petroleum offshore—a status report for the quarter century, 1947–72: USGS Circ. 694.

Bigger, Richard, 1959, The flood problem *in* Flood control in Metropolitan Los Angeles: Univ. of Calif. Publ. Pol. Sci., Univ. of California Press; v. 6, pp. 1–10.

Birkeland, P. W., and Larson, E. E., 1978, Putnam's geology, 3rd ed.: Oxford University Press.

Biswas, A. K., 1972, History of hydrology: North Holland Pub. Co.

Blaise, C., and Mukherjee, B., 1977, Days and nights in Calcutta: Doubleday.

Blum, S. L, 1976, Tapping resources in municipal solid waste: Science, v. 191, pp. 669–77.

Blumenfeld, H., 1967, The modern metropolis, its origins, growth, characteristics, and planning; selected essays, ed. by Spreiregen, P. D.: MIT Press.

Bolt, B. A., Horn, W. L., Macdonald, G. A., and Scott, R. F., 1975, Geological hazards: Springer-Verlag.

Born, S. M., and Stephenson, D. A., 1969, Hydrologic considerations in liquid waste disposal: Jour. Soil and Water Conservation, v. 24, no. 2.

Boyle, R. H., Graves, J., and Watkins, T. H., 1971, The water hustlers: The Sierra Club.

Brabb, E. E., and Pampeyan, E. H., 1972, Preliminary geologic map of San Mateo County, California: Basic Data Contribution 41, San Francisco Bay Region Environment and Resources Planning study: USGS and HUD.

Brabb, E. E., Pampeyan, E. H., and Bonilla, M. G., 1972, Landslide susceptibility in San Mateo County, California: Misc. Field Studies Map MF-360, Basic Data Contribution 42, San Francisco Bay Region Environment and Resources Planning Study, USGS and HUD.

Bredehoeft, J. D. *et al,* 1978, Geologic disposal of high-level radioactive wastes—earth-science perspectives: USGS Circ. 779.

Brobst, D. A., and Pratt, W. P., 1973, Summary of United States mineral resources *in* Summary of U.S. Mineral Resources, by Brobst *et al.,* USGS Circ. 682, pp. 1–8.

Broecker, W. S., 1973, Environmental priorities: Science, v. 182, no. 4111.

Brooks, D. B., and Andrews, P. W., 1974, Mineral resources, economic growth, and world population: Science, v. 185, pp. 13–19.

Brown, Harrison, 1954, The challenge of man's future: Viking.

Brown, L. F., Jr. *et al,* 1974, Natural hazards of the Texas Coastal zone: Bureau of Economic Geology, Univ. of Texas at Austin.

Brown, R. J. E., 1970, Permafrost in Canada, its influence on northern development: Univ. of Toronto Press.

Bruun, P., 1960, Coastal research and its economic justification: Congrès Internat. de Geog. Norden, Royal Danish Geog. Society *in* Steers, J. A., 1971, Introduction to coastline development: MIT Press, pp. 204–25.

Buchanan, Naomi, 1976, Bath [England] Official Guide Book.

Bue, C. D., 1967, Flood information for flood-plain planning: USGS Circ. 539.

Burnham, D. H., 1905, Report on a plan for San Francisco: The City of San Francisco.

Bylinsky, G., 1970, The limited war on pollution: Fortune, Feb. 1970, pp. 102–107, 193–195, 197.

Campbell, R. H., 1975, Soil slips, debris flows, and rainstorms in the Santa Monica Mountains and vicinity, southern California: USGS Prof. Paper 851.

Cargo, D. N. and Mallory, B. F., 1977, Man and his geologic environment, 2nd ed., Addison-Wesley.

Carlson, J. W., 1976, Earthquake forecasting: an opportunity, *in* Earthquake prediction—opportunity to avert disaster: USGS Circ. 729, pp. 2–3.

Carter, L. J., 1974, Con Edison: endless Storm King dispute adds to its troubles: Science, v. 184, pp. 1353-58.

———, 1976, Dade County: the politics of managing urban growth: Science, v. 192, pp. 982–85.

———, 1976, Wetlands: denial of Marco permits fails to resolve the dilemma: Science, v. 192, pp. 641–44.

———, 1978, Nuclear wastes: the science of geologic disposal seen as weak: Science, v. 200, pp. 1135–37.

Castle, R. O., Church, J. P., and Elliot, M. R., 1976, Aseismic uplift in southern California: Science, v. 192, pp. 251–53.

Cherkauer, D. S., 1976, Changes in surface runoff conditions during suburban development: Geol. Soc. of America Annual Meeting, 1976, Program With Abstracts, p. 811.

Christiansen, B. and Clack, T. H., Jr., 1976, A western perspective on energy: a plea for rational energy planning: Science, v. 194, pp. 578–84.

Citizens Advisory Committee on Environmental Quality, 1976, How will America grow?

Clanton, U. S., and Amsbury, D. L., 1975, Active faults in southeastern Harris County, Texas: Environmental Geology, Springer-Verlag, v. 1, pp. 149–54.

CLIMAP Project Members, 1976, The surface of the ice-age earth: Science, v. 191, pp. 1131–44.

Coates, D. R., 1973, Coastal Geomorphology: Publications in geomorphology, State Univ. N.Y., Binghamton, N.Y.

———, ed., 1974, Environmental geomorphology and landscape conservation. Vol. II, Urban areas: Stroudsberg, Dowden, Hutchinson & Ross.

———, ed., 1976, Urban geomorphology: Geol. Soc. of America Special Paper 174.

Cohen, Philip, Franke, O. L., and Foxworthy, B. L., 1968, An atlas of Long Island's water resources, N.Y. Water Resources Comm. Bull. 62: The State of New York.

Cole, L. C., 1969, Thermal pollution: Bioscience, v. 19, pp. 989–92.

Colombo, P., 1972, Rivista Italiana di Geotechnica, v. 6, pp. 7–30.

Colwell, R. N., 1973, Remote sensing as an aid to the management of earth resources: American Scientist, v. 61, pp. 175–83.

Condit, C. W., 1964, The Chicago school of architecture, a history of commercial and public buildings in the Chicago area, 1875–1925: Univ. of Chicago Press.

———, 1974, Chicago, 1930–70, building, planning, and urban technology: Univ. of Chicago Press.

Cook, Earl, 1976, Limits to exploitation of non-renewable resources: Science, v. 191, pp. 677–82.

Cooke, C. W., 1931, Why the Mayan cities of the Petén District, Guatamala, were abandoned: Wash. Acad. Sci. J., v. 21, pp. 283–87.

Cooke, R. U., and Doornkamp, 1974, Geomorphology in environmental management, an introduction: Oxford Univ. Press.

Cotton, J. E., and Delaney, D. F., 1975, Groundwater levels on Boston Peninsula, Massachusetts: USGS Hydrologic Invest. Atlas HA-513.

Council on Environmental Quality, 1970, Ocean dumping: a national policy.

———, 1973, Environmental quality—1973.

Crandell, D. R., and Mullineaux, D. R., 1975, Technique and rationale of volcanic-hazards appraisals in the Cascade Range, northwestern United States: Environmental Geology, v. 1, pp. 23–32.

Crandell, D. R., and Waldron, H. H., 1969, Volcanic hazards in the Cascade Ranges, in Geologic hazards and public problems, Conf. Proceedings, Olson, R., and Wallace, M., eds.: U.S. Govt. Printing Office, pp. 5–18.

Cronin, E. L., 1967, The role of man in estuarine processes in Estuaries, Lauff, G. H., ed.: AAAS Publ. No. 83, pp. 667–89.

Cullen, G. C., 1971, The concise townscape: Van Nostrand Reinhold.

Dahinden, Justus, 1972, Urban structures for the future, trans. by Gerald Onn: Praeger.

Damon, P. E., 1976, Global cooling?: Science, v. 193, pp. 447–53.

Dantzig, G. B., and Saaty, T. L., 1973, Compact city, a plan for a liveable urban environment: W. H. Freeman.

Davey, N., 1976, Building stones of England and Wales: Bedford Square Press of the National Council of Social Service.

Davis, J. H., 1956, Influence of man upon coast lines in Man's role in changing the face of the earth, Thomas, W. L., Jr., ed.: Univ. of Chicago Press, pp. 504–21.

Davis, R. L., 1975, A method for locating potential sites for sanitary landfills with an example: Monroe County, New York: Geol. Soc. of America Northeastern Section, 1975, Abstracts With Programs, pp. 46–47.

Day, J. R., 1964, Railways under the ground: Weidenfeld and Nicolson.

de Laguna, Wallace, 1968, Importance of deep permeable disposal formations in location of a large nuclear-fuel reprocessing plant in Subsurface disposal in geologic basins—a study of reservoir strata, ed. by J. E. Galley: AAPG Mem. 10, pp. 21–31.

de Marsily, G., Ledoux, E., Barbreau, A., and Margat, J., 1977, Nuclear waste disposal: can the geologist guarantee isolation?: Science, v. 197, pp. 519–27.

Denser, W. G. et al, 1976, Glacial and pluvial periods: their relationship revealed by Pleistocene sediments of the Red Sea and Gulf of Aden: Science, v. 191, pp. 1168–70.

Detwyler, T. R., 1971, Man's impact on environment: McGraw-Hill.

Deutsch, M., 1965, Natural controls involved in shallow aquifer contamination: Journal of Groundwater, v. 3, pp. 37–40.

Dolan, R., 1972, Barrier dune system along the

Outer Banks of North Carolina: a reappraisal: Science, v. 176, pp. 286–88.

Dolan, Robert, Godfrey, P. J., and Odum, W. E., 1973, Man's impact on the Barrier Islands of North Carolina: American Scientist, v. 61, pp. 152–62.

Doughty, C. M., 1931, Travels in Arabia Deserta, an abridgement by Edward Garnett: Doubleday Anchor ed. 1955.

Doxiadis, C. A., 1968, Ekistics, an introduction to the science of human settlements: Oxford Univ. Press.

Dobrovolny, E. and Schmoll, H. R., 1968, Geology as applied to urban planning: an example from the Greater Anchorage Area Borough, Alaska: Proc. XXIII Int. Geol. Congress, v. 12, pp. 39–56.

Dudley, D. R., 1967, Urbs Roma, a source book of classical texts on the city and its monuments: Phaidon Press.

Easterbrook, D. J., 1975, Mount Baker eruptions: Geology, v. 3, pp. 679–82.

Ehrlich, P. R., and Ehrlich, A. H., 1972, Population, resources, environment, issues in human ecology, 2nd ed.,: W. H. Freeman.

Eisbacher, G. H., 1973, Vancouver geology, a short guide: Geol. Assc. of Canada, Cordilleran Section.

Eliade, M., 1959, Cosmos and history: the myth of the eternal return: Harper and Row.

———, 1961, The sacred and the profane: Harper and Row.

Ellis, D. W., Allen, H. E., and Nochre, A. W., 1963, Floods in Elmhurst Quadrangle, Illinois: USGS Hydrol. Invest. Atlas HA-68.

English, P. W., and Mayfield, R. C., 1972, Man, space, and environment, concepts in contemporary human geography: Oxford Univ. Press.

Evans, D. M., 1966, Man-made earthquakes in Denver: Geotimes, v. 10, no. 9, pp. 11–18.

Evans, J. R., 1973, Extraction of sand and gravel in Orange County, California—a technical and planning problem: Calif. Geology, v. 26, p. 255–66; 271–72.

Ferrians, O. J., Jr., Kachadoorian, R., and Greene, G. W., 1969, Permafrost and related engineering problems in Alaska: USGS Prof. Paper 678.

Feth, J. H., 1973, Water facts and figures for planners and managers: USGS Circ. 601-1.

Finger, H. B., 1971, Environmental planning for community needs in Environmental Planning and Geology: USGS, pp. 190–201.

Fisher, W. L., McGowan, J. H., Brown, L. F.,

Jr., and Groat, C. G., 1972, Environmental Geologic Atlas of the Texas Coastal Zone —Galveston-Houston Area: Bureau of Economic Geology, Univ. of Texas at Austin.

Flawn, P. T., 1970, Environmental geology: Harper and Row.

Flawn, P. T., Turk, L. J., and Leach, C. H., 1970, Geologic considerations in disposal of solid municipal wastes in Texas: Texas Bureau of Economic Geology Circ. 70-2.

Flint, R. F., and Skinner, B. J., 1977, Physical geology, 2nd ed.,: John Wiley & Sons.

Fried, J. J., 1973, Life along the San Andreas Fault: Saturday Review Press.

Galantay, E. Y., 1975, New towns: antiquity to the present: George Braziller.

Garner, H. F., 1974, The origin of landscapes, a synthesis of geomorphology: Oxford Univ. Press.

Gilbert, G. K., 1917, Hydraulic mining debris in the Sierra Nevada: USGS Prof. Paper 105.

Gilmore, J. S., 1976, Boom towns may hinder energy resource development: Science, v. 191, pp. 535–40.

Goddard, J. E., 1971, Flood-plain management must be ecologically and economically sound: Civil Engineering, v. 41, pp. 81–85.

Goeller, H. E., and Weinberg, A. M., 1976, The age of substitutability: Science, v. 191, pp. 683–89.

Godfrey, P. J., and M. M. Godfrey, 1973, Comparison of ecological and geomorphic interactions between altered and unaltered barrier island systems in North Carolina, in D. R. Coates, 1973, pp. 239–58.

Goldman, H. B., 1959, Urbanization and the mineral industry: State of Calif. Div. of Mines, Mineral Information Service, v. 12, pp. 1–5.

Grava, S., 1969, Urban aspects of water pollution control: Columbia Univ. Press.

Greenfield, S. M., 1972, EPA—the environmental watchman in Underground waste management and environmental implications, T. D. Cook, ed., AAPG Memoir 18, pp. 14–18.

Greensfelder, R., 1971, Seismologic and crustal movement investigations of the San Fernando earthquake in California Geology, April–May, 1971.

Grey, A. L., 1972, Foreword in Westerlund, F. V., Urban and regional planning utilization of remote sensing data: a bibliography and review of pertinent literature: USGS interagency report USGS-242, NITS PB 211 101, Eros Program Tech. Rept. No. 1, pp. vi–xi.

Griffin, J. I., 1959, The port of New York: City College Press, Arco Publishing Co.

Gutenberg, B., and Richter, C. F., 1954, Seismicity of the Earth and associated phenomena: Princeton Univ. Press.

Guy, H. P., 1970, Sediment problems in urban areas: USGS Circ. 601-E.

Halderson, J. L., Hall, G. W., and Rimkus, R. R., 1975, Field application of fluid wastes: Amer. Soc. Agricultural Engineers, 1975, Paper No. 75-2533.

Hall, E. T., 1969, The hidden dimension: Anchor Books, Doubleday.

Hall, Peter, 1974, Urban and regional planning: Penguin.

Hamill, T. D., and Krellen, F. R., 1976, Trip report on California methane recovery facilities: City of New York Environmental Protection Adm. Solid Waste Task Force.

Hamilton, D. H., and Meehan, R. L., 1971, Ground rupture in the Baldwin Hills: Science, v. 72, pp. 333–44.

Hamilton, R. M., 1976, The status of earthquake prediction, *in* Earthquake prediction—opportunity to avert disaster: USGS Circ. 729, pp. 6–7.

Hammond, A. L., 1973, Earthquake prediction (II): prototype instrumental networks: Science, v. 180, pp. 940–41.

———, 1974, Modeling the climate: a new sense of urgency: Science, v. 185, pp. 1145–47.

Hammond, M., 1972, The city in the ancient world: Harvard Univ. Press.

Harris, W. H., 1975, Heavy metal ratios as indicators of dispersal and origin of waste solids in the New York Bight: Geol. Soc. of America Northeastern Section, 1975, Abstracts With Programs, p. 72.

———, 1976, Spatial and temporal variation in sedimentary grain size facies and sediment heavy metal ratios in the New York Bight apex: Am. Soc. Limnol. Oceanogr. Spec. Symp. 2, pp. 102–23.

Harrison, J. M., 1963, Nature and significance of geological maps *in* Albritton, C. C., Jr., The fabric of geology: Addison-Wesley, pp. 225–32.

Hauf, H. D., 1973, Architectural factors in earthquake resistance *in* The Great Alaska Earthquake of 1964, Engineering: Nat. Acad. Sciences, pp. 340–45.

Hays, J. D. *et al,* 1976, Variations in the earth's orbit: pacemaker of the ice ages: Science, v. 194, pp. 1121–32.

Heath, R. C., Foxworthy, B. L., and Cohen, P., 1966, The changing pattern of ground-water development on Long Island, N.Y.: U.S.G.S. Circ. 524.

Heckscher, A., 1977, Open spaces: Harper and Row.

Hill, I. T., 1953, The ancient city of Athens, its topography and monuments: Methuen and Co.

Hill, M. R., 1971, The San Fernando earthquake, 1971: Calif. Geology, v. 24, nos. 4–5, pp. 59–60.

Hitheman, 1973, London holding the tides at bay: Lloyds List; Lloyds of London Press, Ltd., Jan. 4, 1973.

Holden, C., 1978, Panel throws doubt on vitrification: Science, v. 201, p. 599.

Holmes, A., 1965, Principles of physical geology, 2nd ed.,: Ronald Press.

Hoover, D. B., and Dietrich, J. A., 1969, Seismic activity during the 1968 test pumping at the Rocky Mountain Arsenal disposal well: USGS. Circ. 619.

Housner, G. W., 1973, Engineering, *in* The Great Alaska Earthquake of 1964, Summary and recommendations: Nat. Acad. Sciences, pp. 74–88.

Housner, G. W., and Jennings, P. C., 1973, Intro. to Part II, Structural Engineering *in* The Great Alaska Earthquake of 1964, Engineering: Nat. Acad. Sciences, pp. 245–46.

Howe, C. W., 1969, Economics of large-scale transfers *in* McGinnies, W. G., and Goldman, B. J., 1969, Arid lands in perspective: AAAS and the Univ. of Arizona Press, pp. 374–82.

Hoyt, W. G., and Langbein, W. B., 1955, Floods: Princeton Univ. Press.

Hubbert, M. K., 1973, Survey of world energy resources: The Canadian Mining and Metallurgical Bull., v. 66, pp. 37–54.

Hunt, C. B., 1972, Geology of soils, their evolution, classification, and uses: W. H. Freeman.

———, 1974, Natural regions of the United States and Canada: W. H. Freeman and Co.

Idso, S. B., Jackson, R. D., and Reginato, R. J., 1975, Detection of soil moisture by remote surveillance: American Scientist, v. 63, pp. 549–60.

Izaak Walton League of America, 1973, A citizen's guide to clean water, 94 pp.

Jackson, E. L., and Mukerjee, T. 1974, Human adjustment to the earthquake hazard of San Francisco, California *in* Natural hazards, White, G. F., ed., Oxford Univ. Press, pp. 160–66.

Jackson, J. B., 1972, American space, the centennial years 1865–1876: W. W. Norton.

Jacobsen, T., and Adams, R. M., 1958, Salt and silt in Ancient Mesopotamian culture: Science, v. 128, pp. 1251–58.

Jellicoe, G. A., 1966, Studies in landscape design, v. II: Oxford Univ. Press.

Jenkins, C. T., 1961, Floods at Boulder, Colorado: USGS Hydrologic Investigations Atlas HA-41.

Johnson, J. H., 1972, Urban geography, 2nd ed.: Pergamon.

Johnson, S. L., and Sayre, D. M., 1973, Effects of urbanization on floods in the Houston, Texas metropolitan area: USGS Water-Resources Invest. 3-73.

Jones, E., 1966, Towns and Cities: Oxford Univ. Press.

Judeich, W., 1931, Topographie von Athen: C. H. Beck'sche Verlag., Munich.

Judson, S., 1968, Erosion of the land, or what's happening to our continents?: American Scientist, v. 56, pp. 356–74.

Karkheck, J., and Beardsworth, E., 1977, Prospects for district heating in the United States: Science, v. 195, pp. 948–55.

Katznelson, E., Buium, I., and Shuval, H. I., 1976, Risk of communicable disease infection associated with wastewater irrigation in agricultural settlements: Science, v. 194, pp. 944–46.

Kaye, C. A., 1976, The geology and early history of the Boston area of Massachusetts, a bicentennial approach: USGS Bull. 1476.

Kellogg, W. W., and Schneider, S. H., 1974, Climate stabilization: for better or for worse?: Science, v. 186, pp. 1163–72.

Kiersch, G. A., 1965, The Vaiont reservoir disaster: Mineral Information Service, Calif. Div. of Mines and Geology, v. 18, no. 7, pp. 129–38.

King, C. A. M., 1972, Beaches and coasts, 2nd ed.,: St. Martins Press.

———, 1974, Coasts in Cooke, R. U., and Doornkamp, J. C., Geomorphology in environmental management, an introduction: Oxford Univ. Press, pp. 188–222.

Kirby, R. C., and Prokopovitsh, A. S., 1976, Technological insurance against shortages in minerals and metals: Science, v. 191, pp. 713–19.

Klein, H., 1973, Managing the water system in Resource and land information for south Dade County, Florida: USGS Investigation I-850, 1973, pp. 18–25.

Kraft, J. C., Biggs, R. B., and Halsey, S. D., 1973, Morphology and vertical sedimentary sequence models in Holocene transgressive barrier systems in Coates, D. R., Coastal Geomorphology: Publ. in Geomorphology, State Univ. of N.Y., Binghamton, 1972, pp. 321–54.

Krauskopf, K. B., 1971, Preface in The Great Alaska Earthquake of 1964, Geology: Nat. Acad. of Sciences, pp. ix–xiii.

Krynine, D. P., and Judd, W. R., 1957, Principles of engineering geology and geotechnics: McGraw-Hill.

Kubo, A. S., and Rose, D. J., 1973, Disposal of nuclear wastes: Science, v. 182, pp. 1205–11.

Kutcher, A., 1973, The new Jerusalem, planning and politics: Thames and Hudson.

Ladenbruch, A. H., 1970, Some estimates of the thermal effects of a heated pipeline in permafrost: USGS Circ. 632.

Lane, F. C., 1973, Venice, a maritime republic: Johns Hopkins Univ. Press.

Lang, M., 1968, Waterworks in the Athenian Agora: Amer. School of Classical Studies at Athens: Princeton, N.J.

Langer, W. H., 1972, Thickness of material overlying principal clay unit, Hartford North Quadrangle, Connecticut: USGS Folio Map I-784F.

———, 1972, Thickness of principal clay unit, Hartford North Quadrangle, Connecticut: USGS Folio Map I-784E.

Legget, R. F., 1973, Cities and geology: McGraw-Hill.

Le Grand, H. E., 1968, Environmental framework of groundwater contamination: Journal of Groundwater, v. 6, pp. 14–18.

———, 1968, Monitoring of changes in quality of ground water: Journal of Groundwater, v. 6, pp. 14–18.

Leighton, F. B. 1976, Urban landslides: targets for land-use planning in California in Urban Geomorphology, D. R. Coates, ed., Geol. Soc. of Amer. Special Paper 174, pp. 37–60.

Leopold, L. B., 1968, Hydrology for urban land planning—a guidebook on the hydrologic effects of urban land-use: USGS Circ. 554.

———, 1969, Quantitative comparison of some aesthetic factors among rivers: USGS Circ. 620.

———, 1974, Water, a primer: W. H. Freeman.

Leopold, L. B., Clarke, F. E., Hanshaw, B. B., and Balsey, J. R., 1971, A procedure for evaluating environmental impact: USGS Circ. 645.

Leopold, L. B., and Maddock, T., Jr., 1954, The flood control controversy, sponsored by The Conservation Foundation, Inc.: Ronald Press.

Leveson, D., 1971, A sense of the earth: Natural History Press.

Lewis, W. V., 1932, The formation of the Dungeness Foreland *in* Steers, J. A., 1971, Applied coastal geomorphology: MIT Press, pp. 64–83.

Lindholm, R. C., 1976, Climatic change—past, present and future: Jour. Geol. Ed., v. 24, pp. 156–64.

Litton, R. B., Tetlow, R. J., Sorensen, J. and Beatty, R. A., 1974, Water and landscape, an aesthetic overview of the role of water in the landscape: Water Information Center, Inc.

Luce, J. V., 1969, The end of Atlantis, new light on an old legend: Thames and Hudson.

Lynch, K. 1960, The image of the city: MIT Press.

———, 1976, Managing the sense of a region: MIT Press.

Macaulay, D., 1977, Underground cities *in* Subways: Cooper-Hewett Museum, p. 12.

MacCoun, T., The island of Manhattan at the time of its discovery (1609), based upon the early colonial surveys of Ratzer, Montresor, Knypthausen, Bradford, Duyckinck, etc., and the Survey of 1867 by Genl. E. L. Viele; compliments of the Underpinning and Foundation Co., N.Y.

Macdonald, G. A., 1972, Volcanoes: Prentice-Hall.

Mackendrick, P., 1962, The Greek stones speak, the story of archeology in Greek lands: Mentor Books, 1966.

Mackenthun, K. M., 1972, Magnitude of wastewater treatment and disposal problem facing the nation *in* Underground waste management and environmental implications, T. D. Cook, ed.,: AAPG Mem. 18, pp. 19–23.

Mader, G. G., and Crowder, D. F., 1971, An experiment in using geology for city planning—the experience of the small community of Portola Valley, California *in* Environmental Planning and Geology: USGS, pp. 176–89.

Mallon, H. J., and Howard, J. Y., 1971, Land use determination by remote sensor analysis: USGS interagency report USGS-220, NITS PB 204 246.

Mathewson, C. C., and Font, R. G., 1974, Geologic environment: forgotten aspect in the land use planning process *in* Ferguson, H. F., Geologic mapping for environmental purposes: Geol. Soc. of America Engineering Case Histories no. 10, pp. 23–28.

Maugh II, T. H., 1973, ERTS: surveying earth's resources from space: Science, v. 180, pp. 49–51.

Mayer, H. M., and Wade, R. C., 1969, Chicago: growth of a metropolis: Univ. of Chicago Press.

Mazar, A., 1975, The aqueducts of Jerusalem, *in* Jerusalem revealed, archeology in the holy city, 1968–1974: Israel Exploration Society and Shikmona Pub. Co., pp. 79–84.

McCullough, D., 1972, The great bridge: Simon and Schuster.

McDermott, J. E., 1970, Significance of the national community water supply study *in* Water quality in a stressed environment, W. A. Pettyjohn, ed.,: Burgess, 1972, pp. 3–11.

McGauhey, P. H., 1968, Manmade contamination hazards: Groundwater, v. 6, pp. 10–13.

McGauhey, P. H., 1969, Physical implications of large-scale water transfers *in* McGinnies, W. G., and Goldman, B. J., 1969, Arid lands in perspective: AAAS and Univ. of Arizona Press, pp. 358–63.

McGill, J. T., 1964, Growing importance of urban geology: USGS Circ. 487.

McGinnies, W. G., and Goldman, B. J., 1969, Arid lands in perspective, including AAAS papers on water importation into arid lands: AAAS and Univ. of Arizona Press.

McGowan, J. H., 1974, Coastal zone shoreline changes: a function of natural processes and man's activities, *in* Approaches to environmental geology, Wermund, E. G., ed.: Rept. of Investigations No. 81, Bur. of Econ. Geol. Univ. of Texas at Austin, pp. 184–203.

McHarg, I. L., 1969, Design with nature: Natural History Press.

McKelvey, V. E., 1976, A federal plan for the issuance of earthquake predictions and warnings *in* Earthquake prediction—opportunity to avert disaster: USGS Circ. 729, pp. 10–12.

McNeill, W. H., 1963, The rise of the west, a history of the human community: Univ. of Chicago Press.

Meigs, P., 1969, Future use of desert seacoasts *in* McGinnies, W. G., and Goldman, B. J., 1969, Arid lands in perspective: AAAS and Univ. of Arizona Press, pp. 101–18.

Meinel, A. B., Meinel, M. P., and Shaw, G. E., 1976, Trajectory of the Mt. St. Augustine 1976 eruption ash cloud: Science, v. 193, pp. 420–22.

Mikesell, M. W., 1968, Landscape *in* Internat. Encyclopedia of the Social Sciences, D. L.

Sills, ed.: Crowell, Collier and Macmillan, v. 8, pp. 575–80.

Mitchell, C., 1973, Terrain evaluation: Longman.

Moran, J. M., 1975, Return of the ice age and drought in peninsular Florida?: Geology, v. 3, pp. 695–96.

Morgan, F. W., 1952, Ports and harbours: Hutchinson's University Library.

Morisawa, M., 1976, Channelization: impacts and solutions: GSA Annual Meeting, 1976, Program With Abstracts, p. 1019.

Morton, D. M., 1971, Seismically triggered landslides above San Fernando Valley: Calif. Geology, v. 24, nos. 4–5, p. 81.

Morton, D. M., and Streitz, R., 1967, Landslides: Mineral Information Service, Calif. Div. of Mines and Geology, v. 20, no. 11, pp. 135–40.

Morton, R. A., 1976, Effects of Hurricane Eloise on beach and coastal structures, Florida Panhandle: Geology, v. 4, no. 5, pp. 277–80.

Mumford, L., 1938, The culture of cities: Harcourt, Brace and World.

Mumford, L., 1961, The city in history, its origins, its transformations, and its prospects: Harcourt, Brace and World.

Murray, C. R., and Reeves, E. B., 1977, Estimated use of water in the United States in 1975: USGS Circ. 765.

National Shoreline Study, 1973, 93rd Congress, 1st sess. House Doc. No. 93-121, Chief of Engineers, Dept. of the Army.

Nichols, D. R., and Buchanan-Banks, J. M., 1974, Seismic hazards and land-use planning, USGS Circ. 690.

Nichols, D. R., and Wright, N. A., 1971, Preliminary map of historic margins of marshland, San Francisco Bay, California: USGS Basic Data Contribution 9.

Noble, J. V., 1965, The techniques of painted Attic pottery: Watson-Guptill Publications and the Metropolitan Museum of Art.

Norberg-Schulz, C., 1971, Existence, space and architecture: Praeger.

Oakeshott, G. B., 1971, California's changing landscapes, a guide to the geology of the state: McGraw-Hill.

———, 1976, Volcanoes and earthquakes, geologic violence: McGraw-Hill.

———, 1971 The geologic setting *in* California Geology, April–May, 1971.

O'Connell, J. C., 1976, Chicago's quest for pure water: Public works historical society, Essay no. 1.

Orni, E., and Efrat, E., 1976, Geography of Israel, 3rd rev. ed.: Israel Univ. Press.

Osborn, E. F., 1974, Coal and the present energy situation: Science, v. 183, pp. 477–81.

Ostrom, V., 1953, Metropolitan Los Angeles, a study in integration, VIII, water supply: The Haynes Foundation.

———, Water and politics: a study of water policies and administration in the development of Los Angeles: The Haynes Foundation.

Panitch, M., 1977, Alaskan gas: impact of pipeline on Canadian north stirs debate: Science, v. 195, pp. 1308–11.

Page, R. A., Blume, J. A., and Joynes, W. B., 1975, Earthquake shaking and damage to buildings: Science, v. 189, pp. 601–608.

Parizek, E. J., 1978, Geology beneath a city —Kansas City: Abstracts with programs, v. 10, no. 7, GSA annual meeting, 1978, p. 467.

Pashley, E. F., Jr., and Wiggins, R. A., 1971, Landslides of the northern Wasatch Front: Utah Geol. Assc. Publ. 1-K, *in* Environmental Geology of the Wasatch Front, 1971, Utah Geol. Assc. Pub. 1.

Pessl, F., Jr., Langer, W. H., and Ryder, R. B., 1972, Geologic and hydrologic maps for land-use planning in the Connecticut Valley with examples from the folio of the Hartford North Quadrangle, Connecticut: USGS Circ. 674.

Pestrong, R., 1968, The role of the urban geologist in city planning: Mineral Information Service, Calif. Div. Mines and Geology, v. 21, no. 10, pp. 151–52.

Pilkey, O. H., Jr. Pilkey, O. H., Sr., and Turner, R., 1975, How to live with an island, a handbook to Bogue Banks, North Carolina: North Carolina Dept. of Natural and Economic Resources, Raleigh, N.C.

Pimental, D. *et al.*, 1976, Land degradation: effects on food and energy resources: Science, v. 195, pp. 149–55.

Piper, A. M., 1965, Has the United States enough water?: USGS Water Supply Paper 1797.

———, 1969, Disposal of liquid wastes by injection underground—neither myth nor millennium: USGS Circ. 631.

Pirenne, H., 1925, Medieval cities, their origins and the revival of trade, trans. by Halsey, F. D. Princeton Univ. Press; Doubleday Anchor, 1956.

Poland, J. F., 1969, Land subsidence in Western United States *in* Geologic hazards and public problems, May 27–28, 1969 Conf. Proc. Olson,

R. A., and Wallace, M. W., eds.: U.S. Govt. Printing Office, pp. 77–96.

———, 1971, Land subsidence in the Santa Clara Valley, Alameda, San Mateo, and Santa Clara Counties, California: Misc. Field Studies Map MF-332, USGS.

———, 1972, Subsidence and its control *in* Underground waste management and environmental implications, T. D. Cook, ed.: AAPG Mem. 18, pp. 50–71.

Poland, J. F., and Davis, G. H., 1969, Land subsidence due to withdrawal of fluids *in* Reviews in Engineering Geology, Geol. Soc. of America, v. 2, pp. 187–269.

Poland, J. F., Lofgren, B. E., Ireland, R. L., and Pugh, R. G., 1973, Land subsidence in the San Joaquin Valley, California, as of 1972: USGS Prof. Paper 437-H.

Pratt, W. P., and Brobst, D. A., 1974, Mineral resources: potentials and problems: USGS Circ. 698.

Press, F., and Siever, R., 1978, Earth, 2nd ed.: W. H. Freeman.

Pritchard, J. B., 1962, Gibeon, where the sun stood still, the discovery of a biblical city: Princeton Univ. Press.

Pushkarev, B., 1977, How subways can make cities *in* Subways: Cooper Hewitt Museum, pp. 1, 20–21.

Raleigh, C. B., Healy, J. H., and Bredehoeft, J. D., 1976, An experiment in earthquake control at Rangely, Colorado: Science, v. 191, pp. 1230–38.

Rapoport, A., 1969, House form and culture: Prentice-Hall.

Rasmussen, S. E., 1969, Towns and buildings: MIT Press.

Ray, R. G., 1960, Aerial photographs in geologic interpretation and mapping: USGS Prof. Paper 373.

Rex, R. W., 1971, Geothermal resources in the Imperial Valley *in* Seckler, D., 1971, California water, a study in resource management: Univ. of Calif. Press, pp. 190–205.

Reyman, J. E., 1976, Astronomy, architecture, and adaption at Pueblo Bonito: Science, v. 193, pp. 957–62.

Robins, F. W., 1946, The story of water supply: Oxford Univ. Press.

Robinson, A. R., 1970, Sediment, our greatest pollutant?: Paper 70-701, 1970 Winter Meeting, Amer. Soc. Agric. Engin.

Rohl, A., Langer, A. M., and Selikoff, I. J., 1977, Environmental asbestos pollution related to use of quarried serpentine rock: Science, v. 196, pp. 1319–22.

Romero, J. C., and Hampton, E. R., 1972, Maps showing approximate configuration and depth to the top of the Laramie-Fox Hills Aquifer, Denver Basin, Colo.: USGS Misc. Invest. Map I-791.

Rowan, L. C., 1975, Application of satellites to geologic exploration: American Scientist, v. 63, pp. 393–403.

Rudofsky, B., 1969, Streets for people, a primer for Americans: Doubleday.

Ruedisili, L. C., and Firebaugh, M. W., 1978, Perspectives on energy: Oxford Univ. Press.

Ryder, R. B., 1972, Availability of ground water, Hartford North Quadrangle, Connecticut: USGS Folio Map I-784K.

Savini, John, and Kammerer, J. C., 1961, Urban growth and the water regimen: USGS Water Supply Paper 1591-A.

Schick, A. P., 1971, A desert flood: physical characteristics; effects of Man, geomorphic significances, human adaptation—a case study of the southern Arava watershed: Jerusalem Studies in Geography, v. 2, pp. 91–155.

Schneider, W. J., 1970, Hydrologic implications of solid-waste disposal: USGS Circ. 601-F.

Schneider, W. J., Rickert, D. A., and Spieker, A. M., 1973, Role of water in urban planning and management: USGS Circ. 601-H.

Schneider, W. J., and Spieker, A. M., 1969, Water for the cities—the outlook: USGS Circ. 601-A.

Schuberth, C. J., 1968, The geology of New York City and environs: Natural History Press.

Schumann, H. H., 1974, Land subsidence and earth fissures in alluvial deposits in the Phoenix area, Arizona: USGS Misc. Invest. Map I-845-H.

Scott, M., 1959, The San Francisco Bay Area: Univ. of California Press.

Scott, R. F., 1973, Behavior of soils during the earthquake *in* The Great Alaska Earthquake of 1964, Engineering: Nat. Acad. Sciences, pp. 49–72.

Scully, V., 1962, The earth, the temple, and the gods, Greek sacred architecture: Yale Univ. Press.

Seckler, D., 1971, California water, a study in resource management: Univ. of California Press.

Seed, H. B., 1973, Landslides caused by soil liquefaction *in* The Great Alaska Earthquake of

1964, Engineering: Nat. Acad. Sciences, pp. 73–119.

Selkregg, L., Crittenden, E. B., and Williams, N., Jr., 1970, Urban planning in the reconstruction *in* The Great Alaska Earthquake of 1964, Human Ecology: Nat. Acad. Sciences, pp. 186–242.

Seyfert, C. K., and Sirkin, L. A., 1973, Earth history and plate tectonics: Harper and Row.

Shapley, D., 1976, Earthquakes: Los Angeles prediction suggests faults in federal policy: Science, v. 192, pp. 535–37.

Sheaffer, J. R., Ellis, D. W., and Spieker, A. M., 1970, Flood-hazard mapping in Metropolitan Chicago: USGS Circ. 601-C.

Shepard, F. P., 1964, The earth beneath the sea: Atheneum.

Shimer, J. A., 1959, This sculptured earth: Columbia Univ. Press.

Shimer, J. A., 1972, Field guide to landforms in the United States: Macmillan.

Simpson, H. J., Olsen, C. R., Trier, R. M., and Williams, S. C., 1976, Man-made radionuclides and sedimentation in the Hudson River Estuary: Science, v. 194, pp. 179–82.

Skinner, B. J., 1976, A second iron age ahead?: American Scientist, v. 64, pp. 258–69.

Smith, R., 1958, Economic and legal aspects *in* Landslides and engineering practice, Highway Research Board Spec. Rept. 29, Comm. on Landslide Investigations, Eckel, E. B., ed.: NAS-NRC Publ. 544, pp. 6–19.

Snethen, D. R., 1976, A review of damages caused by expansive soils: Geol. Soc. of America Annual Meeting, 1976, Abstracts with Programs, pp. 1113–14.

Soleri, P., 1969, Arcology, the city in the image of man: MIT Press.

———, 1973, The bridge between matter and spirit is matter becoming spirit: Anchor Press, Doubleday.

Soren, J., 1976, Basement flooding and foundation damage from water-table rise in the East New York section of Brooklyn, Long Island, New York: Geol. Soc. of America Annual Meeting, 1976, Abstracts with Programs, p. 1115.

Spangle, W. *et al,* 1974, Application of earth science information in urban land-use planning, state-of-the-art review and analysis: USGS Report GD-74-038, NTIS PB-238 081.

California Dept. of Water Resources Bull. No. 200, 1974, Calif. state water project, v. 1, history, planning, and early progress.

Stauffer, T. P. Sr., 1973, Kansas City: a center for secondary use of mined-out space: Proc. of the Eng. Found. Conf. South Berwick, Maine, June 1973, pp. 50–79.

Steers, J. A., 1953, The East Coast floods, 31 January–1 February, 1953: Royal Geog. Soc. *in* Steers, J. A., 1971, Applied coastal geomorphology: MIT Press.

———, 1971, Applied coastal geomorphology: MIT Press.

———, Introduction to coastline development: MIT Press.

Steinbrugge, K. V., 1968, Earthquake hazard in the San Francisco Bay Area: a continuing problem in public policy: Inst. of Gov. Studies, Univ. of California, Berkeley.

Steinbrugge, K. V., and Cluff, L. S., 1968, The Caracas, Venezuela earthquake of July 29, 1967: Mineral Information Service, Cal. Div. Mines and Geology, v. 21, no. 1, pp. 3–11.

Taylor, F. A., and Brabb, E. E., 1972, Map showing distribution and cost by counties of structurally damaging landslides in the San Francisco Bay Region, California, winter, 1968–69: Misc. Field Studies Map MF-327; Basic Data Cont. 37, San Francisco Bay Region Environment and Resources Planning Study, USGS.

Thiel, C. C., 1976, Possible loss-reduction actions following an earthquake prediction *in* Earthquake prediction—opportunity to avert disaster: USGS Circ. 729, pp. 13–16.

Thomas, D. M., and Edelen, G. W., Jr., 1962, Tidal floods, Atlantic City and vicinity, New Jersey: USGS Hydrol. Invest. Atlas HA-65.

Thomas, G. W., and Box, T. W., 1969, Social and ecological implications of water importation into arid lands *in* McGinnies, W. G., and Goldman, B. J., 1969, Arid lands in Perspective: AAAS and the Univ. of Arizona Press, pp. 363–74.

Thomas, H. E., and Schnieder, W. J., 1970, Water as an urban resource and nuisance: USGS Circ. 601-D.

Thomas, M. P., 1972, Flood-prone areas, Hartford North Quadrangle, Connecticut: USGS Folio Map I-784M.

Thompson, H. A., and Wycherley, R. E., 1972, The Athenian agora, results of the excavations conducted by the American School of Classical Studies at Athens, vol. XIV: American School of Classical Studies at Athens, Princeton, N.J.

Tice, G. A., 1972, Paterson: Rutgers Univ. Press.

Travlos, J., 1960, Poleodomiki ton Athainon.

Tuan, Yi-Fu, 1968, Discrepancies between environmental attitude and behavior: examples from Europe and China: Canadian Geog. v. 12, pp. 176–91.

———, 1974, Topophilia, a study of environmental perception, attitudes, and values: Prentice-Hall.

Turner, R. H., 1976, Social, economic, and political implications of earthquake prediction *in* Earthquake prediction—opportunity to avert disaster: USGS Cir. 729, pp. 17–19.

U.S. Army Coastal Engineering Research Center, 1966, Shore protection, planning and design, Tech. Rept. No. 4, 3rd ed.

U.S. Army Corps of Engineers, Honolulu Dist., 1960: Report on survey for tidal wave protection and navigation.

U.S. Army Corps of Engineers, 1975, Atlantic coast of New York City from East Rockaway Inlet to Rockaway Inlet and Jamaica Bay, N.Y., Beach Erosion and Hurricane Protection, Project Description and Information.

USGS, 1973, Investigation I-850, Resource and land information for south Dade County, Florida, 1973.

U.S. Water Resources Council, 1971, Regulation of flood hazard areas to reduce flood losses, v. I.

Van Burkalow, A., 1959, The geography of New York City's water supply: a study of interactions: Geog. Review, v. 49, pp. 369–86.

van Veen, J., 1962, Dredge, drain, reclaim! —the art of a nation, 5th ed.,: Martinus Nijhoff.

Varnes, D. J., 1958, Landslide types and processes *in* Landslides and Engineering Practice, Highway Research Board Spec. Rpt. 29, Eckel, E. B., ed.: NAS-NRC Publ. 544.

Vecchioli, J., Ehrlich, G. G., and Ehlke, T. A., 1972, Travel of pollution-indicator bacteria through the Magothy aquifer, Long Island, New York: USGS Prof. Paper 800-B, pp. B237–39.

Visvader, H. and Burton, I., 1974, Natural hazards and hazard policy in Canada and the United States *in* Natural hazards, White, G. F., ed.: Oxford Univ. Press, pp. 219–31.

von Engelhardt, W. *et al*, 1976, Earth resources, time, and man—a geoscience perspective: Environmental Geology, v. 1, pp. 193–206.

von Hake, C. A., 1973, Assessment and interpretation of data on seismic history *in* Earthquake Research in NOAA, Stepp, J. C., ed., NOAA Tech. Rept. ERL 256 ESL 28, p. 92.

Walker, T. D., 1971, Perception and environmental design: PDA Publishers, West Lafayette, Ind.

Wallace, R. E., 1974, Goals, strategy, and tasks of the earthquake hazard reduction program: USGS Circ. 701.

Walton, W. C., 1970, Groundwater resource evaluation: McGraw-Hill.

Wang, W. C., Yung, Y. L., Lacis, A. A., Mo, T., and Hansen, J. E., 1976, Greenhouse effects due to man-made perturbations of trace gases: Science, v. 194, pp. 685–90.

Warner, D. L., 1968, Subsurface disposal of liquid industrial wastes by deep-well injection *in* Subsurface disposal in geologic basins—a study of reservoir strata, J. E. Galley ed.,: AAPG Mem. 10, pp. 11–20.

Warnick, C. C., 1969, Historical background and philosophical basis of regional water transfer, *in* McGinnies, W. G., and Goldman, B. J., Arid lands in perspective, incl. AAAS papers on water importation into arid lands: AAAS and the Univ. of Arizona Press, pp. 340–52.

Weinberg, A.M., 1974, Global effects of man's production of energy: Science, v. 186, no. 4160.

Weinberg, E., 1969, Intrastate, interstate, and international legal and administrative problems of large-scale water transfer *in* McGinnies, W. G., and Goldman, B. J., 1969, Arid lands in perspective: AAAS and the Univ. of Arizona Press, pp. 352–58.

Weller, C. H., 1924, Athens and its monuments: Macmillan.

Wendorf, F. *et al*, 1976, The prehistory of the Egyptian Sahara: Science, v. 193, pp. 103–14.

Westerlund, F. V., 1972, Urban and regional planning utilization of remote sensing data: a bibliography and review of pertinent literature: USGS interagency rpt. USGS-242, NITS PB 211 101, Eros Prog. Tech. Rept. No. 1.

White, G. F., and Haas, J. E., 1975, Assessment of research on natural hazards: MIT Press.

Whitham, K., Milne, W. G., and Smith, W. E. T., 1970, The new seismic zoning map for Canada, 1970 ed.: The Canadian Underwriter, June 15, 1970.

Wiegel, R. L., 1964, Oceanographical engineering: Prentice-Hall.

Williams, R. S., Jr., 1976, Diversion of lava by water cooling during the eruption of Eldfell

Volcano, Heimaey, Iceland: Geol. Soc. America Program, Annual Meeting, NE/SE Sections, 1976, pp. 300–301 (abstract).

Williams, S. J., 1975, Anthropogenic filling of the Hudson River (shelf) channel: Geology, Oct. 1975, pp. 597–600.

Winter, F. E., 1971, Greek fortifications: Univ. of Toronto Press.

Wohlrab, B., 1969, Effects of mining subsidence on the ground water and remedial measures: Pub. Int. Assoc. Scie. Hydr., v. 89, pp. 502–12.

Wolman, A., 1976, Ecologic dilemmas: Science, v. 193, pp. 740–42.

Wolman, M. G., 1964, Problems posed by sediment derived from construction activities in Maryland: Report to the Maryland Water Pollution Control Comm. Annapolis, Md.

Wright, H. E., Jr., 1976, The environmental setting for plant domestication in the Near East: Science, v. 194, pp. 385–90.

Wright, R. H., Campbell, R. H., and Nilsen, T. H., 1974, Preparation and use of isopleth maps of landslide deposits: Geology, v. 2, pp. 483–85.

Wulff, H. E., 1968, The qanats of Iran: Scientific American, v. 218, no. 4, pp. 94–105.

Wycherley, R. E., 1969, How the Greeks built cities: Doubleday-Anchor; Macmillan, 1962.

Yelverton, C. A., 1971, The role of local government in urban geology *in* Environmental Planning and Geology: USGS, pp. 76–81.

Zaruba, Q., and Mencl, V., 1969, Landslides and their control: Elsevier.

Zetler, B. D., 1947, Travel times of seismic sea waves to Honolulu: Pacific Science, v. 1, no. 3, pp. 185–88.

Index

Illustration Credits

Chapter 1

1.1 After Berry, 1968.

1.2 After Dantzig and Saaty, 1973.

1.3 After Population Reference Bureau, World population data sheet, 1972.

1.4 Data from Ehrlich and Ehrlich, 1972.

1.5 Data from Legget, 1973.

1.6 Data from Jones, 1966.

1.7 From C. A. Doxiadis, Ekistics (Oxford University Press), © 1968 by Constantinos A. Doxiadis, Fig. 432. Reproduced by permission of Oxford University Press, Inc., and Hutchinson Publishing Group Ltd.

Chapter 2

2.1 After McNeill, 1963.

2.3 After Scully, 1962.

2.5 After W. Judeich, Topographie von Athen (C. H. Beck'sche), 1931, Fig. 7. Reproduced by permission of C. H. Beck'sche, Munich.

2.6 and 7 After J. B. Pritchard, Gibeon, where the sun stood still: The discovery of the biblical city (copyright © 1962 by Princeton University Press), Fig. 5, p. 58. Reproduced by permission of Princeton University Press.

2.10 After H. E. Wulff, The qanats of Iran, Scientific American, April 1968. Copyright © 1968 by Scientific American, Inc. All rights reserved. Reproduced by permission of Scientific American, Inc.

2.12 Aerofilms.

2.13 After H. Blumenfeld, ed., The Modern Metropolis (MIT Press), 1967, Fig. 1 a–d. Reproduced by permission of The MIT Press.

2.15 After F. C. Lane, Venice, A maritime republic (John Hopkins), 1973, map, p. 3. Reproduced by permission of the Johns Hopkins University Press.

Chapter 3

3.12 and 13 From River of life, USDA Conservation Yearbook series, v. 6.

3.14 From Piper, 1965.

3.15, 18, 19, and 21 After Klein, 1973.

3.22 From G. B. Oakeshott, California's changing landscapes: A guide to the geology of the state (Copyright © 1971, McGraw-Hill Book Co., Inc.) Reproduced by permission of McGraw-Hill Book Co.

3.25 After Ostrom, 1953.

3.29 and 30 From R. C. Heath, B. L. Foxworthy, and P. Cohen, The changing pattern of ground-water development on Long Island, N.Y., USGS Circ. 524.

3.31 After Cohen et al, 1968.

3.34 Redrawn from A. N. Strahler and A. H. Strahler, Geography and man's environment (Wiley), 1977, p. 108. Copyright © 1977 by John Wiley and Sons, Inc. Reprinted by permission of John Wiley and Sons, Inc.

Chapter 4

4.9 After R. H. Brown, 1961.

Chapter 6

6.10 After Schmoll and Dobrovolny, 1974.
6.12 Chicago Historical Society.

Chapter 7

7.1 W. C. Mendenhall, USGS.
7.2 Alaska Earthquake 76, USGS.
7.3 After Clark and Hauge, 1973.
7.4 From P. W. Birkeland and E. E. Larson, Putnam's geology (Oxford University Press), 1978, Fig. 19-18 (after Toksoz).
7.5 After Whitham *et al,* 1970.
7.6 R. E. Wallace, USGS.
7.7, 8, and 9 From D. R. Nichols and J. M. Buchanan-Banks, Seismic hazards and land-use planning, USGS 690, 1974.
7.10 From The Great Alaska Earthquake of 1964: Geology (National Academy of Sciences), p. 328. Reproduced by permission of the National Academy of Sciences.
7.12 U.S. Army Corps of Engineers.
7.13 From R. Greensfelder, "Seismologic and crustal movement investigations of the San Fernando Earthquake," California Geology, April–May 1971.
7.14 Modified from G. B. Oakeshott, California's changing landscapes: A guide to the geology of the state, 1971 (Copyright © 1971, McGraw-Hill Book Co., Inc.) Reproduced by permission of McGraw-Hill Book Co.
7.15 From K. Whitham, W. G. Milne, and W. E. Smith, "Seismic zoning map of Canada," 1970 ed., Canadian Underwriter, June 15, 1970. Reproduced by permission of Wadham Publications Ltd., Toronto.
7.16 From P. W. Birkeland and E. E. Larson, Putnam's geology (Oxford University Press), 1978, Fig. 17-14 (after Algermissen).
7.17 From Urban geology master plan for California, 1973.
7.18 and 19 From Community safety, The comprehensive plan of San Francisco, 1974. Reproduced by permission of the San Francisco Department of City Planning.
7.20 From B. D. Zetler, "Travel times of seismic sea waves to Honolulu," Pacific Science 1 (3): 185–88. Reproduced from Pacific Science by permission of The University Press of Hawaii (formerly Univ. of Hawaii Press).
7.21 U.S. Army Corps of Engineers.
7.22 After R. L. Wiegel, Oceanographical engineering (copyright © 1964 Prentice-Hall,

Inc.) Fig. 5-11, p. 108. Reproduced by permission of Prentice-Hall, Inc.
7.23 U.S. Coast and Geodetic Survey.

Chapter 8

8.1 From "Report on the great landslide at Frank, Alberta," Annual Report, 1903, pt. 8 (Can. Dept. Interior). Reproduced by permission of the Geological Survey of Canada.
8.4 and 8.5 From P. W. Birkeland and E. E. Larson, Putnam's geology (Oxford University Press), 1978, Figs. 9-14 and 9-2 (after Kiersch).
8.7 and 9 After E. B. Eckel, ed., Landslides and engineering practice, 1978, Transportation Research Board Spec. Report 29, copyright by the National Academy of Sciences. Reprinted with permission.
8.8 George Cleveland.
8.11 After Aune, 1966.
8.12 After Brabb *et al,* 1972.

Chapter 9

9.1 After Macdonald, 1972.
9.2 After J. V. Luce, The end of Atlantis (Thames and Hudson, 1969), Fig. 11. Reproduced by permission of Thames and Hudson Ltd.
9.5 Brown Brothers.
9.7 From D. R. Crandell and D. R. Mullineaux, "Volcanic hazards in the Cascades," in Environmental geology, v. 1, no. 1 (Springer-Verlag), 1975, Fig. 4. Reproduced by permission of Springer-Verlag, New York, Inc.
9.8 After Crandell and Waldron, 1969.

Chapter 10

10.1 U.S. Army Corps of Engineers.
10.3 From R. U. Cooke and J. C. Doornkamp, Geomorphology in environmental management (Oxford University Press), 1974, Fig. 5.2 (after Kesseli and Beaty, from Schick, 1971).
10.5, 6, and 7 From J. R. Sheaffer, D. W. Ellis, and A. M. Spieker, Flood-hazard mapping in metropolitan Chicago, 1970, USGS Circ. 601-C.
10.8 After Jenkins, 1961.
10.9 From Hydrologic investigations atlas (USGS), 1961.
10.11, 12, 13, 14, and 15 From L. B. Leopold, Hydrology for urban land planning, USGS Circ. 554, 1968.
10.16 U.S. Army Corps of Engineers, Pa. Div.
10.19, 20, and 21 From U.S. Water Resources

Council, Regulation of flood hazard areas, v. 1.

10.22 and 24 After Environmental development guide (Regional Planning Comm., Los Angeles), 1971.

10.23 After a map from the Los Angeles County Flood Control District, 1973.

Chapter 11

11.8 Varig Brazilian Airlines.

11.9 From J. C. Draft, R. B. Biggs, and S. D. Halsey, ''Morphology and vertical sedimentary sequence models in Holocene transgressive barrier systems,'' in D. R. Coates, ed., Coastal geomorphology (SUNY, Binghamton), 1973, Fig. 22. Reproduced by permission of Donald R. Coates.

11.10 and 11 From Environmental atlas of the Texas coastal zone—Galveston-Houston area (Bureau of Economic Geology, U. of Texas), Fig. 7. Reproduced by permission of the Bureau of Economic Geology, Univ. of Texas at Austin.

11.12 After Brown, Jr. et al, 1974.

11.13 After USGS Investigation I-850.

11.14 and 15 After Thomas and Edelen, Jr., 1962.

11.16 After R. L. Wiegel, Oceanographical engineering (copyright © 1964 Prentice-Hall, Inc.) Fig. 14.36. Reproduced by permission of Prentice-Hall, Inc.

11.17 and 19 From O. Pilkey et al, How to live with an island, a handbook to Bogue Banks, North Carolina, 1975, Fig. 3. Reproduced by permission of the North Carolina Dept. of Natural and Economic Resources.

11.20 U.S. Army Coastal Engineering Research Center.

11.21 Photo: U.S. Army Coastal Engineering Research Center; map: U.S. Army Corps of Engineers.

11.23 After O. Pilkey et al, How to live with an island, a handbook to Bogue Banks, North Carolina, 1975, Fig. 6. Reproduced by permission of the North Carolina Dept. of Natural and Economic Resources.

11.24 U.S. Army Corps of Engineers.

11.25 After MacCoun.

11.27 U.S. Army Corps of Engineers.

Chapter 12

12.1 From Environmental atlas of the Texas coastal zone—Galveston-Houston area (Bureau of Economic Geology, U. of Texas), Fig. 18. Reproduced by permission of the Bureau of Economic Geology, Univ. of Texas at Austin.

12.2 After Poland, 1969.

12.3 Dept. of Oil Properties, City of Long Beach.

12.4 From P. H. Hamiliton and R. L. Meehan, ''Ground rupture in the Baldwin Hills,'' Science, v. 172, pp. 333–34, Fig. 1, 23 April 1971. Copyright 1971 by the American Association for the Advancement of Science. Reproduced by permission of the AAAS and Douglas H. Hamilton.

12.5 and 6 From J. F. Poland, ''Land subsidence in western United States,'' in R. A. Olson and M. W. Wallace, eds., Geologic Hazards and Public Problems, May 27–28, 1969 Conf. Proc.

12.7 After J. F. Poland and G. H. Davis, ''Land subsidence in Mexico City,'' Reviews in Engineering Geology, 1969, v. 2, pp. 182–269. Courtesy, The Geological Society of America, 1969.

12.8 After Colombo, 1972.

12.9 After ''Effects of land subsidence caused by mining to the groundwater and remedial measures,'' no. 89, v. II, I.A.H.S. Symposium of Tokyo on Land Subsidence, 1969, Fig. 1.

Chapter 13

13.1 From A. McIntyre, ''The surface of the Ice-Age earth,'' CLIMAP, Science v. 191, pp. 1131–37, Fig. 1, 19 March 1976. Copyright 1976 by the American Association for the Advancement of Science. Reproduced by permission of the AAAS and Andrew McIntyre.

13.2 From C. J. Schuberth, The geology of New York City and environs (Natural History Press), 1968, Fig. 70. Reproduced by permission of Christopher J. Schuberth.

13.6 From P. W. Birkeland and E. E. Larson, Putnam's geology (Oxford University Press), 1978, Fig. 11.3 (after Meigs).

Chapter 14

14.2 After Warnick, 1969.

14.4 From H. L. Berryhill, Jr., The worldwide search for petroleum offshore, USGS Circ. 694, 1974.

14.5 From B. J. Skinner, ''A second Iron Age ahead?,'' American Scientist 64, 1976. Reproduced by permission of American Scientist, journal of Sigma Xi, The Scientific Research Society.

14.6 From E. Cook, "Limits to exploitation of nonrenewable resources," Science v. 191, pp. 677–82, Fig. 1, 20 Feb. 1976. Copyright 1976 by the American Association for the Advancement of Science. Reproduced by permission of the AAAS and Earl Cook.

14.7 From Hubbert, 1973.

14.9 From J. Karkheck et al, "Prospects for district heating in the United States," Science, v. 195, pp. 948–55, Fig. 1, 11 March 1977. Copyright 1977 by the American Association for the Advancement of Science. Reproduced by permission of the AAAS and John Karkheck.

14.10 David Leveson.

Chapter 15

15.7 David Leveson.

15.8 Japanese Consulate, New York.

15.9 David Leveson.

15.11 After E. Orni and E. Efrat, Geography of Israel (Keter), 1971, p. 61. Reproduced by permission of Keter Publishing House Ltd., Jerusalem.

15.12, 14, and 15 From A. Kutcher, The new Jerusalem (Thames and Hudson), 1973, Fig. 12, 11, and 2g. Reproduced by permission of Thames and Hudson, Ltd.

15.13 Woodfin Camp.

15.22 David Leveson.

15.24 David Leveson.

15.25 and 26 After Eisbacher, 1973.

Chapter 16

16.2 New York Public Library.

16.5 From E. Jones, Towns and cities (Oxford University Press), 1966, Fig. 7.

16.6 From the Regional Plan 1970: 1990 (Assc. of Bay Area Governments, San Francisco), 1970.

16.7 From G. G. Mader and D. F. Crowder, "An experiment in using geology for city planning . . . ," in Environmental geology and planning (USGS), 1971, pp. 176–89.

16.10 and 11 After Preliminary regional plan for the San Francisco Bay region (Assc. of Bay Area Governments), 1966.

16.12 After the Regional plan 1970: 1990 (Assc. of Bay Area Governments, San Francisco), 1970.

16.13 From C. A. Doxiadis, Ekistics (© 1968 by Constantinos A. Doxiadis), Fig. 200. Reproduced by permission of Oxford University Press, Inc., and Hutchinson Publishing Group Ltd.